Founder's Library

Renewals & Information: 01784 4/·

Frae Ither Tongues

TOPICS IN TRANSLATION
Series Editors: Susan Bassnett, *University of Warwick, UK* and Edwin Gentzler, *University of Massachusetts, Amherst, USA*
Editor for Translation in the Commercial Environment:
Geoffrey Samuelsson-Brown, *University of Surrey, UK*

Other Books in the Series
Annotated Texts for Translation: English - German
 Christina Schäffner with Uwe Wiesemann
'Behind Inverted Commas': Translation and Anglo-German Cultural Relations in the Nineteenth Century
 Susanne Stark
Constructing Cultures: Essays on Literary Translation
 Susan Bassnett and André Lefevere
Contemporary Translation Theories (2nd Edition)
 Edwin Gentzler
Culture Bumps: An Empirical Approach to the Translation of Allusions
 Ritva Leppihalme
Literary Translation: A Practical Guide
 Clifford E. Landers
Paragraphs on Translation
 Peter Newmark
Practical Guide for Translators
 Geoffrey Samuelsson-Brown
The Coming Industry of Teletranslation
 Minako O'Hagan
The Interpreter's Resource
 Mary Phelan
The Pragmatics of Translation
 Leo Hickey (ed.)
The Rewriting of Njáls Saga: Translation, Ideology, and Icelandic Sagas
 Jón Karl Helgason
Translation, Power, Subversion
 Román Alvarez and M. Carmen-Africa Vidal (eds)
Translation and Nation: A Cultural Politics of Englishness
 Roger Ellis and Liz Oakley-Brown (eds)
Translation-mediated Communication in a Digital World
 Minako O'Hagan and David Ashworth
Time Sharing on Stage: Drama Translation in Theatre and Society
 Sirkku Aaltonen
Words, Words, Words. The Translator and the Language Learner
 Gunilla Anderman and Margaret Rogers
Written in the Language of the Scottish Nation
 John Corbett

Please contact us for the latest book information:
Multilingual Matters, Frankfurt Lodge, Clevedon Hall,
Victoria Road, Clevedon, BS21 7HH, England
http://www.multilingual-matters.com

TOPICS IN TRANSLATION 24
Series Editors: Susan Bassnett, *University of Warwick* and
Edwin Gentzler, *University of Massachusetts, Amherst*

Frae Ither Tongues
Essays on Modern Translations into Scots

Edited by
Bill Findlay

MULTILINGUAL MATTERS LTD
Clevedon • Buffalo • Toronto • Sydney

Library of Congress Cataloging in Publication Data
Frae Ither Tongues: Essays on Modern Translations into Scots/edited by Bill Findlay.
Topics in Translation: 24
Includes bibliographical references and index.
1. Scots language–Translating. 2. Translating and interpreting–Scotland–History.
3. Literature–Translations into Scots–History and criticism. I. Findlay, Bill. II. Series.
PE2103.F73 2004
491.6'3802–dc22   2003017735

British Library Cataloguing in Publication Data
A catalogue entry for this book is available from the British Library.

ISBN 1-85359-700-7 (hbk)

Multilingual Matters Ltd
UK: Frankfurt Lodge, Clevedon Hall, Victoria Road, Clevedon BS21 7HH.
USA: UTP, 2250 Military Road, Tonawanda, NY 14150, USA.
Canada: UTP, 5201 Dufferin Street, North York, Ontario M3H 5T8, Canada.
Australia: Footprint Books, PO Box 418, Church Point, NSW 2103, Australia.

Copyright © 2004 Bill Findlay and the authors of individual chapters.

All rights reserved. No part of this work may be reproduced in any form or by any means without permission in writing from the publisher.

Typeset by Wordworks Ltd.
Printed and bound in Great Britain by the Cromwell Press Ltd.

For my guid freend and collaborator
frae Québécois intil Scots

   MARTIN BOWMAN

an Angus Pict in farawa Canada
and (quo his Monikie mither, Jean Scott)
an aftimes gwamish moudiewort

'If Scots is to be something worth the keeping, then [...] we should be able to take the biggest of books and stretch the tongue beyond what we think it can do, make the tongue new by including things we'd never before have dreamt of saying in Scots, to build the language we lack out of the otherness of a different tongue.'

(Brian Holton, *infra*)

'[A]t times when states are anxious to establish their national identity and to prove the virtues of their language, they have very often in history indulged in widespread translation from other cultures; yet in the process of doing this they subtly alter their own language, joining it in many unforeseen ways to a greater continent of almost undefined and non-specific human expression. Whether one would take this as far as George Steiner does in *After Babel* when he calls translation "a teleological imperative" in the search for an eventual linguistic unity [...], it is probably true that the translator must come to a very peculiar awareness of the way in which the quest for the most native will turn out to draw him into the most universal. He pauses in an astounding landscape, almost afraid to move. When he moves, he is no longer himself. And that is it.'

(Edwin Morgan, [1976] repr. in 1990b: 234–5)

Contents

Editor's Introduction
Bill Findlay. 1

Part 1: Translators on Translating

1 Wale a Leid an Wale a Warld: *Shuihu Zhuan* into Scots
  Brian Holton 15

2 Translating Homer's *Odyssey*
  William Neill 38

3 Dario Fo's *Mistero Buffo* into Scots
  Stuart Hood. 53

4 Translating Register in Michel Tremblay's Québécois Drama
  Martin Bowman and Bill Findlay 66

Part 2: Studies of Translations

5 Robert Kemp's Translations of Molière
  Noël Peacock 87

6 Triumphant Tartuffification: Liz Lochhead's Translation of Molière's *Tartuffe*
  Randall Stevenson. 106

7 Edwin Morgan's *Cyrano de Bergerac*
  David Kinloch. 123

8 Mayakovsky and Morgan
  Stephen Mulrine. 145

9 Robert Garioch's Translations of George Buchanan's Latin Tragedies
   Graham Tulloch 171

10 Robert Garioch and Giuseppe Belli
   Christopher Whyte 188

11 *The Puddocks* and *The Burdies* 'by Aristophanes and Douglas Young'
   J. Derrick McClure 215

12 Translation and Transplantation: Sir Alexander Gray's Danish Ballads
   Peter Graves and Bjarne Thorup Thomsen 231

References 252

Contributors 262

Index 266

Editor's Introduction

BILL FINDLAY

Although this collection of essays was conceived independently, it can be seen as complementary to an earlier volume in the 'Topics in Translation' series, John Corbett's *Written in the Language of the Scottish Nation: A History of Literary Translation into Scots* (1999). Both books are firsts: Corbett's book is a pioneering account of Scots translation from the fifteenth to the twentieth century, and the essays gathered here together represent the first extensive analysis of writers' use of Scots as a translation medium in the modern (or any[1]) era. Both books, too, share being stimulated into life by the extraordinary output of translators into Scots over the past half-century or so. That this has been a period unprecedented in the history of Scots-language writing in the quantity of work and the range of languages and genres translated, and in translators' sustained exploration of the creative resources of Scots as a target medium, will be expanded on below; but some historical and cultural context to the selected translations discussed should first be offered. While John Corbett's comprehensive survey supplies that in detail, a brief summary (drawing on Findlay, 2000a: 36–8) may be helpful for readers here.

* * * * *

In common with its literary tradition, Scotland's literary translation heritage is multilingual, featuring translations into Gaelic, Scots, English and, in the past, Latin. Although Gaelic translation has continued to feature in the modern period, as exemplified by John Maclean's *Odusseia Homair* (Mac Gilleathain, 1976), discussed in William Neill's essay in this volume, translations into Scots and English predominate in quantity. Of the two, translation into Scots has a longer history, reflecting the Scots language's older lineage in Scotland (Gaelic, of course, is oldest of all).[2]

Whilst Scots has a sustained literary history stretching back to about 1300, literary translation has been practised more fitfully. The two periods of most significance are the sixteenth and twentieth centuries. The sixteenth century saw Scots secure as a national language, with demotic to courtly and literary registers, and with a literature boasting poets of the stature of William

1

Dunbar, Robert Henryson and Sir David Lindsay. The maturity of the language is evident in the translation of Virgil's *Aeneid* (1513) by Gavin Douglas (Coldwell, 1957–1964). Douglas firmly states in a Prologue that his translation is 'Writtin in the langage of Scottis natioun'. This national assertiveness through language can be identified with a Renaissance and Europe-wide mood of translating classics into national vernaculars as both a culturo-patriotic act of linguistic independence and a means of making available to a wider readership the works of classical antiquity. The sixteenth century saw other Scots translations, including translations of Latin prose works by Livy (*History of Rome*) and Boece (*The History and Chronicles of Scotland*), the entire New Testament and parts of the Old Testament, and a Latin *comoedia* (*Pamphilus speakand of Lufe*). In the last two decades of the sixteenth century, the poet-king James VI brought together his 'Castalian Band' of court poets. There is a connection with the motivation behind Gavin Douglas's work earlier in the century, in that James, taking as his model what the Pléiade poets had achieved for French in the 1550s and 1560s, promoted the writing *and translation* of poetry as a means of advancing the literary status of Scots. The King himself translated Salluste Du Bartas's *Uranie,* and encouraged court writers to translate, for example, Ariosto's *Orlando Furioso,* Petrarch's *Trionfi,* and Machiavelli's *Il Principe.* He also had other members of his poet band produce versions of Ronsard and poets of the Pléiade.

With King James's accession to the English throne in 1603 and the departure of the Scottish court to London, the Castalian Band of poets dispersed. Royal patronage of and commitment to an independent Scots tradition in literature and translation departed with James. Nonetheless, the Scots literary tradition flowed on, reaching high points in the poetry of Allan Ramsay, Robert Fergusson and Robert Burns in the eighteenth century, and in the novels of Sir Walter Scott, John Galt, James Hogg and Robert Louis Stevenson in the nineteenth century. But translations into Scots were scant: some classical Latin verse in the eighteenth century, some Scandinavian folk poetry and songs and parts of the Bible in the nineteenth century (see Corbett, 1999: 100–25).

* * * * *

The catalyst for the twentieth-century revival of literary translation into Scots was the 'Scottish Renaissance Movement' (so named by the French critic Denis Saurat) which began in the 1920s. The moving force was the poet and nationalist Hugh MacDiarmid. MacDiarmid argued for the revitalisation of Scots as a literary language, and in his own work he developed a 'synthetic Scots' medium that borrowed from earlier literature, reference works and dictionaries. It was an approach that looked back to the Golden Age of Scots in the fifteenth and sixteenth centuries (including Scots as a translation medium) and forward to a hoped-for new age of political and literary independence in which Scots would once again become a national language. In this context, translating into Scots was an arm of cultural politics. MacDiarmid advocated a reorientation away from England towards Europe and a reconnection with Scotland's 'ancient policies' as in the days of Gavin Douglas and James VI when Scotland was a European nation. MacDiarmid saw translation as a key means by which that reorientation could be advanced, for it united two of the guiding principles of the Scottish Renaissance Movement as enunciated by him: to 'refecundate Scottish arts and letters with international ideas and tendencies [and without] the automatic filterscreen of the English language' (1929), and to advance 'a systematic exploration of the creative possibilities of Braid Scots' (1933) (MacDiarmid, 1997: 163, 202). The latter was of particular importance to MacDiarmid's modernist agenda and ambition for Scots to be 'aligned with contemporary tendencies in European thought and expression', believing as he did that '[t]he Scots Vernacular is a vast store-house of just the very peculiar and subtle effects which modern European literature in general is assiduously seeking', and that '[a] *vis comica* that has not yet been liberated lies bound by desuetude and misappreciation in the recesses of the Doric' (quoted in Glen, 1964: 41, 81, 80). MacDiarmid led by example in releasing that potential, not just in his poetry but in translating or adapting modern poetry from several languages.

MacDiarmid's lead was followed by a number of others, including writers in the second wave of the Scottish Renaissance Movement that emerged in the 1940s, such as Douglas Young, Robert Kemp and Robert Garioch (all subjects of essays in this collection). Douglas Young, described in 1947 as 'the acknowledged pillar' of that second wave,[3] penned a verse-letter of homage, 'Letter to Hugh MacDiarmid, 1940', in which he admiringly wrote:

> Icelandic and Scots and German and whiles Greek,
> Provençal, Chinese, and the lave that ye speak, –
> aa your galvanic energie fizzan and sputteran. (Young, 1945: 27)
>
> [Icelandic and Scots and German and occasionally Greek, / Provençal, Chinese, and the rest that you speak, – / all your galvanic energy fizzing and sputtering.]

That galvanic energy infected Young, too. A polemicist, poet, critic, university classicist and polyglot, he translated Greek drama into Scots, as well as poetry from Greek, Latin, French, German, Italian, Russian, Chinese, Hebrew and Gaelic. Following his mentor, he considered translation 'indispensable' for advancing Scots, calling in the 1940s for a society to be formed 'to sponsor and subsidise translations into Scots' (Young, 1949: 19). It is little surprising, then, that by the 1940s MacDiarmid could write with approval of his younger disciples, at whose head was Young:

> These new Scottish poets ... are internationalists in their literary sympathies ... and have translated into Scots a great body of poetry from German, French, Russian, and other European languages ... [These] healthy intromissions with the whole range of European literature ... have been a notable feature of our recent literary history, like a veritable return to the Good Europeanism of our medieval ancestors. (MacDiarmid, [1940] 1948: xxiv)

Thus the ground was laid, too, for a reconnection with the Golden Age of translation in an earlier 'Scottish Renaissance', that of the sixteenth century. (For discussion of MacDiarmid's translation work and that of his second-wave progenitors, including more than those named here, see Corbett, 1999: Ch. 7.)

* * * * *

The effects of the philosophies and achievements of MacDiarmid's Scottish Renaissance Movement have continued to ripple through Scotland's literary culture. Whether one can categorise Scots-medium writers from the 1960s on as 'followers' is problematic, but what can be said with confidence is that MacDiarmid, as the most significant twentieth-century Scottish writer, has cast a long shadow of influence. One fruitful effect of the revivifying change he brought about is that for the past seventy years there has been a sustained output of translations into Scots; sufficient, in fact, to constitute a modern tradition.

Poetry has been translated from most of the European languages and some of the Asian ones, with work from French, Russian and the Classical languages prominent. Translations of collections of poetry by single authors that have attracted particular praise are Robert Garioch's translations of Giuseppe Belli, Edwin Morgan's of Vladimir Mayakovsky, and William Neill's of Homer. Sir Alexander Gray's translations of European balladry and folksong have also been acclaimed. (Hence Gray, Garioch, Morgan, and Neill are all the focus of essays herein.) Most postwar translators of verse have tended to follow the Scottish Renaissance Movement's example in employing a 'synthetic' Scots; that is, one aggrandised by borrowings to create a medium of greater literary range than demotic Scots alone allows. That said, demotic Scots does sometimes feature, as in Garioch's translations of Belli's sonnets. It can also be harnessed to an experimental approach that at the same time draws on a literary Scots, as in Morgan's matching of Mayakovsky's modernist exuberance.

While a substantial corpus of poetry has been translated into Scots in the period since the 1920s (anthologised in France & Glen, 1989), much less prose has been translated. This deficiency reflects the historic loss of a prose register – as a compound consequence of the Union of Crowns in 1603 and the Union of Parliaments in 1707 – and the lack of a settled grammar and orthography. However, one outstanding prose translation has been produced: William Laughton Lorimer's *The New Testament in Scots* (1983).[4] This translation can be seen as a late fruit of the twentieth-century Scottish Renaissance, for Lorimer was of the same generation as Hugh MacDiarmid and shared some of the same motives in wishing to see Scots revitalised. A Scots prose translation-in-progress which, to judge by instalments published so far, bids fair to rival Lorimer's in achievement is *Men o the Mossflow*, Brian Holton's translation of the Chinese medieval epic novel *Shuihu Zhuan* (known in English as *The Water Margin*). Holton contributes an essay here in which he casts light on some of the specific challenges involved in forging a recreated Scots prose fit for his demanding task.

A significant development dating from the 1940s has been the translation of drama into Scots (examined in detail in Findlay, 2000b). Robert Kemp's translations of plays by Molière led the way, and there have since been translations by different hands of a number of other plays by Molière, making him the most translated dramatist (two essays on Molière translations by Kemp and Liz Lochhead, respectively, have been included here). Other classical playwrights whose work has been translated include Aristophanes, Aeschylus, Sophocles, Euripides, Racine, Goldoni, von Kleist, Holberg, Beaumarchais, Ibsen, Rostand, Hauptmann, Gorky, Gogol, Chekhov and Brecht.[5] George Buchanan's sixteenth-century Latin tragedies have also been translated (and are the subject of an essay here), and Shakespeare's *Macbeth* has been translated twice (Lorimer, 1992; Purves, 1992; both compared in Kinloch, 2002). The translation of contemporary plays into Scots got underway only as recently as the 1980s, since when a number of plays by Dario Fo and Michel Tremblay (eight alone in the latter case) have been translated. (Fo and Tremblay are the subject of separate essays in this volume.) Also, there have been translations of single plays by Enzo Cormann, Michael Vinaver, Ludmilla Petrushevskaya, Daniel Danis, Raymond Cousse (the topic of Findlay, 2000c), Pavel Kohout, Teresa Lubkiewicz and Jeanne-Mance Delisle (for the published translation, see Delisle, 2000). If we combine the number of classic and contemporary plays translated, we find that more Scots translations of plays have been produced in the period since 1980 than in any previous period (see Findlay,

1996a), and that, in quantity and length, translations of plays comprise the bulk of modern translations into Scots. To put this in a wider perspective, and to emphasise how rich the modern period has been for Scots translation generally, remarkably, before Robert Kemp's pioneering *Let Wives Tak Tent* (*L'École des femmes*) in 1948, the only previous translation of a play into Scots was, seemingly, John Burel's translation of *Pamphilus speakand of Lufe* in the late sixteenth century (see Findlay, 1998a: 47–50). Today, with the gains made, Scots translations have become an established and popular feature of the Scottish theatre scene, and this trend shows every sign of continuing in the new century.

Translations of classic plays have tended to draw on a literary or 'traditional' Scots, albeit with a spoken base. But in some cases, such as Liz Lochhead's *Tartuffe* (1985) and Edwin Morgan's *Cyrano de Bergerac* (1992a), this has been blended with a street Scots and other registers to create an idiosyncratic 'theatrical Scots'. In contrast, contemporary plays have in the main been rendered into an urban demotic Scots. Taken as a whole, the corpus of classic and contemporary plays translated demonstrates the unusually varied resource available to the Scottish translator. In addition to Standard English and 'Scottish Standard English' (distinguished by Scotticisms in grammar and lexis), there is Scots in its many forms: urban or rural, regional or 'standardised', historic or contemporary, literary or experimental. As appropriate, a translator may employ any of these singly, counterpoint varieties of English and Scots, or devise a hybrid Scots–English instrument. Thus, the distinguishing feature of modern Scottish translations, in drama particularly, is diversity of medium. John Corbett (1999: 3) usefully summarises how exploitation of that diversity developed in translations in stages over the decades, from MacDiarmid's literary synthesising to subsequent borrowing of localised rural and urban varieties of vernacular Scots speech. One could add that the spurt in translating drama (the most speech-based genre), greatly assisted the liberation and acceleration of those developments in the latter decades of the twentieth century.

* * * * *

Why translators of poetry, prose and plays are motivated to use Scots invites many answers, some of which are provided in the essays here. Reasons commonly given are that translation into Scots extends the capacities of the medium in meeting the challenge of a foreign-language work, and that the status of Scots, through its association with the prestige work translated, is enhanced. (Often linked to the latter motivation in the case of the older, more directly MacDiarmid-influenced generations of translators is that such association and demonstration assists efforts to re-establish Scots as a national language along the lines of what was achieved in Norway with Landsmaal.[6]) Another reason is the sense that translators have of working within a literary and linguistic tradition retaining a national, and therefore a political, dimension, and within a national culture that is hospitable to published and performed Scots, as demonstrated by public interest (most markedly in the immediacy of audience reception in theatres – an overt enthusiasm that has in itself encouraged theatre managements and translators). Translation is thus a means of adding to and advancing that tradition; and, paradoxically, it is also one of the means of expressing a national culture because of the translation medium used.

Translators may also be motivated by a belief that, for certain work, Scots (or Scots and English in combination or contrast) is more effective than English in rendering the letter and/or spirit of a source work. For example, for the translator of poetry this might be bound up in part with the phonaesthetic qualities of Scots,[7] and/or the enlarged choice of vocabulary and pronunciation (and therefore rhymes) that Scots and English afford. Translators of prose and drama may be influenced by considerations of linguistic approximation in matching a dialect or non-standard source medium, or with the opportunities that Scots affords for stylistic and tonal variety and register shifts.

Whatever the range of reasons, the sum effect is that the period of the past seventy years has, in terms of quantity and the variety of languages and literary genres translated, been the richest in Scotland's literary and theatre histories for translations into Scots. Moreover, that body of translations rivals the quantity of original work written in Scots over the same period, emphasising the important contribution that translation has made to modern Scottish literature and drama. Further, in terms of non-standard varieties of English around the world, there is wider significance in this, in that no other 'major branch of the English language' (Jones, 1997: vii) – to cite one of the many formulations that, understandably, struggle adequately to convey with brevity the special and complex nature of Scots as a historic sister language to English – enjoys such a differentiated modern translation corpus, or has had a book given over to discussion of its translation products as here.

* * * * *

This volume comprises essays of two different but complementary kinds: reflections by translators on their practice in a given work, and critical analyses of the use of Scots in individual translations. Although the editor's choice of translations for discussion in both cases has been made to provide a mix of generations and a spread of languages, genres and approaches, the essays throw up certain recurring issues in the use of Scots for translation.

A seemingly negative issue is the difficulty in forging a wholly satisfactory register of an elevated nature; for, as Graham Tulloch remarks in his essay (Chapter 9) on Robert Garioch's translations of George Buchanan's Latin tragedies, '[o]ver the last few centuries Scots has been particularly creative in colloquial language and has become extremely rich in that register, but there has been a corresponding decline in distinctively Scots formal language'. Tulloch examines how that decline posed Garioch particular challenges in seeking to extend the range of literary Scots, making his 'search for appropriate Scots diction ... one of the most interesting aspects' of his Buchanan translations. Noël Peacock (Chapter 5) notes, too, in his discussion of Robert Kemp's translations of Molière, that '[t]he major linguistic problem for Kemp was ... parody of tragic diction'.[8] As mentioned earlier, this predicament stems from the loss of the Scottish royal court and parliament, and the concomitant loss of an 'official' or literary register for Scots. In discussing his translation of *Shuihu Zhuan*, Brian Holton (Chapter 1) diagnoses the consequence of this complication for the modern translator of prose: '[T]he kind of text which sits easily in Scots is not so much one which reflects the ornate elegance of a vanished court, as one which speaks with the funky and irrepressible voice of the bad soldier, the dissenter, or the marketplace storyteller'. However, as Holton also points out, that deficiency can be turned to advantage:

> Scots ... precisely because it is defective, allows us to be more adventurous: since there are few rules and precedents, not only do we have more freedom to invent, we often have no choice but to invent – words, structures, registers – because if we do not, we will have a poorer, thinner, tongue to work with. ... Our tongue is our toolkit, and where it is defective, we must make it new.

He goes on:

> We must build the language we lack. Any good writer transforms his own language, just as any translator worth his salt will transform his own tongue. [...] [W]e should be able to take the biggest of books and stretch the tongue beyond what we think it can do, make the tongue new by including things we'd never before have dreamt of saying in Scots, to build the language we lack out of the otherness of a different tongue.

There is an echo of all of this in Christopher Whyte's analysis (Chapter 10) of Robert Garioch's translations of Giuseppe Belli's poetry, which seem to have brought forth a linguistic adventurousness in response to challenges that encouraged extending the boundaries of what is possible in Scots. Whyte claims that there is 'a very real sense in which the Belli translations are an investigation of the Scots language, of its possibilities. ... The presence of an original meant that Garioch was able to focus more closely than anywhere else in his work on this investigation'. Whyte argues that translation thus proved a form of liberation for Garioch, encouraging inventiveness and enabling him 'to break free of the limitations of the stigmatised linguistic medium he had chosen, in a way that "original" work of a "purely Scottish" nature might never have allowed'.

An aspect of the inventiveness called forth by the condition of the language is the practice of aggrandisement and eclecticism. As outlined before, this was initiated by Hugh MacDiarmid, who described the goal as a recreated medium 'which is a synthesis of all the dialects into which Scots has degenerated and of elements of Scots vocabulary drawn from all periods of our history' (MacDiarmid, [1940] 1948: xxiv). Such synthesising is a feature of many of the translations discussed below. William Neill (Chapter 2), for example, employs it in translating Homer's *Odyssey*, and comments: '[W]here a word from another dialect within the whole Scots-speaking area seemed a better fit, I selected it quite without shame'. One sees the technique at work, too, in Garioch, Young and others, and, less reverentially, in the 'experimental Scots' of Edwin Morgan's Mayakovsky translations and the highly individualistic 'theatrical Scots' of Liz Lochhead's *Tartuffe* and Morgan's *Cyrano de Bergerac*. Yet all are linked by the same impulse to build creatively on a spoken Scots base, whether traditional, country or urban-demotic in nature.

Related to this tendency to inventiveness is the rich capacity that Scots has for register shifts; between varieties of Scots, and between Scots and standard English. It is noticeable, for example, that virtually every essay here makes mention of such shifts, whether discussing the translation of historic or modern source texts. Douglas Young in his translations of Aristophanes' plays uses a colloquial Scots as his basic register but with 'passages in different styles standing out in relief', displaying, in J. Derrick McClure's words (Chapter 11), a 'kaleidoscopic range of styles and registers'. Robert Garioch stated that he used 'Scots of different styles for different purposes', as Graham Tulloch (Chapter 9) analyses in relation to his Buchanan translations. Liz Lochhead in *Tartuffe* employs 'gradations of register within Scots speech, elaborated by contrasts with standard or adapted English' (Randall Stevenson, Chapter 6); in *Cyrano de Bergerac*

Edwin Morgan 'birls [spins] through a kaleidoscope of styles and registers' (David Kinloch, Chapter 7); Bowman and Findlay (Chapter 4), in their translations of Michel Tremblay's plays, draw on a range of registers in conveying Michel Tremblay's similar technique in the Québécois originals; and so on. In short, as Brian Holton says, citing his own experience as a translator: 'Register has got a lot to do with the success or failure of translations into Scots.'

To succeed, Holton adds, 'the kind of Scots to be used can't be a simple, aefauld [one-dimensional] creature but must be as multifaceted and as flexible as our grasp of the tongue allows'. A direct echo of this view can be found in Randall Stevenson's analysis of Liz Lochhead's success in her translation of *Tartuffe*: '[T]he range of registers employed suggests they [the characters] are effectively polylingual and correspondingly *multifaceted* [editor's emphasis], as indeed is the whole translation medium itself.' Such multifacetedness may reflect the linguistic or tonal nature of the original work being translated, thereby informing the translator's choice of Scots over standard English as his/her core medium (as in the motivation shaping the choices made by many of the translators represented here). Sometimes, however, it is driven by the demands of Scots rather than by the letter of the original work. This can have a positive consequence, as with Molière translations. In his essay, Randall Stevenson says of Lochhead's *Tartuffe* that 'the happy houghmagandie [intercourse] of dialects and registers in Scots surely offers Molière more satiric opportunities than are to be found in English, or moreover, in his native French'. Detractors might argue, of course, that, effective though such texts might be, what they are presenting is 'MacMolière' rather than Molière. Of relevance here, Stephen Mulrine (Chapter 8), in discussing Edwin Morgan's translations of Mayakovsky's poems, concludes that, 'To paraphrase, *c'est magnifique, mais ce n'est pas Mayakovsky*'; but, that said, he notes how, in the original, 'the sense I have of a pencil sketch, however detailed and lively, [becomes in the Scots] transmuted to a full-colour rendering'. He pinpoints the reason for this in the way that Scots brings a 'rise in emotional temperature' and has a concreteness of imagery which 'works a peculiar magic':

> The overall effect ... is to make Mayakovsky sound much older and wiser. That instructional, occasionally hectoring tone in the original, which both contemporaries and later critics have found tiresome, seems more acceptable in Morgan's Scots, where categorical statements appear as folk-wisdom, and not ideology. And whether it comes with the language or no, the significantly higher incidence of *things* – solid, tangible objects – in Morgan's translation, tends to the same purpose.

Mulrine's observations about Morgan's Scots being characterised by directness, concrete imagery, raised emotion, and a folk quality are echoed in other essays. The sense of Scots as resembling a folk-speech is identified by Stuart Hood (Chapter 3) as a reason for believing that Dario Fo's *Mistero Buffo* would translate well into Scots; William Neill (Chapter 2) sees Scots, 'with its ballad and story-telling tradition', as more suited than standard English to the story episodes in Homer; and Peter Graves and Bjarne Thorup Thomsen (Chapter 12) note, too, how that aspect to Scots provided Sir Alexander Gray with an appropriate medium to translate Danish folk ballads, for 'the ballad translator ... in Scots may draw on a rich stock of suitable vocabulary and constructions at the same time as having access to the hoard of appropriate imagery and formulaic phrasing provided by the native ballad tradition'. Noël Peacock remarks how a feature of Robert Kemp's Molière translations is that he turns 'abstract nouns into concrete expressions'. Brian Holton says: 'What Scots seems to bring out is an earthiness, an immediacy and a strength ... and spikier rhythms'. Randall Stevenson judges that in comparison with Molière's French, Lochhead's Scots is 'gutsier and more down to earth', consistently favouring 'pungency over elegance'. And alongside all of this, David Kinloch concludes of Edwin Morgan's virtuoso handling of Scots in *Cyrano de Bergerac* that it 'shows off the huge emotional range Scots can encompass from the nostalgic and the deeply lyrical to the flippant and sublimely combative'. That 'shows off' also points to an aspect noticeable in many of the translations discussed here; that the medium is in a sense consciously being 'performed' by the translator. For example, Randall Stevenson detects in Liz Lochhead's *Tartuffe* 'a sense of language as performance', of the medium drawing attention to itself and fulfilling a dramatic function in doing so. Stevenson writes: 'This self-conscious awareness of language both develops from, and highlights, the richness and energy available in Scots vocabulary.' Thus, not only can this performative dimension be harnessed for literary and dramatic effects, but it can be used consciously to demonstrate the creative capacities and distinctiveness of Scots – sometimes, indeed, in the flaunting spirit of Cyrano the Gascon strutting his verbal pyrotechnics in one of his *tirades* and throwing out 'pure deid brilliant whigmaleeries' [extremely brilliant fanciful imaginings] (Morgan, 1992a: 25).

Earthiness, concreteness, strong imagery, spikiness, energy, immediacy, lyrical power, emotional directness and range, medium as performance: recurring references in the essays to these and other qualities in Scots as a target medium, and to characteristics of Scots-language writing such as verbal inventiveness and register exploitation, demonstrate the insights that the contributors here provide both to the nature and practice of modern Scots translation generally and to specific considerations flowing from such defining qualities and characteristics as they affect translators' choice of source text and translation approach in this unique national area of translation within the larger international world of 'Englishes'.

Notes

1. That said, relevant discussion on the French and Italian influences on Scottish Literature in earlier periods, including translations into Scots, features in, respectively, Smith (1934) and Jack (1972, 1986).
2. For a succinct history of Scots see Murison (1979); and for a book-length history see Jones (1997).
3. [Anon.], 'Scots Whae Hae No. 13 – Douglas Young', in *The Scots Review* 8 (1) (April, 1947), p. 10.
4. It had been hoped to include an essay on Lorimer's masterwork here, but that has not proved possible. However, it is discussed in Ogston (1988), where he compares aspects of Lorimer's Scots with the Greek original.
5. The Scots version of Hauptmann's *The Weavers* is discussed at length in Findlay (1998)c; and Victor Carin's Scots translations of plays by Molière, Goldoni and Heinrich von Kleist are the subject of Findlay (2001b).
6. In 1925 MacDiarmid wrote that he could 'see no reason why an artificially and quite arbitrarily contrived "generalised" Scots should not yet become an effective medium just as the Norwegian *Landsmaal* has done'; and in 1932, 'The course taken in Norway in fashioning the *Landsmaal* on the basis of Old Norse was one of the models I had in mind for Scotland; and I was also influenced by the example of Mistral and the subsequent Provençal and Catalan developments' (quoted in Glen, 1964: 32 and 32, n. 1).
7. MacDiarmid, for example, described Scots as 'an inexhaustible quarry of subtle and significant sound' (quoted in Glen, 1964: 81).
8. A recent effort has been made by Edwin Morgan, in his translation of Racine's *Phaedra*, to create a Scots medium capable of rendering the formal rhetoric of French classical tragedy (see Morgan, 2000).

Part 1
Translators on Translating

Chapter 1
Wale a Leid an Wale a Warld: Shuihu Zhuan *into Scots*

BRIAN HOLTON

By Way of Beginning

In a complex linguistic environment, where several choices are open to us, what factors influence our decision to use one tongue rather than another? If we choose to use Scots, we choose to use/abuse the following associations:

- marginality;
- couthiness [agreeability];
- familiarity;
- antiquarianism;
- self-conscious literariness;
- hameliness [intimacy].

And if we choose to write prose in Scots, we must expect our readers to react in varying ways:

- some will expect the text to be comic;
- some will be puzzled by the spellings;
- some will say 'A cannae read this' [I can't read this];
- some will simply not bother;
- some will think of it as 'Old Scots';
- some will be delighted by the appropriateness of the match between text and tongue.

If we choose to translate into Scots, the first question will always be 'Why not English?' – though you wouldn't ask a Dutchman or a Dane, 'Why not German?' At least with translation there is a series of clear answers to 'Why Scots?':

- because this text demands non-metropolitan language;
- because we hear this authorial voice in Scots;

- because another tongue would impede or destroy the flavour of the original;
- because with this text the translator is happier in this tongue.

And this is to ignore for the moment wider issues such as:
- every tongue needs to grow;
- living languages are stretched best by cross-cultural contact;
- translations challenge the scope and accuracy of tongues;
- social/political/cultural factors demand the use of this tongue rather than that;
- the translator ignores/subverts/colludes with social/political/cultural factors.

Mossflow Tales

I began translating *Shuihu Zhuan* into Scots, as *Men o the Mossflow*, in the early 1980s, at a time when I had become convinced of the suitability of Scots as a medium for extended prose narrative (Holton, 1981, 1982, 1984, 1986, 1987, 1993, 1995a). I had for some time been attempting to make an English version of *Shuihu Zhuan* (Chen, *et al.*, 1981), with little or no success: the language was clumsy, and refused to bend to either my will or the lithe grace of the original. Stymied, I turned, despite an initial scepticism over my aptitude, to Scots. And the first chapter wrote itself, fell off the typewriter onto the page. It later became necessary to try other experiments: was this just a freak, a one-off? Or could other Chinese texts survive the transition into Scots? With practice it became obvious that some texts not only survived, but even seemed to prosper in their new environment. It all depended on the individual voice of the original. So it could work, in at least some contexts.

The next development came when I asked myself, 'What *kind* of Scots do I want to use here?' This question was to some extent limited by my own background – born into a Border family, brought up in Edinburgh, Falkirk and Selkirk, schooling finished at Gala Academy, university in Edinburgh. So the choice of a Lothian standard Scots with Border tinges, while it may seem to fit the profile of the Makars (Scots poets of the fifteenth and early sixteenth centuries) – and I couldn't help but be influenced by them – actually grew as much from my own linguistic background as it did from conscious literary imitation.

When it came to spelling, the Makars gave me the lead, too: again, Lothian standard with local tinges. At first I used a pure *Scots Style Sheet* approach,[1] but as the years have gone on I seem to have settled into a modified and simplified version that reflects a balance I try to hold between my ear, my own idiolect, and a vaguely-defined idea of what the general reader might be comfortable with.

So to translate a seventeenth-century text written in a close approximation of daily speech, which is not entirely colloquial (like Hugh MacDiarmid's 'Synthetic Scots', it's a literary imitation of colloquial language), I tried to make a kind of Scots that could be spoken with ease, and that had enough elasticity to accommodate the shifting registers of the original. Since comic effects in *Shuihu Zhuan* often build on dialect differences or on jarring shifts of register, these must all come into the translation, so the kind of Scots to be used can't be a simple, aefauld [one-dimensional] creature, but must be as multifaceted and as flexible as our grasp of the tongue allows.

One of the main influences on me has been ballad Scots: with its subtle shifts and turns between broad vernacular and high, almost biblical, language, it provides a marvellous vehicle for lively narrative. Legal language too, with its high and stately tone, its magical invocations of Latin, its evocative and timeless terms of art, is a treasure house – and a very handy one when you're working on a text that hinges on outlawry and bristles with legal terms. Sir Walter Scott's grasp of the language of the law, and the rich ballad-primed Scots of James Hogg's prose works – especially *The Three Perils of Man* (Hogg, 1972) – were early and profound influences, as was the language of folk song. There's no doubt that there are resources to hand – and I haven't even mentioned the resonant prose of religious dispute or the pawky [astute, witty] precision of old saws and speaks, or even that peculiarly salty register known at polite Border tea-tables as 'mill talk', which owes a great deal to the discourse of the public bar.

Register has got a lot to do with the success or failure of translations into Scots. As in any translation, get the register wrong – and in particular, the subtle modulations of register that make so much poetry work – and the whole piece limps. That's especially true of *Shuihu Zhuan*, which relies for many of its effects – mocking wit, savage irony, gentle humour, sly backdoor allusion – on very subtle shifts of emphasis and of register.

While translating *Shuihu Zhuan* whole and entire, I have worked on translating other Chinese texts into Scots. I have to confess here that I have worked only on those texts that made sense to me: with some texts (poems, especially), I just didn't get it, just couldn't see the joke, or could make no sense of some allusion, some catchphrase perhaps, on which a whole passage might turn. Translators all do this to a greater or lesser extent, of course. Our imaginations work better with some writers than with others, just as our conversations with some humans are better than those with others. Hence the measure of truth in the old saw that Chinese poetry was invented by Arthur Waley: he was a great translator, but he translated only the poems that sound like Arthur Waley's. He could do nothing else, and I don't claim to be any better or any wiser or any more adaptable than him. We must work with the voices that echo within us, whose timbre we can reproduce with confidence. Register is one of the keys here, and this raises a problem that is specific to Scots. When we translate into Scots we are using a defective language; that is to say, 'defective' as Latin verbs are in missing some part or parts. Scots lost its high register prose somewhere between the Union of the Crowns in 1603 and the Union of Parliaments in 1707. High register verse lingered on, and the high prose register was picked up by English, but the vernacular revival led by Allan Ramsay, Robert Fergusson, and Robert Burns in the eighteenth century didn't bring prose back to life. When Sir Walter Scott began to use Scots for dialogue, despite some wonderful passages, he didn't encourage high-register prose writing, and Scots has still not regained the registers it lost. So the kind of text that sits easily in Scots is not so much one that reflects the ornate elegance of a vanished court, as one that speaks with the funky and irrepressible voice of the bad soldier, the dissenter or the marketplace storyteller .

A digression: a problem I found with trying to use English for *Mossflow* was that I couldn't get the language to bend enough for me to apply it to what is essentially a medieval novel. Walter Scott did devise a sub-Shakespearian patois for historical fiction, but Zounds, lads!, it's been done to death by his imitators. All this pishery and tushery couldn't do the job (and I would have been embarrassed to have been caught trying).

Scots, on the other hand, precisely because it is defective, allows us to be more adventurous: since there are few rules and precedents, not only do we have more freedom to invent, we often have no choice but to invent – words, structures, registers – because if we do not, we will have a poorer, thinner tongue to work with. For a translator, particularly for a translator working with a book whose original language is new-made, inventive, playful and varied, that would be an impossible restriction. Our tongue is our toolkit, and where it is defective, we must make it new.

It's also true that I can hear one kind of text in Scots and another in English. Though I have made Scots versions of some of Yang Lian's poetry (Yang, 1999), as a youngish internationally-inclined modernist poet with surrealist leanings, he speaks to me more often in English (Yang, 1994, 1995), whereas the down-to-earth subversiveness of an outlaw novel brings out the Border reiver in my blood, and I can't help hearing Scots behind the Chinese when I read *Shuihu Zhuan* nowadays. With Yang Lian, however, it seems to me that the essential hameliness [familiarity and intimacy] of the Scots paradoxically enhances the strangeness at the heart of his poetry, just as the ordinariness of his poetic diction in Chinese contrasts with the oddness of his vision. What Scots seems to bring out is an earthiness, an immediacy and a strength which, together with the spikier rhythms of the Scots, can transmit Yang's voice more powerfully than English versions have so far been able to. This is how he looks in Scots:

WHAUR THE DEEP SEA DEVAULS

blue's aye heicher yet   same as yir weariness
    hes walit the sea   same as a bodie's glower gars the sea
        get twice as dreich
        gaun back same as aye
ti the wrocht stane lug whaur the drumbeats is smoorit
    peerie coral corps   a yowdendrift

        gairie spreckles on deid fish
    same as the lift at bields yir ilka want

    gaun back ti the meiths   same as the enless gaun back
        ti the scaurs   storm heids aa about ye

yir pipes weirdit ti skirl on efter yir daith   tunes o corruption i the
                                                    howe o the flesh
    whan blue's been kent at the last   the mishantert
        sea   millions o caunles   blinters an devauls.
                                (Yang, 1999: 164)

[WHERE THE SEA STANDS STILL

        blue is always higher   just as your weariness
            has chosen the sea   just as a man's gaze compels the sea
                to be twice as desolate
                going back as ever
    to that carved stone ear where drumbeats are destroyed
        where tiny coral corpses   fall in a snowstorm

            gaudy speckles on dead fish
        like the sky that holds all your lust

        go back to the limit   like limitlessness
        going back to the cliffs   stormheads all around
    your pipes doomed to go on playing after your death   tunes of corruption
                                                            deep in the flesh
        as blue is recognised at last   the wounded
            sea   a million candles   stands dazzlingly still.]

This is not the ornate and elegant poetic diction of, say, eighth-century Tang poetry, whose effortless ease and grace are not easily rendered into European tongues. (The linguistic need to clumsily insist on explicit markers for tense, gender, number, etc., is a dead weight that cramps the sinewy allusiveness and simplicity of classical Chinese verse to such an extent that there are few poets who survive the exchange with anything like their native grace.)[2] This is strong, muscular poetry, with a pronounced Beijing accent and a profound sense of place; perhaps these are some of the qualities shared by Scots, and perhaps this may explain why these versions work. But in the end, it's all down to your ear, and your grasp of your ain [own] tongue, as well as your grasp of the other language.

What is *Men o the Mossflow*?

In the early twelfth century the Song dynasty had a succession of calamities, and the north was lost to the Jin Tartars. The Court and the Son of Heaven himself were forced to flee south leaving the homeland in the hands of foreigners, national humiliation, gross loss of face: all round, a pretty bad business from the Chinese point of view. The causes were of course believed to have been corruption at court, the emperor (infallible, by convention) getting bad advice from self-serving mandarins, peculation diverting funds for frontier defence, and so on. In these last years before the loss of the north, when corruption held sway and government was failing the people, there were expressions of popular dissent. Starving peasants rioted, high-ranking officers deserted, individuals made heroic attempts to change the course of history and stem the tide of dynastic decline. And stories were told about some of them. Twice the official Song History briefly mentions one Song Jiang, who with his 36 companions, roamed around terrifying the northern provinces before being defeated and captured.[3] In the century following the loss of the north, stories began circulating in the countryside and among the professional storytellers of the marketplaces and teahouses. These stories told of the exploits not just of Song Jiang, but of other figures too – some historical, some entirely fictional – and whole cycles of stories grew up around them. We know that street theatres as well as the theatres patronised by the gentry were putting on plays based on these outlaw heroes in the same period, and we even have surviving lists of paintings of these heroes as they appear in dramas of the time.

Thus story-cycles were circulating, immensely popular plays were being performed, and at some point in the fourteenth or fifteenth century a novel appeared under the title *Shuihu Zhuan*, which I have rendered as *Men o the Mossflow*.[4] (It is also known in English under the title *The Water Margin*.[5]) It has been attributed to Shi Naian, a shadowy figure who may never even have existed, and to Luo Guanzhong, a slightly more substantial figure who seems to have been associated with the early publication of other novels. The textual history is convoluted and uncertain, but whoever the author was, and whoever Shi Naian might have been, this is a splendid piece of work.

Shuihu Zhuan is the first masterpiece to be written in the vernacular language, and its putative author is the first master of the vernacular. The language is racy and vivid, with a freshmade feeling like the smell of new paint. Over all the registers it uses there is a feeling of mastery and control. Now, it may be the case that, as some scholars still think, Luo Guanzhong simply edited the text from the performance of some great storyteller (perhaps this is where Shi Naian comes in – as the marketplace storyteller whose performance enthralled Luo). Or it may be that Shi Naian, as another theory holds, was a storyteller who took the guild's promptbooks and from them wrote the novel. We'll probably never know. But whoever was responsible, he (or they) made one of the world's great books.

But before we come to why and how it's a great book, there's one other name to be mentioned: Jin Shengtan. He was born around 1608 and was executed in 1661.[6] In all the long and book-haunted history of China, perhaps there was no greater literary mind than Jin's. An unorthodox, thrawn [stubborn] kind of character, he was celebrated for his erudition and the astonishing breadth of his learning, despite the fact that he passed only the lowest of the exams for the mandarinate. In his day the Yangtse delta was, as it had been for centuries, the intellectual and creative heartland of all China, and his hometown of Suzhou was celebrated as a city of great culture and elegance. But, because of a breakdown in the bureaucratic system, few appointments were being made, the civil service was in steep decline, and as a consequence there were large numbers of men who had spent their lives in prolonged and abstruse study, preparing for the entrance examination that would make mandarins of them (see Huang, c1981). And they had no jobs.

In those wonderfully rich and creative times, much new work was being done: Feng Menglong and Ling Mengchu were collecting stories from professional and amateur storytellers, working them up into a new genre, and the novel, which had made its first appearance in the early years of the Ming dynasty,[7] began to eclipse the theatre as the most popular of narrative forms. Jin was part of this ferment. Born Jin Renrui, he early in life took as his byname (a practice common among the literati) the style *Shengtan*. This phrase appears twice in the *Analects* of Confucius, meaning 'the sage

[Confucius] sighed': once over the genius of one of his disciples, and once over the wicked ways of the contemporary world. So Jin calling himself *Shengtan* was not unlike a punk musician taking the stage name *Jesus Wept*. And like the Johnny Rottens and Sid Viciouses of the punk movement, Jin saw his duty as a sustained assault on convention. He set up, in direct competition to the canonical *Six Classics* (which had scriptural authority), his own list of *Six Works of Genius*; they included:

- the poems of the great Tang poet Du Fu (Cooper, 1973; Hinton, 1989);
- the strange shamanistic masterpiece *Encountering Sorrow* by Qu Yuan (Hawkes, 1989);
- the work of the Taoist philosopher Zhuangzi (Graham, 1981);
- the popular drama *Romance of the Western Chamber* (Wang, S., 1968);
- the brilliant historian Sima Qian's groundbreaking *Historical Records* (Sima, 1974);
- *Shuihu Zhuan* (*Men o the Mossflow*, and other titles) (Buck, 1957; Jackson, 1963; Dars, c1978; Shapiro, 1981; Holton, 1981, 1982, 1984, 1986, 1987, 1993; Dent-Young, 1994, 1997, 2001, 2002a, 2002b).

This list was heterodox, almost blasphemous, in that the works were chosen for their literary merit and not for their powers of moral edification. A further shock for the pedant lay in the fact that both *Mossflow* and *The Western Chamber* were popular, both in the sense that they were widely read and admired, and in the sense that they sprang, not from the world of the academies and ministries, but from the streets and marketplaces. As for the fact that *The Western Chamber* dealt frankly with issues of romantic love, while *Mossflow* explored highly political issues such as the nature of loyalty and the reasons for rebellion – well, that just beat all! Jin made many enemies among the ultra-conservative Confucian pedants of his day.

Jin took hold of the *Mossflow*, which had been circulating in editions of varying lengths, and re-edited it, cutting it down to a mere 70 chapters and a prologue. In doing so he claimed, quite rightly, to have excised much that was otiose and repetitive in order to make the book's fundamental structure clearer. His other innovation, no less bold, was to add to the book a series of prefaces, chapter commentaries and interlinear commentaries in the style of scriptural exegesis, in which he gives an idiosyncratic but blindingly revelatory series of insights into the structure of the novel, and into the possible motivation of the author (see Rolston, 1990). It was a brilliant move: overnight his 1641 edition became a best seller, and remained so, to such an extent that all other versions were eclipsed and almost entirely forgotten until the literary renaissance of the early twentieth century disinterred them.

In his recension, the book has a clear subtext: what do good men do about bad government? The story is set in the early twelfth century, in the closing years of the Northern Song dynasty, just before the loss of the north to the Jin Tartars: the government is corrupt, enervated and in terminal decline, totally unable to prevent the imminent invasion. Local hardmen and gangsters are intimately entwined with government at every level, bandits terrorise the countryside, and the forces of law and order are totally incapable of either protecting the innocent or deterring the vicious. In this context, we encounter first of all a number of individuals who meet with a particular injustice, do the right thing in the situation, yet fall foul of corrupt officials or incompetent government, and can save themselves only by taking to the hills as outlaws. (A good example is Lu Da, who, in order to protect Emerant Lilly and her old dad, goes round to teach the West Mairch Crusher a lesson: not knowing his own strength, he inadvertently kills the Crusher, gets a murder rap laid on him, and has to go on the lam.) One by one these good men are driven into outlawry, and slowly they begin to band together in twos and threes, then in larger groups, until finally they are a formidable army, whose aims are to remind the emperor of the wrongs being done in his name and to redress the injustices committed by avaricious or wicked officials.

Well and good, but about halfway through the book, after a series of chance meetings and coincidences ('He's a useful man, wouldn't it be good if he was with us?' – and lo and behold, he turns up!), the leaders of the band begin to seduce otherwise decent and upright individuals into joining them. Then in one horrific incident, a child is murdered in such a way as to throw the blame onto his guardian, whose skills the outlaws urgently need for the next big battle with the authorities. Weren't they supposed to be the good guys? Slowly disillusion sets in until, under Jin Shengtan's guidance, the discerning reader begins to see that these people have become as ruthless and as morally corrupt as the government they set out to reform.

So the subtext, brilliantly elucidated by Jin Shengtan, using a radical mixture of scriptural exegesis, tactical rewriting and judicious cutting, is one about institutionalisation. Many an upright man does the right thing but is forced to step outside the law, having no alternative but to take to the hills. Each man says to himself that it's only a temporary measure, but is drawn into a horrific nightmare of rebellion and slaughter. And that process is the natural and inevitable end of banding together into a unit so large that it takes on its own momentum, regardless of the aims of its founders. In its own time, this was a dangerous doctrine. *Shuihu Zhuan* has always been dangerous, of course, and has been banned many times in its history, but in the closing years of the Ming dynasty, when invasion by

Manchu nomads seemed imminent, and the symptoms of dynastic decline seemed to mirror those shown in the book, it was especially so. Was Jin Shengtan rousing the masses to rebellion? Whose side was he on? Jin, like any wise man, knew that simple answers are for simple minds. Previous recensions had ended either with the heroes dying in battle, or with them receiving an amnesty from the emperor. Jin, by pruning away the final chapters and ending the book with a dream of retribution at a climactic moment when all the 108 heroes are gathered together, lets the reader make up his own mind: this version is morally ambiguous. Just as each of the major heroes exemplifies one of the answers to the question of what good men do about bad government – no easy, one-size-fits-all answer, but a different response for each individual – so the ending challenges each reader to ask what he or she would do if faced by this same dilemma.

The political questions raised in this book are dynamite in any era, but *Men o the Mossflow* is not afraid to explore the dark side of the psyche either. What does 'heroism' mean? What is a 'hero'? Here are men who booze and brawl their way through their lives, causing mayhem and murder all around them, under the collective rubric of 'Justice and Righteousness'. Cannibalism, rape, indiscriminate slaughter, robbery and violence: are these the distinguishing marks of the hero? In dark and difficult times, times when the leaders of the nation seem to be stuck with their heads in the trough of peculation and pilfering, what is heroism? Does the term have any meaning? What, as decent individuals, can we do about it? No easy answers, but a great and challenging book here, one whose astonishing scope and range dawn on the reader afresh with each re-reading.

Why use Scots?

It's not simply a question of just *choosing* a language, of course. We must build the language we lack. Any good writer transforms his own language, just as any translator worth his salt will transform his own tongue. If Scots is to be something worth the keeping, then it should be able to handle the biggest of books that we can throw at it. Or, to put it another way, we should be able to take the biggest of books and stretch the tongue beyond what we think it can do, make the tongue new by including things we'd never before have dreamt of saying in Scots, to build the language we lack out of the otherness of a different tongue.

And why not a transfusion of Chinese? It's the oldest surviving literary language in the world, and in its vast literature you can find anything you want, from the bawdiest, coarsest speech to the most refined and elliptical of diction. Why not transfuse some of that richness into oor ain [our own] tongue? If the Scots tongue can handle Chinese, it can handle anything. That's one reason for doing it: to show that this 'elegant and malleable' tongue (as Robert Louis Stevenson called it) has still the pith and the virr [vigour] in it to encompass all that the Chinese can do, to show that Scots, bereft of some registers though it may have become, can still bend and stretch and expand, can still become a major player again.

And as for the choice of *Shuihu Zhuan* as a vehicle for Scots: 'Why not Scots?' is, of course, another perfectly reasonable response to the question 'Why use Scots?' As if we needed a reason ...

A Guide for the Perplexed

To begin with what might seem an *outré* sort of passage, take the point where Lu Da is taking orders as a Buddhist monk. It fairly bristles with technical terms, few of which have any proper equivalent in English, let alone Scots.[8] Even the word *buddha*, for instance, I render as *Salvator*. Though I am well aware of the theological distinction between the Buddha and Christ, there seems to be a kind of functional equivalence that helps the narrative along. In cases like this, my first priority is the narrative; clotting up the story with abstruse technical terms may produce a kind of accuracy, but it doesn't help to make a rattling good yarn.[9] And in any case, *Salvator* [saviour] is a lovely old word that we don't see or hear enough of these days. Similarly, the term *zhai*, meaning vegetarian food, such as is served in Buddhist monasteries, prompted the use of the old term *lentren* [Lenten]: doubly useful, as *zhai*, like *lentren*, also has connotations of 'fasting'. Here is how part of the ceremony goes:

> The Elder grippit the blank lines an spak this halie-rhyme:
> Ane blink o leivin licht ti see
> Is mair nor warld's gear nor fee;
> The Salvator's law is braid ti see:
> PROFUNDITAS is the name A gie.
> An whan the Giein o the Name wis by the Elder haunit the priestline ti Brither Quairmaister for him ti transcrieve the name an pass it on ti Profunditas Lu ti keep. Neist the Elder gied forth the cassock an the vestments for Profunditas ti pit on, the Procurator led him afore the Throne o the Law for the Layin on o Hauns, an the Elder gied him the Admonition:
> ANE: beild ye in consent o the Enlichtencie o Divinitie
> TWA: beild ye in observe o the Law o Veritie

THRIE: beild ye in reverence o the freins an dominies o the Order.
Thir is the THRIE PERFUGIA. The FIVE ABSTINENTIA is
ANE: takna nae life
TWA: reivena nor spulyie nane
THRIE: deboshna nor hure nane
FOWER: louna strang drink nane
FIVE: tellna nae lees.
Kennin naethin o the SAE SALL A or SAE SALL A NANE at maun be reponit afore the Offrin Table, Profunditas juist cam out wi 'Ay, A'll mind o that', an aa the brithers laucht. (Holton, 1987: 79)[10]

[The Elder took hold of the blank certificate and spoke this holy-rhyme:
One blink of living light to see
Is more than world's gear or fee;
The Saviour's law is broad to see:
PROFUNDITAS is the name I give.
And when the Giving of the Name was over the Elder handed the priest-certificate to Brother Bookmaster for him to transcribe the name and pass it on to Profunditas Lu to keep. Next the Elder gave out the cassock and the vestments for Profunditas to put on, the Procurator led him before the Throne of the Law for the Laying on of Hands, and the Elder gave him the Admonition:
ONE: shelter in consent of the Enlightency of Divinity
TWO: shelter in observance of the Law of Truth
THRIE: shelter in reverence of the friends and teachers of the Order.
These are the THREE PERFUGIA. The FIVE ABSTINENTIA are
ONE: take no life
TWO: rob not nor plunder
THREE: debauch not nor go whoring
FOUR: love not strong drink
FIVE: tell no lies.
Knowing nothing of the SO SHALL I or SO SHALL I NONE that must be answered before the Offering Table, Profunditas just came out with 'Yes, I'll remember that', and all the brothers laughed.]

A few notes will no doubt be in order here. *The Salvator's law* renders the Chinese *fo fa*: both of these terms are themselves translations from the Sanskrit. *Fo* renders *buddha* ['enlightened one'], while *fa* renders *dharma* ['the law, the teachings of the Buddha, the way things work/are']. In this straightforward exchange here, a little theological detail is lost, but much of the sense is kept. *Salvator*, being a little archaic nowadays, also gives a nice high-register feeling, and is also more detached from the image of Jesus Christ than the English 'saviour' would be in this context, which is all to the good here. *Profunditas* is of course a Latin coinage (yes, reader, I made it up). The original Chinese is *Zhi Shen*, literally 'Wisdom Deep', hence my translation. I admit to stealing the wonderfully evocative and astonishingly handy

Latinising of names – especially priestly names and titles – from the master of Chinese-English translation, David Hawkes (e.g. see Hawkes & Minford, 1973–1986). Latin helps to make names less opaque by giving some clue as to their meaning (they are quite transparent to the Chinese reader), and also gives some feeling of the high-register liturgical language that creeps into the text at this point. And, of course, when the grandly and ecclesiastically titled Profunditas starts to get roaring drunk and fight with the other monks, it retains a great deal of the comic effect of the original. By contrast, a mere *Zhi Shen* would mean nothing to the reader of the translation.

Ecclesiastical titles in *Mossflow* were produced in various ways. There exist Latin titles for the various offices and functionaries of a monastery. Many of these were taken over as they stand; other titles were Scotticised from the Chinese (e.g. *Brither Quairmaister* [Brother Bookmaster]); some, such as *Procurator* or *Rector*, adapted secular roles to suit the sense or the function of the Chinese title. Some others had to be invented from scratch, such as *Praepositor*, which is a Latinising of the Chinese *shouzuo* ('head seat' – the senior monastic administrator).

Titles in general present the translator with a set of tricky problems. In the case of our source text, which is set within the context of a formal and highly bureaucratised society that was extraordinarily fertile in its proliferation of ranks, titles and forms of address, these problems are compounded by the fact that many of the titles used are in fact unhistorical: some are anachronistic, some are inaccurately applied – as when the character's rank and duties are clearly those of an NCO, whereas his title seems to denote HQ staff officer level – and some are just plain made up. There can be no ready-made solution. By drawing on the records of the Royal Burghs, legal records, minute books of Craft Guilds and so on, some titles can be found and some can be adapted for use. Some are blindingly obvious, and need only to be translated. For example, *Chief Justiciar o the Southron College o Kaifeng* [Chief Justice of the Southern College in Kaifeng], or *Lord Collegiar o* [Collegiate Lord of] *the Royal Registry*, are clearly high offices, and need little or no modification. Similarly, *jiaotou* is an arms instructor: *jiao* is the normal verb 'to teach', while the *tou* suffix is a noun-former. This becomes *Leirsman* [from *leir* = to teach] with little or no friction. *Tixia*, on the other hand, is problematic: first, in that it's not at all clear what the title means, and secondly, the responsibilities of the *tixia* are unclear. It does seem likely that it is a high military rank; yet Profunditas, as we have him in the novel, is clearly not much more than an unarmed combat instructor, an NCO. So I've called him *Controller*, for lack of anything more specific to go on.

Others are as tricky: *yuanwai* was a title awarded to those who had qualified to hold office but never actually did so. Its sense is 'outside the [register of] personnel', and at times this rank could be purchased: it was often used by rich and idle landowners, and is widely glossed as equivalent, at least in later Imperial times, to the English 'squire'. Now this may have a kind of social appropriateness – which is what led me to use *Laird* [a rank deriving from landownership] in early versions – but in fact it tells you nothing about the holder except that he is of middling to high rank. It doesn't tell you that he belonged to the literati class, for instance. Perhaps *Supernumerary* carries something more of the feeling of being an unattached mandarin. But I remain on the lookout for a better version.

Some titles will remain bafflingly obscure whatever we do: in these few cases, the best that can be done is to invent something that has a vague ring of what we think the character's position might have entailed. Colour is often the thing: if the original suggests a musty pettifogging sort of job, or a dashing, heroic, make-up-the-rules-as-you-go role, responding to that is often as important as formal accuracy. (It ought to go without saying that much research is needed: you can't get the feeling of a title until you have thoroughly investigated the what, when, where and how of it.)

Forms of address present particular problems in pre-modern Chinese, since politeness and polite language demanded that personal pronouns be avoided in favour of honorifics and humilifics: this is what produces 'Johnnie Chinee' horrors such as 'your honourable house'. Clearly, I don't want characters talking like Fu MacChu, but it is a fact that 'your house' was rendered by *gui fushang* [literally 'your noble palace']. Hence the use of terms like *yir guid hous* [your good house] or *yir guid sel* [your good self] and so on. Conversely, a man of middle years, while talking to a social superior, would use the term *laohan*, which becomes *this auld bodie* [old person] and so demands the sort of obsequious third person once used by genteel shop assistants. Other forms, such as *honest brither* [brother], spring from respect language and have been influenced in their making by ballad Scots as much as anything else.

Dialogue presents other problems, but here I'll focus only on the problem of dialect. *Shuihu Zhuan* is admired for the ease with which it handles different dialects, and while much of that is today so obscure as to be invisible to the general reader, there are occasions where a character is so clearly identified by his own shibboleths that the translator can't ignore them. A case in point is Lu Da, whom we met as he metamorphosed into Profunditas Lu. A native of Gansu province in the far northwest, a wild frontier area on the fringes of the Gobi desert, he has a pronounced Gansu accent, marked mainly by his use of the unusual first-person pronoun *sajia*. What can we do about this? Clearly there is no Scots equivalent. One possibility is to draw on forms used by writers to represent Gaelic-speakers' difficulties with Scots, such as *her nainsel* [*ainsel* = oneself], but it won't do, because it was used patronisingly (if not insultingly) for so long that it's hard to wash away that tone, and we have no evidence that the use of *sajia* carried the same negative connotations. My first version attempted to give Profunditas a strong local accent: I thought Buchan might do, but soon found out that I couldn't write a convincing Buchan accent, so I simply ignored *sajia*. It later occurred to me that, though we have no first-person pronouns, we do have to hand the Shetland *de, du, dy* [thee, thou, thy] forms, which, if I used them and them only, would give the same faint whiff of an accent that is given by the use of *sajia* unsupported by other dialect forms. So the next recension of *Mossflow* will make use of this feature, and Profunditas will have a touch of the Shetlander about him.

Profanity, vulgarity, swearie-words, 'mill talk' – what do we do about them? Well, if we're honest, we'll reproduce all of it, no matter how foul we might think it, and we'll reproduce it as closely as we can, because our job is to let the text speak – not to bowdlerise, gut or rewrite it. One word that has raised eyebrows is a great favourite among the braw lads o [brave boys of] the Mossflow: *zhiniang zei*. This would be rendered in English as *motherfucking bandit*, but I didn't like the way this sounded so much like an Americanism, so I took advantage of the fact that *niang* can be used for other female relatives, and came up with *granny-shaggin* for the first part. *Bandit* was another thing: *cateran* or *reiver* were near-hand, but they didn't seem to roll off the tongue the way the original undoubtedly does. So I opted for alliteration – always a good idea with swearie-words, I think – and came up with *granny-shaggin get* [bastard] instead, which is both satisfactorily obscene and satisfyingly rhythmic. Another common term of abuse is *si*, usually in phrases such as *ni zhe si*. Its history is clear as an archaic term for a domestic servant, as is its use as a generalised vaguely offensive appellation. But we don't have an equivalent, so I took instead (with apologies to travellers, Romanies and others to whom it has been misapplied) *tink*, which is a similarly mild though abusive term. And *ni zhe si* (literally, *you this tink*) becomes quite happily *ye tink, ye*.

Proverbs and saws are scattered liberally through *Shuihu Zhuan*, and the difficulty there is to give them that worn-down, used feeling that a good proverb has. The best advice I can give is to trust your ear: go about repeating your various versions, chant them like mantras, sing them in the bath, until one falls into a loose easy rhythm that sticks in your head. Some examples:

- atween the fower seas, we're brithers aa
  [between the four seas, we're brothers all];

- whan twae ill-willers meet, byornar shairp's their een
  [when two enemies meet, very sharp are their eyes];
- you an me we'll leive thegither, an thegither we'll dee
  [you and me we'll live together, and together we'll die].

The saw should roll off the tongue like a ballad verse: rhythm is the key here. And when, as is often the case, the little saws are themselves in rhyme, we've just got to set to and do what we can. For instance:

> Afore the Nine-League Hills there wis a battle,
> Whaur herd-lads nou finds spear an sword;
> As sweet winds riffle owre the Blackwatter River,
> E'en sae did Lady Yu bid fareweill ti her lord. (Holton, 1987: 81)
>
> [Before the Nine-League Hills there was a battle,/Where shepherd-lads now find spears an swords;/As sweet winds ripple over the Blackwater River,/Even so did Lady Yu bid farewell to her lord.]

Now the reader doesn't actually need to know what all Chinese readers would: that this verse refers to the tragic story of the favourite concubine of warlord Xiang Yu, who killed herself as her lord was about to be defeated in his last battle.[11] The main thing is that in the text it appears as a comic counterpoint to Profunditas getting his comeuppance from the Abbeymaister. Similarly, this:

> Bi yir bunnet's bonnie leam
> Ye're ti be the groom at een!
> Bi yir jimp an narra shift
> Ye're ti be guidson this nicht! (Holton, 1993: 102)
>
> [By your bonnet's pretty gleam/You're to be the groom this evening!/By your scanty and narrow shirt/You're to be a son-in-law tonight!]

This is no more than a simple folk song sung at a wedding, and need be no more (and no less) elegant than a folk song. Again, as with the saws, the songs have to be repeated again and again until they turn into something you can *hear*, and can imagine yourself singing, at the very least.

Then there are puns. Of all the great world languages, Chinese is the poorest in speech sounds, and hence the richest in homophones. What a tongue this is for punning! There was even a fashion in the thirteen–fourteenth century for verse forms that involved long palindromic puns, and still today a form of multi-level punning called *xiehou yu* ('wait-a-bit words') is very popular in China. *Shuihu Zhuan*, being an action novel, contains far fewer word games than would, say, a novel set among the idle literati class, but they still crop up. One example will be enough here: when Profunditas is first creating havoc in the monastery he gets into an altercation with a monk who tries to stop him sleeping in the meditation hall. *'Shan zai!'* [Oh, wonderful!], says the monk sarcastically. Profunditas hears this as *shanyu*, meaning 'eel'. I had to resort to *'ye're daein weill!'* [you're doing well], which Profunditas hears as *daimen-eel* – so the pun has a kind of transferable sense. Here's the passage (*haive-eel* is a 'conger-eel', *daimen-eel* an 'occasional eel'):

> 'Ay, ye're daein weill!' says the bodie.
> 'Daimen-eel?' rairs Profunditas. 'Haive-eel A've etten, but whit's a daimen-eel?'
> 'Och, it's wersh wark', says the bodie.
> 'Wersh? It's got a muckle fat belly, the haive-eel, guid fat sweet eatin – hou's it wersh?' quo Profunditas. (Holton, 1987: 80)

> ['Yes, you're doing well!' says the chap./'Daimen-eel?' roars Profunditas. 'Conger-eel I've eaten, but what's a daimen-eel?'/'Oh, it's a tough job', says the chap./'Tough? It's got a big fat belly, the conger-eel, good fat sweet eating – how is it tough?' says Profunditas.]

It's not easy to deal with puns, and serendipity is often all that can help. Puns are always a problem.

So, too, are the obscurities, the *hapax legomena*, the words or expressions rendered wholly opaque by the passing of time. Trust to luck, be bold, revise and revise, ask for help, do as much research as is feasible, try to know your text as well as you possibly can – and it's still down to a lucky hit much of the time. For instance, while I was working on a version of a fourteenth-century poem cycle by Qiao Jifu (Holton, 1995b) I met a very obscure word. Chinese dictionaries came up with nothing much: *a kind of water bird, possibly purple*, or *a water bird, bigger than a duck* – that was as much help as I got. So I did what you do, inserted a splint, and decided to come back to the problem later. Much later, while looking for something else in the *Concise Scots Dictionary* (1985: 194) I found this: *'fewlume, n. some kind of bird*, e16' [early sixteenth century], with the helpful thought that it might be related to *faoileann*, the Gaelic word for a seagull. Bingo! In went *fewlum*, and in fact, in went *fewlums in flauchts* [flocks/flights]. It's as obscure as the original, but since it appears in a long list of birds that were being startled into flight, it's comprehensible. Hits as lucky as that are rare, though.

Names present their own delights. Each of the main characters in *Mossflow* has more than one name, for a start. Lu Da becomes *Profunditas* after his ordination, but also has the byname of *The Flourist Freir* [Tattooed Friar]. One of Song Jiang's bynames is *Timeous Rain* [Timely Rain], Li

Zhong's is *General Toober-the-Tiger* [Thrash-the-Tiger], and so on. Like the Border reivers, each one has his byname, and like the reivers' bynames, they are often very colourful. *The Reid Deil* [Red Devil], *Braid Daylicht Rottan* [Broad Daylight Rat], *The Sleikit Staur* [Cunning Star], *The West Mairch Crusher* [West March Crusher] all appear in the list of *Mossflow* characters. These I would render as closely as possible to the original. Names – in the usual Chinese order of family name first and personal name after – I have not changed, except to follow the sinological convention of translating female names, while leaving male names in transliterated form. This may not be entirely ideal, since male names are as transparent to the Chinese reader as female ones (personal names are all invented by the family, and are chosen for their meaning) but it does have the merit of burdening the text with fewer Chinese names, and giving a more positive identification to the female characters. So *Auld* [Old] *Jin's* daughter becomes *Emerant Lilly* [Emerald Lily] rather than Jin Cuilian, and the famous besom [loose woman] Pan Jinlian will appear as *Gowden Lilly* [Golden Lily].[12] Another habit is to name sons by their sequence in the family: Mr and Mrs Wang's second son would be *Secundo Wang*, his brothers *Tertio, Quarto, Octavo* and so on. I have used this convention for minor characters, and have sometimes translated their names in full – *Lucky Li* for Li Ji, for example. This helps to keep the translated text free of too many opacities, and helps (I hope) to keep the heroes distinct from the walk-on parts.

Place names I will, in future recensions, Scotticise as much as I can. *Xiao Hua Shan* has already become *Smaa Glore Hill* [Small Glory Hill], and *Dongjing, The Eastren* [Eastern] *Capital*. Similarly, *Xinzhou* could be rendered as *Faithlands*, *Jiangnan* as *Besouth the Watter* [South of the River], and so on. This is again to prevent the text from being cluttered up with words that are meaningless to the general reader.

How to Do It Yourself
Read everything

It's all useful if it's written in Scots – the Makars, Hugh MacDiarmid, S.R. Crockett and Annie Swan, *Para Handy*, Edwardian doggerel, folk song and ballads, Wilson's *Tales of the Borders* (which you'll have to mentally translate back into Scots), Sir Walter Scott, James Hogg, Robert Fergusson, Robert Burns, John Galt, Robert Garioch, Robert McLellan, W.N. Herbert, Irvine Welsh, nineteenth-century newspaper serials, eighteenth-century correspondence, chapbooks, Burgh Court records, Pitcairn's *Trials*, Stair's *Institutes*, Murray's *The Dialect of the Southern Counties of Scotland*, Barbour's

Brus and Blin Hary's *Wallace*, thirteenth-century romances and twentieth-century transcriptions of tales and reminiscence – as well as anything and everything published by the Scottish Text Society. Nothing like an exhaustive list, of course – just what comes up at random – but the point is not to exclude anything. You're not reading for good taste.

Read the dictionaries, too. Don't just consult them. Graze them, browse on them, follow chains and trails of words through each one, and from dictionary to dictionary. You can never have access to too many dictionaries or glossaries: they are your tools. No matter how obsolete or jejune or incomplete a dictionary, there may come a time when it is the only tool to help you out of a jam. Know your dictionaries as well as you know your texts. And make your own. No matter how helpful a shelf of dictionaries and glossaries may be, what you will need is a reference to your own idiolect. (Computers make it easy.) A dictionary for each text you translate will help you with consistency and accuracy, of course, but it will also help you to develop the individual authorial voice that each text will need.

What you must do is read to sensitise your ear to the possible rhythms, to the allowable or potentially useful structures. You must learn your own language as thoroughly as you can (if you don't think that's necessary, go and read the instruction leaflet for your Japanese video, and reflect on the way non-native speakers write English). Scots prose is, for almost all of us, gey near [very nearly] a foreign tongue, and unless we make a conscious effort to master this discourse, we will never be able to translate into it.

Listen

Listen to everything: on the streets, in the pubs, on the radio and the TV. Scots is still a living language – you can't write it naturally if you don't speak it naturally, and the best way to learn its cadences and its rhythms is to listen to unselfconscious, *natural* speakers. Get yourself away to the landart airts [country places], listen to your granny and her pals, speak to the bairns [children]. Be the chiel amang fowk takin notes [the one taking notes in a crowd].[13] As your ear develops, learn to trust it. Always read your drafts aloud: if something doesn't sound right to you, keep working at it until it does. And once you're happy with it, read to an audience: having an audience is a great concentrator of the mind – and the audience will be on your side if you're getting it right, and can be a great help to you.

Make it new

There are no rulebooks. There may be strategies and canons (such as grammatical acceptability, dialect preference and so on), but there is no one single way that is right. Our job is to reflect and to use the incredible fecundity of the tongue, and, if we are successful, to lay our wee chuckie stane on the cairn [add our little stone to the pile – make our small contribution]. Defer to the wisdom of experience, but don't let anybody else tell you what's right and what's wrong. You're going to be making it new, and that can be a daunting experience. You'll need faith in yourself, too, because there'll aye be the hoodie craws [always be the carrion crows – Jeremiahs] to tell you that it's a doomed enterprise, and that you're wasting your time. NEVER HEED THEM! You're making it new, you're working for the future, not for the past.

Wale a Leid an Wale a Warld (Choose a Language and Choose a World)

If you choose a text from a distant time or place, you've already chosen your world as you read it, as you silently collude with the authorial voice to make it all new again – each reader has a different text, each re-reading changes the text. Then if you choose to translate the text into another medium, you create another text whose relationship with the *ur*-text bears some relationship to the author–reader collusion, filtered through the medium of the translator's voice. And the translator – ventriloquist and dummy together – must let his text speak in the best way he knows how. Ego is not a factor here, as the voice of the translator is not the point. The authorial voice and the translator's voice must sing together in a kind of unison, neither wholly obscured by the other, each separate and distinct, but both sharing the same modes of delight. To quote Scottish poet W.S. Graham:

> Each word is touched by and filled with the activity of every speaker. Each word changes every time it is brought to life. Each single word uttered twice becomes a new word each time. You cannot twice bring the same word into sound.
>
> It is a good direction to believe that this language which is so scored and impressed by the commotion of all [of] us since its birth can be arranged to in its turn impress significantly for the good of each individual. Let us endure the sudden affection of the language. (Graham, 1986: 43)

Let us indeed learn to love language, to love its quirks and intricacies, its coinages and its clumsinesses. And let us express that love in action. Show the tongue what it's capable of by offering it the greatest challenge we can imagine, the greatest stretching of its powers.

I.A. Richards (1932) imagined that 'the greatest challenge ever undertaken by the human mind' was the translation of Chinese philosophical texts into English. Now, we can't deny the enormous difficulty of that task, but isn't every act of speech an act of translation no less stupendous? (If you doubt it, try telling your neighbour about the taste of that wine you drank on holiday, or tell your loved one precisely what was the feeling-tone of that dream that so scared you.) Every act that involves the transfer of thought/emotion/sensation into language is an act of translation, and though the hidden springs of the process may not make it appear so to us, that transfer involves huge resources of brainpower: imagination, intuition, comparison, analysis, are all parts of this process. To translate a work of imagination from one tongue to another requires these same extraordinary resources to be used to the full, and to be used in a conscious, directed way. It is, they say, impossible.

Now, when we use sound or stone, or daubs of bright colour on a flat surface, or the urbane and elegant tongue that is mathematics, then clearly we are trying to express what may not be susceptible of expression via the medium of language. But when, as in a poem, we try to use language against itself, to use our tongue to say the unsayable, then we are at the heart of the mystery that is language. And does it compound the absurdity to try to transfer that mystery from one tongue to another? Well, it's daft, of course – yet it works. *Eppur si muove* ... Here is the Impossible Machine we inhabit. Here is the mystery of that angelic meta-language that Walter Benjamin imagined, where the transfer of meaning takes place.

It's daft, but we do it. And maybe that is the best rationale of all for what we do as translators. It's daft, it's maybe theoretically or philosophically dubious. But it works. Walter Benjamin remarks:

> Fragments of a vessel which are to be glued together must match each other in the smallest details, though they need not be like each other ... [and so translation] must lovingly and in detail incorporate the original's mode of signification, *thus making both the original and the translation recognisable as fragments of a greater language.* (Benjamin, 1973: 78; my emphasis)

It works, in that we can – by whatever means, miraculous or otherwise – make a rendering in our own tongue of a text from the other end of the world and/or from a time we have never known. Benjamin again:

A real translation is transparent; it does not cover the original, does not block its light, but allows the pure language, as though reinforced by its own medium, to shine upon the original all the more fully. (Benjamin, 1973: 79)

My grandfather once said to me that nothing was worth having unless you shared it – and this, he felt, applied especially to knowledge. Here is your rationale. You may sit in your study beikin bi the fire [basking by the fire], lost in your books, but unless ye tak yir quair [you take your book] in hand like Robert Henryson did,[14] and tell those to whom the book is eternally shut, 'Look, here's a story, boys, here's something that might change your life' – then what is the good of your knowing, of your reading, if no one but you knows the tale? Hence the need for folk like us – owresetters,[15] takers-over: translators. That's the point.

Notes

1. *The Scots Style Sheet* was drawn up in 1947 by a group of writers concerned to standardise the spelling of Scots.
2. For some of my versions of Classical Chinese poetry in Scots, see Douglas and Stokes, 1994.
3. Some scholars take the view that, since no other evidence for Song Jiang exists, he was in fact a fictional character who was included in the histories by mistake.
4. This is still a working title: *Shui* signifies water, *hu* is an obscure term denoting the edge of a river or a riverbank, and *Zhuan* denotes a chronicle. Since much of the action revolves around the bandits' lair in the vast marshes of Liangshanbo, John Scott's suggested title *The Fenland Saga* (personal communication) has much to commend it. We don't have in Scotland this type of geographical feature (though the mid-reaches of the Forth may once have been similar), so it hasn't been easy to find an equivalent. A *mossflow* is a loose boggy bit of moorland: that and the echoes of S.R. Crockett's fine tale of Border Covenanters, *Men of the Mosshags* (Crockett, 1895), persuaded me to stick with the current title for the present. But I'm still not wholly convinced.
5. This title was used by J.H. Jackson for his translation (Jackson, 1963). Titles settled on by other translators include: *All Men Are Brothers* (Buck, 1957), *Outlaws of the Marsh* (Shapiro, 1981), and *The Marshes of Mount Liang* (Dent-Young, 1994, 1997, 2001, 2002a, 2002b). Sadly, none of these translations can be wholly recommended (and the first two are to be avoided). To my knowledge, the best version available is in French (Dars, c1978). I cannot comment on the accuracy or otherwise of versions in other languages, but there are Czech, Swedish and, I believe, Norwegian translations. Experienced translators will recognise in the multiplicity of versions of the title some of the inherent difficulties of rendering the sense of *shuihu*: Jackson and Dars attempted it, while Buck, Shapiro and the Dent-Youngs all executed body-swerves of various degrees of neatness. (As indeed have I so far ...)

6. The details of his life are obscure: because he was executed, his name appears nowhere in any officially-sanctioned publication. Non-persons weren't a Soviet invention: the Manchus were pretty ruthless at suppressing all traces of those who disagreed with them. For Jin's life and work, see Wang, J., n.d.
7. The Ming dynasty ran from 1358 to 1664.
8. Most of these terms have come in to English as unnaturalised Sanskrit words, and I didn't feel that I ought to impose on the reader the necessity of learning Sanskrit, on top of having to cope with the unfamiliarity of Chinese names.
9. Here I part company with many (sadly, very many) of my sinological colleagues. I cannot see the point of taking a spare and beautiful text and translating it in such a way that, constipated with abstruse and ugly technical terms, it becomes unlovely. However accurate such a version may be, if it fails to render the grace and elegance of the original, it fails as a translation. To render beautiful prose in ugly prose is art murder, no less. The perpetrators, unless their aim is solely the production of an unlovely undergraduate crib, should be ashamed of themselves.
10. Here and in subsequent quotations from the published extracts there are minor authorial modifications.
11. This story is the basis for the Beijing Opera *Bawang Bie Ji*, as shown in Chen Kaige's film *Farewell my Concubine.*
12. It should be noted that the resonances and hidden allusions of the names in *Shuihu Zhuan* are much appreciated by connoisseurs as adding flavour and subtlety to the narrative: perhaps the only way to bring any of that out would be to take all the names, both male and female, and translate everything into Scots. Wang Jin would then have to appear as *King Promoter.* I'm not too happy about that. It seems to me to be about as accurate as translating *January* as 'the month of the Roman god of boundaries who faces both ways'. A bit over the top, really.
13. Derived from a line – 'A chield's amang you takin' notes' – in Robert Burns's poem 'On Captain Grose's Peregrinations through Scotland'.
14. This reference is to an early stanza in a late-medieval poem 'Testament of Cresseid' by Robert Henryson (1968: 62, ll. 36–40). The poem begins with Henryson's description of how, chilled by winter cold, he settled down to write his tragedy: 'I mend the fyre and beikit me about,/Than tuik ane drink, my spreitis to comfort,/And armit me weill fra the cauld thairout./To cut the winter nicht and mak it schort/I tuik ane quair – and left all vther sport'. [I banked the fire and warmed myself,/Then took a drink to raise my spirits,/Protecting myself well from the cold outside./To pass the winter night and make it short/I took a book – and ignored all other diversions.]
15. Scots for 'translators'.

Chapter 2
Translating Homer's Odyssey

WILLIAM NEILL

Why Scots? Probably because like Gavin Douglas 'I had nane other choys' [no other choice]. There are many translations of Homer into English verse and prose. I thought that I could contribute a little to the canon by trying to add another. As to the efficacy of Scots for translation, I had no doubts whatsoever. Scots is a flexible and full medium with no scarcity of suitable lexis with which to come at least as near to Homer as standard English does, and in some instances even nearer. The Scots language retains allophones no longer heard in English, and these make for sensible differences in words that sound like homonyms in English. *Whales* and *wails* are not confused in Scottish minds; the vowel difference between *tied* and *tide* indicates a difference of meaning not apparent in the English of England. Scots, like the English of America (now the most widely spoken form), retains older lexical items such as the past participle *gotten*. To refer to such a retention as *archaic* is hardly reasonable in a world context. As for nouns, Scots does not fall short. *Nieves* are clenched fists, *loofs* have an open palm, and a *gowpen* is formed by the cupping of hands together. Scots is not only strong and vivid, it is precise and detailed. You may slap with a *loof*, but you must use your *nieve* to punch and you may give someone a *jundie* [jolt] with your elbow. And you can, with a *nieve*, dish out blows of different kinds such as *dunts, dunches, clours* and *blaffarts*. And what Irus gets from Odysseus in the beggars' brawl is a *clamihewit*, a *hey-ma-nanny*, a good hammering.

    On one occasion, after a reading, I was asked why I had used an English word where a Scots word could have been used. I was not ignorant of the word the objector thought I should have used (and could have kicked myself for not using it), but it spurred me to spend time thinking about the whole business of translation into tongues whose status is contested. The fact that words are shared between languages sheds no light on the *mere dialect/separate development* controversy. A Scots speaker might well be asked why he used Beethoven's last words *mehr licht* (Scots: *mair licht*) when he might have chosen the standard English *more light*, or why he used the French *assiette* (Scots: *ashet*) for a certain kind of dish. I know instantly the shape of an *ashet* [a large, flat, oval serving plate], but I would require at least one adjective to define the type of dish. The Scots word has an immediate impact, whereas the use of English causes a delay, however slight. The use of universal Italian words in Belli's sonnets does not prove, one way or the other, that *romanesco* is a separate development or a dialect of standard Italian (the Florentine dialect), but who would doubt that Belli's verse must have had a more immediate impact on the Roman citizens of his day than did the verse of Dante?[1] As far as literature is concerned, one dialect/ language is as good as another provided it is understood by the people for whom it is intended. One must try for Coleridge's 'best words in the best order' (Coleridge, 1990: 90) provided the audience well understands them, and irrespective of the size of the audience.

Scottish classical translation is not lacking in examples. There is the sixteenth-century Scots version of the *Aeneid* by Gavin Douglas (Coldwell, 1957–64), the first full-length translation of a classical text in Britain. In the eighteenth century there is Ewen MacLachlan's partial translation into Gaelic of the *Iliad* (Macdonald, 1937) – though MacLachlan's translation does not stick very closely to the text and makes no attempt to echo its metre. As to more recent translations, I was much more impressed by John Maclean's Gaelic *Odusseia Homair* (Mac Gilleathain, 1976), a full translation by a scholarly member of a talented and poetic family. There are fine translations by Robert Garioch (1973: 42–3) of Hesiod's *Works and Days,* and by Douglas Young (1958, 1959) of Aristophanes' plays *The Birds* and *The Frogs*. Remembering the assertions of Gavin Douglas, and the fine example of John Maclean, started me thinking that perhaps a Scots translation of the *Odyssey* might be made, as this was an open field.

I deliberately chose the *Odyssey* rather than the *Iliad* simply because I liked its 'surge and thunder'.[2] The crafty Odysseus strikes me as the most human (if not the most proper) of all the heroes who gathered on the plains of Troy, and it seemed to me that Scots, with its ballad and story-telling tradition, was more suited to the story episodes that attracted me than is standard English. To one who is old enough to remember a time when many a small Ayrshire farm made its own butter and cheese, and in which *bines lippen-fu* [shallow tubs full to the brim] stood around in cool dairies waiting for the cream to be skimmed, the domestic arrangements of Polyphemus were not all that strange. The Scottish cannibal Sawnie Bain's name conjured up horrors that matched those of the Cyclops, and Fingal's cave, which I had sailed past in a small dinghy on a glorious summer holiday, was indeed that of a giant. Nor is Scotland short on giant-tales and how these monsters may be defeated by guile. The Gaelic *Fionn ann an Taigh a' Bhlàir Bhuidhe* is one such story, and tells how the unfortunate Fingal is rescued by Diarmaid from the clutches of a giant. There is a whiff of Circe in the ballads of *True Thomas* and *Tam Linn*; nor is fierce and bloody revenge absent from the canon in the story of *Fair Helen* of *Kirkconnel* and *The Douglas Tragedy*. As for trouble at sea, there is the ruinous voyage of *Sir Patrick Spens*, while *The Wife of Usher's Well* has something of a visit to the underworld about it. I heard all these ballads at school, on the tongue of an English master whose usual classroom Scottish Standard English was exchanged for the broad Ayrshire Scots of his youth, which enlivened and enriched these ballads.

George Bruce, in the foreword to my published translation, makes the point that 'there is a demand in the Scots ... that it be spoken out loud' (Neill, 1992: 14), and indeed this is the way in which the first Greeks must have heard these tales. The original audience for the ballads lived in an oral tradition, as did the hearers of the adventures that form the episodes of the *Odyssey*. The folk-tale elements remain even in the Homeric versions: the noble Nausicaa does the family washing, albeit with the help of the maids of the palace. The repetitive kennings, like those of *Beowulf*, are enough to establish that the verses (like the Border Ballads) were first recited by a minstrel to an audience who could not read them. This is very far from saying that the listeners were what we think of nowadays as 'illiterate'. The variety of the tales, the structure of the verse, the mnemonic formulae and the consistency of the characters all show that they were as intelligent as an audience of today. The *sound* of the verses was important to them just as sound was important to the eighteenth-century poet Duncan Ban MacIntrye, who could not read or write Gaelic, but could compose and hold in memory many complicated verse forms, and could remember enough of them to dictate six thousand lines to the lettered Gael who transcribed them. It is then a proper aim that a translator of the *Odyssey* should aim at a version that can be spoken to advantage or sound in a reader's ear.[3]

There is a great deal of nonsense talked about translation: the leading myth being that one should not use dictionaries, cribs or other translations as this is somehow 'cheating'. But in a long work such as the Homeric poems, the passage of time and the arguments of scholars about doubtful renderings make such reference not merely prudent but necessary. I had access to Butcher and Lang's (BL) version (1887) and A.T. Murray's (ATM) version (1919) in the Loeb Classical Library. I make no excuses for the use of prose versions since I see that other verse translators have not been ashamed to refer to such assistance. However, in making the Scots translation, the original text was always before me, and every Greek word in each line was studied for the Scots word or phrase I thought most suitably fitted. I also tried to match the Greek version line for line, though for obvious reasons this was not always successful. I may say also that I was aware of Pound's disputes with scholars on the grounds that some of his translations were flawed. I resolved, therefore, to attempt a fair degree of accuracy while trying to retain at least some of the poetic qualities of the original. In pursuit of this, although eschewing any immediate reappraisal of English verse translations (for fear of unconscious imitation), I studied the Gaelic versions of MacLachlan and Maclean. As John Maclean says in his 1968 paper, 'Translating Homer', read to the Gaelic Society of Inverness (published within Mac Gilleathain, 1976: n.p.), MacLachlan's version is really a paraphrase. Furthermore, though his Gaelic and classical learning is profound, the form of his verse owes a deal more to Ossian than to Homer. John Maclean (Iain Mac Gilleathain) uses hexameters excellently well, as in this example from Book IX:

> Nēriton einosiphullon, ariprepes; amphi de nēsoi
> pollai naietaousi mala skhedon allēlēsi
> Doulikhion te Samē te kai hulēessa Zakunthos.
>
> Néritoin, 's critheanach duilleach 's as sònraichte sealladh, mu'n cuairt di
> 's iomadach eilean a th' ann, 's iad a' laighe ro-dhlùth air a chéile,
> Dùlichion agus Samé is Sacuntos, innis nan coilltean.
> (Mac Gilleathain, 1976: n.p.)
>
> [Neriton, clothed in waving woods, seen from afar and circled by many isles that lie close to one another, Dulichion and Same and forested Zakynthos.]

Maclean's Gaelic not only translates the accurate sense of the Greek but matches the native metre. Gaelic has a lexical and accentual structure that allows this. However, English and Scots do not produce hexameters easily. Attempts to produce them have been for the most part unsuccessful, though Robert Garioch's 'Sisyphus' is a much better than average example:

> Bumpity doun in the corrie gaed whuddran the pitiless whun stane.
> (Garioch, 1966: 79)
>
> [Bumpity down in the hillside hollow went rushing the pitiless whinstone.]

Word order makes little difference in Greek or Latin verse, where a comprehensive case-ending system resolves any syntactical doubts, but requires a deal of strained shuffling in English. For example, George Meredith attempts the hexameter and rearranges the order of words:

> As rose then stupendous the Trojans' cry and Achaians',
> Dread upshouting as one when together they clashed in the conflict.
> ('Clash in Arms of the Achaians and Trojans', Meredith, 1912/1928: 559)

And Samuel Taylor Coleridge, translating from Schiller, has:

> Strongly it bears us along in swelling and limitless billows,
> Nothing before and nothing behind but the sky and the ocean.
> ('The Homeric Hexameter described and exemplified',
> Coleridge, 1969; repr. 1978: 307)

Yet perhaps it would be difficult for a translator less skilful than Coleridge to sustain this metre in a Scots poem of any great length. Scots, being of the same Germanic origins, is no better than English in this respect. When long lines are required, iambic pentameters are usually chosen by both English and Scottish poets as the structure of their tongues falls naturally into such a rhythm. But again I did not think that I could deal with a close rendering of the Greek line, fitting Greek to Scots almost word for word and retaining some echo of the poetry, if I struck rigidly to insistent iambic feet. I resolved to attempt a kind of free verse that sounded like verse in accordance with T.S. Eliot's dictum in 'Reflections on *Vers Libre*' that 'the so-called *vers libre* which is good is anything but "free"' and 'the ghost of some simple metre should lurk behind the arras in even the "freest" verse' (Eliot, 1953: 87, 90). It is notable that in the same essay Eliot points out that words may come into currency again after a period of seclusion. So much for the critics who seem not to have read Shakespeare and make a point of objecting to 'archaisms'. These are the main precepts I held in mind while translating.

On the whole, when faced with the problem of matching lexical meaning, conveyance of mood, and retention of poetical values, it seemed better to adopt the looser structure found in Ezra Pound's first canto. For Homer's *Odyssey XI*, 51–55, Pound has:

> But first Elpenor came, our friend Elpenor,
> Unburied, cast on the wide earth,
> Limbs that we left in the house of Circe,
> Unwept, unwrapped in sepulchre, since toils urged other.
> (Pound, 1975: 4)

This becomes in my version:

> The first tae come wes the ghaist o ma fere Elpenor
> wha hadna syne been lairt ablo the braid-weyed grunn
> for we lea'd his corp back yonner in Circe's haa,
> athoot greetin or yirdin, for anither daurg proggit us on. (Neill, 1992: 59)

[The first to come was the ghost of my comrade Elpenor/who hadn't then been buried below the broad-wide ground/for we left his body back there in Circe's hall,/neither wept for nor buried, for another task drove us on.]

This seemed to me a satisfactory compromise.

The Scots version was based on the language I heard in the Ayrshire of my youth, where the old tongue was and is still strong. Radio, television and downright hostility have taken their toll, but a neighbour of mine who was recently threatened by a bull did not express his disquiet by saying 'he really scared me'; what he said was 'he gied me a richt fley' [gave me a right fright]. The young man who came to repair my garden path, from beneath which the soil had fallen away, thumped the surface with his boot and said 'yon's gey boss' and not 'that's very hollow'. But where a word from another dialect within the whole Scots-speaking area seemed a better fit, I selected it quite without shame. Since the language used by Homer (or those bards whose work he may have conflated and polished) contains words from many dialects of the Greece of his time and many that had fallen out of use, any translator of his work could do this also without a qualm of conscience. There are those who object to what they consider to be a fusion of dialects. These are very often speakers of an imagined 'pure' English who do not seem to realise that English is not merely a fusion of the original Anglo-Saxon and Old Norse dialects, but that *modern* English is an amalgam of two very different root languages, Low German and Norman French. There are further considerable borrowings from Latin, Greek and many other tongues. Perhaps my use of the Aberdeenshire *quine* [young woman] falls into the category of such purist objections. But this word, albeit with a flat vowel rather than a diphthong, is used by Burns and other poets of southern Scotland. On the other hand, I nowhere used the North-Eastern phonetic replacement of *wh* by *f* as in *futtret* [*whutret* = weasel], *fulp* [whelp], etc., on the grounds that this is not universally used in the wider Scots-speaking area. I hasten to add that I am as willing to accept these variants as any other dialect of Scots, and indeed I find North-Eastern Scots pleasant to listen to. As previously stated, where a form seems equally favoured, I chose that nearest to home: *yae* for *ae* [one, single, same], *yin* for *ane* [one], *faur* for *ferr* [far].

It may well be, as some assert, that no language can precisely express the nuances first expressed in another tongue, but it does seem to me that Scots, at least in some cases, often comes nearer Homer's intent than does English. Much English translation of Homer is almost *too* grand. In *The Oxford Book of Classical Verse in Translation*, it is said in the introduction that:

Far too many nineteenth-century translations are written on their knees, as it were. Pound and the modernists will not have anything to do with this cripplingly reverential position. It is unsurprising that much of the most creative translation in English this century has come from poets with their roots in America, Ireland, and Scotland. Our selection has deliberately emphasised the resilience of the resources on which Scots poets have drawn, from Gavin Douglas and Allan Ramsay to Douglas Young and Robert Garioch. (Poole & Maule, 1995: xlv–xlvi)

Of course we do not know how the Greek of Homer sounded in its heyday, but we may possibly make a shrewd guess that the labial consonants and stops of '*anamormureske kukōmenè*' are meant to imitate the physical sound of what Butcher and Lang have as 'seethe up through all her troubled deeps'. A.T. Murray has the slightly better 'seethe and bubble'. But the Scots, in contrast to these, supplies an onomatapoeic:

hotterin up the faem an plapperin sapple

[seething up the foam and bubbling lather]

The stops and sibilants imitate the sounds of a boiling cauldron and the muddy sand of the great deep.

The first episode that I had written as an example was *The Muckle Yin-Eed Etin* [The Big One-Eyed Yetin]. The spelling I used comes nearest to the Western Scots I know from my youth; and, indeed, the majority of Scots speakers I have met do not seem, any more than myself, to have any fierce objections to *yae/ae* or *yin/ane*. I appreciate the desire of the Scots Language Society to standardise spelling, and in fact, this translation adheres to its principles most of the time. I do not, however, agree that a language without a standard spelling will necessarily perish. A standard orthography in English and most other European languages is of comparatively recent origin. Attempts to rid English (or any other language) of redundant letters, or even the fairly useless apostrophe, does not meet with universal approval. Nevertheless, despite my own shortcomings in the matter of standardisation, it is my view that the letters of European languages should represent true sounds wherever they can; European words are not intended as ideograms, though many of them seem to be becoming such. So, if the Cyclops has *yin ee* [one eye] rather than *ane ee*, I trust that East-Coast readers will not be too upset by my departure from uniformity in favour of accurate phonetics.

It seemed to me fairly natural to start with the Cyclops episode. Giants are the familiar monster of folklore, from the Scottish *Lang Johnnie Moir* to the Cornish giant who could 'smell the blood of an Englishman'. And I had first read an English prose version of the Cyclops story in a textbook at school. The story does not come first in Homer, but it is the first to spring to my mind when thinking of the *Odyssey*. People, especially young people, have always enjoyed being 'gart ti grue' [made to shudder].

It has been remarked that, if Dr Johnson had in some strange manner been transported from the London of his day to the Athens of Socrates, he would have been surprised by the clean houses and superior sanitary arrangements. An early twentieth-century farmer translated to the subsistence economy of the Cyclops would, on the contrary, not be all that surprised by it, apart from the attachment to sheep and goats rather than sheep and cattle. In the Scotland of the 1920s we may have used reaping-machines to mow, but the fields were opened up by scythes, cattle were hand-milked by milkers sitting on *creepies* [flat stools] with *luggies* [milking pails] between their knees, and the milk for butter was stored in *bines* (or *boynes*) [metal bowls] for skimming. Thirsty haymakers consumed the buttermilk, and the nutritious whey of cheesemaking was fed to the pigs. The Scots vocabulary of agriculture is rich, even though words such as *stots, queys, stirks* and *kye* have almost been replaced within a generation by 'bullocks', 'heifers', 'yearlings', and 'cows'. So my Etin also has *luggies, bines, fanks* [sheepfolds] and *tups* [rams].

Sex and violence are not a new invention, as the Homeric poems amply demonstrate. Where violence occurs in the *Iliad* both the combats and the resultant damage are discussed in graphic detail; indeed it has been pointed out that the wounds are so accurately described as to be almost a medical record. If the *Iliad* has more violence and the *Odyssey* more dalliance, nevertheless, where violence does occur, its description is no less vivid than on the plains of Troy. The horrifying description of the putting out of the eye of Polyphemus must be one of the most bloodthirsty passages in literature. The giant is guilty not only of killing men of the crew and eating them, but of an offence against hospitality. However deserving of punishment these crimes of Polyphemus, the description of his horrid fate makes pity possible:

ōs tou siz'ophthalmos elaineō peri mokhlō

sae hisst his ee aroon the olive stang

[so hissed his eye around the [burning hot] olive shaft]

He 'raised a great and terrible cry' and 'plucked out the stake': here Butcher and Lang have 'brand bedabbled in much blood', and Murray has 'stake all befouled with blood,' but the Scots has 'pluckt oot the slockent stob' [plucked out the quenched stake]; the Greek word in Autenrieth, *phurō* (elsewhere used to describe tears), gives the idea of wetness in the same sense as the Scots *slocken* [moisten, drench, soak]. One of the word's meanings, to *slocken* [quench] one's thirst, is an activity that brings pleasant relief – and its deliberate use in this context emphasises by contrast the pain of the Cyclops.

The story of Nausicaa is far removed from the dire perils and bloody encounters of the Cyclops' cave. My translation opens with the shipwrecked mariner's struggles to gain safety:

> An as he swithered sae in harns and hairt
> a muckle swaw heized him tae the craigie shore
> an thare his skin wad hae been flyped an his banes brak
> hadna the goddess, yon bricht-eed Athene,
> pit in his hairt a thocht.
> In his bygaun he raxt baith haunds oot tae a craig
> an held on wi a grane until the swaw gaed bye.
> But back it breenged its wey an duntit him
> an flung him oot yince mair intil the deep,
> an lik the hosack ruggit frae his byke,
> the paibles hingin frae the sookers,
> sae wes the hide scartit frae his strang haunds
> an the muckle swaw gaed ower him. (Neill, 1992: 17)

[And as he hesitated in head and heart/a great wave lifted him to the rocky shore/and there his skin would have been flayed and his bones broken/had not the goddess, that bright-eyed Athene,/put in his heart a thought./In being carried along he reached out both hands to a rock/and held on with a groan until the wave went bye./But back it suddenly rushed and struck him/and flung him out again into the deep,/and like the cuttlefish pulled forcibly from its den,/the pebbles hanging from the suckers,/so was the flesh torn from his strong hands/and the great wave went over him.]

As regards my rendering of the third line here and the reference to 'his skin wad hae been *flyped*' (my emphasis), I was not entirely ignorant of translations into Scots of Greek classics other than the *Odyssey.* I had, for example, often read Robert Garioch's 'Anatomy of Winter' (Garioch, 1973: 42–3), a Scots version of Hesiod's *Works and Days* (ll. 503–553), in which the Greek word *boudora* occurs. Liddell and Scott (1895), in *A Greek–English Lexicon*, give the meaning as 'flaying oxen; galling'; and Evelyn-White (1936: 41) translates *'kak' ēmata, boudora panta'* as 'days ... fit to skin an ox'. Garioch treats the same passage as 'days that wad flype a nowt'. *Flype,* I remember from my childhood, was what my grandmother said she did with her gloves. The first definition in the *Concise Scots Dictionary* (1985: 204) gives 'fold back; turn wholly or partially inside out'; the second definition gives 'tear off (the skin) in strips, peel'. Garioch's felicitous choice of *flype* amply demonstrates that there are literary contexts where a word still current in Scots can express a fact more accurately than today's English. So, where Homer has:

entha k' apo rhinous druphthē, sun d' ost arakhthē

and Butcher and Lang (1887: 89) have:

there would he have been stript of his skin and all his bones been broken

my version has:

an thare his skin wad hae been flyped an his banes brak.

It seems to me, too, that in point of onomatopoeia, the Scots 'banes brak' [bones broken] comes nearer the Greek, where *arakhthē* echoes the crashing of the waves on the rocks.

Odysseus escapes with a whole skin, and his later embarrassment at having to appear with only a leafy branch between his nakedness and the disporting maidens is not without humour. As 'a man o monie ploys' [of many undertakings and stratagems] (*polutropos*), he is prepared for the situation. His speech seems to be a mixture of deliberately overblown rhetoric and crafty wheedling, which I tried to catch in the Scots. Greek is not the only ancient story-telling tradition in which royalty does its own domestic chores; it is common in other folklore traditions, Gaelic among them. Nausicaa and her handmaidens are playing ball while waiting for the washing to dry and she sharply reproves their timidity at the sight of the stranger Odysseus:

Stēte moi, amphipoloi; pose pheugete phōta idousai

Bide thare nou, lasses. Whit for dae ye flee et the sicht o a man?

[Stay there now, girls. Why do you flee at the sight of a man?]

The word 'halt' (BL) is a little too military and peremptory. After all she is trying to reassure them. Nausicaa is rightly afraid of plebeian gossip because

... some coorse ouf micht say
 gin he saa us:
*Wha's yon wi Nausicaa ... a yauld callant an braw,
an a streinger? Whaur did she finn him?* (Neill, 1992: 28)

[some coarse lout might say/if he saw us:/*Who's that with Nausicaa ... a strong, handsome fellow,/and a stranger? Where did she find him?*]

I based these lines not only on Homer but on *heard* conversations from my own youth. Those who assert, as I have somewhere read, that Scots was dying in Ayrshire at the time of Burns, must have been reading the more accurate assertion that *Gaelic* was dying in the Carrick district of Ayrshire at that time. My grandmother, on being told that a stranger's surname was Robertson, say, would enquire 'Wha's he for a Robertson?', which meant that she wished to know his family background. I remember Will Orr, a byreman [cattleman], when I protested about the weight of a burden I was carrying, admonishing me with 'That wee wecht shouldna bother a big yauld callant like yirsel!' [That small weight shouldn't bother a big strong chap (or youth) like yourself]. These are the kind of words that the Scottish commonalty would have used in similar circumstances to Nausicaa, and they are by no means far removed in spirit or lexical agreement from:

Tis d' ode Nausikaa epetai kalos te megas te xeinōs?

The description and actions of the dog Argos is for many one of the most illuminating sections of the great poem, showing as it does that concern for the welfare of animals is not merely a modern phenomenon. The old dog very nearly betrays the sought anonymity of his master on hearing his voice:

an de kuon kephalēn te kai ouata keimenos eskhen

a dug that lay thare liftit up his heid,
an cockit up his lugs (Neill, 1992: 75)

[a dog that lay there lifted up his head,/and cocked his ears]

The description is so accurately doglike. I tried to echo Homer's description of the dog's disgraceful condition – 'he lay neglected, his master gone, in the deep dung of mules and cattle full of vermin' (Murray, 1919: Vol. II, 173) – with:

... negleckit
he lay deep in the sharn o kye an cuddies
... craalin wi flaes (Neill, 1992: 76)

[neglected/he lay deep in the dung of cattle and mules/crawling with flies]

The exchange of blows in the beggars' contest for the reward of what amounts to the Greek equivalent of a black pudding or a haggis goes easily into Scots. Irus is not a heroic figure, but a mean-spirited bully; nor does

Odysseus want to be seen in any guise other than a poor vagabond. The scene has more to do with a common brawl than a noble Homeric encounter, so it seemed to me that the translation should reflect this. The hectoring manner of Irus is immediately apparent:

Eike, geron, prothurou, mē dē takha kai podos elkē

The Scots seems to be more fitting here than the English of Butcher and Lang (1887: 295): 'Get thee hence, old man, from the doorway, lest thou be even haled out soon by the foot'; and of A.T. Murray (1919: Vol. II, 197): 'Give way, old man, from the doorway, lest soon thou be even dragged out by the foot'; for both seem a little too 'costumed'. The desire of Irus to get rid of a possible rival's access to the luxurious leavings of the suitors requires an urgency and violence that the Scots captures:

Haud aff, auld man, haud aff frae this durestane,
sae I dinna hae tae rugg ye bi the fuit. (Neill, 1992: 78)

[Clear off, old man, clear off from this threshold,/so I don't have to pull you [away] by the foot.]

To be *ruggit* [pulled or tugged] is a much less gentle action than to be simply dragged, and as George Bruce pointed out in his foreword (Neill, 1992: 15), the *durestane* [a flagstone in front of the threshold of a door] paints a vivid image in the minds of those who, like myself, can remember the careful scrubbing of this step by the matrons of the village who completed the work by whitening it with a block of chalk-like stone, sometimes adding a design of curly lines around the edges. The *durestane* was a particularly private appendage to a house and for a stranger to sit on it was seen by Irus (as by Scottish housewives) as an infringement of a privilege. But Odysseus is not to be seen off so easily from what is, after all, his own doorstep; it is Irus who has infringed propriety. Odysseus replies reasonably enough, pointing out that there is plenty of room on the step for the two of them. Nevertheless he answers in a manner that Irus would have been wise to heed. Murray (1919: Vol. II, 199) has 'But with thy fists do not provoke me overmuch, lest ... I befoul thy breast and lips with blood', and Butcher and Lang (1887: 295) has the somewhat stronger 'Provoke me not overmuch to buffeting'. Scots has a ready vocabulary for this sort of bare-knuckle squaring up:

[T]his durestane will haud us baith,
...
Sae dinna lift yir nieves tae gie me dunts
an gar me fyle yir breist an lips wi bluid. (Neill, 1992: 78)

[This threshold will hold us both, /.../ So don't lift your fists to give me blows / and make me dirty your breast and lips with blood.]

Mankind has always enjoyed tales in which the villain or villains are subjected to the just revenge of the heroes. Anyone who remembers the cinemas of the thirties, filled with children at the Saturday matinée, will remember the uninhibited cheers of the juvenile audience when the purveyors of such ready justice came galloping over the hill. The tale of the archery contest and the subsequent undoing of the insolent suitors contains the same elements of suspense and retribution that delighted the young cinema-goers.

Eurimachus mac Polybus (for Greek patronymics throughout the translation I used the similar Gaelic method, as did both MacLachlan and Maclean) does not want the disguised Odysseus to compete in the archery contest because he fears that:

... yin o the keelie kind sud say:
Deed aye, but gey peelie-wallie men are wooin
the wife o a nobil man, an canna string his glaizie bou;
but a tink, that cam on his traivels, eithlie did,
an shot thro the airn forbye. (Neill, 1992: 95)

[one of the rough type should say: / *Indeed yes, but very pallid, sickly men are wooing/the wife of a noble man, and cannot string his glossy bow; /but a tinker, that came on his travels, easily did, /and shot through the iron besides.*]

This, I feel, is a good example of where the translation follows the Greek fairly closely, but it is not enough merely to translate this with simple lexical exactness; it must be given words that match the mood of the Greek in a *Scottish* way. 'Peelie-wallie [pallid, sickly] men' paints a more vivid native Scots image than 'men far too mean' (BL). For *kakōteros,* 'base fellow' (ATM), or 'one of the base sort' (BL), are perfectly good translations, but 'yin o the keelie [rough] kind' strikes more closely home in Scots; and a 'tink that cam on his traivels', for similar reasons, fits the Greek better to Scottish minds than 'a beggar, that came on/in his wanderings' (ATM/BL). In the same context Maclean in his Gaelic translation uses the word *suarach* [trifling, contemptible] for *kakōteros.* Eurymachus is looking down his nose at the very idea that an unkempt and socially inferior stranger should be allowed to compete on equal terms with the noble suitors, and he is horrified by the prospect of plebeian mockery should they fail. (Those who are conditioned by present-day mores to laugh at the idea of aristocrats speaking in 'braid [broad] Scots' should remember that until the end of the eighteenth century many of them would have done just that: Lord

Braxfield's quashing of an eloquent villain by saying, 'Ye're a verra clever chield, man, but ye wad be nane the waur o a hingin' [You're a very clever man, fellow, but you would be none the worse of a hanging] is valid linguistic evidence whatever one's forensic attitude; as is the fact that eminent and highly educated divines preached their sermons to their congregations in Scots.)

At last, after the bickering of the suitors and Penelope's ready support, Odysseus shoots his *flain* [arrow] through the holes worked in the axe heads and allows himself to boast to Telmachus that:

> Ma virr is wi me yit, for aa the wooers snirk
> an lichtlie me.
>
> [My strength is with me yet, for all the wooers snigger/and despise me.]

Again, to *snirk* [snigger] and to *lichtlie* me [despise me] is more telling – Scottice – than 'scornfully to slight me'.

It may be that disputing the status of Scots is a barren pursuit. What matters in the end is not what the linguistic rank of Scots *is*, but what is *done with it*. If it is a 'mere dialect' of English, it must be pointed out that it is the *only* dialect outside that of Standard Southern English (itself only a privileged dialect) that has a literary tradition going back eight centuries and containing many works that have a prestigious status. One need only mention William Dunbar, Robert Henryson, Robert Burns and Hugh MacDiarmid to make the point, but there are many excellent anthologies that make it more strongly (e.g. Crawford & Imlah, 2000). Of course, like Standard English, Scots is richly informed by borrowing, but the source of this (even where the borrowings are from French) is different from that of English. Scots is more strongly influenced by Scandic sources, as seen in the *kirk/circ* dichotomy (hard *k* sound as opposed to Anglo-Saxon *ch* as in 'church') and the retention of words such as *gar* (Norse *garre* = compel). There are more borrowings from Gaelic words and syntactical constructions than there are in English. Scots contains more words of a recognisably Germanic origin as well as a retention of Germanic fricatives lost (except in spelling) to Standard English. Scots vowels are flat where many English consonants have a diphthong. I have deliberately written *thare/thair* for *there/their* to emphasise this level vowel. Many of the differences mentioned are found in my *Odyssey* translation: *beseek* has Norse [k] for southern [ch]; *ben* = 'within', from Old Northumbrian *binna* (not to be confused with *ben* = 'mountain', from Gaelic *beann*); *wale* = 'choose' (Norse *val*, German *wahlen*); *hairns* = 'brains' (M High German *herne*); and so forth.

In reviewing my *Tales frae the Odyssey o Homer owerset intil Scots*, Harry Smart (1993: 50) said in *Lines Review* that it was a pity that means could not be found to allow the translation and publication of the whole of the *Odyssey*. I would have been more than willing to make such a translation could this support be found. I admire John Maclean's assiduity and expertise in translating the whole of the *Odyssey* (Mac Gilleathain, 1976), knowing the difficulty of getting Gaelic into print. He died before its publication, but his brother, the great Gaelic poet Sorley Maclean, and many Gaelic organisations and eminent Gaels, saw that it was published eventually. The Saltire Society, with much more limited resources than are now available for Gaelic, has made possible publication of my translation of some of the great Homeric verses. The chief motive of John Maclean must have been his sheer delight in translating the voyagings and adventures of the *'andra polutropon'* – in Gaelic, as he put it, the *'gaisgeach nan iol-char'* – into the language nearest his heart. I share his sentiments, and if I have come near his achievement with 'the aunters o the man o monie ploys' [the adventures of the man of many undertakings], I am well content.

Notes

1. For my translations of Belli into Scots, see Neill (1995, 1998).
2. Kenneth Farrow has translated the *Iliad* into Scots (see Corbett, 1999: 146–7). His translation awaits publication but a copy has been deposited in Glasgow University Library. [Ed.]
3. An audiocassette recording of passages from my translation can be obtained by Mail Order from Scotsoun Productions, PO Box 7015, Glasgow G44 3WJ.

Chapter 3
Dario Fo's Mistero Buffo *into Scots*

STUART HOOD

Mistero Buffo, which is one of Dario Fo's best known and most successful works, is a collection of dramatic monologues (see Fo, 1988). It dates from the 1960s when it was played to huge audiences – 25,000 on one evening in Milan, for example, and 14,000 in Turin. The global audience for the piece in Italy in those days of radicalism was, Fo estimates, more than a million. It is a 'mystery' in the same sense that those medieval plays that make up the York cycle are mystery plays. Thus it draws in large part on scriptural material for its story lines, which include the Massacre of the Innocents, the Raising of Lazarus, the Marriage at Cana, and the Passion of Mary at the Cross. All these are incidents narrated by Fo, who exploits in his writing his genius for mimicry and mime, and his command of theatrical space, as was evident in performance when he played all the characters involved.

If the *Mistero* is also *buffo*, it is so in the same sense as comic opera is *opera buffa*. This is in line with the medieval tradition: in the York cycle, for example, there is room for humour in the exchanges between the shepherds at the Nativity. In Fo, however, humour predominates. Laughter is a weapon, he maintains, with which one can disarm an audience, catching them as it were off guard, making them vulnerable to the shafts of wit and irony and – in the case of *Mistero Buffo* – to a reading of the Christ's being and actions as life-affirming, socially critical: a reading that has inspired the worker-priests and the liberation theologians of today's Roman Catholic church.

In its original conception and as first performed *Mistero Buffo* was an extended lecture on the art of the *giullare* – a word best rendered by the French *jongleur* – a wandering minstrel and actor. The *giullari* in Fo's reading of history were the bearers of subversive readings of scriptural and other texts, the representatives of that tradition which produced the boy bishops and the lords of misrule and inspired the carnival – in short, the burlesque and mockery that was one of the safety-valves of medieval society.

Mistero Buffo is written and performed not in 'Italian' but in dialect. Fo grew up near the Lago Maggiore in a community of fishermen, smugglers and peasants who habitually used dialect in their daily speech, and in the storytelling that was a notable element in their social life. Fo draws on the linguistic thesaurus of these men and women from whom, as he says, he 'learned the structure of a primordial, integral language' (Fo, 1990: 22). The first lines of the episode dealing with the Raising of Lazarus are typical:

> *'Oh, scusé! Oh l'è questo ol simitéri, campusanto, duè che vai a fa ol süscitamento d'ul Lassaro?'*
>
> *'Si, l'è quest.'*
>
> *'Ah, bon.'*
>
> *'On mument, des palance par entrár.'* (Fo, 1974: 102)

This in 'Italian' would be:

> *'Scusi! questo il cimitero, camposanto, dove vanno a fare il resuscitamento, resurreaione, del Lazzaro?'*
>
> *'Si, è questo.'*
>
> *'Ah, bene.'*
>
> *'Un momento, dieci soldi per entrar.'*

The Scots version would run:

> 'Hey, mister! is this the cemetery, the kirkyaird, whaur they're gaunae raise Lazarus?'
>
> 'Aye, that's richt.'
>
> 'That's fine than.'
>
> 'A wee minute – a saxpence tae come by.'
>
> 'Saxpence?'
>
> 'Thrippence than.'[1]
>
> ['Hey, mister! is this the cemetery, the churchyard, where they're going to raise Lazarus?'/'Yes, that's right.'/'That's fine then.'/'[Wait] A wee minute – a sixpence to come by.'/'Sixpence?'/'Threepence then.']

There seemed to be two reasons why the work as a whole would go well into Scots. One was linguistic and stylistic: Scots would convey the feel of the dialect original more expressively than Standard English would. The other was that Fo's characters (who are clearly based on Italian peasant types) have a mode of feeling, speaking and thinking which I feel to be congruent with certain Scottish attitudes, derived from similar social backgrounds. In the language and psychology that Fo depicts, there is the same toughness, the same down-to-earth quality combined with a scepticism that I recall from my early years in the Angus countryside, with its bleak cottar houses from which the farmhands flitted at term time with their family and bits and pieces of furniture piled on horse-drawn carts. That note is struck at the beginning of the episode dealing with the Raising of Lazarus which, to follow on from the excerpt above, goes:

'Thrippence? Whit for, dammit?'

'Becus I'm in chairge o this kirkyaird and ye fowk come breengin in ram-stam an spile the hedges and traimple doun the girss ana and I maun get a bob or twa fir aa the baither ye gie me. Thrippence or ye dinna see the miracle.'

'Ye're a fly ane, ana.'

'Thrippence ye tae and I dinna care if ye hae yer bairns wi ye – it's aa the same tae me – they can keek as weel, no? Richt than, a bawbee. Get affen that wa, ye muckle eediot. He'd like fine tae see the miracle fir nocht. Are ye gaun tae pey or no? Thrippence – no, ye didna pey. Thrippence, you anes – thrippence tae come by.'

['Threepence? What for, damn it?'/'Because I'm in charge of this churchyard and you folk come rushing headlong in and spoil the hedges and trample down the grass as well and I must get a shilling or two for all the bother you give me. Threepence or you don't see the miracle.'/'You're a fly one, right enough.'/'Threepence the rest of you too and I don't care if you have your children with you – it's all the same to me – they can peep as well, can't they? Right then, a halfpenny. Get off that, you big idiot. He'd like fine to see the miracle for nothing. Are you going to pay or not? Threepence – no, you didn't pay. Threepence, you ones – threepence to come in.']

Fo's original Italian with its mixture of dialect and archaisms gives expression to a voice which, it seems to me, is consonant with the one I was familiar with: a voice that was laconic, sceptical, ironical. Those who spoke it lived in a society in which a man passing another on the road would confine his greeting to an 'Aye man' and be answered with the same formula: 'Aye man'. It was a society in which a woman waiting at the church door for a hastily wedded bride to emerge commented to another: 'Aye, white fur chastity'; or the ploughman watching a pregnant girl go past remarked: 'she liked the rammin fine, we'll see hoo [how] she likes the lambin'.

The moment when Jesus at last arrives to perform the miracle is accompanied by a chorus of voices that transfer very naturally into Scots:

'He's comin. He's comin. He's here.'

'Whit yin is he?'

'The yin wi the black face? I dinna like the wey he glowers.'

'No, no. That yin's Mark.'

'The yin ahint?'

'The big yin?'

'No, the wee yin.'

'The halflin?'

'The yin wi the beard ana.'

'He luiks like a halflin tae me, dammit if he disnae.'

'Luik! There's the Madonna as weel! There's aa his kith an kin. He's aye got them aa wi him.'

'They dinna lat him oot alane – he's no richt i the heid.'

'Jesus! Oh I like that yin. He gied me a wink ana.'

'Jesus, Jesus, dae that miracle wi the laifs an the fishes like that ither time whan they were that guid.'

'Haud yer wheesht! Blasphemer, behave yersel.'

['He's coming. He's coming. He's here.'/'Which one is he?'/'The one with the black face? I don't like the way he glowers.'/'No, no. That one's Mark.'/'The one behind?'/'The big one?'/'No, the wee one.'/'The youth?'/'The one with the beard as well.'/'He looks like a youth to me, dammit if he doesn't.'/'Look! There's the Madonna too! There's all his kith and kin. He's always got them all with him.'/'They don't let him out alone – he's not right in the head.'/'Jesus! Oh I like that one. He gave me a wink as well.'/'Jesus, Jesus, do that miracle with the loafs and the fishes like that other time when they were that good.'/ 'Be quiet! Blasphemer, behave yourself.']

Here there was the problem of how to render the Italian *quello*, meaning 'that one'. Should it be *wan, ane* or *yin*? I settled for *yin* – a choice in which I was influenced by memories of Billy Connolly's early monologues, which have the same tone as the scene in which the miracle takes place, hence my translation runs:

'Jesus! – luik! They've taen up the muckle stane. There's the deid man – in there – it's Lazarus fair stinkin. Feech! Whit's that awfy stink?'

'Christ!'

'Whit's wrang?'

'Wheesht!'

'Lat me see!'

'He's fou o wurms – o creepie-crawlies. Feech! he maun hae been deid a month – he's aa fa'in apairt. That's a fine like thing they've dune tae him. Tae Jesus. It's nae joke. I fear he'll no can dae it this time, puir thing.'

'I'm sure he'll no can dae it – he cannae dae it. There's nay wey he cin mak him come oot. He's stinkin rotten. That's a fine thing – tellin him he wasna deid mair nor three days! It's a month or mair. Puir Jesus!'

'I say he'll manage jist the same – that yin's a holy man at cin dae the miracle even if they've been stinkin rotten for a month an mair.'

'And I say he canna.'

'Will ye wager?'

'I'll wager ana.'

'Right than! Saxpence! Whitiver ye like!'

'Gie's it. I'll haud it. Dae ye trust me? He dis. We aa trust each ither. Fine, I'll tak the money.'

['Jesus! – look! They've taken up the big stone. There's the dead man – in there – it's Lazarus fair stinking. Yuck! What's that awful stink?'/'Christ!'/'What's wrong?'/'Quiet!'/'Let me see!'/'He's full of worms – of creepy-crawlies. Yuck! he must have been dead a month – he's all falling apart. That's a fine like thing they've done to him. To Jesus. It's no joke. I fear he'll not be able to do it this time, poor thing.'/'I'm sure he'll not be able to do it – he can't do it. There's no way he can make him come out. He's stinking rotten. That's a fine thing – telling him he wasn't dead more than three days! It's a month or more. Poor Jesus!'/'I say he'll manage just the same – that one's a holy man that can do the miracle even if they've been stinking rotten for a month and more.'/'And I say he can't.'/'Will you wager?'/'I'll wager too.'/'Right then! Sixpence! Whatever you like!'/'Give me it. I'll hold it. Do you trust me? He does. We all trust each other. Fine, I'll take the money.']

So the bet is laid, the wager is won, but at the moment of the miracle the purse with the money is stolen:

'Whit's he daein?'

'He's there prayin.'

'Wheesht will ye!'

'He's there, Lazarus, git up noo!'

'Wheesht! he's on his knees.'

'Wha? Jesus? No! Lazarus. God, luik at that.'

'Get awa wi ye – it's nae possible.'

'Lat me see.'

'Luik, luik – he's waukin, he's fawin doon. He's staunin! On his twa feet!'
'Weel doun, Jesus.'
'I hae won the wager. Gie's the money. Dinna try ony tricks wi me!'
'Weel doun, Jesus.'
'They've stawn mi purse. Thief!'
'Weel doun, Jesus. Jesus! Weel doun! Thief ... !'

['What's he doing?'/'He's there praying.'/'Be quiet will you!'/'He's there, Lazarus, get up now!'/'Quiet! he's on his knees.'/'Who? Jesus? No! Lazarus. God, look at that.'/'It can't be – it's not possible.'/'Let me see.'/'Look, look – he's waking, he's falling down. He's standing! On his two feet!'/'Well done, Jesus.'/'I have won the wager. Give me the money. Don't try any tricks with me!'/'Well done, Jesus.'/'They've stolen my purse. Thief!'/'Well done, Jesus. Jesus! Well done! Thief ... !']

The same tone comes across in the account of the Marriage at Cana. The narrator is a drouthy [thirsty] wedding guest who arrives to find the place in an uproar:

There wis I invited tae a waddin at a place at the fowk in these pairts ca Cana – Cana – whit is why aifterwards they'll ca it the waddin at Cana. I wus invited – as I wus sayin – I gat there – there wus a' the table ready an set fur the waddin wi a' the fuid but there wasna ane o the waddin fowk set doon tae eat. They wur a' staunin there an gien great kicks at the flair an cursin an sweerin. There wus the bride's mammy greetin. There wus the bride's daddy bangin his heid even on agin the wa – he wus fair wuid.

'Whit's wrang?' I speired. 'Oh, it's affey.' 'The bridegroom's up an awa?' 'Whit's wrang than?' 'It's affey – we've fand oot a hail barrel o wine, a hail cask, is gaen aff – turned intae vinegar.' 'A' the wine turned intae vinegar! that's awfy. That maun bring bad luck ana.' An them a' greetin an cursing and sweering, an the bride's mammy tearin her hair, the bride greetin, the bride's daddy bangin his heid even on agin the wa.

[There was I invited to a wedding at a place that the folk in these parts call Cana – Cana – which is why afterwards they'll call it the wedding at Cana. I was invited – as I was saying – I got there – there was all the table ready and set for the wedding with all the food but there wasn't one of the wedding folk sat down to eat. They were all standing there and giving great kicks at the floor and cursing and swearing. There was the bride's mother crying. There was the bride's father banging his head continuously against the wall – he was fair beside himself with rage. //'What's wrong?' I asked. 'Oh, it's terrible.' 'The bridegroom's up and away?' 'What's wrong then?' 'It's terrible – we've discovered a whole barrel of wine, a whole cask, has gone off – turned into vinegar.' 'All the wine turned into vinegar! that's terrible. That must bring bad luck too.' And them all crying and cursing and swearing, and the bride's mother tearing her hair, the bride crying, the bride's father banging his head continuously against the wall.]

Or again later, when Jesus, having turned the water into wine, offers some to the Madonna:

Than, suddenly, he catches sicht o his Mammy. 'O guid wummin, oh Madonna, oh Mammy! I've gane and forgotten ye, dinna be angry, tak a drap tae, drink a wee drappie.' 'No, no laddie, thank ye, but I canna touch it, I'm nae used tae wine, it maks me dizzy and aifterwards I canna haud mi tongue.'

[Then, suddenly, he catches sight of his Mother. 'O good woman, oh Madonna, oh Mother! I've gone and forgotten you, don't be angry, take a drop too, drink a wee drop.' 'No, no laddie, thank you, but I can't touch it, I'm not used to wine, it makes me dizzy and afterwards I can't hold my tongue.']

Fo, as indicated earlier, conceives of the episodes of *Mistero Buffo* as being enacted by a *giullare* whose territory is Northern Italy, from the great lakes across the Po valley to the Apennines, which still mark a linguistic frontier with Tuscany. Until the 1950s when the migration of the peasantry into the towns destroyed the agricultural society that sustained them, this was a region rich in dialects. As an escaped prisoner of war making my way in 1943 along the Apennines between Emilia and Tuscany (see Hood, 1963) I came to recognise how the vocabulary and accent, and the word formations, varied from village to village and from valley to valley. Fo postulates that his *giullare*, in order to make himself understood to his various audiences, must have used a language that was based on living dialect but which incorporated local variations and forms. He cites a *giullare* from Bologna who in one sentence used four synonyms for 'girl': *zovina, fiola, tosa, garsonetta*. An equivalent in Scots would be to use 'lassie' as a gloss on 'quinie'. A more obvious example occurs at the beginning of the Raising of Lazarus episode when 'cemetery' is glossed as 'kirkyaird'. The result, according to Fo, was a dialectal lingua franca intelligible over most of Northern Italy.

For *Mistero Buffo,* Fo elaborated a language he had first used in radio monologues and so produced an artificial construct, a theatrical language based on dialect and enriched by archaisms, which is vivid, expressive and sharp. The dialectal forms are drawn from Italy north of the Apennines, a linguistic zone that has modified vowel sounds as in *fueg* for the Italian *fuoco*, nasalisations, and apocopes as in *vin* (with a nasal) for *vino*. Such differences distinguish it from that other language that the peasants called *italiano*. (My first encounter with a peasant in Emilia was brief; he did not, he explained, speak 'Italian'.)

The dialects had difficulty in surviving the various internal migrations that took place in Italy from the 1950s onwards as the *mezzadri* (the sharecroppers) and the agricultural labourers left the land and made for the towns or for the small factories that sprang up in so many places in Northern Italy. They were joined by internal immigrants from the South with their own (to the others) incomprehensible dialects. What died with the internal immigrations was the peasant life with its skills and customs, its self-sufficiency and hard unrelenting regime driven inexorably by the seasons – a life about which, having shared it (see Hood, 1963), I cannot feel sentimental. With the end of *la civiltà contadineca* (peasant culture and the life that sustained it) two things happened. First, dialects in general died out (and with them a whole lexicon connected with the working methods of the peasants became obsolete), although regional accents are still marked. Second, there was a levelling out of Italian into what Pasolini called *koinè*, a generally accepted and understood language, in the formation of which television has played an important part. A similar process can, I believe, be seen in the development of modern Scots.

Where dialect has survived is in towns like Brescia, prosperous and with a strong local tradition. Here I have heard dialect spoken round a dinner table by professional people. It can be an expression of that brand of local patriotism that has nourished the politically dubious Northern League with its anti-southern racism.

When Fo wrote and first performed his *Mistero Buffo* in the 1960s, the social process that had led to the dying away of dialects was already far advanced; one must therefore ask why he chose to write a text so strongly anchored in dialect. There was undoubtedly a certain linguistic nostalgia. But his use of dialect and archaisms can be interpreted differently and more positively as a request to his audience to make an effort to understand his text, to work at it and to reach back into a cultural past when the vocabulary of the ordinary person had a vigour and edge lacking in today's homogenised linguistic patterns. Above all there was the intention to recreate the tradition of the *giullare* – to revitalise a tradition of disrespect that could be adapted as a political tool to mock the corruption of twentieth-century Italy.

Given the nature of the language employed by Fo, the translation of *Mistero Buffo* clearly presents problems for a publisher. The publisher is concerned to reach the largest possible readership and will naturally opt for a linguistic equivalent to Fo's text that is easily accessible. The result is that inevitably the published text of *Mistero Buffo* in Britain is in English (Fo, 1988) – good, colloquial English which, since we are talking of the work of an experienced translator, is eminently actable. But the transposition into current English cannot, to my mind, reproduce the demotic accent of the original.[2] Perhaps in an ideal world the publishers would have settled for a literal translation that could then be rendered into local dialect (where dialect still exists), or at least into demotic speech, which could be that of the Afro-Caribbean community – the language of Kwesi Johnson, for instance – or of that Glasgow tongue of which James Kelman shows himself to be a master in *How Late It Was, How Late* (Kelman, 1994).

To me, it therefore seemed that a rendering into Scots was appropriate, notwithstanding the difficulty some people appear to experience with that language. In a recent radio programme a man who, to judge by his accent, was Scottish, found both comical and incomprehensible the old saying that one must *'pit a stoot hert tae a stey brae'* [put a stout heart to a steep hill]. Another speaker on radio, when discussing Robert Louis Stevenson's *Weir of Hermiston*, found the dialect 'difficult'.

I felt I was qualified to make the effort to turn the text into Scots because like Dario Fo, who spoke dialect but was educated in 'Italian', I grew up to be bilingual. At home we used English, due in part to my father's role as village dominie [teacher] and keeper of the 'purity' of Spoken English, and in part to the fact that my mother, who came from Nairn, apparently had not been exposed to Scots. Yet certain Scots words were part of our vocabulary, such as *drouth* [drought/thirst], *bauchles* [slippers], *semmit* [vest], *spaver* [the front slit in trousers], *douce* [pleasant], *thrawn* [stubborn], and *shauchle* [shuffle] – although they were on certain occasions and in certain company placed, as it were, in inverted commas to show that the speaker was aware of deviating from the cultured norm. But my lexicon was considerably wider than this. I went to school and grew up alongside the children of ploughmen and farm labourers. From them, and from helping to drive sheep and cattle to the market, I learned a large vocabulary that extended from processes such as *biggin* [building] and *stookin* [setting sheaves of corn to stand in groups in a field], to the identification of various beasts as *stots* [castrated bullocks], *stirks* [young bullocks], *hoggs* [young sheep] and *staigs* [young horses], and to knowing which of them would be or had been *libbed* [castrated]. I knew that the *weesh* was the command to make a carthorse turn to the right, just as *hi* meant to turn to the left, and that a horse was *lowsed* [released from the yoke] at the end of the working day – at what was called for man and beast alike *lowsin time*. This language of the countryside and the country economy I heard all around me – in shops, at the mart, on the farms. Much of it I learned from a village woman called

Jean Moir, who sometimes looked after me and who pronounced her name in the old manner as 'More', just as in the Middle Scots of the fifteenth and sixteenth centuries *rois* was pronounced 'rose'. That language became a permanent part of my lexicon.

The attempt to make a translation of Fo into Scots required a number of decisions. One was concerned with the variety of Scots to be used, another with orthography, and the third with the number of archaisms that could be used.

I had grown up speaking the North-East Scots native to Angus. It was distinguished by the substitution of *f* for *wh*, as in: *fit* for 'what'; *fa* for 'who' – as in *Fa's echt this?* [Who does this belong to?]; *far* for 'where' – *Far's he frae?* [Where's he from?]; and *foo* for 'why', as in *Foo no?'* [Why not?]. Other characteristics included a tendency to metatheses as in *girss* for 'grass' and *brod* for 'board', although these were rare usages. (It was considered daring in my puritanical family to make a punning reference to a chequered pattern on a length of cloth as a *dam-brod* [draughtboard] one.) There was also the plentiful use of dimunitives, as in *sweetie-wifie* [a garrulous, gossipy person].

It seemed to me, however, that Angus Scots was too local and that I should use something closer to what the *Concise Scots Dictionary* (1985: xxxiv–xxxv) defines, with reference to a more general geographic spread, as 'Mid Scots'. This was a dialect of Scots I was familiar with: my father hailed from Stirling, and although, for the reason indicated before, he made a point never to use Scots as a spoken language, his working-class relations did, and from them I heard it.

Fortunately, in his eyes Scots as a literary vehicle was another matter. Through him I was familiar with Scots as used by Charles Murray, from whose book of poems *Hamewith* he liked to read aloud, just as he would quote Hew Ainslie's poem 'The Hint o Hairst' or Violet Jacob's love poem 'Tam i' the Kirk'. It was through him that in my teens I got to know Robert Burns, Robert Fergusson and Allan Ramsay, and, looking further back, Robert Henryson's 'The Testament of Cresseid'. When I came to learn German he introduced me to Alexander Gray's Scots translations of Heine's *Dichterliebe* (see Gray, 1920). In due course, as a student I was familiar with the work of Hugh MacDiarmid, William Soutar and Robert Garioch – a line of poets of which Raymond Vettese is a modern representative.

In dealing with orthography I faced a problem which I was interested to learn had confronted that great translator, William Laughton Lorimer (1983: xvii–xx), when translating The New Testament in Scots: whether to opt for a phonetic rendering of pronunciation or to adopt a standard spelling. But there again, what is the standard spelling of Scots? How for instance does one spell the past tense of the verb 'to be'? Is it *was, wuz* or *wiz*? How does one render the possessive adjective 'my'? Is it *my, ma* or *mi*? The latter is a form which, I am told, I naturally and normally use in certain contexts – 'mi bed', 'mi hands', 'mi shoes' – and in which the vowel would be rendered in the phonetic alphabet as ∂. For 'awful', is it *awfu* or *awfy* – or, as my ear tells me, *affy*? How should one write the Scots form of the English 'pay'? As *pey* or as *py*? My inclination is to settle for the diphthong *pey*, which phonetically is 'p∂y'.

I preserved one characteristic that my brand of Scots shared with Dario Fo's northern dialect; namely, the use of a modified *u* – what is described by the *Concise Scots Dictionary* (1985: xxiii) as 'a more or less rounded front vowel, ranging in quality from the vowels in French *lune*, German *über* to those in French *peu*, German *schön*. To my ear this is precisely the sound in *guid* [good], in *doun* in the sense of 'done', in *luik* [look].

Then there is the question of archaisms. When I first came across Lallans as practised by Hugh MacDiarmid, I was not convinced that it was wise, as in his practice, to use Jamieson's *Etymological Dictionary of the Scottish Language* (1808 and 1825) as a quarry, or to favour archaisms. MacDiarmid, it was true, used them with great effect in some of his best poems, but I did not believe that they could easily be resurrected and made to fit into a modern Scots that was anything other than the language of poetry. 'Archaism', however, is a term that requires definition. If in translating Fo into Scots I have relied on the lexicon I acquired over seventy years ago, is that lexicon not in the nature of things replete with archaisms? When a few years ago I visited the village school where I spent my first years, the headmistress told me that today's children no longer spoke the same language that I had. So in whose mouth – apart from those of some of my contemporaries – are many of these words still alive? What I would consider an archaism would be an archaic form like the *-and* ending of the present participle, as in *bydand* [remaining in readiness], which was the motto on the badge of the Gordon Highlanders. In short, I made the arbitrary decision that words that were no longer in common use when my lexicon was formed were 'archaic'.

Thus, at the beginning of the story of how the water was turned to wine at Cana, the narrator tells how he had been invited to a wedding, which I prefer to render as *wadden* rather than the archaic *tryst*, although the latter is a possible rendering. But there is an inconsistency in my practice, for when he describes the miracle and the bouquet rising from the wine, I use the archaic *nosthrils* [nostrils] in the following passage:

I wus a wee bit tae ae side fur as I wus sayin watter gars me grue whan I see it, an I wasnae lookin, I was staunin there richt cast doon whan suddenly I feel in my nosthrils a perfume o squashed grapes – it had tae be, it wus wine. An sic a wine! They raxed me a jug – I pit it tae my lips – I swallied doon a drap – Guid Lord what a wine! An abody clappin for Jesus. 'Jesus, ye're a richt yin – ye're divine.'

[I was a wee bit to one side for as I was saying water makes me feel repulsion when I see it, and I wasn't looking, I was standing there right cast down when suddenly I feel in my nostrils a perfume of squashed grapes – it had to be, it was wine. And such a wine! They passed me a jug – I put it to my lips – I swallowed down a drop – Good Lord what a wine! And everybody clapping for Jesus. 'Jesus, you're a right one – you're divine.']

In the Raising of Lazarus episode there are a couple of archaisms in the passage where the narrator is searching for the grave:

I maun see whaur this Lazarus is. There maun be his name abune the tomb ana. That ither time I cam here tae see the miracle wrocht on another wan and I wis here aamost hauf the day just wytin and than they gaed an haid the miracle doun by. Here was I staunin like a gowk. But this time like I ken the name. I fand it oot. I'll finnd the name on the grafstane. I'll be the first like. I'll staun there richt afore the tomb an I'll see aathing frae the beginnin.

[I must see where this Lazarus is. There must be his name above the tomb too. That other time I came here to see the miracle wrought on another one and I was here almost half the day just waiting and then they went and had the miracle down there. Here was I standing like an idiot. But this time, like, I know the name. I found it out. I'll find the name on the gravestone. I'll be the first, like. I'll stand there right before the tomb and I'll see everything from the beginning.]

In this context the use of *wrocht* [wrought] seemed permissible, as did *grafstane* [gravestone]. Both were in my terms archaic, although I had occasionally heard a joiner spoken of as a *wricht* [wright]. Whether *gowk* [fool or cuckoo] can be defined as an archaism is more dubious. I remember it being used in the sense of 'a stupid person', and also in the context of to *hunt the gowk* – to 'go off on a fool's errand'. I do not believe that I ever heard it in its literal sense as the word for 'cuckoo'.

Fo has not been without his critics. There is a debate over his use of dialect and archaisms, about his sources and his interpretation of them. There are some who consider his invented medium a macaronic jargon. The point, however, is that in performance it works, in the sense that it is an excellent vehicle for Fo's talents and that it was understood and savoured by the large Italian audiences to whom it was first addressed. However, what is increasingly obvious today is that Fo is a figure of the 1960s and 70s. Along with his immensely talented wife, Franca Rame, he tackled subjects relevant to that period in plays that are still eminently performable but are somewhat dated nonetheless. *Mistero Buffo*, in contrast, is less obviously and directly linked to issues that were important at a specific conjuncture in Italian political history. It has a lasting appeal derived in large part from Fo's use of a distinctive and dialect-coloured language which is, to my mind, best reproduced by a rendering into Scots.

Notes

1. A short section of my translation into Scots of *Mistero Buffo* has been published: see Fo (1988: 120–2). Parts of that section are quoted here (sometimes with minor modifications), but the translation is otherwise unpublished.
2. This linguistic consideration contributed to the popularity of Fo's plays in Scotland in the 1980s and early 1990s when they were given a Scottish voice and, at times, a Scottish adaptation – including *Mistero Buffo*, staged in 1990 and starring Robbie Coltrane. One of the Scottish adaptors of *Mistero Buffo*, and author of a biography of Fo, Joseph Farrell (2000: 123–5) discusses the reasons why 'there have been more productions [of Fo's work] of a high standard in Scotland than elsewhere [in the UK]', and how Fo thereby 'entered the [theatrical] mainstream of Scotland'. For other discussion of the popularity and Scotticisation of Fo, see: Findlay (1996a: 189) and Corbett (1999: 153–4 and 173–4). [Ed.]

Chapter 4
Translating Register in Michel Tremblay's Québécois Drama

MARTIN BOWMAN AND BILL FINDLAY

We are a transatlantic translation partnership. Martin Bowman, who lives in Canada, is a born-and-raised Montrealer whose parents were immigrants from Scotland; Bill Findlay is a Scot and lives in Scotland. We have described the consequences of this distance for our collaborative method thus:

> The transatlantic nature of our collaboration no doubt affects the form our translations finally take. Martin Bowman produces a literal draft into unidiomatic English from Tremblay's original. This first draft is a kind of French-in-English which avoids as much as possible any kind of English literary interference such as the translation of idiomatic expressions into English equivalents. This translation is accompanied by an explanation of usage, catching passing irony, word play, and humour, and explaining cultural elements unfamiliar to a Scot. Before Bill Findlay casts this draft into Scots, there is an exchange of questions, answers, clarification, and qualification after which a first Scots draft is completed. Then follows a working through of the Scots text with close attention to the original, and if possible this part of the process is done face to face. Finally, of course, changes are made during rehearsal.
> (Bowman & Findlay, 1994: 72)

As Sirkku Aaltonen has noted in her discussion of our work:

> [t]his procedure introduces a clear division of labour where one of the translators is assumed to have the necessary knowledge of the foreign language of the source text and the conventions which were followed when it was written, while the other is the master of the target language as well as the systemic norms and conventions of the stage in the target system. (Aaltonen, 2000: 44)

Translating Register in Michel Tremblay's Québécois Drama 67

Although we have translated single plays by three other contemporary Québécois playwrights using this method of approach, our principal application of it has been in translating Michel Tremblay's drama.

Just as the frequency and popularity of Scots translations of Molière has given rise to him being dubbed 'MacMolière', as if he had become a Scottish playwright by adoption (witness Peacock, 1993, and his chapter in this volume), a similar phenomenon has arisen with Tremblay, who has been dubbed 'McTremblay' (Pautz, 2000). Between 1989 and 2003, eight of Tremblay's plays, in Scots translations by us, will have been professionally staged in Scotland. Indeed, the popularity of one of those, *The Guid Sisters* [*Les Belles-Soeurs*], led to the production being revived twice for Scottish tours and taken on invited visits to Toronto and Montreal, where it ran for a month at the premier English-language theatre as part of the city's 350th anniversary celebrations. Another, *The Real Wurld?* [*Le Vrai Monde?*], was invited to an international theatre festival in the USA, and *Solemn Mass for a Full Moon in Summer* [*Messe solennelle pour une pleine lune d'été*] played at London's Barbican Centre, again as part of a festival of international theatre. Therefore, in addition to the remarkable reception given Tremblay's work in Scotland, productions of his plays have made a contribution to promoting Scottish theatre in other countries.

Scottish reviewers have regularly noted the special appeal that Tremblay's work seems to have for Scottish audiences. Typical are comments such as these: 'In the translations into Scots by Martin Bowman and Bill Findlay the plays of Tremblay achieve an astonishing affinity of class, religion, voice and emotional oppression for Scottish audiences' (*The Herald*, 11 April 1994); 'Tremblay is contemporary theatre's great melancholy realist; he fits Scotland like a glove, and it was a stroke of luck that we had the translators with the vision to see this' (*The Scotsman*, 9 February 1998); '[I]f Scotland is to adopt a playwright, there could be no better candidate than Tremblay' (*The Scotsman*, 11 April 1994); '[Tremblay is] the best playwright Scotland never had' (*The Guardian*, 29 October 1992).

Consideration of possible reasons for his special appeal in Scotland is beyond the scope of this essay. In any event, it has been touched on elsewhere by us and others – along with discussion of, variously, our 'ideology', collaborative method, fidelity of approach, and so on – in the critical literature that our Scots Tremblays have generated (e.g. Aaltonen, 2000: 69–72; Bowman, 1988, 2000a, 2000b, 2000c, 2003; Bowman & Findlay, 1994; Corbett, 1996; Findlay, 1988, 1992, 1996b; Foucheraux, 1995; Harvie, 1995; Hastie, 2000; Kinloch, 2000; Lockerbie, 2000a; Salter, 1993; Woodsworth, 1996). However, one important source of appeal for a Scottish audience must be mentioned because of its relevance here, and that is our choice of

Scots as a translation medium. That choice was made partly because of the fit we saw between Québécois and Scots, and partly because we wanted to challenge and extend the capacities of modern vernacular Scots in rendering Tremblay's bold experimentation with the creative resources of Québécois. We have been fortunate in that theatre critics, appreciatively, have recognised these impulses. For example, of our first translation, *The Guid Sisters*, one commented that 'the Tremblay dialogue – written in the once-despised *joual* French dialect of Quebec – translates into urban Scots as though the two languages were long lost twins' (*The Guardian*, 5 May 1989); and of our seventh, *Solemn Mass for a Full Moon in Summer*, another opined, 'Bowman and Findlay have created a new dramatic language for Scottish theatre by capturing in the Scots idiom the lyricism and energy of Québécois' (*The Sunday Herald*, 7 May 2000). It should be noted that ours has by no means been an isolated exploration of the potentialities of Scots as a stage language, for this has been a defining characteristic of modern Scottish theatre. It is a development that took on a new energy in the 1970s (see Findlay, 2001a: ix–xxvi) and has continued since. Thus, as Randall Stevenson states in *Scottish Theatre Since the Seventies*, 'it is probably Scots speech that is the most fundamental influence on the drama' over the past thirty years (Stevenson & Wallace, 1996: 4).

The same is true of Quebec theatre since the mid-1960s in its assertion of the validity of Québécois as a serious stage language and in writers' engagement with its artistic potentialities. We have discussed elsewhere the history and modern development of Québécois, the distinctive variety of French spoken in Quebec (Bowman & Findlay, 1994: 63–5). Suffice to say here that, until the primacy of metropolitan French (as well as English) was challenged by writers and intellectuals as part of the 1960s' '*Révolution tranquile*', it held a privileged position, along with Parisian-French cultural products and norms, in Francophone Quebec society, including in the theatre. Michel Tremblay was a key figure in challenging that hegemony through his harnessing of *joual* (or *montréalais*), the working-class dialect of his upbringing in Montreal's east-end. Jane Moss explains of *joual*:

> [T]he term was coined in the early 60s by André Laurendeau, editor of the Montreal French-language newspaper *Le Devoir*, who along with a priest named Jean-Paul Desbiens, wrote a series of articles denouncing the quality of French spoken and taught in Quebec. To illustrate his point about the poor pronunciation of the average Québécois, he used the example of the word 'cheval' which was mispronounced 'joual'. The term was picked up by other critics and the debate was on over the purity of the French language. 'Joual' is not merely a matter of pronun-

ciation; it refers to the mixture of Anglicisms, Old French, standard French and neologisms, which has become the popular idiom of the province. To some critics, 'joual' was a degenerate form of French, a symbol of the decadence of Quebec society, the ignorance of its people, the contaminating effect of contact with English. To others, 'joual' was a symbol of Quebec's unique cultural identity and a rallying point for nationalist and separatist sentiments. (Moss, 1996: 207, n. 3)

Tremblay's 1968 play *Les Belles-Soeurs* was a *succès de scandale* because it proved just such a rallying point in both its unapologetic assertion and celebration of Quebecness and its groundbreaking exploitation of *joual* for serious artistic effect. Tremblay remarked two decades later:

> The *joual* language in the '60s and early '70s was like [...] a political and cultural arm because we in '68, and a whole generation, took culture from the élite in songs and films, in theatre and literature. We took it from them and twenty years after we still have it. We never gave it back.
> (Tremblay, 1989: 32)

The artistic and political impact of Tremblay's now more than twenty plays has made him the most important playwright in Quebec history.

Whilst it is problematic to claim that there are close parallels between the linguistic, cultural and political experiences of Quebec and Scotland, nonetheless there are sufficient points of similarity to create a sense of kinship (see Bowman & Findlay, 1994: 66). An area of approximate similarity, of particular importance to us as translators, is a language-related one, as described by Ian Lockerbie:

> Historically, the sense of a distinctive identity in both Quebec and Scotland has been strongly sustained and projected through the vernacular form of French and English that is spoken in each country. These vernacular languages have evolved over time and are continuing to do so at an increasing rate. The use of the vernacular has considerably receded in everyday life in favour of more standard forms of each language, although these standard forms continue to be flavoured and coloured by the older usages. Standard English in Scotland is not quite the same as standard English elsewhere, and the same is true of the standard French of Quebec. Yet the vernacular has not disappeared. Quite on the contrary, it has not only retained but strengthened its role in the domain of the language arts, by becoming the principal vehicle of expression in theatre, television and the cinema, while still maintaining a presence in the novel and poetry, which were its original strongholds.

It is the extension of the vernacular from the realm of the local and the everyday into that of the symbolic and the *imaginaire* which distinguishes both Québécois and Scots from regional dialects, as these are normally defined. Québécois and Scots, while sharing many of the formal features of dialects, find themselves being used, not simply for local everyday matters (the domain of the dialects), but for the most sophisticated and valued forms of language use in society: those that occur in the expressive arts. Hence their centrality to collective identity: it is often through the vernacular in the theatre, cinema or literature that people in Quebec and Scotland gain their most significant insights into their culture, their history and their shared values, and thus reinforce their collective sense of belonging. (Lockerbie, 2000b: 1)

A common element is language variety and the exploitation of that by modern writers, including Tremblay. Just as the Quebec writer may draw on standard French, the Quebec variant of standard French, and a range of country and urban vernacular forms of Québécois (of which *joual* is one), the Scottish writer can draw on standard English, Scottish standard English, and urban and country dialects of Scots. One consequence of this rich linguistic mix in Scotland's case is, both historically and continuing through to today, the employment of style-shifting by writers for literary and other effects. Since this is also an aspect of Tremblay's dramaturgy, in part as a reflection of Quebec reality, the Scottish translator is arguably in a privileged position in attempting to render the distinctive qualities of his stage language. We have therefore chosen to focus on this particular aspect of our work in the discussion that follows.

A simple example of the kind of register contrast found in Tremblay, and how we convey this, can be taken from our translation *The Guid Sisters* [pun on *guid* = 'good,' and *guid sister* = 'sister-in-law']. This example also illustrates the kind of inferioristic attitude towards *joual* that that pioneering 1968 play challenged, and in its time scandalised. The one socially aspiring and would-be standard speaker among the 15 working-class women in *Les Belles-Soeurs*, Lisette de Courval, embodies and voices that attitude, including deferring to France as the arbiter of taste (though, for comic and ridiculing effect there are little tell-tale signs that she has not succeeded in wholly suppressing her vernacular speech):

And as for Europe! Everyone over there is so well brought up. They're far more polite than here. You'd never meet a Germaine Lauzon over there. Only people with class. In Paris everyone speaks so refined. There they speak proper French. No like here. Leopold [her husband] was right. These people are inferior. They're nothing but keelies [vulgar, lower-class persons]. We shouldn't be mixing with them. We shouldn't even waste breath talking about them ... They should be hidden away somewhere out of sight ... My God, I'm so ashamed of them. (Tremblay, 1991: 31)

(For discussion of the reasoning behind using *keelies* to represent Tremblay's anglicism *cheap*, see Bowman & Findlay, 1994: 75.) What Lisette de Courval is ashamed of, linguistically speaking, is tellingly illustrated by the register clash with the *joual* (or urban Scots) of the other women; as here, when one of them turns on her when she is patronisingly boasting about getting a new fur stole:

> Shut yir gab, ya bloody leear ye! We ken damn fine yir man's up tae his erse in debt acause ae your mink stoles an yir fancy trips tae Europe. Ye cannae take us in wi aw that shite aboot bein weel-aff. Ye've nae mair money nor the rest ae us. Christ, ah've had it up tae here wi that slaverin bitch bummin her load. (Tremblay, 1988: 45)[1]
>
> [Shut your mouth, you bloody liar you! We know damn fine your husband's up to his arse in debt because of your mink stoles and your fancy trips to Europe. You can't take us in with all that crap about being well-off. You've no more money than the rest of us. Christ, I've had it up to here with that rubbish-spouting bitch's boasting.]

Were it not possible to represent in translation this contrast in speech and therefore outlook between characters – and the ideological point behind it – the full import of what Tremblay is doing in his original would be diluted or lost.

To jump from our first to our eighth and latest Tremblay translation, *If Only ...* [*Encore une fois, si vous permettez*] (1998), staged by Edinburgh's Royal Lyceum Theatre in 2003, here we find register contrast, too, but used for a different purpose. Here it is used to mark a change brought about by age and intellectual/artistic development. The play is a two-hander featuring a successful middle-aged playwright and his long-dead mother, who died in the 1960s before the playwright enjoyed first success, but had a formative influence in encouraging his imagination through her own flights of fancy and colourful command of *joual*. The play is strongly autobiographical, being an act of homage by Tremblay to his own mother, who died in 1963, five years before *Les Belles-Soeurs* launched his stellar career. The play opens with the playwright character, the son/narrator, addressing the audience in a prologue in which he makes reference to, and at times quotes from, classic drama by authors such as Shakespeare, Chekhov, Ibsen, Ionesco, Lorca, Tennessee Williams and others. In keeping with the intellectualising nature of his discourse, he speaks in standard language, one effect of which is that the first entry of his larger-than-life mother is all the more dramatic because of the surprise factor in the unanticipated switch in registers:

> THE NARRATOR: You'll've often come across her at the theatre, in the audience and on the stage. You'll've met her in real life, she's one of you. She was born at a particular period in our country's history, is the product of a city like ours. I'm certain she's one of many. And universal. She is Rodrigo's aunt, Electra's cousin, Ivanov's sister, Caligula's godmother, Mistress Quickly's little niece, Ham's mother or Clov's ... maybe both. And when she expresses herself in her own words, those who speak a different language understand her in their own words. She is found throughout history and is part of all cultures. She has always been there and will be there always. I wanted to see her again, to hear her once more. If only for the pleasure of it. If only so's to laugh and cry. I'd like to see her once more, if you'll allow me. (*He looks in the direction of the wings.*) I can hear her coming. She'll speak ten to the dozen, because words, for her, have always been the most effective weapon. (*He smiles.*) As they put it in the classics, 'Behold she enters'.
>
> *Enter Nana. She is visibly angry.*
>
> NANA: Get tae yir bedroom right this minute! Daein that at your age! What wis in that heid ae yours? At ten year ae age yir auld enough tae know right frae wrang! Aye, but no auld enough tae actually pit it intae practice, eh no?! Naw, for stupit ten-year-auld weans are stupit and behave stupit! You've nae excuse for what you did!
>
> THE NARRATOR: Ah didnae mean tae dae it.
>
> NANA: What d'ye mean ye didnae mean tae dae it?! Ye flung a big dod ae ice under a passin caur! Don't sit there and tell me ye didnae mean tae dae it. The dod ae ice didnae fling itsel! (Unpublished translation)
>
> [NANA: Get to your bedroom right this minute! Doing that at your age! What was in that head of yours? At ten years of age you're old enough to know right from wrong! Yes, but not old enough to actually put it into practice, isn't that right?! No, for stupid ten-year-old kids are stupid and behave stupid! You've no excuse for what you did!/THE NARRATOR: I didn't mean to do it./NANA: What d'you mean you didn't mean to do it?! You flung a big piece of ice under a passing car! Don't stand there and tell me you didn't mean to do it. The piece of ice didn't fling itself!]

In the prologue, and at other points in the play, the Narrator is 50 years old; but he is also represented at ages 10, 13, 16, 18 and 20, when he is still at home, and still subject to his mother Nana's verbal and other influence. As exemplified by this passage, he style-shifts in accordance with his age, and, since he is played by the same actor at all ages and in the same clothes, the register contrasts help to signal whether it is the boy/youth or the middle-age adult speaking.

In *The House Among the Stars* [*La Maison suspendue*] (1990) three generations of the same family, separated by time, and by the consequences of geographic and social mobility, occupy the stage simultaneously, and their respective speech forms help to differentiate and characterise them. Each of Tremblay's registers finds an unforced Scottish equivalent: the 1910 characters, who live in a remote country area, speak a lyrical, rural Québécois/Scots; their children, in 1950, live in the city as first-generation working class, and they speak an urban-demotic Québécois (i.e. *joual*)/Scots; and in 1990 their middle-class, city-dwelling grandson, an academic by profession, and his male lover, speak a relatively prosaic standard French/English, which is Quebec-/Scottish-accented and features some Quebec/Scottish features. The brief excerpts below are representative of the speech of the 1910, 1950 and 1990 characters, respectively. In the first, Josaphat is enthralling his son with the story of how, while he is asleep, their house magically sails into the sky at night, pulled by a rope attached to a birch-bark canoe:

> The canoe it curses awaa tae itsel as it wrastles wi the wecht ... It pu's an pu's, an the men in the sky sterts paddlin like billy-oh ... A hoose, ye'll appreciate, is a fair wecht! [...] The forest passes aneath us ... Duhamel seems toattie ... The haill o' the Laurentian Mountains slip oot ae sicht intae the daurk ... The hoose is held in perfect balance, swee in jist a wee, wee bittie [...] The haill sky unfolds in front us as the hoose birls slow at the end o' its rope ... It's maist byordinar braw!
> (Unpublished translation)

> [The canoe curses away to itself as it wrestles with the weight ... It pulls and pulls, and the men in the sky start paddling like billy-oh ... A house, you'll appreciate, is a fair weight! [...] The forest passes beneath us ... Duhamel seems tiny ... The whole of the Laurentian Mountains slip out of sight into the dark ... The house is held in perfect balance, swaying just a wee, wee bit [...] The whole sky unfolds in front of us as the house revolves slowly at the end of its rope ... It's most extraordinarily beautiful!]

In the second, Edouard is defending himself against his sister's aggressive disapproval of his transvestism and brazenly camp behaviour:

> Mind last summer at Roger Beach? Ye wur ashamed ae me cos Ah actit the poof in front ae a gang ae nyaffs ... Mind that? Well, if Ah hidnae

played the poof fur the benefit ae that shower, they'd've smashed ma gub in [...] Hid Ah tried tae hide it, they'da made a full ae us, pestered us the haill day, spiled oor picnic, an at the feenish-up they'd've goat me in a coarner somewhere, humiliated me, an smashed ma puss in! But Ah wiggled ma erse at thum, pit a hankie oan ma heid and sung thum some golden oldies fae afore they wur boarn ... and they laughed! Laughed the haill day! (Unpublished translation)

> [Remember last summer at Roger Beach? You were ashamed of me because I acted the poof in front of a gang of contemptible good-for-nothings ... Remember that? Well, if I hadn't played the poof for the benefit of that shower, they'd've smashed my face in [...] Had I tried to hide it, they'd've made a fool of us, pestered us the whole day, spoiled our picnic, and finally they'd've got me in a corner somewhere, humiliated me, and smashed my face in! But I wiggled my arse at them, put a handkerchief on my head and sung them some golden oldies from before they were born ... and they laughed! Laughed the whole day!]

And in the third, Jean-Marc, the academic, expresses his utter disenchantment with his job, in a register that reflects at times, in its prim semantics and invited 'refined' Scottish accent, both his occupation and a certain stiffness in his character:

Until not very long ago, whenever I saw one of my older colleagues at the university indulge in the time-honoured and suspect practice of taking a sabbatical year out, I always said to myself, 'There goes another chancer who's contrived an excuse to do sweet nothing for a year at the taxpayer's expense!' I would watch said person depart, walking on air as if a prison-door had swung open after twenty years of forced labour at the chalkface. [...] I told myself naively that I'd never do the same as them. I enjoyed my work too much, my students enthused me as much as ever. I could never imagine myself taking a sabbatical. The very thought was preposterous. [...] But then ...
(Unpublished translation)

John Corbett (1997: 20) has written of this 'code-mixing', as he terms it, that it renders 'a dramatic strategy which would be lost if only one variety of the language had been used for the translation'. Certainly, it was our wish as translators that, following Tremblay, the language contrasts should have a poignancy complementing the play's elegiac tone and the thematic concern with change and with how geographic and social mobility can lead a later generation to a troubling sense of deracination, loss and aridity; as thrown into relief in this family's history by language shift, from rural dialect to urban vernacular to standard.

Translating Register in Michel Tremblay's Québécois Drama

Of course, such shifts in language variety also allow Tremblay to harness them for artistic effect, as seen in the play in his careful crafting of exits and entrances, and of overlaps and contrapuntal simultaneous speeches when characters of different generations and registers are on stage at the same time and in the same house but oblivious of one another. They are effects that demonstrate Tremblay's abiding interest in the musicality of language and in the application of musical forms to dramatic structure and technique. This was evident as early as his breakthrough play *Les Belles-Soeurs*, with its use of solos, duos, trios, quartets and choruses, and has remained a characteristic of his work. His most daring experiment with musical form is *Messe solennelle pour une pleine lune d'été* [*Solemn Mass for a Full Moon in Summer*] (Tremblay, 1996). The play was inspired by the discovery of a lost mass by the composer Hector Berlioz, and takes the form of a traditional Catholic mass into which is integrated the pagan element of lunar worship. Each numbered and named part of the mass is also given a musical direction, such as 'III. EXULTATE JUBILATE *allegro vivace*'. The play is set on the balconies of six flats in Montreal's Plateau Mont-Royal district on a hot, humid night in August. The eleven characters – young and old, gay and straight, partnered and bereft – reveal their innermost thoughts about love and lost love, often in a confessional- or prayer-like manner. The play has been compared to a spoken cantata, alternating naturalistic dialogue with lyrical and ritual address to God and the moon. The constant interplay of vernacular and standard speech – the latter usually in a heightened poetic/religious mode – creates a double music where the one is enriched by the other. The effect, involving solo, unisonal, antiphonal and contrapuntal voices, with the liturgical elements allowing for the integration of choral set pieces into the quotidian lives of the characters, has been likened to high church meeting spoken opera. The complexity and startling originality of what is achieved instances again how one of the attractions for us in translating Tremblay's drama is the challenge of capturing in Scots – and, we hope, importing fruitfully into Scots – the artistic ambition he shows in stretching the capacities of his vernacular stage language, often through register contrast and a creative tension with standard language.

The following excerpts give a flavour of the work. At the end of section IV, headed 'DE PROFUNDIS et GLORIA *largo*', the characters in their separate and joint miseries address the moon in a standard register (Tremblay uses a form of bracketing to indicate where characters speak simultaneously):

> THE NINE CHARACTERS: O moon, O blood of Christ. O moon, O blood of Christ, in your passage across the sky. O moon, O blood of Christ, in your passage across the sky, bring me peace. Bring me a little peace. Grant me a little of your glory. Bring a little peace to my sufferings. Bring me peace.
>
> JEANNINE: Higher!
>
> LOUISE: Higher!
>
> THE WIDOW: Hang your glory in the heights of heaven!
>
> ROSE: But grant me jist a little.
>
> LOUISE: Let your milk-white gaze ...
> ... pour over me
> JEANNINE: Your milk-white gaze ...
> ... your healing light.
> MIREILLE: Your healin light.
>
> THE NINE CHARACTERS: Your light. Your glory. Your peace. O moon, let your milk-white gaze pour over me. O host of heaven, let your light flow over me. Let your light flow over me. Bathe me in your peace. Bathe me in your peace. Your peace. Peace. Peace. Peace. Peace ...
>
> (Tremblay, 2000: 31)

The section that then follows, 'DIES IRAE *allegro agitato*', dovetails by having characters in precise unison pick up and repeat that last word 'peace' to musico-linguistic effect. We see, too, Tremblay's regular alternation in the play between incantation and naturalistic dialogue (though even in the naturalistic dialogue one finds verbal and rhythmic patterning). The latter is exemplified by Mireille and Yvon, who bitterly address their respective dependant cohabitants; in Mireille's case, her widowed father who has lost both arms in a work accident caused by his drunkenness, and in Yvon's case, his gay partner who is dying from Aids contracted from a male prostitute. As well, we see in this passage how Tremblay has two or more characters in different situations share the same line to describe their own individual circumstances, and how he cross-cuts their respective stories:

> JEANNINE, LOUISE, ROSE, MATHIEU, GASTON, GÉRARD, THE WIDOW
> (*Very slowly [in unison] throughout all of this fast 'movement'*)

JEANNINE: I've no peace ... I've no peace anymore.

LOUISE: I've no peace ... I've no peace anymore.

MATHIEU: I've no peace ... I've no peace anymore.

ROSE: Ah've no peace ... Ah've no peace anymair.

GÉRARD: Ah've no peace ... Ah've no peace anymair.

WIDOW: Ah've nae peace ... Ah've nae peace anymair.

GASTON: Ah've nae peace ... Ah've nae peace anymair.

(The outer pair of the following four lines are said four times)

YVON: Ah've no peace ...
... Ah've no peace anymair.

MIREILLE: Ah've nae peace ...
... Ah've nae peace anymair.

YVON: Ah've had enough.

MIREILLE: Ah've had enough.

MIREILLE, YVON: Ah cannae cope anymair.

MIREILLE: Ah've had it up tae here wi skivvyin fur ye, dad. Ah've had ma fill ae daein fur ye – waashin yir face, wipin yir erse, seein tae yir ivry need. Ah'm sick ae no hivin a life tae masel, ae no hivin a life tae caw ma ain. Aw cos ah've tae look eftir you. Wance'n fur aw, ah waant a bit ae peace!

YVON: Ah cannae cope wi goin on like this, understand? Ah cannae go on actin the nurse, comin back here fae ma work and no knowin in what state ah'll find ye. Ah cannae go on any longer. Ah've had enough ae it! Ah'm worn oot. Worn oot and sick wi worry. D'ye understand? Ah spend aw ma time at work watchin the telephone. Ma nerves are shot tae hell!

(MIREILLE *and* YVON *repeat the same two speeches, saying them at the same time)*

YVON: Ah've had enough!

MIREILLE: Ah've had enough!

YVON, MIREILLE: Ah've had enough ae cleanin up your shite!

YVON: Your shite, Gérard, your shite! Ah'm sick ae cleanin up your shite! Ah'm sick ae wipin yir arse, ae washin yir arse while fightin back ma tears and tryin no tae spew up, sick ae changin the sheets, disinfectin ivrythin, then startin again, startin aw ower again wi nae prospect ae it ever comin tae an end, wi nae hope it'll ever finish, unless ... *(He stops suddenly and looks at* GÉRARD*)* ... unless you ... My God, unless you pass away!

MIREILLE: Ever since ah wis wee, ever since ma mum passed away cos she couldnae take anymair ae it, ah've hid tae dae her duties. But noo it's ma turn no tae be able tae cairry oan. It's ma turn tae waant tae pack it aw in. Ever since ah wis a lassie ah've served ye hand and fit – been yir cook, yir cleaner, yir nurse, yir skivvy. But ah'm seeck-scunnered skivvyin fur ye! (Tremblay, 2000: 32–3)²

[From after the choral speeches:] [YVON: I've had enough./MIREILLE: I've had enough./MIREILLE, YVON: I can't cope anymore./MIREILLE: I've had it up to here with skivvying for you, dad. I've had my fill of doing for you – washing your face, wiping your arse, seeing to your every need. I'm sick of not having a life to myself, of not having a life to call my own. All because I've to look after you. Once and for all, I want a bit of peace!/YVON: I can't cope with going on like this, understand? I can't go on acting the nurse, coming back here from my work and not knowing in what state I'll find you. I can't go on any longer. I've had enough of it! I'm worn out. Worn out and sick with worry. D'you understand? I spend all my time at work watching the telephone. My nerves are shot to hell!/ *(*MIREILLE *and* YVON *repeat the same two speeches, saying them at the same time)*/ YVON: I've had enough!/MIREILLE: I've had enough!/YVON, MIREILLE: I've had enough of cleaning up your shite!/YVON: Your shite, Gerard, your shite! I'm sick of cleaning up your shite! I'm sick of wiping your arse, of washing your arse while fighting back my tears and trying not to spew up, sick of changing the sheets, disinfecting everything, then starting again, starting all over again with no prospect of it ever coming to an end, with no hope it'll ever finish, unless ... *(He stops suddenly and looks at* GÉRARD*)* ... unless you ... My God, unless you pass away!/MIREILLE: Ever since I was little, ever since mum passed away because she couldn't take any more of it, I've had to do her duties. But now it's my turn not to be able to carry on. It's my turn to want to pack it all in. Ever since I was a girl I've served you hand and foot – been your cook, your cleaner, your nurse, your skivvy. But I'm sick-fed-up skivvying for you!]

Where we differ from Tremblay's original is in our use, as here, of phonetic spelling to signal precisely subtleties of sound and register. Early in his career Tremblay employed phonetic spelling with his *joual*. However, shadowing political advances in Quebec and the enhanced status for Quebec-French that followed (see Bowman & Findlay, 1994: 65), Tremblay is now less concerned to signal persistently on the page the minutiae of Québécois pronunciation and is much more restrained in doing so than previously. Also, he can now depend on actors to bring Québécois pronunciation to written standard forms as appropriate. However, there is less confidence in relying on this in Scottish theatre, and there is a continuing convention of writers employing phonetic spelling, often in an idiosyncratic manner. This is particularly so with urban Scots, and is a feature not just of drama but of fiction and poetry. One reason for this practice is the reality in Scottish vernacular speech of fluctuating choices in word forms. A writer can play with that fluctuation creatively but in order to do so has to pin down on the page which choice is preferred at any given moment. Both the speech fact and the opportunity it affords for artistic exploitation are conveyed in Tom Leonard's prose piece 'Honest', which itself is written in a highly individualistic phonetic Glaswegian:

> [I]fyi write down 'doon' wan minute, nwrite doon 'down' thi nixt, people say yir beein inconsistent. But ifyi sayti sumdy, 'Whaira yi afti?' nthey say, 'Whut?' nyou say, 'Where are you off to?' they don't say, 'That's no whutyi said thi furst time'. They'll probably say sumhm like, 'Doon thi road!' anif you say, 'What?' they usually say, 'Down the road!' the second time – though no always. (Leonard, 1976: 47)

> [[i]f you write down 'doon' one minute, and write down 'down' the next, people say you're being inconsistent. But if you say to somebody, 'Where are ye aff tae?' and they say, 'What?' and you say, 'Where are you off to?' they don't say, 'That's not what you said the first time.' They'll probably say something like, 'Doon the road!' and if you say, 'What?' they usually say, 'Down the road!' the second time – though not always.]

The conditions prevailing in the Scottish context, then, inevitably affect the form our target text takes – as does our awareness of the Québécois theatrical context in which Tremblay operates and the way his spoken, performed text can differ from its form on the page. This makes somewhat problematic the reading of the text by someone who is unfamiliar with the sound of Tremblay's Quebec-French voices, particularly in the case of a play such as *Solemn Mass* where, because of the unusual musical elements, the written text has to be 'heard' by the reader even more than usual. Our Scotland–Canada partnership is helpful in providing us with the necessary bifocalism here. It also allows us to arrive at the reasoned acceptance that it is difficult to avoid a degree of creative latitude in where and how we render vernacular speech on the page in situating each character on a standard-vernacular scale appropriate to his/her Scottish voice/social level. Honouring both the sociolinguistic realities of Scotland and the conventions influencing the written presentation of Scots-medium scripts in Scottish theatre thus led us in *Solemn Mass* to use a wider range of stylistic variation between the characters than is evident in the source text *as written*. In the main, Tremblay does not build modulations of register between the respective characters' everyday speech, but on the page only distinguishes the secular mode from the sacred (with Québécois items peppering the former). In the extract above, for example, the opening line, 'I've no peace ... I've no peace anymore', is given in variant forms by us, with extra notational bracketing, partly for the reasons just given, partly to aid the subtle speech contrasts (flowing from those reasons) that we have built in between characters in our target text, and partly to serve Tremblay's intended musico-linguistic effect. In the published original, Tremblay (1996: 55) simply gives the same line to the seven opening speakers, with one Québécois item included: '*J'en ai pus de paix! ... j'en ai pus jamais!*'

In view of the above, it might seem contradictory to state that Tremblay's characters in the source text are universally more able to employ vernacular in their secular speech than is the case in our translation. A consequence of this is that there is less differentiation between them in the source text than in our target one, where we individualise their language more and do not make them all Scots speakers (though most of them are to differing degrees). A sense of the distinctions we introduce, sometimes marked and sometimes small, can be gained from the passage that closes the 'KYRIE *lento*' section, where nine of the characters speak simultaneously, in a cacophony that achieves resolution in their joint appeal to God in shared words:

> (*The following lines are repeated nine times in crescendo.*)
> JEANNINE: If you've nothing more to say to me, then shut it!
> LOUISE: Your wish is my command. My lips are silent.
> ROSE: Ah do what ah kin tae help ye, ah do what ah kin. . .
> MATHIEU: It does no good thinkin about it, it's done with.
> GASTON: If ah need somethin, ah'll tell ye, okay!
> MIREILLE: Ah'll stey wi ye, ah'll stey in, awright!
> YVON: Ah do what ah can tae help ye, ah do what ah can.
> GÉRARD: If ah need somethin, ah'll tell ye, okay!
> THE WIDOW: There's nae point thinkin aboot it, it's done wi.

THE NINE CHARACTERS: (*Twice, very loud*) My God! Christ Jesus! Lord! HAVE MERCY UPON US!   (Tremblay, 2000: 19)[3]

The sudden solemnity of that appeal to God is the more tellingly affecting – and the more theatrically effective – because of the shift into the sacred standard register in contrast to the preceding, mostly vernacular, babble of the profane 'novena'. This follows Tremblay, but we signal a wider range of register modulations.

At opposing polarities of the sliding scale that we used, because of Scottish circumstances, are the Scottish standard English of the lesbian couple Jeannine and Louise, and the relatively broad urban Scots of armless Gaston and his long-suffering carer daughter Mireille. To instance the difficulty we had in following Tremblay in putting a vernacular wash through Jeannine's language is an utterance such as this, taken from when she is soliloquising about how her love for Louise has turned to hate:

> JEANNINE: Tonight, I could bare my claws. I could tear and slash the sky apart, could rip the moon out like a cyst, gouge it out as if it were a malignant tumour! [...] Tonight, there's a storm rampaging across the little peace I have. (Tremblay, 2000: 38)

It is difficult not to read Jeannine as a middle-class, well-educated incomer to Plateau Mont-Royal, where Tremblay sets the play. Traditionally it was a working-class area but it has gradually been undergoing gentrification, with the old guard working class living alongside the more gentrified incomers in the same tenement. In Scottish terms, that and the kind of imagery and language that Jeannine uses (e.g. *'J'ai été son Pygmalion sans jouer les Pygmalion et j'ai pensé l'aimer pour toujours!'* and *'[C]'est la lune blanche qui vogue haut dans le ciel comme un énorme galion!'*), drive one to 'hear' standard English as her typical speech. To have coloured her language with vernacular items would have risked inauthenticity for a Scottish audience in terms of social class and her 'cultivated' utterances – ironically, to the detriment of the source text in theatrical effectiveness when received by its target audience.

At the other polarity, that Gaston and Mireille are poor, working-class characters indigenous to the district, demanded from us an insistent, phoneticised urban demotic, as in this speech by Mireille:

> Ah cannae go oan feedin ye, faither, huddin yir soup spoon, yir foark, wipin yir mooth when ye dribble! It drives me dementit! Fur fifteen years, dad, ah've fed ye three times a day, and three times a day doon aw thae years ah've felt like stranglin ye! What could you dae, dad, eh? What could you dae wi thae piggin wee stumps if ah wis tae try tae strangle ye! Eh? Wi thae piggin wee stumps that've stoapped us livin like ither folk aw thae years? Ah feel like smashin ivrythin, settin fire tae the place, poisonin the two ae us, cuttin ma throat even, leavin you tae fend fur yirsel wi yir bastardin work accident! (Tremblay, 2000: 34–5)
>
> [I can't go on feeding you, father, holding your soup spoon, your fork, wiping your mouth when you dribble! It drives me demented! For fifteen years, dad, I've fed you three times a day, and three times a day down all those years I've

felt like strangling you! What could you do, dad, eh? What could you do with those bloody wee stumps if I was to try to strangle you! Eh? With those bloody wee stumps that've stopped us living like other folk all these years? I feel like smashing everything, setting fire to the place, poisoning the two of us, cutting my throat even, leaving you to fend for yourself with your bastarding work accident!]

The original reads:

Chus pus capable de te faire manger, de tenir ta cuiller à soupe pis ta fourchette, pis de t'essuyer la bouche quand ça coule! Ça me rend folle! Ça fait quinze ans que j'te fais manger trois fois par jour, papa, pis depuis des années j'ai envie de t'étouffer trois fois par jour! Qu'est-ce que tu pourrais faire, papa, qu'est-ce que tu pourrais faire avec tes deux Christ de p'tits mognons si j'essayais de t'étouffer? Hein? Avec tes deux p'tits Christ de mognons qui nous empêchent de vivre tout le monde depuis des années? J'ai envie de tout détruire, papa, de mettre le feu, de nous empoissoner tous les deux ou ben de crever en te laissant tout seul avec ton maudit accident de travail! (Tremblay, 1996: 57–8)

Tremblay clearly incorporates *joual* words and forms here, but our Scots medium 'exaggerates' these, as it were, by employing a more 'unthrottled' spoken vernacular in keeping with Scottish sociolinguistic reality and Scots writing conventions. We should add, too, that in forging our target medium we 'heard' unbidden the bitter verbal battles between Gaston and his daughter in the language that we have spelled out on the page. In other words, it seemed spontaneously right to us that that was how they should sound in their Scottish voice – and our thinking selves, conscious, too, of how anger or heightened emotion tends to bring about an intensification of Scots, told us, after due deliberation, that we should trust our instincts on this occasion. In doing so, we were working within the grain of Tremblay's intention in the juxtaposition of vernacular and standard registers, and in the abrasive, musico-linguistic effect that is thereby achieved. For, were standard English the sole register of a translation of this play, a crucial aspect of Tremblay's artistry would be lost.

Whereas, then, with Jeannine and Louise we give them more standard language than Tremblay, obversely, we give Gaston and Mireille a denser spoken vernacular than Tremblay (on the page at least). Such decisions are not made wilfully, as our general policy is to attempt to replicate what Tremblay does, even if not always where he does, or even how he does (as instanced in *Solemn Mass* by our greater modulation of register). Effecting that policy can be described as 'translation-as-negotiation', since inevitably we win some and lose some.[4] The negotiation – both with the source text and between ourselves as collaborators – is often a subtle business, and can be difficult to recover in fine detail in retrospect. But we like to believe that we *knowingly* 'lose', and do so usually because of the requirement to balance fidelity to Tremblay with fidelity to the Scottish ear and context. Perhaps paradoxically, the latter consideration ultimately has to be the overriding one if we are to serve Tremblay effectively.

Notes

1. The reason for taking the two quotations from *The Guid Sisters* from different editions is that the publisher of the 1991 edition chose to Anglicise the spelling of the Scots in order to make the text more accessible to a non-Scottish readership, whereas the 1988 edition gives the text in its original orthography (and in its original West-Fife Scots as against the Glasgow-Scots adopted for the Tron's performance version. For more about the latter revision, see Bowman and Findlay (1994: 67–8).
2. The translation was published before the script went into rehearsal, during which we made some refinements. There are therefore a few small discrepancies between the quotations here and the published version of the translation.
3. See note 2 above. The reason for the discrepancies here is that hearing the script in rehearsal alerted us to the need to achieve similar line lengths to allow the voices in crescendo to end together.
4. For discussion of other win–lose aspects of our Tremblay translations, such as the general tendency for Scots to be more figurative and idiomatic than Tremblay's Québécois, see Bowman and Findlay (1994: 70–80).

Part 2
Studies of Translations

Chapter 5
Robert Kemp's Translations of Molière

NOËL PEACOCK

Perhaps one of the most curious aspects of post-war Scottish theatre history has been the upsurge of interest in the seventeenth-century French comic dramatist, Molière (see Peacock, 1993). One of the most significant factors contributing to this theatrical phenomenon has been the plethora of adaptations in Scots, particularly in the 1980s, which gave birth to the anachronistic neologism, oft repeated if not coined by theatre reviewers, 'the MacMolière industry'. In the 1990s and since, Robert Kemp's work on Molière, though recognised by some adaptors and translators (e.g. Hector MacMillan, Edwin Morgan and Bill Findlay), has been largely ignored by directors, exceptions being the production of *Let Wives Tak Tent* by Pitlochry Festival Theatre in 2001 and of *The Laird o' Grippy* by Dundee Rep Theatre in 2003. Yet, in 1948 and 1955, Kemp played a pioneering role in adapting two of Molière's masterpieces for the Scottish stage; respectively, *L'École des femmes* [*Let Wives Tak Tent*] and *L'Avare* [*The Laird o' Grippy*] (Kemp, 1983, 1987). The aim of this essay is to reassess Kemp's achievement, both historically and linguistically.

Genesis

Before Kemp's translation of *L'École des femmes* there seemed to be no (extant) Scottish translation of Molière. Kemp's undertaking in 1948 therefore proved a landmark in Scottish theatre. It came at a time when generally flat, stilted translations of Molière in English had given countless problems to actors and to not a few box-office managers. The genesis of *Let Wives Tak Tent* may be traced to Louis Jouvet's production of *L'École des femmes* at the first Edinburgh Festival in 1947. First staged in 1936, Jouvet's interpretation had already in France become one of the most signicant productions of Molière in the twentieth century. It was recognised as an important theatrical event on the Scottish stage, and caused *The Scotsman*'s reviewer to issue a challenge to British theatrical practitioners:

Louis Jouvet's company [...] played Molière's comedy with such verve, grace and humour that it might be wondered why British actors have neglected Molière. The time when he was an important influence upon our stage and adaptations of his work were made in English has long since passed, but to play him now, in all his comic plenitude, would be only to reciprocate the homage which France has rendered to Shakespeare. (*The Scotsman*, 9 September, 1947)

That Kemp responded to the challenge, not so much from *The Scotsman*, but from Jouvet's realisation of Molière's play, is well attested from a letter Jouvet sent Kemp on 23 January 1948:

> *Notre visite à Édimbourg provoque indirectement cette naissance de* Let Wives Tak Tent *au Gateway Theatre. Ainsi Molière une fois encore, gagne le coeur d'un public sensible dont nous nous souvenons avec une profonde gratitude.* (From a letter held by the late Arnold Kemp, Robert Kemp's son)

> [Our visit to Edinburgh has (indirectly) induced the birth of *Let Wives Tak Tent* at the Gateway Theatre. In this way Molière once again is reaching the hearts of an appreciative audience which we remember with deep gratitude.]

Kemp's translation was also influenced by actorly considerations. During visits to Paris before and after the war (when he was working for the BBC Features Department in London), Kemp was struck by similarities, particularly in the use of mime and in the flowing body language, between the French style and that of certain Scottish comedians and actors, in particular, Duncan Macrae. The performance of Jouvet, one of the most celebrated actors in France in the 1930s and 1940s, gave Kemp a timely reminder of this. Kemp created the roles of Oliphant (in *Let Wives Tak Tent*) and the eponymous Laird o' Grippy for Macrae. Macrae made the role of Oliphant his own, performing it in different venues from 1948 to 1961, but to Kemp's disappointment, Macrae declined the part of The Laird in 1955, on financial grounds (by that time, he was earning considerable sums of money in pantomime).[1]

In *Let Wives Tak Tent* and *The Laird o' Grippy* Kemp followed Molière's texts closely and sacrificed literal exactness only when faithfulness would be unidiomatic. The choice of prose was justified on account of the difficulty of translating rhymed Alexandrines of an evenly accented tongue to a heavily stressed dialect of the Teutonic group. 'Rhymes that are needed to point the flow of the French may hammer themselves home too heavily in English or Scots' (Programme Note to *Let Wives Tak Tent*, 1948). The Scots chosen was a synthesis of North Eastern Doric and Ayrshire Lallans as well as of modern vernacular.

Setting and Topography

Molière's unidentified outdoor topography in *L'École des femmes* ('*la scène est une place de ville*') is changed to a house on the Canongate (a residential district at the foot of the Royal Mile in late seventeenth-century Edinburgh), with a garden that can be opened and closed at will. While Kemp's scenes take place outdoors, the frequent lifting of walls, indicated in the stage directions, allows the audience to see what is happening inside the house and in the garden. Jouvet had already developed the idea (first introduced in the nineteenth century) of a garden on stage to give greater plausibility to the intimate scenes between Arnolphe and Agnès. Kemp exploited the broader scenic perspective to provide more action on stage.

Molière's vague references to location in *L'Avare* are made more precise in *The Laird o' Grippy*: '*en ces quartiers*' and '*pas loin d'ici*' become 'up by the Lawnmarket' (part of the Royal Mile in Edinburgh's Old Town); '*aller dans d'autres lieux*' is rendered 'to flee awa to London'. The Scottish setting entails consequential emendations in the recognition scene. The '*désordres de Naples*' (which took place in 1647) are transposed to the Highland Jacobite rising of 1715 (referred to by Cramond (Anselme) as 'after the '15'). The shipwreck involved only Hector, Mirren and their mother. This allows Cramond to return after sixteen years to seek pardon and the return of his lands. The reunion takes place not in the country of exile but in Scotland. Molière's parody is maintained: Dom Thomas d'Alburcy is MacRory o' MacRory; Hector was rescued by a 'ship frae Leith' ('*vaisseau espagnol*'); the family were thought to have drowned in 'the cauld [cold] North Sea'; Mirren and her mother stayed with 'fisher-folk' until they could return to Auld Reekie (Edinburgh). The choice of the 1715 uprising, regarded by historians as a 'genteel affair',[2] is particularly appropriate for Kemp's Highland Puss-in-Boots.

Names

The common practice in English translations is to keep the names in French. Even Miles Malleson, whose adaptations in a modern idiom of *L'École des femmes* (Molière, 1954) and of *L'Avare* (Molière, 1950) took great liberties with the text, retained the original names. Kemp sought to transfer to the Scottish context the comic suggestiveness of Molière's names, which could otherwise be lost on a non-French audience. In *Let Wives Tak Tent* [*tak tent* = be careful], Arnolphe (patron saint of cuckolds) is rendered by Oliphant, a Scottish surname (*oliphant* being both the obsolete Scots word for 'elephant' and Old French for 'elephant' and 'trumpet'); Monsieur de la

Souche, glossed by Chrysalde as *'un vieux tronc pourri'*, is translated The Laird of Stumpie, which contains both the idea of the owner of lands over which he has feudal rights and the metaphorical associations of a truncated tree. The blunderer, Horace (with the ironic connotations of the legendary Roman conqueror of Alba), is given the Germanic name Walter ('ruler of people') – and, in Scots, the word *walter* further suggests 'a change or an upset that causes confusion'. The Scottish names given to the characters in *The Laird o' Grippy* similarly provide expectations of comedy: Grippy [*grippy* = 'grasping'] for Harpagon [*harpago* = 'grappling hook']; Mistress Frizell [*frizzle* = 'to coax' or 'to flatter'] for Frosine, the ingenious servant [*Euphrosine* = stock name for matchmaker]. Kemp has added colour to other names: Maître Jacques, the slow-witted valet who thinks he is clever, becomes Jock ('a countryman'); Maître Simon, the stereotypical broker, a fount of all financial wisdom, is called Solomon; Mariane is given the expressive surname Clatterinshaws [from Scots *clatteran* = 'a babbler'].

Structural Changes

One of the problems for English-speaking audiences, versed in the action-packed theatre of Shakespeare, is that most of the physically-expressive moments of *L'École des femmes* occur off-stage and are conveyed through a series of narrations (*récits*) by Agnès and Horace.[3] Kemp retains all the *récits* and soliloquies but lets the audience witness Agnès throwing a stone at her young lover and the latter climbing the ladder and falling, and Agnès's escape. Molière reports these incidents (which have taken place between Acts II and III, and IV and V, respectively) in Horace's *récits* in Act III scene iv and Act V scene ii. Similarly, the interval between Acts III and IV is occupied by scripted stage business, which Molière conveys through Horace's *récit* in Act IV scene vi:

> (*He runs into the house. The servants stare in amazement at one another. Almost immediately he is seen at the upper window, from which he angrily throws pens, papers, books, into the garden.*)

In some of the Kemp scripts held in the Scottish Theatre Archive at the University of Glasgow, Oliphant is given two additional lines at the end of Act III scene v, which convey his attempts at self-deception (apportioning the blame for his discomfiture on reading and writing materials) and develop the stage business suggested above:

> Her buiks, her pens, her papers – they hae brocht me to this! O them at least I can mak an end. (Scottish Theatre Archive, STA 2G C. 2)

[*buiks* = books; *hae brocht* = have brought; *mak* = make]

Directors have still felt disquiet at the conjunction of Acts III and IV, and have tended to include further stage business, even to the point of adding one additional scene between Oliphant and the servants. Appended to the Kemp script for The Sherek Players' production (at the Lyceum Theatre in Edinburgh, 16–21 April 1956 and at the King's Theatre in Glasgow, 23–28 April 1956) is the following accretion at the end of Act III scene v:

ALISON: My certes, what a tirrivie!   [Assuredly, what a commotion!]
ALAN: His glower was as black as the Earl o Hell's weskit!   [waistcoat]
ALISON: This bodes ill for our young birkie!   [conceited lad]
ALAN: It bodes ill for you and me!
ALISON: Oh, I wonder what next will befall us!
ALAN: What will descend upon our innocent heids?   [heads]
(*The books come flying out of the window on top of* ALAN *and* ALISON *who shield their heads and try to escape from the rain of literature and inkpots*)
CURTAIN

Elsewhere Kemp has interpolated in the *récits* an occasional, brief exclamatory aside to break up the narrative and to give comic emphasis to the main character's discomfiture. For example, compare Molière and Kemp:

AGNÈS: *Hélas! qui pourrait, dis-je, en avoir été cause?*
Sur lui, sans y penser, fis-je choir quelque chose?
'Non', dit-elle, 'vos yeux ont fait ce coup fatal'.
(*L'École des femmes*, III.v. 515–17)

AGNES: 'Waes me', said I, 'what could hae been the cause o that? Did I let something faa on him without kennan?'

OLIPHANT: (*aside*) Wad tae God it had been a causey! ['chanty' in 1981 production]

AGNES: 'Na', said she, 'your een hae struck this fatal stound ...'.
(Kemp, 1983: 17)[4]

[AGNES: 'Woe's me', said I, 'what could have been the cause of that? Did I let something fall on him without knowing?'/OLIPHANT: (*aside*) Would to God it had been a cobblestone! ['chamberpot' in 1981production]/AGNES: 'No', said she, 'your eyes have struck this fatal blow...'.]

The introduction of Indians at the end of *L'École des femmes*, an invention imported from the Jouvet production, conveyed pictorially the theatrical apotheosis depicted by the verbal fantasia of Molière's rhyming couplets, which in the prose translation is not fully captured. The roles of Brindavoine and La Merluche have been omitted from *The Laird o' Grippy*: their lines in Act III scene i are cut (with the loss of jokes about Harpagon's parsimony) and elsewhere are redistributed. Mariane's role is changed from Molière's rather douce, dutiful, polite girl to a more spirited, down-to-earth, even frivolous young woman who accepts Grippy's ring without demurring, and whose language is direct and at times blunt (e.g. Mariane's more abstract expression of horror *'tourment effrayable'* is rendered without precious refinement 'the very idea o this auld man's eneuch to gar me boke' [the very thought of this old man's enough to make me vomit] (III.iv)). The change in the role, or rather the incongruity between Mirren's present state and true status, is indicated by the new surname, Clatterinshaws.

Verbal Humour

Underpinning Kemp's translations was a desire to preserve Scottish humour. In a broadcast on French radio on 5 February 1950, Kemp seemed keen to distance himself from the raucous American humour so popular in schools, and from the convulsive English comedy which he likened to the braying of a donkey:

> [C]e qui n'est pas caractéristique des Écossais, c'est le rire immodéré, à pleine gorge des Anglais. Si par exemple, à Édimbourg vous entendez un rire bruyant et envahissant résonner sur la plate forme d'un tramway, tel le braiement d'un âne, vous pouvez être sûr qu'il émane d'un colon anglais.[5]

> [[W]hat is not characteristic of the Scots is convulsive, full-throated laughter. If, for example, in Edinburgh you hear raucous laughter resounding like the braying of an ass all around the platform of a tram you can be certain that it is coming from an English ex pat.]

The pawky [sly, quiet] humour that pervades his translations is, Kemp acknowledges in the same broadcast, sometimes *'sinistre'*, even *'macabre'*, and not always 'funny', at least to the non-Scot, provoking no more than a smile. This dry humour, not dissimilar to the new comedy Molière was seeking to provoke in 1662 in *L'École des femmes*, was essentially verbal, and constituted for Kemp a form of poetry:

> ... un humour qui se signale davantage par la discrétion que par l'éclat. ... Par la confiance qu'il accorde aux mots eux-mêmes, (ipsissima verba), l'humour ressemble beaucoup à la poésie.

[... a type of humour distinguished more by understatement than by exuberance ... by the trust placed in the impact of words, *(ipsissima verba)*, this humour is very much like poetry.]

In *Let Wives Tak Tent*, Kemp had the courage to transpose into the Scottish idiom all of the topical humour in *L'École des femmes* (apart from the *tarte à la crème* joke). The literal renderings of many other adaptations in English must have fallen flat on twentieth-century audiences. The nobiliary pretensions of Pierre Corneille's brother, Thomas, are depersonalised:

> *Je sais un paysan qu'on appelait Gros-Pierre,*
> *Qui, n'ayant pour tout bien qu'un seul quartier de terre,*
> *Y fit tout à l'entour faire un fossé bourbeux,*
> *Et de Monsieur de L'Isle en prit le nom pompeux.*
> (*L'École des femmes*, ll. 179–82)

I ken a crofter body caa'd Creeshy Pate. He had nae mair than an ell a land, but he delvt a glaury sheugh around it, and titled himsel the Lord o the Isles. (Kemp, 1983: 6)

[I know a crofter called Greasy Pete [or Head]. He owned no more than an ell of land, but he dug a muddy ditch around it, and titled himself the Lord of the Isles [ancient Scottish title].]

The allusion (l.118) to Rabelais in '*Ce que Pantagruel à Panurge répond*' is more obviously caricatural in the form 'I reply as Jamie Fleeman did to the Laird o Udny' (Fleeman, a historical character from North-East Scotland, was renowned for his wise-fool utterances to his master). Agnès's reported remarks about 'auricular conception' which some have taken as a parody of the Annunciation, are turned into a stock comic illustration of ingenuousness:

> *L'autre jour (pourrait-on se le persuader?)*
> *Elle était fort en peine, et me vint demander*
> *Avec une innocence à nulle autre pareille,*
> *Si les enfants qu'on fait se faisaient par l'oreille.*
> (*L'École des femmes*, ll. 161–64)

The other day – you'll hardly believe this – she was fair bombazed, and cam to spier at me, wi an innocence you never saw the marrow o, if bairns were taen out o the hearts o green kail! (Kemp, 1983: 5)

[The other day – you'll hardly believe this – she was very perplexed, and came to ask me, with an innocence you never saw the like of, if babies came from the hearts of green cabbage!]

However, in the prompt script for the Scottish Theatre Company's production in 1981, the insertion of an afterthought, 'Well I thought it was funny', anticipates the audience's failure to grasp or to laugh at the joke. (For discussion of other emendations and updating made in 1981, see below, and Peacock, 1993: 57–8.)

In *The Laird o' Grippy* Kemp's manipulation of register and of lexis captures the essential comic differences between the main characters in the French texts. Hector (Valère) protests his love in exaggerated metaphors:

> *Je vous vois soupirer, hélas! au milieu de ma joie! je vous aime trop pour cela, et mon amour pour vous durera autant que ma vie. ... Ne m'assassinez point, je vous prie, par les sensibles coups d'un soupçon outrageux.* (*L'Avare*, I.i)

> Waes me, I hear ye sigh! And that nips my pleasure in the bud like ony frost! ... My love's far owre strang for that. I swear, it will endure till aa the seas gang dry! ... Lassie, dinna murder me wi the fearsome dirk-wounds o suspicion – (Kemp, 1987: 2)

> [Woe's me, I hear you sigh! And that nips my pleasure in the bud like any frost!... My love's far too strong for that. I swear, it will endure till all the seas run dry! ... Lassie, don't murder me with the fearsome dagger-wounds of suspicion –]

Grippy's son is more given to plain speaking:

> *[J]e brûlais de vous parler, pour m'ouvrir à vous d'un secret ... J'aime.* (*L'Avare*, I.ii)

> I'm fair burstan to let ye intil a secret! [...] I'm in love. (Kemp, 1987: 5)

> [I'm absolutely bursting to let you into a secret!]

Grippy's economy of words is conveyed immediately as in Molière by his elliptical opening line: 'Out o here wi ye this very instant' (*'Hors d'ici tout à l'heure'*) and by his repeated 'without a tocher [dowry]!' (*'sans dot'*). Kemp has preserved Harpagon's mock-romantic declaration:

> [*C]'est avec des lunettes qu'on observe les astres, et je maintiens et garantis que vous êtes un astre le plus bel astre qui soit dans le pays des astres.* (*L'Avare*, III.v)

> [I]t's wi glesses that we observe the heavenly bodies, and I'se maintain and uphaud that you're a heavenly body, the heavenliest body in aa the clanjamphrey o heavenly bodies! (Kemp, 1987: 41)

> [[I]t's with glasses that we observe the heavenly bodies, and I do maintain and uphold that you're a heavenly body, the heavenliest body in the whole crowd of heavenly bodies!]

Harpagon's uninventive imitation of the lover's astral vocabulary is undermined phonetically by the assimilation of *des* and *astres* (= *désastres*), which for an audience provides an unconsciously ironic comment on Harpagon's amatory declaration. Grippy's stratospheric, linguistic flights are grounded by similarly inept repetition and the use of 'clanjamphrey', with its pejorative connotations.

Kemp's depiction of the inventory of Harpagon's hoard broadens the comic cultural and historical allusions in Molière's text:

> ... *un pavillon à queue, d'une bonne serge d'Aumale, une tenture de tapisseries des amours de Gombaud et de Macée ... un luth de Bologne, garni de toutes ses cordes, ou peu s'en faut. Plus, un trou – madame et un damier, avec un jeu de l'oie renouvelé des Grecs ....* (*L'Avare*, II.i)

> A canopy o Paisley silk ... Tapestry hangings representing the love of Patie and Jeannie in the Gentle Shepherd ... an auld fiddle of Neil Gow's, wi a crack in the belly and but ae string. Item the acht, a dambrod, a set o curling stanes, and a quiver o arrows suitable for onybody intending to join the Royal Company o Archers. (Kemp, 1987: 22–3)

> [A canopy of Paisley silk ... Tapestry hangings representing the love of Patie and Jeannie in the Gentle Shepherd ... an old fiddle of Neil Gow's, with a crack in the belly and only one string. Item the eighth, a draughtboard, a set of curling stones, and a quiver of arrows suitable for anybody intending to join the Royal Company of Archers.] [*The Gentle Shepherd* = an eighteenth-century ballad opera by Allan Ramsay; Neil Gow = a famous fiddler (1756–1823); Royal Company of Archers = Sovereign's bodyguard in Scotland]

Stereotypical references to Turks, whose invasion of Austria in 1663–1664 had given them a reputation for barbarity and unchristian behaviour, are adapted to a caricature of a particular trait of inhabitants of the kingdom of Fife:

> *Il est Turc, là-dessus, mais d'une turquerie à désespérer tout le monde.* (*L'Avare*, II.iv)

> He's as dour as a Fifer, but o a Fifishness that'll drive ye wud! (Kemp, 1987: 26)

> [He's as humourless as a native of Fife, but of a Fifishness that would drive you to distraction.] [*Fifish* = eccentric, slightly deranged]

Juxtaposition of contraries are similarly localised:

> [J]*e marierais le Grand Turc avec la République de Venise.* (*L'Avare*, II.v)

I could marry the Moderator o the General Assembly to Mistress
Bellamy o the Theatre Royal. (Kemp, 1987: 28)

[Moderator of the General Assembly = annually appointed head of the Church of Scotland; Mistress Bellamy = eighteenth-century actress]

The *dialogue de sourds* between Arnolphe and Le Notaire (IV.ii) affords Kemp an occasion to display the full gamut of register and lexis, from the lawyer's accumulation of technical terms with which Scots law is replete and which are not readily accessible to the non-professional (e.g. 'byordinar', 'reversionary, non reversionary', 'donatio inter vivos', 'acquerenda') to Oliphant's vituperative retorts (e.g. 'Plague upon this tyke-faced [dog-faced] scoundrel'), which are only too transparent.

The major linguistic problem for Kemp was, as he admitted himself, parody of tragic diction, particularly in *Let Wives Tak Tent*. To reclothe his nobiliary self-image, Arnolphe has frequent recourse to the verbal costume of the tragic hero, particularly after encounters with Horace during which he is confronted with the spectacle of his folly. Molière exposes holes in the linguistic habit through the *imaginaire*'s inability to sustain the high-flown diction:

Jamais trouble d'esprit ne fut égal au mien.
Avec quelle imprudence et quelle hâte extrême
Il m'est venu conter cette affaire à moi-même! (*L'École des femmes*, ll. 358–60)

Never was man tortured in the spirit like me! But what a hasty bletherskate he is to come blabban his tale to me, of all men! (Kemp, 1983: 12–13)

[*bletherskate* = person who talks foolishly; *blabban* = blabbing]

Molière's deflation of Arnolphe derives from the subtle comic descent from the highly literary abstract lexis (*trouble d'esprit, imprudence, conter*) to the more prosaic *affaire*. However, Kemp's more colourful concrete expression (e.g. 'bletherskate' and 'blabban') hardly allows Oliphant to entertain delusions of tragic grandeur. In Act II scene i, Arnolphe misapplies the language of a Racinian hero to bemoan a ten-day business trip into the country:

Éloignement fatal! Voyage malheureux! (*L'École des femmes*, l. 385)

Here Kemp's prose version fails to capture the mock-pathos of Arnolphe's plaint, which is heightened by balanced repetition of quasi-synonymous expressions:

Oh why did fate send me on yon unchancy [that ill-fated] journey!
(Kemp, 1983: 13)

On the other hand, in Act IV scene iv, Kemp captures better than most modern adaptors Arnolphe's inability to sustain the elevated language of the heroic lover:

> Sans cesse nuit et jour je te caresserai,
> Je te bouchonnerai, baiserai, mangerai. (L'École des femmes, ll. 1594–95)

> Nicht and day without halt will I fondle ye, clap [stroke affectionately] ye, kiss ye, devour ye. (Kemp, 1983: 49)

Molière's juxtaposition of gallant expression (*caresserai, baiserai*) and ambiguous vocabulary with equine and culinary connotations (*bouchonnerai, mangerai*) is reflected in Kemp's bringing together of 'fondle', 'kiss', and 'clap', 'devour'. Whereas most adapters are content to paraphrase Arnolphe's mock-heroic declaration, Kemp follows Molière's text closely. Particularly felicitous is his rendering of Molière's caricature of Arnolphe's threats of self-mutilation, a motif of French tragedies of the 1630s. Kemp retains the over-precision that undermines the tragic resonance of Oliphant's threat and at the same time reflects the mercenary bourgeois spirit, conscious of the cost of every gesture:

> Veux-tu que je m'arrache un côté de cheveux? (L'École des femmes, l. 1062)

> Wad ye hae me rive out a lock o hair? (Kemp, 1983: 49)

> [Would you have me tear out a lock of hair?]

Horace's mock-heroic speeches pose perhaps an even greater challenge to the translator. In many English versions the lover comes over as an extremely colourless figure forever emitting abstract platitudes. However, Kemp turns many of the abstract nouns into concrete expressions that give Walter some of the verbal characteristics of the *imaginaire*. Take, for example, Horace's speech in praise of the tutelage of love. Horace's unconscious irony, which provokes subtle reflective comedy in L'École des femmes, is given broader comic emphasis in Let Wives Tak Tent:

> Il le faut avouer, l'amour est un grand maître
> ...
> D'un avare à l'instant il fait un libéral,
> Un vaillant d'un poltron, un civil d'un brutal;
> Il rend agile à tout l'âme la plus pesante,
> Et donne de l'esprit à la plus innocente. (L'École des femmes, ll. 900, 906–09)

Ye maun allou, there's nae schulemaster like love ... In a flash he maks the grippy man free wi his siller, the cowardie as brave as an eagle, and a gentleman out o a boor. He gies quickness o mind to the maist dosent lump and wit to the simplest. (Kemp, 1983: 29)

[You must allow, there's no schoolmaster like love ... In a flash he makes the miserly man free with his money, the coward as brave as an eagle, and a gentleman out of a boor. He gives quickness of mind to the stupidest lump and wit to the simplest.]

The categorical tone, set by the replacement of the indefinite article in '*un grand maître*' by a superlative 'nae ... like', prepares the more colourful detailed enumeration.

Reception

As Tom Fleming (1965: 25) records, the title of *Let Wives Tak Tent* was the subject of many jokes in the Late Night Revues at the Edinburgh Festival in 1961 when the translation was performed by the Gateway Theatre Company: e.g. 'Actually it's a play about married ladies going camping!' Initially, in the 1940s, there was some hostility from London-based critics to Kemp's new medium:

[B]road Scots has a terribly retarding effect on Molière's comic ideas. They march to the skirl of bagpipes, as it were, but they no longer ripple and sparkle on light waves of laughter that are set moving by the influence of tolerance and good sense. (*The Times*, 16 June, 1949)

[Molière] does not, as we know, translate; at best a possible equivalent would be the sort of English Defoe wrote. If dialect is to be used, it must be at least fast moving; Billingsgate possibly, or slum Dublin. But Lowland Scots, be it ever so fine a language (which I am not disputing), is far too slow, uncouth and trundling a vehicle, besides having the disadvantage for benighted Sassenachs of being almost as incomprehensible as French! (*Time and Tide*, 25 June, 1949).

Kemp's pioneering work was nevertheless recognised by a number of Scottish theatre critics:

[Kemp's play] is a triumphant blending of French artistry and Scottish savouriness, making (consciously) clear the Celtic link between two people both of whom combine ruthless logic and common-sense with incurable romanticism. I was charmed by the beautiful Scots tongue. (William Parr, reported in *The Scotsman*, 12 February, 1948)

Kemp has got over an obvious difficulty by making the play completely Scots, in character and in location, as well as in tongue. Yet he hasn't lost Molière. (*The Bulletin*, 25 May, 1948)

Robert Kemp's translation into Scots of one of Molière's finest comedies is indeed an unusual piece. It has wit, charm, and a masterly use of language. (*The Bulletin*, 2 November, 1948)

The language of *Let Wives Tak Tent* is a language understandable in the main by anyone familiar with that of Burns, save for an isolated word or expression now and again. (*The Scotsman*, 24 June, 1949)

Some Scottish reviewers (particularly in the popular press), while sometimes recognising Kemp's achievement, questioned his choice of Scots:

The play is an interesting experiment but now, even after the third showing [in Edinburgh and Glasgow], it remains still only an experiment. One feels that there are more fruitful fields than this for Mr Kemp to till. (*The Evening News*, 2 November, 1948)

It is a little doubtful, despite Robert Kemp's lively and natural text, whether this kind of intensely artificial comedy really 'goes' in a Scottish setting. (*The Glasgow Herald*, 2 November, 1948)

This adaptation by Robert Kemp of Molière's *L'Ecole des femmes* into the Scottish idiom of 17th-century Edinburgh left me with a feeling that the aesthetic appetite had not been completely satisfied. Instead of a full feast, one had only a succession of nibbles.

It was a queer mixter-maxter [jumble], to use the appropriate idiom, of melodrama, burlesque-ballet, mime and straight acting ...

One felt that Scotsmen wouldn't go about carrying their hearts on their sleeves so openly. (J.C., *The Glasgow Observer*, 2 November, 1948)

The ultra broad Scots ... puzzled even Scots last night and will bewilder London when the play goes there soon. (*The Scottish Daily Mail*, 7 June 1949)

When Kemp's adaptation was performed at the Embassy Theatre in London in June 1949, there was (understandably) a measure of incomprehension on the part of the London-based critics:

The Caledonian dialect is rather more difficult than French to understand ... (W.A. Darlington, *The Daily Telegraph*, 16 June, 1949)

The trouble is that the task of solving linguistic problems rather diverts our attention from the comedy of the man who nurses the fantastic hope of 'creating' out of a ward a faithful wife ... Yet for those familiar with the language it may well be an agreeably formalised reading of the comedy. (*The Times*, 16 June, 1949)

[The translation into broad Scots] proves not so good an idea as it might sound. Instead of the supple ease and strength of Molière's language we hear a gnarled and choppy speech which is a slow and clumsy vehicle for this author's urbane moralising [...]. (P.H.W., *The Guardian*, 16 June, 1949)

However, some London critics (for different reasons) found Kemp's adaptation superior to its English counterparts:

Perhaps one reason is that any costume comedy of manners, translated into English, has the inescapable atmosphere of Bath ... Perhaps one savours of a foreign comedy better when it is translated into a semi-foreign tongue. (*The Evening Standard*, 21 June, 1949)

French without English. In theory it seems impermissible and even daft ... The secret of this success lies in something which one can hardly expect the non-Scots to fully understand. It is the centuries-long affinity between Scotland and France ... [I]t is this strong affinity – which makes Molière translate far more smoothly into Scots than I have ever known it in English. Mr Kemp – wisely avoiding the couplets – catches the tang and the wit and the verve but inevitably misses the elegance. (*The News Chronicle*, 18 June, 1949)

I found London critics at the Embassy, Swiss Cottage, last week amazed to find they could follow the broad Scots of *Let Wives Tak Tent* quite comfortably, and also that Molière's play seemed to translate so much better this way than into English. (*The Scottish Daily Express*, 19 June, 1949)

By 1961, despite a savage dismissal of Kemp's adaptation by Bamber Gascoigne:

Robert Kemp has performed another pointless exercise by setting Molière's *L'École des femmes* in Seventeenth-Century Edinburgh and translating it into the meatiest Scots brogue ... The language is not even relevant to his busy burghers ... (*The Spectator*, 1 September, 1961)

London-based critics were becoming attuned to language deemed as incomprehensible as Chaucer's to foreigners south of Berwick:

It is more than ten years since I first heard it [*Let Wives Tak Tent*], and then I found it pretty difficult for any southern ears to follow. Last night I think I got all the jokes pat: which only goes to show what fourteen years of Edinburgh Festivals can do for a barbarian ... (Philip Hope-Wallace, *The Guardian*, 26 August, 1961)

Robert Kemp's free adaptation turned out to be an enjoyable comedy of Jonsonian humours. (*The Sunday Telegraph*, 3 September, 1961)

By 1980, despite a decline in the speaking of a 'traditional' Lowland Scots such as Kemp used, his adaptation was still highly regarded (even if in the Scottish Theatre Company's revival in 1981, the language was occasionally updated – see below):

The resounding achievement of Robert Kemp's drama is its magnificent use of the Scots language. Some of his most vigorous writing is in his adaptation. (Lindsay Paterson, *The Scotsman*, 10 October, 1980)

Kemp's play was written when there was much more interest in the use of lowland Scots. That interest has waned, but Kemp's broad Scots proves a muscular and evocative medium for Molière's wit. (John Fowler, *The Glasgow Herald*, 17 March, 1981)

As to the play itself and its language, it bears up better than many would credit, or would perhaps wish to. Robert Kemp's vigorous translation of Molière has a beefiness which is still very attractive ... (Mary Brennan, *The Glasgow Herald*, March 1981)

Whatever the reservations from certain reviewers, Kemp's *Let Wives Tak Tent* was greatly appreciated by theatrical practitioners from both north and south of the border:

Lawrence Olivier [in a conversation with Tom Fleming with regard to *Let Wives Tak Tent*] said that he thought Molière sounded much better in Scots than in English. (*The Scotsman*, 1 September, 1961)

To begin with I understood not a word. It was like listening to the original French, of which I have none. But after ten minutes I was suddenly listening and understanding as if a part of me locked away had come to life again.

Old Scots words I'd been brought up with flooded back to consciousness and words I'd never heard made their impact directly to my emotions by their sounds. (Fulton Mackay, *The Scotsman*, 9 May, 1977)

Robert Kemp's earthy and expressive translation ... is such a fine partner to Molière's original French ... (Ewan Hooper, Programme Note to the Scottish Theatre Company production, 1981)

One of those few translations which take on a life of their own and which has, as such, become a classic of Scottish drama in its own right. (David Thomson, Programme Note to the Scottish Theatre Company production, 1981)

Let Wives Tak Tent's popularity continued into the 1980s. However, the Scottish Theatre Company felt the need to update and emend some of Kemp's text. The prompt script in the Scottish Theatre Archive indicates a number of omissions, including:

- Oliphant's parodic sketch of contemporary cuckolds, and his denunciation of clever wives and praise of ignorance (ll. 21–72; 82–128);[6]
- some of Oliphant's asides that Kemp had either translated (e.g. 'Oh, I'll bust!' ... 'This pill is sair [hard] to swallow' ... (ll.327, 332)), or added (e.g. 'I'll choke' 'Perdition, damnation, abomination' ... 'My heid'll burst' 'I'll explode' ... 'I could thraw [wring] your neck!' 'Wad God it had been!' ... 'Agnes! No Agnes! Oh the sleekit [sly] jaud!' [*jaud* is a term of abuse for a woman] ... 'Oh has she jinket [dodged] me yet?');
- the references to the garden (no longer relevant in view of a changed set) and to costuming ('ony number o ribbons and feathers, muckle [large] wigs, braw [beautiful] laces' (l. 652));
- the exchange of greetings (ll. 846–52);
- Oliphant's lament over the frustration of his carefully elaborated scheme (ll. 1184–1206);
- some of Walter's ingenuous eulogies (e.g. ll. 904–05, 1412–19).

There seems also to have been some attempt to adapt the text to the acting style of Rikki Fulton. For example, Oliphant's:

Maybe, my friend, ongauns at hame wi you gar ye tremble on my account. I suppose ye conclude by the state o your ain broo that a set o antlers gaes wi ilka marriage! (Kemp, 1983: 1)

[Maybe, my friend, goings-on in your home make you tremble on my account. I suppose you conclude by the state of your own brow that a set of antlers goes with every marriage!]

is rendered in the prompt script:

Oh, is that a fact? Just because you do ne [sic, should be 'nae'] ken what your ain wife is up to does nae mean the rest of us will be sufir [sic] the same fate. You seem to think that a set of antlers goes wi ilka marriage.

The Laird o' Grippy has not been as frequently performed as *Let Wives Tak Tent*. The adaptation was applauded by John Laurie (the first Grippy) and by most reviewers:

Masterly, my boy, masterly. Kemp's command of Scottish, you know. Much better than the English adaptations you see. Vocabulary is so much bigger in Scots. (John Laurie, *The Scottish Daily Mail*, 26 February, 1955)

The play runs merrily in its Scottish mould, and if its success must, in the first place, be credited to the brilliance with which Molière built up his scenes, to his sense of irony and the cross-purpose of much of his dialogue, something is due to the skill with which Mr Kemp has found the equivalent Scottish phrase. (*The Scotsman*, 1 March, 1955)

... splendidly translated by Robert Kemp from Molière's *The Miser* ... (*The Daily Record*, 1 March, 1955)

Alien ill-wishers might suggest that this eternal comedy of a miser's love for his gold is particularly susceptible to translation into Scots, and certainly Mr Kemp has done an excellent job, creating something new and native out of the French masterpiece.

The 'Scots' which he uses is a fine warm language rich in homely imagery ... and full of light and colour. (*The Glasgow Herald*, 10 May, 1955)

To those whose ears are attune to the guid Scots tongue the dialogue is scintillating with wisdom and wit ... (*The Evening Times*, 10 May, 1955)

A less favourable response from two reviewers was prompted by their different perceptions of the French text:

In the original French, Harpagon is the father of all misers, a pitiable creature deluded by his weakness. When one laughs at him, tears also well to one's eyes ... In Robert Kemp's version, The Laird o' Grippy is an absurd figure of fun, a catherine wheel of emotion. One laughs, but one does not want to weep. (*The Edinburgh Evening Dispatch*, 1 March, 1955)

The author's rendering of the pithy old Scots is admirable as in his previous crib from the French, but one cannot feel that the subtlety of the centuries-old classic has been captured. (H. McD., *The Scottish Daily Mail*, 10 May, 1955)

Achievement

At the box-office, Kemp's translations never reached the heights attained by renderings of Molière in the 1980s by Liz Lochhead (*Tartuffe*), Rikki Fulton (*A Wee Touch o' Class*) and Hector MacMillan (*The Hypochondriak* and *Le Bourgeois gentilhomme*). In 1949, The Citizens' production of *Let Wives Tak Tent* showed a modest surplus of £4, though such figures need to be evaluated against losses in the same year of £2600 incurred by Zola's *Guilty* and Barrie's *Dear Brutus*. However, the Scottish Theatre Company's production of *Let Wives Tak Tent* in 1981, starring Rikki Fulton, was the company's most successful commercial venture by far.[7] *The Laird o' Grippy* was performed on BBC1 Television on 27 March 1979, with Rikki Fulton as the eponymous hero. (The Scottish Theatre Company's production of *Let Wives Tak Tent* was offered to the BBC, but it could not be accommodated, because of crowded schedules.) It may be that the success of Kemp's venture was limited by the use of a diction that was sometimes found inaccessible by Scots, and has dated quickly. However, the reconstruction of a largely eighteenth-century idiom has not passed its sell-by date, as is evident from the successful export to Finland in the 1990s of Hector MacMillan's translation of *The Hypochondriak* (see Findlay, 1996a: 195–6, n.14). Nevertheless, the eclectic style of Liz Lochhead, like that of Lady Gregory, whose Anglo-Irish translations proved very popular outside Ireland, more easily transcends linguistic frontiers. However considerable the intrinsic merits of Kemp's work, his greatest achievement lies perhaps in the encouragement given to Scottish dramatists and actors to convey to new generations of theatre-goers masterpieces that had hitherto been considered too demanding, inaccessible or untranslatable.[8]

Notes

1. I am obliged to Kemp's son, the late Arnold Kemp, for information concerning the circumstances of the composition.
2. The Jacobite leader Mar wrote to Argyll to ask him to see that his gardens at Alloa were not damaged by government troops. See Mitchison (1971: 318 ff).
3. Even Molière's contemporaries expressed reservations. Molière sought to refute his critics in *La Critique de L'École des femmes*, assigning strictures concerning the static nature of the play to a ridiculous poet:

[I]l ne se passe point d'actions, et tout consiste en des récits que veut faire ou Agnès ou Horace (scene vi)

[[And in this comedy] no actions take place, and everything consists of the accounts related by either Agnès or Horace.] (Frame, 1967: 197)

Molière's defence was conducted by the sympathetically portrayed Dorante:

[L]es récits eux-mêmes y sont des actions suivant la constitution du sujet; d'autant qu'ils sont tous faits innocemment, ces récits, à la personne intéressée, qui par là entre, à tous coups, dans une confusion à réjouïr les spectateurs ...

[[T]he accounts themselves are actions, according to the nature of the subject; for they are all given innocently to the person concerned, who is thereby thrown at every turn into a confusion that delights the spectators ...] (Frame, 1967: 199)

The long tirades have usually been substantially abbreviated in English translations. Even Hazlitt, who considered L'École des femmes to be Molière's masterpiece, thought the lengthy speeches would never be tolerated on an English stage.

4. This and subsequent references to *Let Wives Tak Tent* and *The Laird o' Grippy* are taken from the versions published after Kemp's death (Kemp, 1983, 1987). However, extensive consultation has been made of scripts used on stage, as these give us insight into the relationship between text and performance, and, perhaps, an indication of Kemp's original composition. It is difficult to know how much actors and directors contributed to Kemp's translation or whether the modifications in performance met with his approval. It may be that, as with Tony Harrison's *The Misanthrope* (Molière, 1973), changes effected were the result of a collaboration between cast and adapter. Molière scholarship is divided as to which text may be regarded as the most authentic: the first printed editions were considered to be the most faithful; recent opinion has favoured the 1682 posthumous edition of his works which was revised by one of Molière's actors, La Grange, taking account of contemporary stage practice. (See Peacock, 1994: 45–61.)

5. National Library of Scotland, ACC 7622, Box 19, RS3.
6. Line references here and subsequently are to Molière's text.
7. For more detailed box office statistics see Peacock, 1993: 230–32.
8. For a more detailed analysis of Molière's fortunes in Scotland, and of the reception of Kemp's work, see Peacock (1993). Kemp's motivation and method with his Molière translations is the subject of Findlay (2000b: Chapter 3); and his founding of a modern tradition of translating into Scots for the stage is the focus of Findlay (2004). [Ed.]

Chapter 6
Triumphant Tartuffification: Liz Lochhead's Translation of Molière's Tartuffe

RANDALL STEVENSON

> Molière's scripts can sometimes seem pretty flat and inert, like the printed notes of an uncommunicative musical score. As a result, his drama is harder to translate well than are the more consciously poetic or naturalistic plays of (say) Shakespeare or Ibsen.

Thus wrote Roger Savage, in a programme note for the Royal Lyceum's 1987 revival in Edinburgh of Liz Lochhead's version of *Tartuffe*. To suggest that Molière is harder to translate than Shakespeare is obviously a large claim: it nevertheless seems to be borne out by the experience of *English* theatres. Bill Findlay explains that 'it is noticeable that Molière has never quite enjoyed the popularity on the English stage that his status warrants'. He goes on to quote a reviewer who suggests that, in English, Molière may be 'the most uninteresting of world dramatists' (Findlay, 1996a: 193) – a view confirmed by *The Oxford Companion to the Theatre*, which concludes that his work is 'not easy for English audiences to understand, either in French or in translation' (Hartnoll, 1983: 556). Yet as Findlay also points out, Molière has enjoyed in the post-war period an almost unique popularity on the *Scottish* stage; one that has made him 'almost a Scottish playwright-by-adoption' and even 'helped define the distinctiveness of modern Scottish theatre' (Findlay, 1996b: 203).

How can this be so? Why should a seventeenth-century French dramatist – presenting the translator, as Roger Savage suggests, with formidable problems – turn out to be so particularly playable on the modern Scottish stage? One of the most popular of modern Scots Molières – both during its first Royal Lyceum run in 1986, and in revivals – that version of *Tartuffe* by Liz Lochhead offers a good place to look for an answer. And Bill Findlay (1996a: 193) suggests an important way of starting to look when he talks of translating Molière into 'a Scots idiom' – if, that is, the term 'idiom' is taken to refer not only to language, but to the kind of broader cultural matters that

Susan Bassnett places among the 'Central Issues' examined in her survey *Translation Studies*. Language, she stresses,

> is the heart within the body of culture ...[i]n the same way that the surgeon, operating on the heart, cannot neglect the body that surrounds it, so the translator treats the text in isolation from the culture at his peril. (Bassnett, 2002: 14)

The heart of this essay's operation will be an assessment of what Scots offers Lochhead as a linguistic medium for translation. A useful first step, however, is to consider what broader affinities of culture or 'idiom' might help account for the facility with which Molière speaks to modern Scotland.

Several of these are apparent in Lochhead's *Tartuffe*, which quickly establishes a convincingly Scottish accent for Molière's concern with religious and other forms of hypocrisy. For example, whereas in Act I scene v Molière's Cléante complains to his brother-in-law Orgon '*De tous vos façonniers on n'est point les esclaves./Il est de faux dévots ainsi que de faux braves*' [We are not the slaves of all your fakers/Falsely pious people are as common as vainglorious ones],[1] Lochhead's translation suggests that 'Piety, like bravery can be put on, – if we're as silly's/To believe in False Heroes and Holy Willies', firmly placing Tartuffe among the figures of monstrous religious self-righteousness who turn up in Robert Burns's 'Holy Willie's Prayer' and at many other points in Scottish literature both before and since. A tradition not only of religious hypocrisy but of religious bigotry offers Lochhead further opportunity for specifically Scottish satire. At a crucial moment in her version, when it looks as though Marianne's unhappiness really might persuade her father Orgon to cancel his scatterbrained plan to marry her to Tartuffe, she unfortunately renews his resolve by hitting on the plea 'Let me turn Catholic! In God's honour, He/ Bids me live my days out in a nunnery' (IV. iii). In the original, Orgon is shocked by what he sees as women's capacity to be distracted from heavenly devotion by the flames of earthly love – '*Ah! voilà justement de mes religieuses,/Lorsqu'un père combat leurs flammes amoureuses!*' In Lochhead's version, however, the stress falls firmly and furiously on 'Catholic' when Orgon asks Marianne 'Did your daddy hear you say a Catholic Convent?' Religious hypocrisy in seventeenth-century France did not much involve soul-destroying divisions and bigotries within the Church itself: Lochhead's scene between Marianne and her father not only finds a precise, highly-energised context for Molière's kind of satire, but there is obvious *additional* scope for it in modern Scotland.

Opportunities like this are developed throughout Lochhead's version, and are established from its very first scene. This shows Pernelle getting herself 'inty [into] a state', not because she values Tartuffe's apparent allegiance to 'God's Good Grace' over the 'worldliness' and 'gauns-oot-and-in' [goings-out-and-in] which she reckons have made her son-in-law's house into 'Paddy's Market' [Glasgow street market or any confused scene – a surprisingly apt translation of Molière's equally-colloquial *'la cour du roi Pétaud'*]. Rather, what most troubles her about the 'pairties and cerd-schools [parties and card-schools] ... socials and swarrys [soirées] and conversat-zionis' is that they make the household 'the talk of the pairrish [parish]' – an occasion of 'Yatterin' fit tae fill the vera tower o' Babel' [chattering fit to fill the very tower of Babel]. Molière's Pernelle registers in her own way 'the talk of the pairrish' – *'on en parle, et cela n'est pas bien'* [it's talked about, which isn't good] – but her complaint concentrates as much on the mass of idle 'conversatzioni' *in* Orgon's house as on talk *about* it. Lochhead's slight adjustment of Molière targets hypocrisies that are especially familiar in Scotland – fears of neighbours' adverse judgement, and the flaunting of morality, church-going and general bourgeois good behaviour as accessories of social as much as religious distinction. Significantly, Lochhead devotes a large part of her introductory stage direction (an addition to Molière), as well as her first scene, to defining Pernelle's 'kirkish [churchish] moral superiority'. Few other characters are given any authorial introduction, Lochhead making of Pernelle a figure almost more useful than Tartuffe in establishing from the outset a very Scottish equation of 'kirkishness' and social standing. The setting of her version in an obviously middle-class household, and at a period earlier in the twentieth century when 'kirkishness' held a stronger influence on middle-class *mores*, further confirms a familiar Scottish focus for Molière's interests in social climbing in the name of religion, and in social climbing generally.

While Lochhead's opening helps contextualise concerns with religion, her conclusion establishes a similarly firm relation to Scottish experience in terms of politics. Most commentators find in Molière's *rex-ex-machina* ending, and its long speeches lauding monarchical power, only an attempt – perhaps exaggerated enough to be a little tongue-in-cheek – to flatter the king. Louis XIV was present at the play's first staging in its three-act form in 1664, and eventually gave permission for it to be performed again, despite the attacks of clergy outraged by what they saw as an attack on faith rather than on hypocrisy. Lochhead, however, finds in *Tartuffe* and develops in her version what her Introduction calls 'an ending of quite explicit political satire which bland English translations totally lost'. Such satire has little to do with monarchical power – she converts the king into the aloof, omnipotent but rather inspecific figure of 'Mr Prince' – but is directed instead on ways in which political power in general is mediated and appropriated by the affluent upper echelons of society. The Officer's suave closing speech satirises, or parodies, the glib certitude with which governments and moneyed classes close ranks against threats to their power, casually assuming their right to manipulate the laws of the land in their own favour:

> Just men who love the Government needny fear the Law. [needn't]
> Is a contract worth the paper that it's written oan? [on]
> Nut at a'! [not at all]
> Thank God Good Government's Sovereign Power can aye [always]
> arrange it
> That if a law isny servin' Justice, well ... they can change it. [isn't]
> (Lochhead, 1985: 62)

Extended from Molière's more modest view of a king who *'d'un souverain pouvoir ... brise les liens/Du contrat'* [with sovereign power, breaks the bonds of the contract], the political resonances of Lochhead's version were unlikely to be lost on Scottish audiences in the 1980s. As Noël Peacock suggests in his useful survey *Molière in Scotland: 1945–1990* (Peacock, 1993: 233), it was 'not accidental' that Molière translations 'flourished during the years of Thatcherism'. Molière's sharp satire of social manners and behaviour offered Lochhead and other translators a vision easy to develop and direct on the 1980s' favouring of the bourgeoisie, and other Tory strategies of which Scotland had particular reason to be sceptical.

Scottish affinities for Molière in religious, social and political terms – extensive as these seem – are nevertheless probably less significant than similarities in theatrical tradition and idiom. Molière's theatrical background was itself fairly international, and the Italian *commedia dell'arte* was a strong influence on the farces he wrote for his company during their early years on the road, and further consolidated when they came back to Paris and shared a theatre with an Italian *commedia* company permanently established there. A cheeky, scatty descendant of the Roman comedy of Plautus and Terence, *commedia* flourished in Italy and France throughout the sixteenth and seventeenth centuries. Based on improvisation by stereotyped characters around standard plots, enriched by brilliant gags and routines, its broad, popular entertainment could work anywhere and appeal to anyone. Its influence is particularly apparent in *Tartuffe*: Dorine is close to the wily, omnicompetent, uppity servants, the *zanni* of *commedia*, while Marianne and Valère are the kind of young lovers sure to be thwarted – initially anyway – by the doddery idiocy of father-figures or *pantalone*. Orgon, however, is a more-than-usually particularised version of this figure. One of Molière's achievements for the European stage – like Carlo Goldoni's later in Italy – was the addition to familiar figures and plots of the kind of characterisation and complexity that could extend the appeal of *commedia* for sophisticated metropolitan audiences at the time.

However wide its contemporary appeal, or however deeply it may draw on supposedly timeless, archetypal comic impulses (such as needs for fertility to triumph over sterility, and for new generations to replace the old) this kind of antique Italianate comedy might seem to have little to do with theatrical styles or interests in modern Scotland. There is no firm record of *commedia* influencing the Scottish stage, although records of theatrical activity in Scotland generally, from the seventeenth century up to and sometimes including the twentieth, can look a little sparse (Findlay 1998a). Where specific forms of theatrical entertainment are concerned, however, the Scottish tradition looks less threadbare, and less remote from some of the models familiar to Molière. As David Hutchison has shown, performance forms such as music hall and variety have been *more* successful in late-nineteenth and twentieth-century Scotland than elsewhere, partly as a result of what he calls their 'fundamental dependence on a shared identity of experience between performer and audience' (Hutchison, 1987: 164). Though music hall itself scarcely exists nowadays, the variety tradition survives in the form of Christmas pantomime, which is still a major feature of the Scottish theatrical scene. Music hall, variety and pantomime are forms far from identical with Molière's theatre or the *commedia* that nourished it, yet there are significant elements in common (with pantomime especially): breadth of appeal, reliance on stock situations, plots or characters, and on wit, improvisation, gags and routines. As Noël Peacock (1993: 11) explains, the pioneer of modern Scots translation of Molière's work, Robert Kemp, was first drawn to it by similarities he perceived between French performances in the 1940s and what he knew of the abilities of Scottish pantomime stars. Kemp's translations of *L'Ecole des femmes* and *L'Avare* – as *Let Wives Tak Tent* (1948) and *The Laird o' Grippy* (1955) – were both written for one of these stars, Duncan Macrae. Ironically, Macrae eventually made so much money from pantomime that he lost interest in performing in the second of these plays. Something of his mantle, however, fell in the 1980s on the shoulders of another doyen of a thousand pantomimes, Rikki Fulton, who was a brilliant lead in *Let Wives Tak Tent* when it was revived by Scottish Theatre Company as its first-ever production in 1981. The experience must have seemed worth repeating, for Fulton returned to Molière in *A Wee Touch of Class* in 1985, a translation of *Le Bourgeois gentilhomme* written in collaboration with Denise Coffey. This was seen by around 70,000 spectators throughout Scotland: perhaps enough even to have satisfied Duncan Macrae, and surely enough to confirm Molière's popularity and adaptibility to local theatrical expectations.

These popular expectations and forms have continued to figure in other modern productions of Molière-into-Scots, as well as shaping much of Lochhead's *Tartuffe*. When Dorine frantically signals Elmire then 'disguise[s] it as an itch as Tartuffe catches her at it' (III.ii), the stage direction for her exit – *'pantomiming as much as possible'* – sums up one of Lochhead's tactics throughout, accentuating pantomime elements in the original and sometimes finding new ones of her own. In the play's first scene, for example, *'Dorine, Elmire and Marianne all mimic Pernelle behind her back as she wheels round to almost but not quite catch each of them'*; later, another stage direction requires that while Dorine is eavesdropping *'bent over at keyhole* [she] *falls into room'* when the door is snatched open by Orgon (II.i). Adding all these stage directions to the original, Lochhead's version shows a related tendency to adapt or extend Molière's dialogue with cracks or one-liners, in doing so often departing decisively from the more sober idiom of other translators. The first complete English version of Molière's works, published in 1739, remains one of the most sober and faithful. Its translators, H. Baker and J. Miller, render – unusually inventively – Cléante's suggestion to his brother-in-law, *'La campagne à présent n'est pas beaucoup fleurie'* (I.iv), as 'The country at present is not very pleasant'. Christopher Hampton's translation – interesting to compare with Lochhead's as it was written around the same time, for production by the Royal Shakespeare Company – just follows the French: 'Nothing much out yet, is there, in the country?'[2] But Lochhead's Cléante asks 'How was the country? Green and stuff?'. This is cheekier, funnier, closer to music-hall patter and exemplary of Scottish wit – perhaps even of its origins among a people whose rugged landscape has never left much place for conventional pastoral concerns.

There may, of course, be losses as well as gains from 'pantomiming as much as possible'. There are critics who find Molière's *Tartuffe* serious and alarming as well as funny, and complexities in the deluded figure of Orgon, or genuine threats in Tartuffe – more a pantomime monster in Lochhead's version than the bourgeois nightmare Molière may have had in mind – may dissolve too far into laughter. Even when dubiously faithful to the letter of her original, however, Lochhead generally does follow it in spirit. Molière's scanty stage directions (though he does include a strange, half-commentary one, *'C'est un scélérat qui parle'* (IV.v), to remind us of Tartuffe's real wickedness) rarely specify actions as explicitly as Lochhead does, but there is usually enough in his text to sanction what she suggests. There are no stage directions in his first scene to indicate what goes on behind Pernelle's back, but it is clear enough from his dialogue that she should be revolving like a kind of moral lighthouse, her caustic assessments transfixing family members in turn. And Dorine's exchange with Orgon in Act II scene ii does end with a rare stage direction – '*Il lui veut donner un soufflet et la manque*' [he tries to slap her and misses] – which confirms a pantomime element in the original just as strong as Lochhead's at this point. Such elements of funny, lively theatricality in any case help provide an alternative to the phoney morality propounded by Pernelle and Tartuffe, and the 'gey [rather] grey life with damn-all fun in it' (I.i) which would result from their rules – each targets of Molière's satire throughout. Finding such fun within the ready resources of Scottish performance tradition probably preserves more of Molière's broad vision than can ever be realised by the more exactly faithful work of translators such as Hampton or Baker and Miller.

Theatrical and other cultural affinities so far discussed assist communication of Molière's vision, but however inseparably culture is bound up with language, like body-to-heart, it is ultimately upon language that the success of any translation most depends. Here too, a 'Scots idiom' may be particularly convenient for the translator of Molière, or in some ways of any French text, since lexical legacies of the Auld Alliance between Scotland and France have left Scots strewn with borrowings from French. The first lines of her translation show Lochhead profiting from one of these when she renders Pernelle's judgement of Marianne's '*doucette*' appearance directly into Scots as 'sae douce' [so sweet]. Coincidences of this kind turn up here and there throughout, perhaps the happiest being the ease with which Dorine's name can be made to sound Scottish simply by accenting its first syllable rather than the second syllable, as in French.

But even if there were many more such coincidences, they would not solve all the problems with *Tartuffe*. Molière is difficult to translate, not especially because he writes in French, but because of the stage French he writes. 'Smooth rhyming verse', Roger Savage calls it in his 1987 programme note – smooth enough, perhaps, to make the scripts sometimes as 'flat and inert' as Savage goes on to suggest, and certainly enough to make it difficult to imitate in English. Molière's rhyming hexameter is a form that very rarely appears in English verse, and has a clumsy quality when it does, at least according to Alexander Pope (1965: 47), who, in his 'An Essay on Criticism' (l. 357), saw it as a measure 'that, like a wounded snake, drags its slow length along'. Translations of Molière have therefore usually opted either for prose – Baker and Miller's choice back in 1739 – or for the kind of rhymed iambic pentameter used in Richard Wilbur's translation of *Tartuffe* (Wilbur, 1982). Christopher Hampton (1984) offers another possibility in the blank verse used in his Royal Shakespeare Company version, but none of these solutions is ideal. Prose translations sound, well, *prosaic*, losing some of the rhythm and colour of the original. Richard Wilbur's verse, on the other hand, is *so* regular in rhythm and rhyme that it eventually seems repetitive and trite. Describing its effects in productions, two critics arrived – presumably independently – at the phrase 'jog-trot'.[3] Sensibly enough, Hampton reasons that, since Molière's hexameters – Alexandrines – were the standard measure of the golden age of French drama, they are most naturally rendered in English by the decasyllabic blank verse used by English dramatists in *their* golden age. Yet, perhaps because it does have such strong associations with the grand vision of Elizabethan drama, his version's blank verse sometimes seems too sober and serious for some of the pantomime-like comedic elements discussed above. One of Molière's main achievements, after all, was to contain the material of *commedia* within the kind of stylish language – and sometimes moral vision – familiar in French theatre from Corneille. Hampton's language sometimes seems instead to stifle rather than to stylise broader or more farcical comic energies.

Hampton is nevertheless helpful in explaining why he avoided rhyme in translating from the French, summing up as follows difficulties he sees created by that language itself:

> The French language has a much more rigid and defined phonetic structure than English; and when one takes into account, additionally, the inflected endings, the regular participial formations, the silent plurals and the verb forms, whether infinitive or conjugated, it will be clear that the business of finding a rhyme is infinitely simpler and more natural in French than it can ever be in English. (Hampton, 1984: A note on the translation)

Finding a rhyme in Scots, however, presents difficulties rather more finite and negotiable. Lochhead's *Tartuffe* often exploits greater phonetic flexibility in a more colloquially-based Scots to sustain rhymes unimaginable in standard English. For example, Orgon's judgement of Tartuffe that 'The felly/Jist turns whit folk haud sacred inty his moral umb'relly' [The fellow/Just turns what folk hold sacred into his moral umbrella] (V.vii) succeeds in creating a rhyme out of unpromising constituents while also preserving much of Molière's original metaphor, which suggests of Tartuffe that *'il sait ... /Se faire un beau manteau de tout ce qu'on révère'* [he is able to make himself a fine overcoat out of all that is reverenced]. (In the original, these words are spoken by Dorine, not Orgon.)

The success of such rhymes, and others that Lochhead creates out of the flexible resources of Scots vocabulary and pronunciation, might seem qualified by Hampton's suggestion that 'there have been a number of admirable rhyming translations of Molière: but the ingenuity they demand cannot avoid drawing attention to itself' (Hampton, 1984: A Note on the

Translation). Lochhead's *Tartuffe*, however, makes a confident comic virtue out of something that Hampton sees as a problem for the translator. In her Introduction, Lochhead recalls basing her treatment of Molière's verse on a decision that 'the really important part, the comic drive, came from the rhyming'. Accordingly, she explains, she:

> set to, in rhyming couplets with a cavalier and rather idiosyncratic rhythm that I justified to myself by calling it 'the rhythm of spoken Scots'. (Lochhead, 1985: Introduction)

As she suggests, the rhythm of her lines seems either natural, wayward or sometimes just missing – helping her couplets avoid the repetitive, jog-trot quality that critics found in Wilbur's version. Her use of rhyme, however, achieves much more than that. The devious routes that her lines sometimes follow in order to find one – and the ingenuity (as in the example above) of the rhyme itself – remind a modern audience as firmly as Molière's Alexandrines did the original audience of the linguistic artifice containing the wayward material of the play. But a tidier containment also appears in rhymes whose neat closures reproduce something of the original's elegant, classical conciseness. Lochhead not only matches Molière's talent for moral maxims, but sometimes even outdoes him in brevity and aphoristic quality; catching, for example, nearly all the sense of four of his lines:

> ... *d'une fille on risque la vertu,*
> *Lorsque dans son hymen son goût est combattu,*
> *Que le dessein d'y vivre en honnête personne*
> *Depend des qualités de mari qu'on lui donne.* (II.ii)

in two of her own:

> To live the virtuous life is awfy chancy
> When a lassie's merrit tae a man she disnae fancy.
>
> [To live the virtuous life is awfully chancy/When a lass is married to a man she doesn't fancy.]

As Lochhead intended, rhyme also adds a continual 'comic drive' to her work, with anticipation of its completion of successive lines often heightened by hilarious expectation of what their conclusion will be. In the Officer's closing speech, for example, quoted earlier – 'sovereign Power can aye [always] arrange it/That if a law isny [isn't] servin' Justice, well ... they can change it' (V. vii) – that judiciously-inserted pause in the last line was regularly filled, in the Royal Lyceum production, not only by a general laughing expectation of the approaching rhyme, but often by spectators actually saying it aloud, speaking Lochhead's satire for themselves. Expectation of words fulfilling established patterns of their own also contributes to a feature that several critics have noticed in this and other productions – a sense of language as performance, of the form as well as the content of what is said, the medium of the play as well as what it expresses, functioning as a comic element as powerful as any character or action.[4]

This self-conscious awareness of language both develops from, and highlights, the richness and energy available in Scots vocabulary. Though the Officer's suave assurances about government power provide a concluding comic climax, they are earlier surpassed in hilarity – or were at any rate in that first Lyceum production – by the language that Dorine uses to deal with Tartuffe (III.ii). When the latter suggests she should cover up her 'whidjies' [whatnots], since 'evil sichts' [sights] of flesh encourage impure thoughts in men, Dorine memorably replies:

> You must be awfy fashed wi' flesh tae fire
> Yir appetites sae quick wi' Base Desire.
> As fur masel', Ah'm no that easy steered.
> If you were barescud-nakit, aye and geared
> Up guid an proaper, staunin' hoat for houghmagandie
> I could lukk and lukk ett you, and no get randy. (Lochhead, 1985: 31)
>
> [You must be awfully afflicted by flesh to fire/Your appetites so quick with Base Desire./As for myself, I'm not that easily aroused./If you were bare-naked, yes and geared/Up good and proper, standing hot for fornication/I could look and look at you, and not get randy.]

An emphatic, terminal position highlights the gallus [cheeky] colloquialism of 'randy', but the wild-sounding 'houghmagandie' asserts itself even more strongly, contributing in these lines to a passage funnier and more powerful in Scots than anything in English translations, or even the original French. Molière's Dorine concludes her speech by remarking only that

> ... je ne suis point si prompte,
> Et je vous verrais nu du haut jusques en bas,
> Que toute votre peau ne me tenterait pas. (III.ii)
>
> [... I am by no means so hasty:
> I could see you naked from head to foot
> And your whole body would not tempt me.]

Christopher Hampton's version has:

... I'm not so easy to arouse:
for instance, I could look at you stark-naked,
and not be tempted by a single inch. (Hampton, 1984: 49)

This is more coldly, pallidly lewd than Lochhead's lines. Audiences, of course, do not compare translations as they sit in the theatre. Yet they can hardly fail to register that, of the many words that might have been used instead of 'houghmagandie', few could rival it in phonetic richness and suggestiveness: certainly not the simple, sombre English translation in the *Concise Scots Dictionary* (1985), 'fornication'. For Scottish audiences, *Tartuffe* becomes at such moments not just entertainment, but confirmation or rediscovery of the resources of their own language, or at any rate – given that 'houghmagandie' would hardly be a term many spectators would daily use – one closely connected with it. Even before the satiric solidarity of the conclusion (when they might find themselves virtually speaking Lochhead's lines for her) spectators of *Tartuffe* are drawn in this way into a version of the 'shared identity ... between performer and audience' which, as noted earlier, David Hutchison (1987) describes as one of the particular strengths of Scottish theatre.

Dorine's speech also highlights other features of Lochhead's version and its use of Scots. Molière is fairly frank about matters physical and sexual: however formally elegant his lines, what they actually express is often raunchy enough, as the above passage shows. Yet as comparison of it with Lochhead's suggests, the latter is often a little gutsier than her original – sometimes almost literally so. Molière, for example, readily refers to Tartuffe belching, even making a joke of Orgon's indulgence of it – '*s'il vient à roter, il lui dit "Dieu vous aide!"*' [if he happens to belch, he says "God bless you"] (I.ii). However, when in the original Tartuffe simply eats a good meal and sleeps dreamlessly until morning, Lochhead doubles his intake – a gigot [leg] of mutton rather than '*une moitié de gigot*' (I.iv) – and adds that 'Riftin', dozent and weel-fed' [belching, stupefied and well-fed] he spends the night 'fartin' ablow [below] the feather quilt'. Details more gross and physical than Molière's appear at several other points; for example, Dorine, naturally enough, uses several to heighten Marianne's terror of marriage to Tartuffe.

Dorine's speech and the translation as a whole are gutsier and more down to earth than Molière metaphorically as well as literally, a factor obvious from the language of the very first lines. Molière's Pernelle hurries her servant away from the family with the words '*Allons, Flipote, allons, que d'eux je me délivre*' [Come on, Flipote, let me get away from them], but Lochhead renders this into the thoroughly colloquial 'C'moan, Flipote, afore Ah get masel' inty a state' [Come on, Flipote, before I get myself into a state]. Particularly in some of Pernelle's later speeches, Molière himself occasionally moves far enough into colloquialism to persuade even Hampton's rather restrained version to follow – his 'discombobulated' making a rare deviation from standard English to register Pernelle's *'ébaubie'* instead of *'ébahie'* (V.v). Colloquialisms, however, scarcely trouble the regular, elegant flow of Molière's lines: even the very first of them, quoted above, flaunts a stylish inversion. Lochhead, on the other hand, consistently favours pungency over elegance, speech-form over stylishness. Her translation's greatest departure from its original is its sustained use of slang, the demotic and the rhythms of ordinary speech, creating a colloquial quality too omnipresent to illustrate more than partially. Molière's Dorine, for example, describes Tartuffe as *'un inconnu ... / ... qui, quand il vint, n'avait pas de souliers'* [an unknown ... who had no shoes when he arrived]. Lochhead describes him as 'a naebody' who 'breenge[d] in here, a raggity bare-fit tink' [a nobody who pushed in here, a ragged, barefoot good-for-nothing] (I.i), adding that 'it makes me mad how everybody / Can see my maister [master] is enamoured o' a *cuddy* [of a donkey]' (I.ii) – a disreputable beast entirely absent from the French. When Orgon finally sees through Tartuffe for himself, Molière has him conclude:

> ... je renonce à tous les gens de bien:
> J'en aurai désormais une horreur effroyable.
> Et m'en vais devenir pour eux pire qu'un diable. (V.i)

Hampton translates this fairly faithfully as:

> he's the last religious man I'll trust;
> in future I'll recoil from them in horror,
> and never miss a chance to be their scourge. (Hampton, 1984: 78)

while Lochhead's Orgon explodes:

> May God damn an' blast and pit a pox on pious folk.
> Ah loathe an' detest them they gie me the boke.
> Ah'll 'In-the name-o'-the-faither-son-an'-Holy-Ghost' them!
> Ah'll hunt-them-tae-Hell, Ah'll roast them! (Lochhead, 1985: 52–3)

[May God damn and blast and put a pox on pious folk./I loathe and detest them they make me vomit./I'll 'In-the-name-of-the-father-son-and-Holy-Ghost' them!/I'll hunt-them-to-Hell, I'll roast them!]

This is hardly an accurate rendering of Molière, but it is well ahead of Hampton in energy and theatricality: an Orgon who decides never to miss a chance to be a scourge is no match for the damning, blasting, poxing, boking and roasting that Lochhead's character promises.

Highly, pungently, colloquial throughout – highly sayable – Lochhead's Scots is in a wider sense thoroughly *playable*. The comic tradition that Molière and his actors worked in would have made the performer playing Pernelle, for example, aware of a whole range of interfering parent-figures from *commedia*. And if that proved insufficient, Molière himself would have been there to put her right, delivering in person the kind of stage direction mostly missing from his text. As Roger Savage's 1987 programme note accepts, Molière's scripts could afford to seem fairly flat on the page, given that he could rely on personal involvement with 'energetic, high-profile, well-integrated players' able to 'give strong life to the words' on stage. As it happened, Lochhead did have a good deal to do with the first production of her translation: nevertheless, one of its strengths is that its speeches are so highly characterised in themselves that they scarcely require further directions. Indeed, after that crucial opening definition of Pernelle, and a few further words on Elmire, her later stage directions generally specify action rather than character. And, even in the case of Pernelle, that first speech gives in itself more than enough for a performer to work on – clues about someone who not only 'gets inty [into] states' but imposes on those around her the threat of doing so. This is all communicated with the broad, lazy, West-of-Scotland confidence that bothers to deliver only about half the syllables and a sprinkling of the consonants that other speakers might use, while twisting and twanging the vowels that remain. Rather like Shakespeare's mechanicals, Lochhead's characters speak their parts all at once, cues – or clues – and all, except that the cues and clues concerned appear not only in straightforward semantics but in the form and style of the language itself; in all that Scots language and dialect immediately suggest about speakers.

Molière's original, of course, is not without cues and clues about the nature of characters – if not in the form of stage directions, at least in certain habits of speech; often ones that Scots allows Lochhead to develop further. Pernelle's tendency to lapse from kirkish superiority into slangy colloquialism has already been discussed, but other members of her family circle have speech patterns that are almost equally distinctive – as of course does Tartuffe, in his pretentious devotions. Elmire and Cléante, for example, sustain a diction more elevated than some around them, with Elmire particularly dextrous in her use of the pronoun *on* [one] to refer simultaneously to Tartuffe, during his attempt to seduce her, and to her husband, unaccountably reluctant to intervene. Always seeking *'le milieu qu'il faut'* [the necessary middle course] (V.i), Cléante's speeches are marked both by reasonableness and often by close, persuasive reasoning – necessarily so, in long speeches with Orgon (I.v), presumably included by Molière to silence the clergy who resisted earlier versions of the play. Like most translators, Lochhead slightly cuts some of these speeches, and creates for the rest of Cléante's part the irony that opinions replete with sweet reason are comprehensively ignored, partly at least because they are almost always delivered in standard English and lack the colloquial forcefulness that might communicate his wisdom effectively. *'Bearsden voiced'*,[5] according to Lochhead's stage direction, and 'a whole generation more bourgeois than her husband', Elmire shares her brother's anglified tones except when affected by another family characteristic – a susceptibility to being knocked off their rhetorical perch, lapsing back into Scots at moments of stress. Cléante does so, for example, when shocked by Orgon's violent rejection of the 'pious folk' who suddenly 'gie him the boke' [make him want to vomit] (V.i). Elmire does so at a number of awkward moments throughout, noticeably with her mother-in-law in the first scene, or when Tartuffe's seduction accelerates and she is too busy signalling her husband with a faked cough to concentrate on what else passes her lips.

Another example – particularly significant for the translation's whole use of Scots – occurs when Elmire exasperatedly concludes of Tartuffe 'the man's a mere balloon!' (V.iii). 'Balloon' [blowhard] marks a departure from plummier tones in favour of a succinct dialect term more appropriate to the crisis in which her family finds itself. A comparable move, though in the reverse direction, appears very early in the translation, in Pernelle's second speech: 'Wait, haud oan [hold on]! I've had an ample sufficiency/Of your good manners, there's no necessity –' (I.i). The change in register from dialect exclamation to the posher anglicism of 'ample sufficiency' separates the second sentence from the first as decisively as 'balloon' is made to stand out by Elmire. Each is enclosed in what the language theorist Mikhail Bakhtin might call 'intonational quotation marks' – ones by means of which:

> the speaker insulates himself from [a] word as if from another 'language', as if from a style, when it sounds to him (for example) too vulgar, or on the contrary too refined, or too pompous, or if it bespeaks a specific tendency, a specific linguistic manner. (Holquist, 1981: 76)

Quotation marks actually are used in the text at other points: for example, in that threat of Orgon's – 'Ah'll "In-the-name-o'-the-faither-son-an'-Holy-Ghost" them!' – 'insulating' himself from a rejected rhetoric of piety. Mostly, Lochhead's additions to the original – such marked incorporations of an extrinsic register, or lapses into one – add to the translation's sense of language as performance, as play and pretence for characters themselves. They also add to an analysis of social roles and manners for which variations *within* speeches are at least as significant as differences of register *between* individual characters. Any dramatist will use distinctive speech forms to distinguish characters: Lochhead creates characters who often exploit different registers in order, literally, to distinguish themselves: to aspire or cling to the social levels such speech forms suggest. As Bakhtin points out, 'intonational quotation marks' are part of 'an argument between languages; an argument between styles of language' (Holquist, 1981: 76) , but an argument of particular significance; one whose:

> important activity is not only (in fact not so much) the mixing of linguistic forms – the markers of two languages and styles – as it is the collision between differing points of views on the world that are embedded in these forms ... [and] set against each other dialogically. (Holquist, 1981: 360)

As Bakhtin suggests, the shifting registers in speeches such as those quoted above hold up social assumptions and points of view as it were for separate inspection and mutual interrogation, establishing critical, satirical angles between attitudes 'embedded' in each.

Finer, firmer gradations of register within Scots speech, elaborated by contrasts with standard or adopted English, offer more potential than was available to Molière for this kind of investigation of social attitudes, for the dialogic collisions that Bakhtin defines, and for the carnivalesque form of comedy to which he sees such conflicts contributing. In *Rabelais and his World,* Bakhtin (1984) retraces a fundament of comedy to medieval carnival practices in which parodic, playful shows half-celebrated and half-mocked or travestied official culture and established social structures. Subversive, carnivalesque energies of opposition as well as engagement with official culture and language are especially apparent in Lochhead's *Tartuffe.* It is fuller of gutsy Rabelaisian physicality than Molière's, and equipped with a language shaped more comprehensively by 'arguments' between styles and forms, and the social stratifications they imply. Lochhead even adds to the range of registers naturally offered by 'the Scots idiom'. Though she points out in her Introduction that most of her characters are 'at least bilingual and consequently more or less "two faced"', in practice the range of registers employed suggests that they are effectively polylingual and correspondingly multifaceted, as indeed is the whole translation medium itself. As her Introduction explains, Lochhead writes in:

a totally invented ... theatrical Scots, full of anachronisms, demotic speech from various eras and areas; it's proverbial, slangy, couthy, clichéd, catch-phrasey, and vulgar; it's based on Byron, Burns, Stanley Holloway, Ogden Nash and George Formby, as well as the sharp tongue of my granny. (Lochhead, 1985: Introduction)

Especially in this highly dialogised form, the range of registers and possibilities offered by Scots helps to provide another answer to those opening questions about Molière's success on the Scottish stage. Bill Findlay (1996b: 204) moves towards it when he suggests that 'the availability of dialect in Scotland' should be seen to present 'special opportunities'. Edwin Morgan found these essential, sometimes supplemented by English, in order 'to meet the range of tones and tongues in the original' when making his celebrated translation of *Cyrano de Bergerac* (Morgan, 1992). Findlay finds that, by contrast, 'wonderful though the English language is' it offers less range, and therefore 'as a translation medium it can have a homogenising effect on foreign work'. His argument, however, goes on principally to consider ways in which Scots is equipped as a vehicle for foreign work in which dialect, or a range of tones and tongues, are already central elements. This is helpful in general, but needs to be particularly adapted in relation to Molière's drama. Molière's tones and tongues do vary in some of the ways suggested above, but by no means enough to define him as a dialect playwright, and not nearly as much as they do in Lochhead's version of *Tartuffe*. It is Molière's range not of tongues and tones but of social or class identities, attitudes and conflicts (so crisply defined in that first scene of *Tartuffe*) that Scots is so well equipped to represent and differentiate – a 'special opportunity' that it might offer to translators of satire and comedy more generally. Translations in each area can clearly benefit from a language so highly varied and dialogised internally, and at such a critical distance from standard English and the official culture that employs it – a language also able to establish with its audience an impression of familiarity and the kind of consensual solidarity of outlook on which satire depends. Whatever Molière might have achieved in *theatrical* presentation with that lively company Roger Savage supposes he worked with, in terms of *linguistic* medium the happy 'houghmagandie' [intercourse] of dialects and registers in Scots surely offers Molière more satiric opportunities than are to be found in English – or, moreover, in his native French. In this way at least, it may be justified to see him as 'almost a Scottish playwright-by adoption', one who does help 'define the distinctiveness of modern Scottish theatre' at least by showing so clearly the potential of 'theatrical Scots'. Further evidence of this might be found in recent decisions by other foreign translators to use Scots versions of Molière, rather than the original, as the basis for their work, presumably because in a whole range of the ways outlined above, it so naturally gives character and colour to what Molière may have left rather flat on the page.[6]

So Scots may naturally be good for Molière, but it would be rash to suppose that all Scots Molières are naturally good. However promising the opportunities offered by any language, or any text, it is the vision of the individual translator that determines how successfully these will be exploited. Lochhead's is, after all, a 'totally invented' Scots. If further evidence of the cleverness and comprehensiveness of its invention were required, it could be based on a single line in Act II scene iii, when Dorine teases Marianne with the threat that her prospective marriage will leave her *'tartuffiée'*. For 250 years, from Baker and Miller in 1739 to Hampton in 1983, Molière's neologism has most often been translated simply – and accurately enough – as 'tartuffed'. In Lochhead's version, however, Marianne risks no less than finding herself 'Tartuffified'. Little extra shimmies like that separate a truly engaging translation from a merely functional one. Liz Lochhead's Scots is full of them.[7]

Notes

1. Quotations from the French original are taken from Molière, 1990. Where it seems useful, they are followed in square brackets by my literal translation. In this and other matters concerning the French original I am grateful for the advice of Helen Stevenson.
2. Baker & Miller (1739, repr. 1956); Hampton (1984). Subsequent references to these translations are to these editions.
3. Irving Wardle and W.A. Darlington (Peacock, 1993: 75, 76).
4. Sarah Hemming talks of 'using the power of rhyme ... to make language part of the theme' in a review in *The Times* in 1986, quoted in Peacock (1993: 90). It is also discussed in Stevenson (1993), which contains an earlier version of several of the ideas in the present chapter.
5. Bearsden is an affluent suburb on the north-western fringes of Glasgow. For Glaswegians it has long-standing, and often caricatured, associations with affected poshness.
6. Hector MacMillan notes that, whereas Finnish translators found difficulty in making Molière funny when translating directly from French into Finnish, when they worked instead from his Scots translation of *The Hypochondriak* there were no such difficulties (see Findlay, 1996a: 195–6, note 14).
7. Other Molières translated by Lochhead are *Les Précieuses ridicule* (*The Patter Merchants*, 1989) (see Peacock, 1993: 22), and *Le Misanthrope* (*Miseryguts*, 2002) (see Lochhead, 2002).

Chapter 7
Edwin Morgan's Cyrano de Bergerac

DAVID KINLOCH

Among the remarkable events of 1992, many Scots will be unable to forget the spectacle of Labour's defeat at the General Election and Edwin Morgan's spectacular version of *Cyrano de Bergerac*. It would be a crude and unjust interpretation that attributed his translation's immediate success simply to the prevalent political atmosphere of gloom and recrimination, but there can be no doubt that the elation experienced at the first performances had something to do with this. It wasn't just card-carrying Nationalists that felt a certain satisfaction that Morgan should confine De Guiche and the foppish marquises to the English language while Cyrano was allowed to soar in Scots. On the other hand, those more sceptical souls among us must have grimaced ruefully at Cyrano's apt self-mockery at the end of the play:

... Fate joketh!
Here Ah am, ambushed, battert like a dog,
Kilt fae behind by a lackey wae a log!
Fair enough – pair death eftir pair love. (Morgan, 1992a: 159)

[Fate joketh!/Here I am, ambushed, battered like a dog,/Killed from behind by a lackey with a log!/Fair enough – poor death after poor love.]

Morgan provided us, on cue, with a 'heroic comedy' whose mixture of passion and passionate self-deflation was both balm and irritant to that unheroic Scottish summer. Indeed it was as if his desire to transpose as acutely as possible had extended even to the conditions of reception prevalent at the time of the première of Rostand's play in 1898; for the original French play did much to cheer up contemporary theatre-goers still smarting from a succession of military defeats, including those of the disastrous Franco-Prussian War of 1870–71. It was not simply the theatrical merits of *Cyrano de Bergerac* that attracted the likes of the then President, Félix Faure, to attend successive performances and confer the *légion d'honneur* on Rostand, but the perceived patriotism of its hero.

Such coincidences do, however, raise the issue of Morgan's purpose in translating this play into Scots. In his introduction to the Carcanet edition,

123

he refers to *Cyrano* as 'one of those rich and challenging works which need to be translated again and again, in different circumstances and for different purposes, readerly and actorly. The time seemed ripe for a Scottish version ...' (Morgan, 1992a: xi). Tantalisingly, however, he goes no further, leaving us free to speculate. The key lies, perhaps, in his use of the word 'need', for it points enigmatically to his conception of writing as a means of controlling and expressing a fundamental human energy. This aesthetic is basic to all Morgan's original poetry, and has been explored by numerous commentators. What emerges clearly from these studies is that Morgan regards writing itself as essentially a form of translation, an energetic interpreting of sometimes silent or hidden messages. As he noted in an interview:

> If I write a poem called 'The Apple's Song', the apple is being translated if you like into human language ... I like the idea particularly that in a sense we're surrounded by messages that we perhaps ought to be trying to interpret. (Morgan, 1988/1995: 154)

Consequently, Morgan has been attracted particularly by types and genres of writing that exhibit a certain adventurous energy. One thinks, for example, of his translations of Mayakovsky (see Stephen Mulrine's chapter in this volume) or his interest in science fiction. In an essay on 'The Whole Morgan', Robert Crawford (1990: 16) has pointed out that the William Dunbar poems he likes best 'manifest energy through controlled, rapid movement'. It may be, indeed, that for Morgan there exist some crucial texts that embody, symbolise even, the whittrick [ferrety] energy that is writing itself. And if they are written in a foreign language they demand, 'need', cry out to be translated. Perhaps a useful point of reference here would be the distinction made by the French thinker, Roland Barthes, between the *écrivain* and the *écrivant*, or in English, the *author* and the *writer*. For Barthes (1972: 143–50), it is the writer who is the true contemporary, a 'transitive man' typified by 'impulses' and 'impatiences'. For him, 'the author's language is an intransitive act (hence, in a sense, a gesture), the writer's an activity'. As we shall see, Rostand is a stimulating mixture of the two, but his play's verbal energy provided a natural temptation to Morgan, whose principal aim was to rekindle and renew it, in other words, translate it, making it accessible to contemporary and future audiences.

This, therefore, is the primary 'purpose' of Morgan's translation and much of what follows will attempt to describe and analyse Morgan's unique renderings of *Cyrano*'s wordplay and to examine the importance to him of the play's styles and genres. It is worth identifying two other 'purposes', however, before continuing.

It is true, for example, that this Scots version of *Cyrano de Bergerac* confirms Bill Findlay's belief that:

> a healthy would-be national theatre culture requires a more extended repertoire of Scots translations than we presently have and that one effect of this would be to allow more consistent exploration of our 'national linguistic resource'. (Findlay, 1993: 21)

Morgan's translation of *Cyrano*, along with those of Molière by Hector MacMillan (Alexander, 2000) and Liz Lochhead (see Randall Stevenson's chapter in this volume), are pioneering works in this regard – as Findlay has been happy to acknowledge. Indeed, it is this aspect of Morgan's translation, rather than any spurious attempt to anticipate or reflect the times, that constitutes the true cultural impetus of the play, one that is at once political and artistic.

There is, however, one other impulse at work in Morgan's translation, one that is both personal in terms of the translator's life and work as a poet, and also political in its resonance. For it is not simply Cyrano's bravura that keeps Rostand's play alive; his vulnerability is also important. Cyrano's need to find a voice capable of interpreting for Roxane an inner beauty betrayed by his physical imperfection is both frustrated and exacerbated by the obligation to translate Christian's handsome contours into their verbal equivalent. The result is pathos as well as humour, a profound sense of lack concealed by a potentially camp excess. Morgan goes to the heart of this dilemma, choosing, at key points in the play, to bring this aspect more clearly but no less subtly into the open than Rostand or any of his other English translators have done.

What then of Cyrano's words and styles? What precisely did Morgan find so attractive about them? Rostand's attempt to catch something of the historical Cyrano's heroic defiance of his age must have had a natural appeal for Morgan, the poet of heroic elegies such as 'Cinquevalli', 'Che', and 'The Death of Marilyn Monroe' (Morgan, 1990a). In his essay quoted above, Crawford (1990: 11) has insisted on Morgan's 'interest in developing a poetry of heroic elegy', and, taken as a whole, this is just what Rostand's '*comédie héroique*' is. Significantly, however, Morgan's heroic elegies have always been characterised by a mercurial eclecticism that has prevented them from becoming either sentimental or simply tragic, and it is precisely this quality that Morgan singles out for special mention in his introduction to the published translation. In fact, it seems that it is present in both Rostand's play and the real Cyrano's character. The play is described as 'robust and boisterous, yet sad also, and it at once inhabit[s] a territory of its own, escaping both gritty naturalism and *fin de siècle* decadence' (Morgan,

1992a: ix); Cyrano himself is seen as fascinating for 'the manysidedness of a man who was a poet, a Guards officer, a dramatist, a musician, a writer of science-fiction, a student of philosophy and physics, a freethinker, and gay' (Morgan, 1992a: ix–x). 'Manysidedness', 'a territory of its own', 'escape' – these are all words and epithets that have importance for Morgan's own poetry and persona. What fascinates Morgan about this play and its hero is *'something less categorisable'* [my emphasis] (Morgan, 1992a: xi). Significantly, Morgan follows this phrase by referring to Cyrano's last act of dramatic bravura as he imagines the plume of his doffed hat sweeping the floor of heaven *'sans un pli, sans une tache'*. This perfectly judged gesture is symbolic, not simply of the complexity of Cyrano's character, but of the entire aesthetic that governs Rostand's play and with which Morgan has a natural affinity. He prefers to make the last words of his translation, *'Ma plume'*, evocative of the qualities they symbolise, but there is something to be said for Anthony Burgess's decision to make Cyrano's 'last English word the same as his last French one' (Burgess, 1991: Introduction), if only because this word, 'panache', encapsulates the genre to which Rostand's play belongs and provides a fresh route into Morgan's own aesthetic.

The best and most succinct guide to this aspect of the play is provided by Geoff Woollen in the introduction to his edition of Rostand's original. He defines it as a *'panaché*, i.e. a mixture, of constituent generic features, be they neo-Romantic, neo-Classical, baroque or burlesque' (Woollen, 1994: xvii). While Woollen is sympathetic to Rostand's achievement and presents the 'genre-problematising aspect of Cyrano' as 'innovative drama', he opens his introduction by relating the enthusiasm that greeted *Cyrano de Bergerac,* the 1990 Rappeneau/Depardieu film of the play, to contemporary 'liking for the "retro", the nostalgic and the emotive' (Woollen, 1994: v). The potential contradiction here may be resolved simply by acknowledging that *Cyrano de Bergerac* has something for everyone. The original play was, as Patrick Besnier (1983: Introduction) has pointed out, a great popular success. This was due, in part, to the familiar and rhetorically ingenious *'grandes tirades'*, but it managed also to enthuse the avant-garde with its virtuoso handling of stychomythia or fragmentation of the line of verse (Woollen, 1994: xxiv), a strategy that Rostand uses sometimes to undercut and satirise Cyrano's verbosity. It is, indeed, in such apparent contradictions that Barthes' opposing *author* and *writer* reappear on the horizon.

Such a mixture of materials and reactions must have fascinated Morgan who, in his own poetry, has always sought to be both genuinely innovative and accessible. He would have felt at home in the mode of *'le panaché'* and it is, perhaps, significant that he worked from Besnier's edition of *Cyrano,* whose introduction is extremely sensitive to the play's more modern resonances.

It is worth spending a little time, therefore, looking at Morgan's renderings of the dazzling *'panaché'* of styles. His determination to find an appropriate equivalent for them all, often at points where other translators simply give up, shows that he recognises how the essence of both the play and its hero lies in their refusal to be easily categorised. Morgan is not interested in virtuosity for virtuosity's sake. In this he joins Cyrano himself, who has little time either for the *préciosité* of noble side-kicks or even of his beloved Roxane. Morgan birls [spins] through a kaleidoscope of styles and registers because he understands that, ultimately, this energy opens on and gives access to the dark and famished soul of a hero who knows and is at once proud and unhappy that he is different.

In this respect, therefore, it is possibly burlesque that is the most important stylistic element in *Cyrano*, since it is by this means that the playwright accedes to other styles, or allows the echo of other styles, tones and registers to be heard. Burlesque *presents* styles and/or precepts even as it satirises them and, as such, is a linchpin of *le panaché*. Thus, Cyrano's duel with Valvert becomes a delightfully light-hearted presentation of the hero's complexity. Cyrano is able to display his skill and erudition both as a poet and a swordsman while gently but determinedly mocking both his opponent and himself for indulging in such antics. Cyrano's burlesque is at once the rapier-sharp instrument of his pride and a shield against ridicule. By strictly observing the rhyme scheme of a ballade royal (*ababbcbc*), a form popular during the seventeenth century, but filling it with a mixture of conceits and insults appropriate to the situation, Cyrano thrusts even as he parries. As Geoff Woollen (1994: xxv) remarks, the chosen French rhymes on *'eutre'*, *'on'* and *'ouche'* are 'not of the easiest to sustain', and Morgan does well to match Rostand/Cyrano's virtuosity while giving it a contemporary twist here and there that teases out an underlying manic hilarity not fully articulated by the original. Hence, Cyrano's *'Il me manque une rime en eutre'* becomes the funny and exclamatory 'It's hellish this rhyming on urrish', and *'Tiens bien ta broche, Larridon'* turns into the colloquial 'It's kebab time now, nothing's barred!' as he prepares to skewer his victim (Morgan, 1992a: 28).

This duel is the direct result of Cyrano's equally outrageous *'tirade'* on the merits of his nose, another example of his unquenchable penchant for the burlesque. Here Cyrano is allowed to demonstrate his familiarity with the verbal pyrotechnics of the baroque poet Agrippa d'Aubigné (1552–1630) while simultaneously pointing to the dangers of such a style as it loses itself in a ridiculous *'préciosité'*. Again, Morgan's method is to mix into a faithful, at times quite literal, translation of the original, humorous contemporary notes that in their range of tone and reference skilfully reflect the impure and heteroclite textures of the tirade. Valvert, Cyrano opines, could have chosen from a whole gamut of styles and registers in his desire to describe his opponent's nose, among them:

> Gracieux: *'Aimez-vous à ce point les oiseaux*
> *Que paternellement vous vous préoccupâtes*
> *De tendre ce perchoir à leurs petites pattes?'* (Besnier, 1983: 73)

In Morgan's version, the unctuous pretentiousness of Cyrano's alliteration – the lordly imperfect subjunctive perfectly undercut by the rhyme with *'pattes'* – is compressed into the tripping consonants of a more whimsical simile, but one that is just as attentive to the discrepancies delineated by the original:

> *Gracious*: 'Ye're a right Saint Francis, ye wheedle
> The burds o the air tae wrap their gentle tootsies
> Roon yer perch and rest their weary Guccis!' (Morgan, 1992a: 24)
>
> [You're a right Saint Francis, you wheedle/The birds of the air to wrap their gentle tootsies/Round your perch and rest their weary Guccis!]

A little further on, Morgan cannot deny himself an invention of his own:

> *Admiring*: 'Logo fur Boady Shoap, better'n a rose!' (Morgan, 1992a: 25)
>
> [Logo for Body Shop, better than a rose!]

Out of context, of course, some of these jokes may strike the reader as simply puerile. Only in the theatre, where the rhymes can be heard and the inextinguishable nature of Cyrano's inventiveness appreciated, do they work properly.

It is significant, however, that the critique of this wonderful nonsense arises within the tirade itself. It is as if the degree of verbal energy required to bring it off forces a kind of spontaneous combustion or implosion as Cyrano, with an indignant flourish, sweeps the carpet away from under his own creativity:

> *Bummin:* 'Nae wind, O hypermacho nose,
> Could gie ye snuffles but blasts fae Muckle Flugga!'
> *Dramatic:* 'Bleeds a haill Rid Sea, the bugger!'
> *Lyrical:* 'It's a conch fur Captain Hornblower!'
> *Naive:* 'Is yer monument open fae nine tae four?'
> *Respeckfu:* 'A badge? Yer Honour disnae need yin!
> It's clear up-front that ye're a real high-heid-yin!'
> *Rustic:* 'Fat's a dae wae noses? Na, na!
> A muckle neep or a scrunty melon, hah?'
> *Military:* 'Pynt yer supergun at the troops!'

Practical: 'Ye kin raffle it, cowp the coops,
Hit the jackpot, snaffle the dosh and away!'
Or lastly, parodying Pyramus in the play:
'See how this nose has blasted the harmony
Of its master's features! It blushes wretchedly!'
– That's a wee tait a what ye could've sayed
If ye'd had wit or kulchur; Ah'm afraid
Ye've nane. Yer wit wis ripped oot fae yer genes,
Yer kulchur, O maist deplorable of bein's,
Comprises five letters, D, U, M, B, O!
But even if ye'd hud the nous tae throw
Sic pure deid brilliant whigmaleeries oot
Intae this deid brilliant audience, Ah doot
Ye'd no could stammer the furst syllable
Before Ah'd shawn it tae be killable:
Thae juicy jests are mine, Ah love them, but
When ithers try tae mooth them, Ah cry, 'Cut!' (Morgan, 1992a: 25)

[*Boastful:* 'No wind, O hypermacho nose,/Could give you snuffles but blasts from Muckle Flugga!'/*Dramatic:* 'Bleeds a whole Red Sea, the bugger!'/*Lyrical:* 'It's a conch for Captain Hornblower!'/*Naive:* 'Is your monument open from nine to four?'/*Respectful:* 'A badge? Your Honour doesn't need one!/It's clear up-front that you're a genuine person in authority!'/*Rustic:* 'What's the matter with noses? No, no!/A big turnip or a shrivelled melon, hah?'/*Military:* 'Point your supergun at the troops!'/*Practical:* 'You can raffle it, overturn the hen-coops,/Hit the jackpot, snaffle the dosh and away!'/Or lastly, parodying Pyramus in the play:/'See how this nose has blasted the harmony/Of its master's features! It blushes wretchedly!'/– That's a little sample of what you could've said/If you'd had wit or culture; I'm afraid/You've none. Your wit was ripped out from your genes,/Your culture, O most deplorable of beings,/Comprises five letters, D, U, M, B, O!/But even if you'd had the nous to throw/Such extremely brilliant fanciful imaginings out/Into this extremely brilliant audience, I doubt/You would be able to stammer the first syllable/Before I'd shown it to be killable:/those juicy jests are mine, I love them, but/When others try to mouth them, I cry, 'Cut!']

It is tempting to see this tirade, which runs without a break for 53 lines, as complete in itself. But, in fact, Valvert's subsequent contemptuous attack on Cyrano's 'borrowed' eloquence:

Whit? A jumped-up squire?
Sich arrogance! You ... you ... ye'd huv tae hire
Gloves, ribbons, tassels, braid, stoakins, the loat! (Morgan, 1992a: 25)

[What? A jumped-up squire?/Such arrogance! You ... you ... you'd have to hire/Gloves, ribbons, tassels, braid, stockings, the lot!]

induces a searingly earnest but no less witty coda that reflects indirectly not so much on the *futility* of the type of literary conceit that Cyrano has just displayed as on the *limiting* nature of indulging in it for too long. Cyrano's 'nose tirade' is like a great baroque tapestry, an amalgam or *'panaché'* of styles and colours. The greatest tapestries are, of course, never static, seeming to burst profusely across the walls, striving to engulf the whole field of our vision. This profusion is of their essence but an essence that will not speak its name; it is 'something less categorisable', to return to Morgan's introduction, one that refuses to be defined as our eye passes from one rich detail to the next; one that *may* perhaps be seized, may *only* be perceived in the very process of such movement.

The multifarious folds of Cyrano's eloquence conceal as they reveal, his speeches an elaborate series of *trompe-l'oeil* typical of a baroque aesthetic. As the French thinker Gilles Deleuze (1988: 5) puts it, '*Le trait du Baroque, c'est le pli* [the 'fold'] *qui va à l'infini'*. And here, it is *va*, the use of the present tense of the verb *aller*, that is perhaps most important, signifying a rapid continual *movement*, a striving quality that is heard throughout Cyrano's coda but with particular clarity at the end of it as he attempts again and again to articulate his difference, his odd panache:

> Ah cannae cut a dash like Valentino,
> It's soul, no flash, Ah press oot fur its *vino*.
> Ah pin oan deeds, no ribbons, tae ma doublet,
> Ah wax ma wit, no ma moustache, tae unstubble it.
> Ah pass through punters, chatterers, orators,
> And shinin truths come ringin oot like spurs. (Morgan, 1992a: 26)
>
> [I cannot cut a dash like Valentino,/It's soul, not flash, I press out for its *vino*./I pin on deeds, not ribbons, to my doublet,/I wax my wit, not my moustache, to unstubble it./I pass through punters, chatterers, orators,/And shining truths come ringing out like spurs.]

'*Cest le pli qui va à l'infini*', 'Ah *pass through* punters, chatterers, orators'. He never stops for long. To do so would be to risk silence, to be dead. When Christian dies at the end of Act 4, Cyrano knows that:

> ... Ah should dee with him the-day:
> She disnae know it's me she's laid away! (Morgan, 1992a: 142)
>
> [I should die with him today:/She doesn't know it's me she's laid away!]

For he can speak to Roxane only through the beautiful, shimmering musculature of Christian's body, soon to be mere dust. This is the real tragedy of

Christian's death, and it is why Cyrano must be silent in the space between Acts 4 and 5, which represents a period of fifteen years.

Morgan's translation of Cyrano's reply to Valvert in Act 1 scene 4, clearly shows that he understands its importance to the play as a whole. This time it is not so much his choice of lexis or cultural reference that is impressive as the way he manages to capture this quality defined above, an urgency of tone and manner. Rostand gradually builds up clause upon clause to the climax of his final lines, creating that climax by separating the infinitive *sonner* from the controlling factitive that he places at the beginning of the previous line:

> *Je fais, en traversant les groupes et les ronds,*
> *Sonner les vérites comme des éperons.* (Besnier, 1983: 75)

If anything, Morgan's strategy actually intensifies these effects, using repetitive verbal structures that convey a real sense of self-discovery while reinforcing our picture of a man continually on the hoof, in pursuit, through metaphor and simile, of an image of himself capable of matching his sense of his own baroque complexity:

> *Ah pin oan deeds,* no ribbons, tae ma doublet,
> *Ah wax ma wit,* no ma moustache, tae unstubble it.
> *Ah pass through punters,* chatterers, orators,
> And shinin truths come ringin oot like spurs.
> (Morgan, 1992a: 26, my emphasis)

[*I pin on deeds*, not ribbons, to my doublet,/*I wax my wit*, not my moustache, to unstubble it./*I pass through punters*, chatterers, orators,/And shining truths come ringing out like spurs.]

If this may seem like special pleading or an attempt to force the text to fit a theory, readers might take a look at Anthony Burgess's (1991) version of the same speech. Burgess's translation is accomplished and elegant, but it fails to reproduce Rostand's careful *pacing* of Cyrano's search. We do not feel, as we do in Rostand and even more so in Morgan, that Cyrano just might be making a discovery about himself *as he speaks*.

A similar sincerity may be heard in the speech to Le Bret in Act 2 scene 8, which Woollen (1994: xx) aptly describes as the '*non merci*! tirade'. Again, we are in the presence of both the baroque and the burlesque as Cyrano scorns his friend's advice to avoid poverty by seeking a rich and powerful patron. Cyrano's language holds up a burlesque mirror to such pretensions, and spectators laugh at the distorted reflections that flash back at them:

Whit wid ye huv me dae?
Suss oot some high-born heavy, take a patron,
Cling like an ivy tae some bigwig, slaisterin
His gummy trunk wi pyson, climb the rungs
No through ma strength but wi the whisperin tongues?
Naw thanks. Dedicate poems, as some dae,
Tae money-men? Pit oan the motley, and play
Before some minister tae get a smile
Fae his thin lips and no a loada bile?
Naw thanks. Eat toad insteeda halesome porridge?
Weer oot ma wame wae crawlin? Fudge and forage
For favours on a hackit glaury knee-cap?
Bend backwards tae Ah need a spinal tap?
Naw thanks. Try bein a right sleekit chap,
Run wi the hounds, run wi the hare, same lap?
Gie a senna-pod tae get some rhubarb,
Daein yer broon-nose at a weel-kent scutard?
Naw thanks! Loup oan fae bed tae bed, a
Wee big guy fur the hostess and the widda,
A seafarer wi madrigals fur rowlocks
And auld wives' sighs tae fan his weary bollocks?
Naw thanks! [...] (Morgan, 1992a: 62–63)

[What would you have me do?/Suss out some high-born heavy, take a patron,/Cling like an ivy to some bigwig, smearing/His gummy trunk with poison, climb the rungs/Not through my strength but with the whispering tongues?/No thanks. Dedicate poems, as some do,/To money-men? Put on the motley, and play/Before some minister to get a smile/from his thin lips and not a load of bile?/No thanks. Eat toad instead of wholesome porridge?/Wear out my stomach with crawling? Fudge and forage/For favours on a scraped, dirty knee-cap?/Bend backwards till I need a spinal tap?/No thanks. Try being a right plausible but sly chap,/Run with the hounds, run with the hare, same lap?/Give a senna-pod to get some rhubarb,/Doing your brown-nose at a well-known defecator?/No thanks! Jump from bed to bed, a/Wee big guy for the hostess and the widow,/A seafarer with madrigals for rowlocks/And old wives' sighs to fan his weary bollocks?/No thanks!]

Baroque in the swift and colourful sequence of images of dependency it considers and discards, it is baroque also in the glimpse it affords us of a more profound reality. As Woollen says, the tirade, as it rages on, turns 'on the hinge of *"Mais ... chanter"*, "But ... sing"'. This figure of the hinge recalls once more Deleuze's (1988) interpretation of Leibniz's baroque philosophy. Cyrano's labyrinthine soul exists and expresses itself on two levels, but, as Deleuze assures us, '[i]t is certain that the two levels communicate with each other'. A door at the top of a flight of baroque stairs swings open on its hinge and we catch a momentary glimpse of that more secretive, higher soul within its *'pièce close privée, tapissée d'une toile diversifiée par des plis'* (Deleuze, 1988: 7) The door swings open and, as before, we can hear a hidden soul breathing in the fresh air as each quick verb proposes a more complete and balanced picture of its existence. Here is the French. Listen to the concatenation of feverish infinitives:

> Non, merci! Non, merci! Non, merci! Mais ... chanter,
> Rêver, rire, passer, être seul, être libre ... (Besnier, 1983: 142)

Now, here is Morgan:

> Naw thanks! Naw thanks! Naw *thanks*! – But ... sing romanzas,
> Dream, laugh, stravaig, alane and free by choice,
> Huv eyes that don't miss much, a ringin voice,
> Tilt ma hat sidieweys when Ah feel like it,
> Fecht this or that – or let a poem strike it,
> Wark withoot chasin eftir fame and glory,
> Traivel tae the muin fur ma best story! (Morgan, 1992a: 63)

> [No thanks! No thanks! No *thanks*! – But ... sing romances,/Dream, laugh, wander, alone and free by choice,/Have eyes that don't miss much, a ringing voice,/Tilt my hat sideways when I feel like it,/Fight this or that – or let a poem strike it,/Work without chasing after fame and glory,/Travel to the moon for my best story!]

The choice of that word 'stravaig' is a happy one, conveying – to this reader/listener at any rate – all the paradoxical whimsy of a purposeful stroll. Similarly, the instinct to preserve the verbal impetus is, as we have suggested, a true measure of this translator's inwardness with his material.

It is not sufficient to say, though, that the ultimate goal of this façade of talk is to pass beyond it to the small quiet room of Cyrano's soul. Cyrano is a hero whose sole appetite is for talk – and then more talk. He fasts poetically while all about him feast contentedly on Ragueneau's pastries and Roxane's pumpkin-like carriage. Cyrano greedily translates everything into a succulent, racy tongue and his very death is a rhetorical flourish. Death can barely get a word in edgeways. This play is a play on words, of words, for words; it is theatre about theatre. The first act depicts the theatre of the Hôtel de Bourgogne, while Molière casts his shadow in the last. As Woollen (1994: xxi) points out, 'both Cyrano and Roxane are doubled by burlesque protagonists', Ragueneau and Lise. The mirror of art continually acknowledges its presence, fragmenting, doubling, suggesting that the true pain and loss experienced by Cyrano, the extremity of his love, may only momentarily be glimpsed in the ceaseless movement of the play's myriad textures, as style after style is taken up and lain down. Patrick Besnier (1983: 23) is correct to remind us that the play is as famous for its deployment of stycomythia, the shattering of the twelve-syllabled Alexandrine and its distribution among a plurality of voices, as it is for its more conventional tirades.

Hence, Morgan's unwillingness to let even the smallest cadence or obscurity of the original slip through the translator's net; because through that crack or *fente* in the weft of his fabric, the true Cyrano, that which makes him who and what he is, might slip away. It is to be as serious about Cyrano's playfulness as Cyrano himself. Indeed, Morgan's Glaswegian-Scots frequently proves to be much more versatile a vehicle than standard English for rendering the variety of registers manipulated by his characters as well as for rendering the play's neologisms and puns. Morgan shows off the huge emotional range that Scots can encompass from the nostalgic and the deeply lyrical to the flippant and sublimely combative. Here, for example, is a remarkable instance of Morgan's ability to derive a powerful lyric charge from Glaswegian accent as distinct from lexis. In the following short speech by the theatre usherette in Act 1, the husky gravel tones of a particular generation and class of Glasgow women are perfectly caught simply by means of the occasional addition or subtraction of a vowel:

Ices, ginger, tea,	[soft drink]
Raspberry yoghurt, Greek yoghurt, aw the yoghurts,	[all]
Lovely Turkish delight, licorice awsorts,	[allsorts]
Popcoarn, hote chestnits, marshmallows,	[hot]
Chewin-gum, candyfloss...	

(Morgan, 1992a: 4)

The catalogue of sweeties is poignantly brief but longer, in fact, than Rostand's French version. Apparently, this expansion was suggested to Morgan by members of the Communicado Theatre Company, and Morgan recognised an opportunity not simply to add a touch of local colour but to reveal a poetry at work in the speaking human voice. Here, Morgan's art reminds one of the unique voices recorded and created in Tom Leonard's Glaswegian poetry and prose (Leonard, 1984). This becomes clearer if the catalogue is given in standard English with no regard to the accent of the usherette. In this case, the catalogue becomes a simple list of sickly foodstuffs. The combination of nicely-judged onomatopoeia and repetition present in the Glaswegian version turns it into a lovely yearning poetry that, in true Proustian fashion, reawakens the tastes and sounds of childhood.

Morgan is also adept at illustrating the bewildering rapidity with which Scots speakers can switch from one register to another, sometimes within the space of a single speech. Cyrano, for example, is fond of Lignière:

[b]ecause this soak,
This tun of muscat, this vodka-sozzled bloke
Done somethin wance that shaws the best a folk:
He saw his lady-love sip holy watter
At the font eftir Mass, envied the blatter
A the sweet draps, and like a fermer at a rowp
Ran and slurped dry that non-alcoholic stowp! (Morgan, 1992a: 37)

[because this soak,/This tun of muscat, this vodka-sozzled bloke/Did something once that shows the best of folk:/He saw his lady-love sip holy water/At the font after Mass, envied the flow/Of the sweet drops, and like a farmer at a public auction/Ran and slurped dry that non-alcoholic receptacle!]

The straightforward pub invective of the first two or three lines acts as a familiar colloquial prelude to a scene that could almost have come from a Ronsard sonnet. Morgan's 'fermer at a rowp' is an invention, but one perhaps more faithful to Rostand's gauche *'fût de rossoli'*, and to the character of Cyrano's own comradely affection for him, than the French author's depiction of a gallant action. Similarly, Morgan's attention to 'the blatter/A the sweet draps' is an aural felicity missing from the original, in which the hero of the episode simply watches *'celle qu'il aimait prendre de l'eau bénite'*.

Again, at the other end of the linguistic spectrum, Morgan is keen to display Glaswegians' fondness for a certain type of earthy humour. Act 2 scene 1 ends with Ragueneau's agonised exclamations as his wife wraps up pastries in the pages of the verses of his 'friends': *'Avec des vers, faire cela!'* moans Ragueneau. Lise: *'Pas autre chose'*. Ragueneau: *'Que faîtes-vous, alors madame, avec la prose?'* Morgan adds one word to this and considerably heightens the comedy. Ragueneau: 'Hoo can ye make poetry intae bags?' [How can you make poetry into bags?].Those bags are typical of the literal-minded genius that animates Glaswegian humour. Other examples are not hard to find. When Cyrano warns Lise against cuckolding her husband, he says: *'Je défends que quelqu'un le ridicoculise'* (Besnier, 1983: 115). In Scots, Cyrano declares he likes his friend, hence: 'And so, Missus, ye're/Out of order if he's ridicuckoldous. Ye hear?' (Morgan, 1992a: 47). Other English versions merely yield bland exhortations 'not to make a fool' of Ragueneau, not to 'take his name in vain'. Again, most English versions are quite foxed by the cadets' wordplay, which verges (but not entirely) on nonsense: *'Milledious! – Capdedious! – Mordious! – Pocapdedious!'* (Besnier, 1983: 129).

Instead, Morgan (1992a: 55), virtuoso of the poem the 'Loch Ness Monster's Song', turns these Provençal oaths into broad Glaswegian: 'Gawds-agawds!– Gawdstoptop!–Gawdsdeddo!– Gawdspapawl!'

Indeed this deeply felt delight and belief in the creative power of polysemy, which Morgan shares with Rostand and the historical Cyrano (Prévot, 1977: Introduction), provokes comments of a more general nature about Morgan's choice of Scots rather than standard English as the language of his principal characters. For there is a sense in which Scots both gives this play an *extra* dimension of the type just outlined and also releases a dramatic energy that is greater even than that displayed by Rostand's original and the many standard English translations of it. The point is best made, perhaps, in relation to Cyrano himself. It is easy enough to forget – until Cyrano reminds you – that, in standard English versions, Cyrano is a Gascon from Gascony and not Parisian. Morgan's decision to let him speak mainly in Scots is tantamount to giving his Gascon identity and voice back to him. Much of the pleasure and shock we get from Rostand's play comes from the pressure that Cyrano puts on standard French. That pressure is a Gascon one. It is the instinctive, subversive revolt of a tongue that does not quite recognise itself in standard French just as Cyrano does not entirely recognise his true self when he looks in the mirror and his nose looks back at him. His virtuosity and restless ventriloquism is in part the product of a suppressed regional identity. Morgan's Scots releases Cyrano and, as one might expect, the result is the much wider variety of accents, tones and registers currently under discussion.

It could be argued that a logical result of allowing Cyrano's Scots tongue a free rein might be a certain dissolution of the 'pressure' referred to above. It is clear, however, that Morgan was aware of this potential problem and resolved it by diverting pent-up emotion into an ongoing flyting (poetic duelling) in English with his upper-class foes. Cyrano is a master of all the metropolitan poetic and social forms and niceties, but his virtuosic attacks on De Guiche and Valvert show how the Scottish tradition of flyting may be used to give backbone to the necessity for English invective. Put crudely, the audience's satisfaction derives partly from seeing the bloke with the long nose and the 'guid Scots tongue in his heid' [good Scots tongue in his head] going one better each and every time in the language of his cultural and social 'superiors'. The audience's enjoyment of clashing linguistic codes thus becomes, almost without their realising it, an awareness of national or regional *difference*.

In fact, Morgan's use of Scots enables us to identify *Cyrano de Bergerac* as a classical piece of multivocal flyting, which, in turn, helps to resolve a number of difficulties relating to the tone of two important scenes and how they should be interpreted on stage. Apparently, several violent acts occur in the course of the drama, and the problem for a director of the play is to decide what weight should be attached to them. The first is the duel with Valvert but, as we have already seen, and as Geoff Woollen (1994: xx) rightly comments, more damage is 'done by the tongue than by the rapier ... [A] theatrical production might do well to prefer a light, though physically incapacitating wound to a comprehensive skewering'. A similar sensitivity to the play's true character as a duel of words, or flyting, would have calmed the kind of worries expressed by the director, Michael Langham, who first commissioned Anthony Burgess to translate the play. In his introduction, Burgess (1991) reports Langham's rather po-faced annoyance at the content of Act 4, and particularly the distracting and 'unrealistic' arrival of Roxane. Because of this, Burgess was forced 'to substitute for Roxane's personal appearance the arrival of a letter from her, which she, distant and disembodied, had to breathe into a microphone while the lights dimmed and perfume was sprayed through the auditorium'. It is difficult to imagine a more comprehensive way of missing the point of this Act, and even Burgess himself confesses that Roxane's 'Platonic rhetoric' sounds unreal 'on speaking lips'. Yet by this stage one would have thought that the continually self-renewing nature of the characters' languages would have bounced such concerns with realism out of court. It doesn't matter if we can't entirely believe Roxane's tale of enemy Spanish gallantry. We *might* care to interpret the catalogue of fantastic foodstuffs she carries out from Paris simply as the entertaining hallucinations of the starving cadets. But even this is not the point. What matters are the words themselves, 'Peacock truffle!', 'cushions ... stuffed wae [with] finches!', 'carafes [of] rubies ... carafes a topazes', and the mercurial speed with which Roxane flashes from one monosyllable to the next, expressing a *joie de vivre* marvellously caught in Morgan's translation:

> Sh! – Rid or white? – Breid fur this hungry brood! –
> A knife! – Yer plate! – Piece a crust? – Mair?–
> Ah'll serve ye! A wing? – Drap a Burgundy? (Morgan, 1992a: 127)
>
> [Sh! – Red or white? – Bread for this hungry brood! –/A knife! – Your plate! – Piece of crust? – More? –/I'll serve you! A wing? – Drop of Burgundy?]

And *what* of Christian's death? There is, after all, something more comic than tragic about poor Christian hauled off to war before being able to consummate his marriage and then instantly sacrificed to the first round of grapeshot. It is pathetic, certainly, but not tragic. Significantly, at the end of the play, Roxane never refers to Christian once she is sure that it is Cyrano's voice she has been listening to all these years. He no longer matters, never *really* mattered in fact because Roxane never *really* loved him. What she really loves is language, poetry, but an inexhaustible language, a language of peacock-coloured bravura, a language that tastes of the 'uncategorisable' taste of truffle, a language that creates even as it reveals ... love, a soul, what Matthew Arnold (1909: 170) called a 'buried life'. It is, in fact, a language that ultimately eschews the 'artificiality' of 'wit', as Cyrano confesses to Roxane while wooing her on Christian's behalf. Well then, Roxane asks, 'What wurds will *you* speak?' and Cyrano replies, his own voice breaking through, a Glaswegian of stuttering eloquence:

>   Aw those, aw those, aw those
> That come tae me, Ah'll bunch them, hurl them, no
> In a neat bouquet: Ah love ye, Ah'm chokin, Ah know
> Ah'm crazy, Ah love ye, Ah'm at the end a ma tether;
> Ma hert's a bell, yer name's there in aw weather,
> It hings and shivers as Ah shiver, Roxane,
> It rings oot, bell and clapper, *Roxane, Roxane*! (Morgan, 1992a: 92)[1]
>
> [All those, all those, all those/That come to me, I'll bunch them, hurl them, not/ In a neat bouquet: I love you, I'm choking, I know/I'm crazy, I love you, I'm at the end of my tether;/My heart's a bell, your name's there in all weather,/It hangs and shivers as I shiver, Roxane,/It rings out, bell and clapper, *Roxane, Roxane*!]

To talk of the 'true' Cyrano is not to subscribe to an essentialist view of personality. What we are speaking of here is something deeper or, rather, something *other* than that, something impossible to name, a fundamental human energy that coalesces and is perhaps most visible in the play of language, bringing all the elements of what we see and interpret as 'personality' into play, juggling them, Cinquevalli-like before our eyes. We are not far, here, from Morgan's concern with the very nature of writing and its existence as a form of translation. Nor from Walter Benjamin's thoughts about the concealed 'language of truth' that it is the 'task of the translator to release in his own language' and which Morgan (1990b and 1992b) quotes in two essays on the art of translation. Here, Morgan writes:

> It is as if the translator had to get *behind* [my emphasis] the words of the foreign poem, through his understanding of them, through his analysis of their meaning and their associations, until he is in touch with a deverbalised poem, a brain pattern (possibly) of nervous or electrical energy which he can then reverbalise into his own language.
> (Morgan, 1992b: 45)

Cyrano de Bergerac is, to date, Morgan's most colourful and successful attempt at 'reverbalising' the 'hidden poem' of which Cyrano himself is perhaps the most perfect metaphor. Not only is this play a play about language and about the theatre, it is a play about translation and the state of 'pure language' which these other languages serve.

At the beginning of this chapter, I identified three main purposes behind Morgan's decision to translate this play and I should like to conclude by turning to the third of these, the issue of Cyrano's marginality.

Morgan's concern with the styles and textures of his translation does not exclude, and indeed is intimately related to, his interest in his hero's vulnerability, his sense of lack. It is, of course, from Cyrano's ugliness, his sense of personal unworthiness, that his verbal energy derives and which it tries to supplement and transform. The connection between the two is best summed up in a couplet from Act 2 scene 10:

CHRISTIAN: Oh tae be able tae express things sweet and clear!
CYRANO: Oh tae be a neat wee handsome musketeer!
(Morgan, 1992a: 70–1)

In the introduction to his edition of the play, Woollen (1994: xii) dismisses what some commentators have seen as an underlying homoerotic element in the play. 'Rostand', he writes, 'does not subscribe to a theory which would drastically alter our interpretation of the interpersonal dynamics in the play'. Morgan, however, in his introduction, after mentioning the historical Cyrano's homosexuality, notes in parenthesis that this element 'could offer the theme of frustrated love an added resonance, scarcely but perhaps just audible in the play itself' (Morgan, 1992a: x). I have been able to identify two moments in the play where Morgan's translation broadens the range of interpretations available to actor and critic in this respect, without in any way gratuitously distorting the characters' relations with each other. It is worth looking at them for this reason, but also because they offer further proof of Morgan's ingenuity as a translator and, in one case at least, of how he possibly improves on Rostand's original.

Shortly after the whimsical reference to the 'neat wee musketeer', Cyrano's vision of what he can do for Christian and Christian for him takes on a breathless, rhapsodic dimension quite in keeping with the urgent, striving character of his love analysed earlier. Cyrano's ambition is to win Roxane 'by perfect fusion' with Christian (Morgan, 1992a: 71). His desire is to infuse his words with such power that they become a kind of flesh; and, significantly, Morgan chooses precisely this word to translate Rostand's more cerebral '*beauté*' (Besnier, 1983: 156), a beauty that is to be the perfect amalgam of Cyrano's wit and Christian's good looks. It is interesting, here, to compare Rostand with both the Morgan and Burgess versions of the play. In Rostand, Christian is astonished, moved even, by Cyrano's apparent generosity. He is also slightly bewildered by it. Rostand conveys this sense of wonderment by using stycomythia to alternate Christian's questions with Cyrano's explanations. Just as Cyrano seems on the point of giving himself away, Rostand inserts the following stage direction: *'se reprenant, et en artiste'*. Cyrano draws back, remembers who he is speaking to and passes off the ploy as a poetic joke he would enjoy. Turning to Morgan and Burgess's translations, it is as if Burgess has paid too much attention to this stage direction and Morgan too little. First of all, Burgess gives much less scope to Christian's bewilderment than either Rostand or Morgan and then, in the passage that follows the stage direction, gives these words to Cyrano:

> CHRISTIAN: I say what I said
> At first: I don't quite –
> CYRANO: Understand. Unsure
> About my motive? Simple: it's pure art.
> The finest lines of the dramatist are dead
> Without the actor's partnership. One whole
> Is made from our two halves – your lips, my soul. (Burgess, 1991: 79)

In comparison with Morgan's version, and even with the original French, this is dry, intellectual, a mere conceit. There *is* conceit, in all senses of the word, present in Cyrano's wordplay as given by Morgan but the difference, surely, is that it is *felt*. It has its origins in the emotions, not the brain. Here is the full exchange:

> CYRANO: Ye willin?
> CHRISTIAN: Why has it meant
> Such pleasure tae ye?
> CYRANO: Ah, it wid ...
>   provide amusement.
> A poet's temptit by sich escapades.
> Ah'll be your hauf, you ma hauf, and the shades
> Will gaird me as Ah gaird you, new and fresh.
> Ah'll be your flashin wit, you'll flash ma flesh. (Morgan, 1992a: 72)

[CYRANO: You willing?//CHRISTIAN: Why has it meant/Such pleasure to you?//CYRANO: Ah, it would ... provide amusement./A poet's tempted by such escapades./I'll be your half, you my half, and the shades/Will guard me as I guard you, new and fresh./I'll be your flashing wit, you'll flash my flesh.]

There is an intimacy here that slightly deepens the relationship with Christian as articulated by Rostand. How does Morgan achieve this? One of the things he does, is to replace the abstract French verb *compléter* with the more physical, colloquial 'hauf'. With *compléter* it is as if Cyrano merely 'adds to' Christian's gifts in some way, whereas Morgan's two 'haufs' offer the image of an ideal whole, a oneness. Then, there is Morgan's poetic, moving use of the Scots verb 'gaird' which has the sense of 'protect' as well as 'guard' and 'keep'. In Rostand, Cyrano simply walks *'dans l'ombre à ton côté'* but in Morgan it is as if Cyrano's longing soul overflows into the surrounding night, animating the shadows of a protective embrace. And then those shadows are pierced, penetrated by the flashing onomatopoeia of the final line, words made flesh indeed. These shadows are 'shades', the supernatural connotations are also present, beckoning both Christian and Cyrano to the dark curtain of the final act.

What this strategy implies, of course, remains in the realm of echo, or 'resonance', as Morgan puts it. There is no attempt to dramatically 'alter the interpersonal dynamics of the play' (Woollen, 1994: 12). Cyrano is not gay. He is in love with Roxane, not Christian. But his anguished outreaching to Christian, which involves him in an epistolary and vocal commitment that goes beyond a vision of the young man as the mere 'completion' of his true self, offers uncanny parallels with classic interpretations of the origins and nature of homosexuality. In such theories the desire for the other's body is grounded in a desire to *be* it because the other offers an image of beauty that the desiring man experiences in himself, perhaps quite erroneously, as a lack. Crudely put, it is a desire not so much for the *other* as for *more* of the *same*; the recipient becomes a mirror that reflects back a slightly different, because perfected, image of the sender. Hence the view of homosexuality as an exacerbated form of narcissism. What Cyrano sees when he looks at Christian is not, ultimately, a handsome young man, but the mirror image of his own inner beauty. And it is appropriate that such reflections should inscribe the baroque textures of this play. Cyrano's desire is not homosexual but its co-ordinates echo a pattern familiar in the history of gay love. Cyrano's love, after all, cannot speak its name except in disguise, except through the shapely contours of another man. Let us listen to how that frustration vents itself in Morgan's version at a significant moment in Act 3 scene 7.

Cyrano, partially hidden, is wooing Roxane who stands, Juliet-like, on the balcony above. She notes with unconscious irony that her lover's voice sounds different, and he replies:

> CYRANO: Aye, it's quite different. The night's ma gaird and grot.
> Here Ah kin daur tae be me, kin daur ...
> But what –
> Ah don't know – aw this – forgie me – stealin
> Ower me, new and wunnerfu, the feelin ...
> ROXANE: It's new?
> CYRANO: It's new ... totally ... tae be sincere ...
> Ma hert ay nippit ... tae be laughed at ... the fear ... (Morgan, 1992a: 90–1)

[CYRANO: Yes, it's quite different. The night's my guard and grot./Here I can dare to be me, can dare ... But what – /I don't know – all this – forgive me – stealing/Over me, new and wonderful, the feeling ... // ROXANE: It's new?//CYRANO: It's new ... totally ... to be sincere ... /My heart always constricted, inhibited ... to be laughed at ... the fear ...]

This is Cyrano at his most touching, most atypical yet most sincere. Note, again, that protective 'gaird', present in his speech to Christian. Here, he catches himself off guard, shocked more by the novelty of sincerity than by the power of the love that inspires it. It is a reaction familiar to those who have been forced to suppress strong and unusual passion, and Morgan catches its poignancy exactly by giving the inarticulate slightly more room to breathe and more space to signify than Rostand does. He allows this by slowing down the pace of the exchange and by reducing the eloquence of Cyrano's remarks and pauses. In Rostand, one is sure that Cyrano's hesitation is that of a poet searching for the *mot juste*, and we expect him to find it. The Scots version, however, is – more movingly – less assured, the momentary stutter of a big bear of a Glaswegian gobsmacked by a sudden vision of the pitiful, wonderful irony of his situation.

That situation is also the situation of the poet, the writer, the translator of hidden and secret messages, here momentarily at a loss for words to express himself adequately. It is the moment, perhaps, that links all these ideas about language, translation, national identity, love and frustration together in one complex and interrelated whole. 'Here is another paradox', Morgan writes:

> [At] times when states are anxious to establish their national identity and to prove the virtues of their language, they have very often in history indulged in widespread translation from other cultures; yet in

the process of doing this they subtly alter their own language, joining it in many unforeseen ways to a greater continent of almost undefined and non-specific human expression. (Morgan, 1990b: 234)

Cyrano turns to Christian, borrows, translates the beautiful lines of his body in order to speak, to express himself to Roxane. But that involuntary turn to the other – in which he yet recognises glimmerings of his own true self – is a shattering experience. You cannot love another human being without being changed, less like yourself, more like the other. As Morgan says, you cannot translate from another tongue without altering your own and discovering how 'the quest for the most native will turn out to draw [you] into the most universal'. Cyrano's moment of epiphany is shockingly and movingly inarticulate. Like the figure of the translator in Morgan's essay, '[h]e pauses in an astounding landscape, almost afraid to move. When he moves, he is no longer himself. And that is it' (Morgan, 1990b: 235).

I should like to end, however, more simply. Much of what has gone before has spoken of Morgan as an extremely skilled and sensitive translator, continually suggesting that this skill and sensitivity derives from his own practice and interests as a poet. Much has been written of Morgan the ludic experimenter, the adventurous manipulator of forms, but this translation also offers confirmation of Morgan's gifts as a poet of exceptional *lyric* power. He has insisted on the contribution that the Scots tongue can make in this sphere, and I should like to draw attention to just one more example that sticks in the mind the way a good poem does – long after the curtain has come down.

At the end of Act 1, Cyrano hails nocturnal Paris and describes the moon '*[qui] coule aux pentes des toits bleus*' (Besnier, 1983: 96). One English translation shows us roofs 'like bright shields braving the moon' (Fry, 1975: 33), but Morgan recognises both the accuracy in the colour of those roofs and the vivid poetic charge to be derived from so palpable a detail. And so we get:

Muinlicht seepin doon blue roofs, a frame
Ower fine fur scenes that huv nae hamely name. (Morgan, 1992a: 38)

[Moonlight seeping down blue roofs, a frame/Too fine for scenes that have no homely name.]

That dash of blue and the care with which Morgan positions it in the line are a sure indication of the quality of Morgan's intelligence as a translator. It doesn't just recall the Impressionist painters that were Rostand's contemporaries but the thing itself, the dark blue evening roofs of Paris, and it makes a poet of Edwin Morgan.[2]

Notes

1. The first line of this quotation is given in the Carcanet edition as 'Aw those, aw those, as those'. Edwin Morgan has confirmed that there is a misprint and that 'as' should read 'aw'.
2. This essay was commissioned for this volume but an earlier version was published in *Scotlands* 5 (2). See Kinloch (1998).

Chapter 8
Mayakovsky and Morgan

STEPHEN MULRINE

Vladimir Nabokov, in the foreword to his English version of Pushkin's *Eugene Onegin*, identifies three kinds of translation, as far as poetry is concerned: *paraphrase*, broadly a free version which may on occasion, he concedes, be stylish and idiomatic, but which should fool no-one; *lexical*, basically word for word; and *literal*, which Nabokov regards as the only 'true' form of translation, since it 'render[s], as closely as the associative and syntactical capacities of another language allow, the exact contextual meaning of the original'. To his declared ideal of literalism, in *Eugene Onegin*, Nabokov claims to have 'sacrificed everything (elegance, euphony, clarity, good taste, modern usage, and even grammar) that the dainty mimic prizes higher than truth' (Nabokov, 1964: viii, x). Surplus to Nabokov's requirements, too, is rhythm. A short passage chosen at random will illustrate what that means. Here are four lines from Pushkin's original, with the stressed syllables in capitals:

> ONEgin BYL gotOV so MNOIyu
> uVIdet' CHUZHdyE stranY;
> no SKOro BYli MY sud'BOIyu
> na DOLgii SROK razVEdenY. (Pushkin, 1984: 29)

Pushkin, the supreme craftsman, orders his iambic tetrameters to rhyme on key words, as one would expect, and the passage flows with consummate ease. Nabokov, however, offers us this:

> Onegin was prepared with me
> to see alien lands;
> but soon we were to be by fate
> sundered for a long time. (Nabokov, 1964)

Pushkin's masterpiece is thus presented to English readers in the form of an unlovely schoolboy crib, and its poetry is surely lost. Nabokov's ineptitude may of course be feigned, but the real victim of his arrogant polemic is Pushkin, and in my view the responsible translator should attempt to render *all* the meanings of a poem, not simply its story.

My own experience as a translator from Russian, chiefly of drama, leads me to conclude that the process may be likened to serving three masters. The first is the original author, and his or her meaning, to the limits of one's comprehension of the language; and the second is one's own language, its idiom and peculiar character. The third master, however, and no less demanding, requires the translator to acknowledge that he or she is engaged in a creative act; that Russian characters, made vocal in English, are new people, engaged in a new play, just as translated poems are new poems. 'Academic' translations not uncommonly fail at that level, because they are made by linguists, not by artists. Poetry, one could claim, should be translated by poets. Of course it may be argued that the relative scarcity of poets who also read Russian makes that impractical, which no doubt explains the very large number of English free verse renderings of tightly-rhymed originals. Like Nabokov's *Eugene Onegin,* such work 'tells the story' of the poem, but amounts to little more than a white flag of surrender.

It goes without saying that the primary requirement of any translation is accuracy, in the sense of avoiding unwitting error, and in that respect, Edwin Morgan's Scots versions of Mayakovsky in *Wi the Haill Voice* [1] (Morgan, 1972) are almost watertight. A rare lapse in 'Mandment No. 2 to the Army o the Arts', has Mayakovsky haranguing his misguided fellow-poets:

That means you –
cooerin wi the mystical leafletfuls,   [cowering with]
yir broos aa runklt like plewland –   [your brows all wrinkled like
futuristicos   ploughed land]
imaginisticos
acmeisticos [2]

The second line appears impenetrable, and in Russian, the stanza opens:

Eto vam –
prikryvshiesya listikami mistiki [3]

The literal meaning, however – 'mystics covered with leaflets' – places symbolist or obscurantist poets at the top of Mayakovsky's hit list, and not even a possible secondary sense for *prikryvshiesya,* of 'cowering behind', rescues Morgan's line from uncharacteristic error. On the other hand, the stanza ends with a description of poets, '*zaputavshiesya v pautine rifm*' – literally, 'entangled in a spider's web of rhyme' – and Morgan's 'trachlt in moosewabs o crambo-doodlin' [bedraggled in spider webs of verse-doodling] leaves the original gasping for breath.

Mayakovsky's side-swipes at his fellow-practitioners, and the art in general, tend to bring out the best in Morgan, and the title poem of the collection, 'Wi the Haill Voice' [With the Whole Voice], offers a fine example of the strengths of this translation. The Russian original engages in some complex word-play (internal rhyme and alliteration mainly):

Zasadila sadik milo,
dochka,
           dachka,
                   vod'
                       i glad' –
'sama sadik ya sadila
sama budu polivat''.
Kto stikhami l'et iz leiki,
kto kropit,
           nabravshi v rot, –
kudrevatye Mitreiki,
                   mudrevatye Kudreiki –
kto ikh k chertu razberet!

[*Literally*: She sweetly planted a little garden, daughter, cottage, water, smooth surface – 'I planted a little garden by myself, and I'll water it.' Some pour verses from watering cans, others gather them in their mouths and spray them out – the ornate Mitreiks, the obscure Kudreiks – who the devil can make them out!] [4] (Mayakovsky is poking fun here at two minor poets of the day, Mitreikin and Kudreikin.)

Morgan not only matches this, but surpasses his original, and the concreteness of his language gives real bite to Mayakovsky's garden metaphors:

Her wee bit gairden was as mim as its gairdner –
denty dochter
           simmer cotter,
                   loch watter,
                           laich lauchter.
'Alone I garden all my garden,
alone I'll water it and sort it.'
Some crambo squeeters through a watterin-spoot,
some makars
           skoot it fae distendit cheeks.
Squirblesome Berrymans,
                   Betjemanly squerrs – hoots,
wha can untaigle the dreichs fae the dreeps!

[Her wee bit of garden was as prim as its gardener –/dainty daughter,/ summer tenant,/loch water,/low laughter./[...]/Some verse flies in all directions from a watering-spout,/some poets squirt it from distended cheeks./ Trickily intricate Berrymans,/Betjemanly squares – pooh,/who can distinguish the bores from the drips!]

Mayakovsky's list *'dochka, dachka, vod', i glad"* is transformed in this version, and 'laich lauchter', entirely Morgan's, introduces an unseen audience to some effect. Here again, Mayakovsky's last line – *'kto ikh k chertu razberet'* – has no particular sound value, and Morgan's solution not only catches the dismissive tone, but plays brilliantly on 'dreichs' and 'dreeps'.

It will be obvious that Morgan expands his original at almost every turn, and at a basic word-count level, that is to be expected. Russian is a highly inflected language, with a much freer word order than English, to the extent that it manages quite comfortably without definite and indefinite articles, and any translation therefore involves a degree of 'unstuffing'. Subtle variations in the meaning of a verb, for example, which would demand a prepositional phrase or an adverbial clause in English, are expressed by a complex system of prefixes, and almost 80% of Volume III, for instance, of the standard four-volume Russian dictionary (Evgen'eva, 1981), consists of words beginning with 'p', as a consequence. Thus a single polysyllabic word in Russian will often be rendered by four or five in English. There is an attendant risk that the English translation will appear less intense and focused than the original, and this is something that Morgan's Scots does not always avoid. In 'Vladimir's Ferlie' [*ferlie* = wonder], for example, Mayakovsky retreats before the advancing sun in a regular quatrain, as neat as a nursery rhyme:

Khochu ispug ne pokazat' –
i retiruyus' zadom.
Uzhe v sadu ego glaza.
Uzhe prokhodit sadom.

[I don't want to show my fear – and I beat a retreat. His eyes are already in the garden. He's already passing through the garden.]

Morgan's version not only incorporates several enjambments, at the cost of Mayakovsky's emphatic rhythm,

wi its fiery stoggin: the sun! And me,
I want naethin but to hide my trimmlin,
I mak a wee retreat. But its ee
's in the gairden noo: and noo it's thrimmlin

richt through
the gairden.

[with its fiery stabbing: the sun! And me,/I want nothing but to hide my trembling,/I make a wee retreat. But its eye/'s in the garden now: and now it's threading/right through/the garden.]

but also an awkward chime on 'gairden', not heard in the Russian *'v sadu/ sadom'*, thanks to its case system.

Morgan's expansive manner very often opens up the poem, filling gaps in the reader's understanding, where both Mayakovsky, and the Russian language, have a tendency to the cryptic. However, Mayakovsky occasionally adopts a simple, almost childlike mode of address, for good agitprop reasons, but Morgan rarely follows him. His version of *'Maiskaya pesenka'*, 'May Day', for example, begins very promisingly:

Leafikie leafikie green!
We ken the winter's awa.
Lat's gang
      whaur's the swire's as bricht's a preen,
me
   and you
      and us an aa.

[Leafikie, leafikie green!/We know the winter's away./Let's go where the dip in the hill's as bright as a pin,/me and you and us as well.]

However, the uncertain shuffle of the ending is no match for the original:
i ya,
  i ty,
    i my.

Also, in succeeding stanzas, Mayakovsky repeats the rhythm of his little refrain as an exhortation:

Krasnye flagi
nesem!
  Nesem!
    Nesem!

which means, literally, 'Let's carry red flags!' While Morgan's expansion may have more charm, the agitprop punch of the original is considerably weakened:

Lat's cairry a lowe mair rid nor thae –
flaggies

and banners
   and streamers an aa.

[Let's carry a flame more red than those –/little flags and banners and streamers too.]

This can be seen even more clearly in Mayakovsky's untitled couplet addressed to the doomed bourgeoisie (here with the stressed syllables in capitals, to point up its emphatic rhythm):

ESH' anaNAsy, RYABchikov ZHUi,
DEN' tvoi poSLEDnii priKHOdit, burZHUi.

In the Russian, the lines are as undecorated as a slogan, like one of Mayakovsky's ROSTA[5] poster captions. They translate literally as:

Eat pineapples, chew grouse,
Your last day is approaching, bourgeois.

In Morgan's version, 'To the Bourgeoisie', this becomes:

Stick in, douce folk. – Pineaipple, feesant's breist:
stuff till ye boke, for thon is your last feast.

[Eat your fill, respectable folk. – Pineapple, pheasant's breast:/stuff till you vomit, for that is your last feast.]

Despite fewer syllables, oddly enough, and a neat internal rhyme, the arrow straightness is gone, and along with it something of the couplet's 'historical inevitability'.

In the great majority of instances, however, Morgan's additions to Mayakovsky's text are felicitous, and make a genuine virtue out of the necessity to expand, which Russian imposes on the translator into English or Scots. Often they take the form of exposition, clarifying Mayakovsky's intention, as in the poem '*A vy mogli by?*' ('Ay, but can ye?'). The Russian is very spare, and distinctly cryptic:

Na cheshue zhestyanoi ryby
prochel ya zovy novykh gub.
A vy
noktyurn sygrat'
mogli by
na fleite vodostochnykh trub?

This might be literally rendered:

On the scales of a tin fish
I have read the cries from new lips.
But could you
play a nocturne
on a flute (made) of drain-pipes?

Without weakening the force of Mayakovsky's metaphor, Morgan's version makes all clear, and manages a side-swipe, not in the original, at the reactionary opposition:

A tin fish, ilka scale a mou –
I've read the cries o a new warld through't.
But you
wi denty thrapple
can ye wheeple
nocturnes fae a rone-pipe flute?

[A tin fish, each scale a mouth –/I've read the cries of a new world through't./But you/with dainty windpipe/can you whistle/nocturnes from a gutter-pipe flute?]

Elsewhere, sheer creative exuberance directs Morgan's hand, and the relationship to the original can be somewhat tenuous. In 'Versailles' ('*Versal*') for example, Mayakovsky reflects on the garden's fountains and ornamental lakes, etc., created to provide a pleasant atmosphere for the courtiers,

chtob zhizn' im
      byla
           svezha

While this translates literally as, 'so that life might be cool/fresh for them', Morgan accepts the idea, but goes his own way:

juist to mak shair
      that their air
           had a surfeit
o douceness and nae foof

[just to make sure that the air had a surfeit/of sweetness and no stink]

And where Mayakovsky's paths are 'full of statues', Morgan's are 'hoatchin wi stooky shades' [heaving with plaster shadows]. Generally, 'Versailles' offers a good illustration of Morgan's tendency to work up Mayakovsky's outline sketch to full-colour portrait. The pleasure-seeking

Parisians, driving past in their shining cars, are simply listed by Mayakovsky thus:

Teper'
    po nei
        veselyi Parizh
gonyaet
    avto rassiyav, –
kokotki,
    rant'e, podschitavshii barysh,
amerikantsy
    i ya.

[Now gay Paris drives shining along it – coquettes, *rentiers* having counted up their profits, Americans, and I.]

But in Morgan's Scots, the procession is even more eye-catching:

Noo
    Paris
        taks its pleesure on it,
caurs flee by
    in a glintin stream ...
wee hures,
    landlords fu o grace and the gear o't,
Americans,
    and me.

[Now Paris takes its pleasure on it,/cars fly by in a glinting stream ... /wee whores, landlords full of grace and the wealth that brought it,/Americans, and me.]

Clearly, the faithfulness of Morgan's translation must be a relative concept, and its very audacity, it might be argued, is a linguistic equivalent of the bold stroke of the Revolution, celebrated by its leading spokesman *'vo ves' golos'*, 'wi the haill voice', and then some. In a Russian context, within a dominant tradition of finely-crafted verse, Mayakovsky's mass-audience address is outrageous, more resembling the 'barbaric yawp' of Whitman, say, than any of his own countrymen. The sprawling *mise-en-page*, the occasional doggerel rhymes, the declamatory manner, all give the sense of a cultivated roughneck at work, and his contribution to freedom of speech, albeit in a restricted sense, is evidenced in the number of his neologisms and eccentric coinages.

However, Mayakovsky's linguistic experiments are nowhere near as radical as those of his contemporaries, such as Kruchenykh and Khlebnikov. Moreover, his word-play, even at its most intense, retains too much meaning to qualify as *zaum* (literally, 'trans-sense'), the abstract sound-poetry invented by the Russian Futurists, who were dismissive of similar experiments by their Italian counterparts because the latter's taste for onomatopoeia was regarded as a concession to meaning. Mayakovsky, indeed, is much closer to the mainstream of Russian poetry than he might appear. His formative years were spent in rural Georgia, before he moved to Moscow in his early teens, and the voice in the poems is that of an educated Muscovite, with little in the way of dialect or archaism. *Wi the Haill Voice* is a relatively small collection, of course, some 25 poems, but they are representative, ranging over the period 1913–1930, and in comparison with Morgan's Scots versions, Mayakovsky's neologising is generally more restrained. In the title poem, for example, Mayakovsky invents a sardonic epithet for fellow poet Sergei Esenin and his ilk:

Ya k vam pridu
       v kommunisticheskoe daleko
ne tak,
       kak pesenno-esenennyi provityaz'.

[I shall come to you, in the far-off Communist [future], not as a melodious Esenin-like super-hero.]

The portmanteau word *pesenno-esenennyi* attaches the notions of 'song' and 'Esenin-like' to an archaic term for 'hero', or 'knight'. Morgan's version is alert to every nuance, both of sound and meaning, and even underscores the irony with a play on 'Esenin' and 'Messiah':

I'll reach ye
       in yon communistic hyne-awa.   [that; far distance]
I'm no
       some yestersingin messeniniah-gent.

Mayakovsky's creativity is perhaps better illustrated in his extended metaphors, and his mass-proletariat *'Atlanticheskii okean'* ('Atlantic Ocean') is an extraordinary flight of fancy, well-matched by Morgan, with 'watter-partisans', 'central widewatter-committee', 'districk wave-committee', etc., and even improved upon, when the straightforward *'ekvatoru v tsirkul"* becomes a resounding 'circumequatoriality'. Mayakovsky's touching little scene of the whale family, awaiting their version of the Constructivist radiant future, is another opportunity that Morgan is quick to seize:

I pod vodoi
  delovito i tikho
dvortsom
  rastet
    korallov pletenka,
chtob legshe zhilos'
    trudovoi kitikhe
s rabochim kitom
    i doshkol'nym kitenkom.

[And under the water, busily and quietly, a wickerwork of coral grows like a palace, so that the labouring whale cow, and her worker bull-whale and infant (pre-school) whale calf, might have a better life.]

And underwatter a thing's growin,
  strang but wary-like,
a palace
  o the skeely
    coral-craturs,
to lichten the burden
  for workin whale-wives,
disjaskit jock-whales
  and garten-whale-kinder.

[And underwater a thing's growing, strong but wary-like,/a palace of the skilful coral-creatures,/to lighten the burden for working whale-wives,/ exhausted man-worker-whales and kindergarten whales.]

One might take issue with Morgan's 'strang but wary-like', for *'delovito i tikho'* (meaning 'quietly and efficiently'), and the wickerwork image of *'pletenka'* is missing, but it is difficult to imagine a more felicitous solution to Mayakovsky's basic whale family than that offered here, outrageous neologism to boot.

The highly inflected character of Russian, with its six noun cases, three grammatical genders, and agreement of adjectives, opens up a vein of comedy in affixing 'inappropriate' endings to words, and Mayakovsky is conforming to a well-established pattern in *'Evpatoriya'* ('Eupatoria'), celebrating the hedonistic delights of the Black Sea spa town. Over the piece, he introduces *'evpatoriiskuyu', 'evpatoriiki', 'evpator'yaki', 'evpator'- yane', 'evpatoryonki', 'evpatoryach'i', 'evpatorstvo'*. It is worth noting, however, that while Mayakovsky's invented suffixes are broadly neutral – masculine and feminine adjectival endings, nationality, 'offspring', abstract noun (cf. English *-ish*, *-ian*, *-let*, *-ation*) – Morgan's equivalents, 'Eupatorium', 'Eupadandycats', 'Eupajollocks', 'Eupataptoos', 'Eupataryan', 'Eupajinkajanks', have a wild life of their own. Thus, where Mayakovsky's sunbathing Muscovites are described as *'moskvichi-evpator'yane'*, with the grammatical ending simply borrowed from words such as *grazhdane* [citizens], *anglichane* [Englishmen], and so on, Morgan's 'Muscovite-Eupataryan' contrives another layer of meaning, suggesting the stereotype pale-skinned Aryan:

And him,
        fair pechin for as dark a skin,   [panting]
puir Muscovite –   [poor]
        Eupataryan!

Again, Mayakovsky's spare commendation of the curative properties of the local mud:

Vse bolezni
    vyzhmut
        goryachie
gryazi
    evpatoryach'i

[Eupatorian hot mud squeezes out every illness]

becomes:

Ilka seikness
    cries Kamerad
        uncondeetional
to the glaury plaisters
        Eupamedeecinal.

[Every sickness cries Kamerad unconditional/to the mud plasters Eupa-medicinal.]

Likewise, in 'The Ballad o the Rid Cadie [of the Red Cap]' (*'Skazka o krasnoi shapochke'*), Morgan responds to some boisterous wordplay in the original:

Zhili pripevayuchi za kadetom kadet,
i otets kadeta i kadetov ded

The literal meaning of the lines is something like:

Cadet after cadet lived in clover,
both the cadet's father, and the cadets' grandfather.

An odd switch is signalled in the original from singular to plural 'cadets', presumably for the sake of euphony. Morgan, typically, overshoots Mayakovsky's wordplay by some distance:

> Like grumphies in claver lived the haill Cadet caboodle,
> the Cadet and his cadaddy and his grampacadoodle.
>
> [*grumphies* = pigs; *claver* = clover; *haill* = whole]

One would have to be utterly humourless not to enjoy lines like these, though their debt to Mayakovsky is not obvious. However, the preceding couplet of this agitprop fairytale presents an aspect of Morgan's translation that I find less engaging. The poem has a few suspect rhymes, but it is in the main regular, both in metre and syntax, and when Mayakovsky's neat and emphatic lines,

> *Uslyshit kadet – revolyutsiya gde-to,*
> *shapochka seichas zhe na golove kadeta.*

become

> He thocht he heard a revo – wheesht thought – LUTION, rid and bluidy!
> The wee Cadet was ready wi his bluid-rid cadie.
>
> [He thought he heard a revo – silence thought – LUTION, red and bloody!/The wee Cadet was ready with his blood-red cap.]

the impression is one of straining for effect.

Morgan occasionally follows Mayakovsky in his excursions into doggerel (this same poem, for example, rhymes 'somebody' with 'body') but more often he opts for euphony, and his attention to half-rhymes and the like is assiduous. The opening lines of 'The Atlantic' are particularly challenging in this respect:

> *Ispanskii kamen'*
>   *slepyashch i bel,*
> *a steny –*
>   *zub'yami pil.*
> *Parokhod*
>   *do dvenadtsati*
>   *ugol' el*
> *i presnuyu vodu pil.*
> *Povel*
> *parokhod*
>   *okovannym nosom*
> *i v chas,*

sopya,
> *vobral yakorya*
>> *i ponessya.*
Evropa
> *skrylas', mel'chas'.*

[Spanish stone, blinding and white, and walls like saw-teeth. The steamer ate coal till twelve o'clock and drank fresh water. The steamer turned its iron-clad nose round at exactly one o'clock, snuffling, weighed anchor and pulled out. Europe disappeared, growing smaller.]

Here, Mayakovsky's first four end-rhymes include the doggerel pairing *pil/pil*, the one meaning 'a saw', the other 'drank'. Russian is easier to rhyme in than English, but rhymes wholly dependent on inflected endings tend to be heard as unsatisfactory. Mayakovsky's grouping of *sopya/yakorya/ponessya* thus sounds weak, and Morgan's rhymes are distinctly more solid:

Spain blins the ee
> wi its white stane,
its waas staun
> like teeth on a saw.
Till twal,
> the steamer lined its wame
wi coals,
> and drank fresh watter an aa.
The steamer's
> airn-ticht snoot
>> gied a trimmle
and at wan o'clock
wi a snort,
> up-anchort
>> and oot o the dock.
Europe
> began to hiddle and dwinnle.

[Spain blinds the eye with its white stone,/its walls stand like teeth on a saw./Till twelve, the steamer lined its stomach/with coals, and drank fresh water as well./The steamer's iron-tight snout gave a tremble/and at one o'clock/with a snort, up-anchored and out of the dock./Europe began to huddle and fade.]

Again, at first sight, Morgan's word-splitting in 'Brooklyn Brig' (*'Bruklinskii most'*) seems perverse, since it appears to match nothing in Mayakovsky:

This makar'll no be blate

at namin
what's guid.
> Blush rid
>> at my praises, you s-
uperunited states-man –
>> rid
>>> as the flamin
flag o Sovetsky Soyuz.

[This poet'll not be shy at naming/what's good. Blush red at my praises, you s-/uperunited states-man – red as the flaming/flag of Sovetsky Soyuz.]

However, the original is equally unconventional, albeit in a different way, rhyming the English word 'of', hung out to dry on the end of its line, with *slov*:

Na khoroshee
> *i mne ne zhalko slov.*
Ot pokhval
> *krasnei,*
>> *kak flaga nashego materiika,*
khot' vy
> *i raz'yunaited stets*
>> *of*
Amerika.

[I'm not sparing of words for the good. Blush red from praise, like our flag, no matter how United States of America you may be.]

In general, though, Morgan 'tidies up' Mayakovsky's prosody, and in poem after poem, demonstrates that he is more than equal to the latter's much-admired sound patterning, as for example in '*Edu*' ('I'm aff' [off]) –

Zasvistyvai,
> *tris', vrezaisya i rezh'*
skvoz' L'ezhi
> *i ob Bryusseli.*
No nozh
> *i Parizh,*
>> *i Bryussel',*
>>> *i L'ezh –*
tomu,
> *kto, kak ya, obruseli.*

[Start whistling, loiter, plunge into and cut through Liège and around Brussels. But Paris, Brussels, Liège, is the knife to a Russified person like me.]

In Morgan's version this becomes:

Gang whusslin,
        skirr and skaig
                and slash
through Liège
        and roon by Brussels toon.
But it's Brussels,
        Paris,
            Liège
                that fash
and slash the hert
        o the Russkatoon.

[Go whistling, scurry and hurry and splatter/through Liège and round by Brussels town./But it's Brussels, Paris, Liège that trouble/and slash the heart of the Russkatoon.]

Even Mayakovsky's consciously provocative *'ob Bryusseli/obruseli'* finds its echo in 'Brussels toon'/ 'Russkatoon'.

Whether it is something inherent in his chosen medium, a certain *Dinglichkeit* (concreteness) peculiar to Scots, perhaps, Morgan's imagery is also often more direct and concrete than that of his original. The dispute between the horse and the camel, for instance, in *'Stikhi o raznitse vkusov'* ('Anent the Deeference o Tastes'), is resolved in the Russian by:

I znal lish'
        bog sedoborodnyi
chto eto -
        zhivotnye
            raznoi porody

[And only grey-bearded God knew that they were animals of a different breed.]

That 'animals of a different breed' is a rather banal conclusion, which Morgan triumphantly animates through his precise kitchen metaphor:

– Ach,
        lat auld Frosty-Pow abune unscrammle
the twa puir craturs;
            he
                kens the brose fae the gundy.

[Ach, let old Frosty-Head above unscramble/the two poor creatures; *he* knows the porridge from the toffee.]

The same rich concreteness is in evidence throughout one of the most charming pieces in the collection, 'A Richt Respeck for Cuddies' ['A Right Respect for Horses'] (*'Khoroshee otnoshenie k loshadyam'*). Mayakovsky opens with a burst of onomatopoeia that would no doubt have earned him a Futurist rebuke, the more stern because his clip-clop words are marginally meaningful:

Bili kopyta ,
Peli bydto:
– Grib.
Grab'.
Grob.
Grub.

However, where Mayakovsky's possible meanings are arbitrary – 'mushroom', 'hornbeam', 'coffin', 'coarse' – Morgan's seem better suited to their equine source:

Horse-cluifs clantert   [horse-hoofs clumped along clog-like]
giein their patter: [giving]
crippity
crappity
croupity
crunt.

Mayakovsky's image of the idle Muscovites, in their flared trousers, hurrying along Kuznetsky Most to gape at the wretched fallen horse, is wonderfully graphic:

i srazu
za zevakoi zevaka
shtany prishedshie Kuznetskim klyoshit'
strudilis',
smekh zazvenel i zazvyakal:
– Loshad' upala!
– Upala loshad'!

[And immediately, gaper after gaper, bell-bottoms sweeping the Kuznetszky, arrived. Laughter rang out again and again: 'The horse has fallen! It's fallen, the horse!']

But Morgan not only matches him, he adds some colour on his own account, the effect of which is to make the spectators appear even more idiotic:

> and wheech
> but the muckle-mou'd moochers werna lang
> in makin theirsels thrang,
> gawpus eftir gawpus, aa gaw-hawin
> alang the Kuznetsky in their bell-bottom breeks.
> 'Aw, see the cuddy's doon!'
> 'Aw, it's doon, see the cuddy!'

> [and whizz-wow/but the big-mouthed moochers weren't long/in making themselves numerous,/gaper after gaper, all gape-guffawing/along the Kuznetsky in their bell-bottom trousers./'Aw, see the horse's down!'/'Aw, it's down, see the horse!']

Especially noteworthy in this translation, moreover, is the manner in which Morgan's Scots places a rural frame around the events, transporting the 'gawpuses' from the streets of a metropolis, a world capital, albeit backward, to somewhere like the small, gossipy Scots town of Barbie in George Douglas Brown's classic Scottish novel *The House with the Green Shutters* (1901). Mayakovsky's *'Loshad' upala!/ Upala loshad'!'* is neutral, whereas Morgan's 'Aw, see the cuddy!' might have been uttered by the village idiot. That bucolic note is something of a bonus in this poem, where the subject is empathy between fellow-creatures. In fact, the comparative refinement of Mayakovsky's Russian puts some distance between narrator and horse, which is even addressed as *vy*, rather than the intimate *ty,* though it could be argued that the former is more respectful:

> *'Loshad', ne nado.*
> *Loshad', slushaite –*
> *chego vy dumaete, chto vy ikh ploshe?'*

A literal rendering might be:

> 'Don't (cry), horse,
> Listen, horse –
> why do you think you're any worse than them? ... '

Morgan's speaker, however, is altogether chummier:

> 'Ned, Ned, dinna greet!
> Listen to me, Ned –
> ye think thae buggers are the saut o the erd?'

['Ned, Ned, don't cry!/Listen to me, Ned –/you think those buggers are the salt of the earth?']

Inanimate objects, also, glow with distinctly more warmth in Morgan's version and, while the subtext of Mayakovsky's 1914 tale of the distraught fiddle, '*Skripka i nemnozhko nervno*' ('Fiddle-ma-fidgin') ['Fiddle-my-fidgeting'], concerns the poet's strained relationship with his public, the narrative follows the pattern of the previous poem – a wounded fellow-creature embraced by compassion. Given the musical context, Morgan's opening lines are markedly more sensitive to sound than the original:

> The fiddle near dwinnilt to naethin wi sichin and beseikin
> till wi a blash it burst oot greetin
> sae like a wean
> that the drum hud to say:
> 'Weel din, weel din, weel din!'
>
> [The fiddle nearly dwindled to nothing with sighing and beseeching/till with a splash it burst out crying/so like a child/that the drum had to say:/'Well done, well done, well done!']

Mayakovsky's fiddle suffers from a bad case of nerves, and keeps up a flow of importunate questioning – '*Skripka izdergalas', uprashivaya...*' [The fiddle was overwrought, asking questions...] – but there is no trace of what Morgan goes on to characterise as 'lang-dringin [long slow-sung] fiddly-bits' in its voice. While Mayakovsky's drum, which attempts to console the fiddle with '*Khorosho, khorosho, khorosho!*', might arguably be a snare-drum, with a fetching rustle, that isn't specified in the Russian *baraban,* Morgan's booming 'weel dins' are more conventionally percussive.

However, it is the rise in emotional temperature that is most notable. Mayakovsky's fellow-feeling is expressed in a significantly more neutral tone of voice than Morgan's, and again, the concreteness of the latter's imagery, which appears to come with the Scots territory, works a peculiar magic. Where Mayakovsky's speaker tells the fiddle that they are literally 'terribly alike' –

> '*Znaete chto, skripka?*
> *My uzhasno pokhozhi:*
> *ya vot tozhe*
> *oru -*
> *a dokazat' nichego ne umeyu!*'
>
> ['Do you know what, fiddle? We are terribly alike – I bawl just like you, and I can't prove anything.']

Morgan's 'decorative' additions are vividly companionable:

'D'ye ken whit, my fiddle?
The gait you're gangin's awfy like my road:
juist like you I
yowp and yowl –
and canny prove a thing to ithers!'

[D'ye know what, my fiddle?/The way you're going's awfully like my direction:/just like you I/howl and wail –/and can't prove a thing to others!]

Likewise, the poet's final offer, the suggestion that they should 'live together' (*'zhit' vmeste'*) is much more particularised in Morgan's Scots:

'D'ye ken whit, my fiddle?
We mun –
set up hoose thegither!
Whit d'ye say?'

[D'you know what, my fiddle?/We should –/set up house together!/What d'you say?]

Russian employs a very wide range of diminutive (and augmentative) noun suffixes typical of low registers, which often suggest an affectionate, but occasionally contemptuous or patronising view of the subject. The general word for 'cap', for example, is *shapka,* and *shapochka* covers both a child's cap and a uniform cap as worn by the military. The title of Mayakovsky's *'Skazka o krasnoi shapochke'* is thus aptly translated here as 'The Ballad o the Rid Cadie [of the Red Cap]'. However, the Russian idiom *'popast' pod krasnuyu shapku'* [literally, 'to end up under a red cap', i.e. in the army] long pre-dates the Revolution, as does an old saying to the effect that a fool is easily recognisable by his red cap. Accordingly, Mayakovsky's employment, later in the poem, of the pejorative *shapchonka,* 'pitiful little cap', is all the more disparaging since it is contrasted with a 'super-augmentative' adjective applied to the wind – *prebol'shushchii* – a neologism of the poet's devising, from *bol'shoi* [large]:

Podnyalsya odnazhdy prebol'shushchii veter,
v kloch'ya shapchonku izorval na kadete.

[One day there arose a mighty great wind and ripped that pitiful little cap on the cadet to shreds.]

Morgan has to admit defeat with *shapchonku,* but his Scots augmentative for the wind (lit. 'boisterous obstreporous') emphasises its mischief-making, rather than simply its force:

But up whupt a rouchlin outstrapolous blad o
wind and rippit thon cadie to a shadda.

[But up whipped a tossing-about obstreperous gust of/wind and ripped that cap to a shadow.]

Scots is also rich in affectionate or disparaging diminutives, and, in 'May Day', Morgan's 'leafikie' is a perfect match for Mayakovsky's *listiki*. In 'Wi the Haill Voice', an entire line of diminutives

ushku devicheskomu
> *v zavitochkakh voloska ...*

[a young girl's little ear, in its little curls of hair...]

goes almost effortlessly, it seems, into Scots:

wee
> curly-haslockt lassies' earickies

[wee curly-fine-haired girls' little ears]

Elsewhere, in 'Goavy-dick!' [*goavy-dick*! = wow!], for example, the Scots usage of 'bit' serves a useful turn, with *rifmishka* [*rifma* = rhyme] becoming 'bit o verse', and *voditsa* [*voda* = water] becoming 'the blue bit sea'. In 'Versailles', again, a disdainful reference to Anna Akhmatova (*stikhi* is the neutral word for 'poetry', *stishki* is a diminutive) in

k kakim-to
> *stishkam Akhmatovoi*

[some sort of little verses by Akhmatova]

is rendered:

amang the bit verses o Akhmatova

A few lines later in the same poem, another of Mayakovsky's nonce-augmentatives, *krasotishche* [from *krasota*, 'beauty'] emerges as 'beautiosity'! Mayakovsky's rousing appeal to youth, *'Tovarishchu podrostku'* [Comrade Teenager!], throws up a stanza fairly packed with patronising suffixes:

Slovom,
> *detenysh,*
bud'te tsvetochkom.
Blagoukhaite mamashe
i –
> *tochka!*

[In a word, young creature, be a nice little flower, smell sweet to your mummy.]

While *detenysh* is the routine word for the young of an animal, *tsvetochkom* and *mamashe* are diminutive forms of *tsvetok* [flower] and *mama* [mum]. Morgan's version, though he overworks the terse *tochka!* [full stop!] of the original, sounds so authentically Scottish as to make one wonder whether his 'Mayakpherson' isn't more than a joke:

In wan word,
        ma mannie,
be a wee modest flooer,
smell sweet to yir mammy,
nae mair's
        in yir pooer.

[In one word, my little man,/be a wee modest flower,/smell sweet to your mummy,/no more's in your power.]

The all-purpose 'wee', which Tom Leonard (1984: 23) famously deconstructs in his poem 'The Voyeur',[6] is also effectively deployed in the satire on Soviet bureaucracy, the non-stop proliferation of meetings and jaw-breaker acronyms, titled '*Prozasedavshiesya*' in the Russian, and masterfully reincarnated here as 'Mayakonferensky's Anectidote'. The original, as ever, is relatively spare, with the poet's attitude indicated in the regular superlative adjective *spokoineishii*, [most mild], and the first-line diminutive *golosok* [from *golos*, 'voice']:

*I slyshu
spokoineishii golosok sekretarya*

[And I hear the calmest little voice of the secretary]

Morgan, however, transforms the secretary into a memorable, and all-too familiar character:

But a wee wee voice, a wee prignickity
voice o a scriever-cum-key-skelper

[But a wee wee voice, a wee pernickety/voice of a shorthand-typist]

This is perhaps an appropriate point to consider Morgan's translation as a totality. In his own introduction to the collection, he suggests that a vein of fantastic satire in Scottish poetry makes it a more sympathetic vehicle for Mayakovsky than is Standard English. He also speaks of:

an element of challenge in finding out whether the Scots language could match the mixture of racy colloquialism and verbal inventiveness in Mayakovsky's Russian. (Morgan, 1972: 16–17)

It should be clear from the foregoing that I am in no doubt whatever of Morgan's success in meeting that challenge, and I would go so far as to say that his own 'verbal inventiveness' at times makes his exemplar appear almost feeble. Mayakovsky's Russian is less 'non-standard' than Morgan's Scots to a very considerable extent and, as I noted earlier, exhibits a degree of compression, which is partly a feature of the language, but may also reflect a certain anti-romantic posture, in keeping with the spirit of the age.

Much of Mayakovsky's work reads like slogans – lines to be shouted, rather than savoured – and while his narratives and extended metaphors are often richly inventive, there is little real kinship with the Scots tradition to which Morgan refers: that of Dunbar, Burns and MacDiarmid, whose language is as fantastical as their imaginings. I am sure this accounts for the sense I have of a pencil sketch, however detailed and lively, transmuted to a full-colour rendering. To paraphrase, *'c'est magnifique, mais ce n'est pas Mayakovsky'*. On page after page of Morgan's *Wi the Haill Voice* the reader's eye lights on some memorable phrase. 'Goavy-dick!', for example, a wry account of one of Mayakovsky's public readings, opens with an image of the moon:

Perjink and roon
    like the arse o a barrel

[Neat and round like the arse of a barrel]

but Mayakovsky merely observes that it was 'like the bottom of a barrel, in the form of a regular disc':

Kak dnishche bochki,
    pravil'nym diskom

And even where both languages felicitously agree on what the famous poet's face looks like on his publicity posters (i.e. round, flat and doughy),

gladyat
   glaza
      blinorozhiya ploskogo

Een
   gawp oot
      fae a sonsy bap-face

[Eyes stare out from a hearty bap-face] [*bap* = bread roll; *bap-faced* = face like a bap, soft and stupid-looking]

Morgan's 'sonsy' adds another dimension to the image.

The overall effect, in my view, is to make Mayakovsky sound much older and wiser. That instructional, occasionally hectoring note in the original, which both contemporaries and later critics have found tiresome, seems more acceptable in Morgan's Scots, where categorical statements appear as folk-wisdom, and not ideology. And whether it comes with the language or no, the significantly higher incidence of *things* – solid, tangible objects – in Morgan's translation, tends to the same purpose. Consider what he does with an already powerful idea in the anti-war poem '*Doloi!*' ('Awa wi it!') [Away with it!]. Mayakovsky's lines,

A khochesh' –
    umri
        pod yadernym gradom, –
tebe
  veka
    vzmonumentyat nagradu

mean something like: 'Die if you wish under a hail of shot – the centuries will reward you by monumentalising you'. Morgan, however, instinctively gives posterity a trade, turns it into a canny maker of things:

But dee
  if ye like
    in the on-ding o cannon –
the future's ay
  a dab haun
    at the cenotaphin.

[But die if you like in the hail of cannon –/the future's always a dab hand at the cenotaphing.]

The truth of the matter is that Morgan uses Mayakovsky as a launching-pad for his own cosmic excursions – these translations fit none of Nabokov's categories, being neither *lexical* nor *literal*, and they are so far removed from what Nabokov describes as *paraphrase*, the work of his despised 'dainty mimics', as to make the term critically worthless. Indeed, one wonders why Nabokov failed to suggest a fourth category, let us call it *re-creation*, to describe the process whereby a master craftsman, an outstandingly gifted poet in his own right, is also enough of a linguist to understand his source, interpret it accurately, and respectfully, and nonetheless produce a wholly new work, unmistakably his own. The fact that Morgan is translating from one 'second' language into another – i.e. from Russian into literary Scots, rather than Standard English – may even be an advantage, but there is no denying the skill with which he goes about his business.

Perhaps the most 'Soviet' piece in this collection is *'Prozasedavshiesya'*, packed as it is with insider references, and in that sense a good test of Morgan's empathy with the experience of Mayakovsky, the frenzied super-activist of the early 1920s, when the poem was written. The first and last stanzas in particular illustrate both the depth of Morgan's sympathetic understanding, and the sturdy independence of his own Muse:

> *Chut' noch' prevratitsya v rassvet,*
> *vizhu kazhdyi den' ya:*
> *kto v glav,*
> *kto v kom,*
> *kto v polit,*
> *kto v prosvet,*
> *raskhoditsya narod v uchrezhden'ya.*
> *Obdayut dozhdem dela bumazhnye,*
> *chyt' voidesh' v zdanie:*
> *otobrav s polsotni –*
> *samye vazhnye!*
> *sluzhashchie raskhodyatsya na zasedaniya.*

[Night has scarcely been transformed into dawn, than I see every day: some going to 'glav', some to 'kom', some to 'polit', some to 'prosvet'; people are dispersing to their organisations. You hardly enter the building, when paperwork showers down – selecting fifty or so, the most important, the office-workers disperse to their meetings.]

Characteristically, Morgan not only outdoes Mayakovsky in the wordplay of the title, with his 'Mayakonferensky's Anectidote', but the translation throughout is also more concrete and directly personal. In the Scots, the merry-go-round of acronymous committees is suggested by having one abbreviated ending begin the next

> folk to CENTGEN
> folk to GENCOM
> folk to COMPOLIT
> folk to POLITCENT

thus providing a neat solution to Mayakovsky's *'glav – kom – polit – prosvet'*, the exploded fragments, presumably, of *Glavnyi politiko-prosvetitel'nyi komitet Narkomprosa* ('Main Political Education Committee of the People's Commissariat for Education'). However, where Mayakovsky's people simply 'disperse to their organisations', and then repeat the action in an equally abstract fashion, such as

raskhodyatsya narod v uchrezhden'ya

and

sluzhashchie raskhodyatsya na zasedaniya

Morgan's bureaucracy is an altogether livelier affair:

hooses skail, offices fill [houses empty]
...
the boys wi the pens are gane like whittricks [gone like weasels]
to committees and cognostins and burroos and statistics. [bureaus]

The most impressive pyrotechnics, however, are reserved for the ending. Here Morgan places himself within a Scots tradition reaching back to Sir Thomas Urquhart, who could blithely double the length of the most overstuffed lists, be they animal noises or legal documents, that Rabelais had to offer (see Boston, 1975; Craik, 1993). Here, Mayakovsky yearns for just one more meeting, on the subject of the eradication of all meetings:

'*O, khotya by
eshche
odno zasedanie
otnositel'no iskoreneniya vsekh zasedanii!*'

[Oh, for one more meeting concerned with the eradication of all meetings!]

Morgan is of course handsomely assisted by the weighty Latinisms of Scots law, bowling club AGMs and the like, but the end result is magical:

'Oh for
yin mair [one more]
sederunt to convene [meeting]
to congree to conclude
to comblasticastraflocate sans avizandum [without judicial consideration]
ilka sederunt and tap-table-tandem!" [each; top-table]

There is a school of thought among translators that maintains that improving the work is no part of the job. Nevertheless, one is often confronted with clumsy locutions, muddled syntax, awkward chimes, etc., in the original, and the temptation to 'correct' them is strong. Russian, for example, has a much smaller vocabulary than English, and is less free with pronouns, so repetition of the sort that betrays slipshod revision in English often passes unremarked. Should one employ synonyms, then, perhaps not even available to the Russian author? Endless variety is so deeply embedded in our literature as to condition our expectations of other literatures, often with very different resources. There is no easy answer, I fear. Translation is always a compromise, and nowhere more so than translation of poetry, but while Nabokov's *Eugene Onegin*, for example, may be the perfect crib, one cannot imagine anyone but a student of Pushkin becoming excited by it, or indeed reading beyond its first page. Morgan's *Wi the Haill Voice*, by contrast, going hell-for-leather to the opposite extreme, is an exhilarating *tour-de-force* on its own terms; Morgan's wiser, warmer, and wittier Mayakovsky does the great Soviet poet no harm, and perhaps even much good.

Notes

1. Morgan's title is taken from one of the poems in his collection, which he has assembled from various Mayakovsky poems ranging from 1913 to 1930.
2. This and subsequent quotations from *Wi the Haill Voice* are taken from Morgan (1972). Since the title of the poem is given in each case, page references have not been supplied.
3. This and subsequent quotations in Russian are taken from Mayakovsky (1958). Since the title of the poem is given in each case, page references have not been supplied.
4. This and subsequent literal translations given in square brackets are mine. Line breaks may on occasion be omitted, where Russian word order differs significantly from English.
5. ROSTA is the acronym for the 'Russian Telegraph Agency', a title used until 1935, when it was re-named TASS, 'Telegraph Agency of the Soviet Union'.
6. Leonard's poem, originally published in 1973, reads: 'what's your favourite word dearie/is it wee/I hope it's wee/wee's such a nice wee word/like a wee hairy dog/with two wee eyes/such a nice wee word to play with dearie/you can say it quickly/with a wee smile/and a wee glance to the side/or you can say it slowly dearie/with your mouth a wee bit open/and a wee sigh dearie/a wee sigh/put your wee head on my shoulder dearie/oh my/a great wee word/and Scottish/it makes you proud' (Leonard, 1984: 23).

Chapter 9
Robert Garioch's Translations of George Buchanan's Latin Tragedies

GRAHAM TULLOCH

Any good translation of a literary work brings into interesting conjunction two creative writers, the original author and the translator. However, the conjunction is not always as interesting as that brought about by the decision of Robert Garioch Sutherland (better known as the poet Robert Garioch) to translate the two sixteenth-century Latin tragedies of George Buchanan, *Iephthes* and *Baptistes,* published together as *Jephthah and The Baptist* (Sutherland, 1959).[1]

In many ways they are very different writers. Buchanan, the internationalist, moved easily back and forth between Scotland and France and on to Spain, entirely at home as a teacher, scholar and writer in the European cultural world of Latin learning. He achieved, and retained for several centuries, an international reputation and was described by his contemporary Henri Estienne as '*poeta sui saeculi facile princeps*' (quoted in McFarlane, 1981: 17). Garioch, though he spent part of his life teaching in England, was much more culturally focused on Scotland; indeed he is, even more specifically, in his original writings as opposed to his translations, the poet of Edinburgh. He won some fame within Scotland but his work was, and is, little read and appreciated outside his native land. However, these differences overlie certain fundamental similarities. Importantly, they were both Scottish writers. Both wrote about Scotland, Buchanan principally in histories of, or satires on, contemporary events, and Garioch in his poetry. They differ in that Garioch further expressed his Scottishness by using Scots as his poetic language, whereas Buchanan wrote only a few works in Scots and mostly chose to write in Latin. However, Buchanan's choice of language should not be seen as involving the same kind of displacement of the writer's own language and culture as sometimes attends a Scot's choice to write in English. Latin had been for centuries an international language and had ceased to be tied to any one country, so a Scottish scholar had as much right as any other European scholar to consider Latin as his own language. Indeed the title pages of Buchanan's plays describe them, in

Latin, as *'Auctore Georgio Buchanano Scoto'*, 'written by George Buchanan the Scot' (Sharratt & Walsh, 1983: [21], [95]). Both writers also obviously share an interest in language. For Buchanan it was part of his professional life as a teacher, and he used his tragedies to give his students practice in speaking Latin (see Findlay, 1998a: 19–24); while Garioch's choice of Scots as a poetic language is in itself an indication of a concern with language. In this context it is significant that both writers are strongly associated with renaissances, Buchanan with *the* Renaissance in sixteenth-century France and Garioch with the so-called 'Scottish Renaissance' in twentieth-century Scotland. Both writers in their chosen medium were dealing with a language that was seen as being revived. The sixteenth-century humanists were trying to restore the pure Latinity of classical Rome after the changes wrought in medieval Latin, while the authors of the twentieth-century Scottish Renaissance were trying to give back to Scots something of the range and status it had in the time of the Middle Scots makars in the fifteenth and sixteenth centuries. Finally, while I have drawn a contrast between the internationalist Buchanan and the more locally focused Garioch, this is only partly true. Garioch, in fact, like many twentieth-century Scots poets, expressed a more international view by translating the work of European poets, most notably in his translations of Guiseppe Belli (see Christopher Whyte's chapter in this volume), but also in occasional translations of other poets (Garioch, 1983). [2]

In view of their similarities, then, it is not surprising that the conjunction of Buchanan and Garioch proves to be an interesting one. Garioch's own sense of his affinity with Buchanan finds expression in his version of Buchanan's lament at the lot of a teacher (translated as 'The Humanists' Trauchles [Struggles] in Paris') and in his own 'Garioch's Repone til [Reply to] George Buchanan'. We should not, moreover, forget the officiant in this marriage of true minds, another Scotsman, Thomas Ruddiman, whose splendid complete works of Buchanan appeared in 1715. In view of what I have just been saying, Ruddiman is an extremely appropriate intermediary, being also the author of a glossary of the most important Middle Scots translation (see Duncan, 1965: 48–59), Gavin Douglas's version of Virgil's *Aeneid* (Coldwell, 1957–64). In his works Ruddiman thus brought together an interest in the language of the Middle Scots poets (which was to provide such an important model and resource for twentieth-century poets such as Garioch), and an interest in Buchanan.

Before considering Garioch's translations of Buchanan's plays, it is helpful to consider the original plays themselves, and their relation to Buchanan's other work. Buchanan published four Latin tragedies but two of these, *Medea* and *Alcestis* (Sharratt & Walsh, 1983: 165-244), were translations from Euripedes. It was Buchanan's two original plays, *Iephthes sive Votum* ['Jepthah or the Vow'] and *Baptistes sive Calumnia* ['The Baptist or False Accusation'] (Sharratt & Walsh, 1983: 21–164) which Garioch chose to translate. According to Buchanan's autobiography, all four works were written in Bordeaux between 1540 and 1543 for his students to perform when he was teaching there in the Collège de Guyenne.[3] They thus belong amongst his earlier work, but were not published until much later (1554 and 1577, respectively) and were possibly revised before publication. In his two original plays, Buchanan follows Euripedes' model in many respects, using a Chorus and many longer speeches, and placing major events offstage. But the use of classical models does not prevent Buchanan from considering contemporary issues. In his writing he was much involved in the issues and events of his own time, in early life attacking the Franciscans in his satire *Franciscanus* and in later life writing in defence of the deposition of Mary, Queen of Scots. It is tempting therefore to speculate that the plays refer to specific events of his time but, in fact, it is hard to find close specific parallels to contemporary events. Various different commentators have attempted to demonstrate that *Baptistes* deals with, for instance, Berquin and Francis I, or Patrick Hamilton and James V, or Thomas More and Henry VIII (Sharratt & Walsh, 1983: 10–19), but the fact that there is no general agreement on its application suggests that it lacks any very specific features of contemporary events. In *Baptistes* in particular the pictures of religious intolerance and royal tyranny are conceived in very general terms that allow them to be applied to any number of specific situations. Indeed, it has been suggested that *Baptistes* was finally first published in 1554 in order to encourage James VI not to be a tyrant, although it was written and performed well before his birth (Sharratt & Walsh, 1983: 5). The two plays together illustrate in general terms that 'rejection of religious and political fanaticism' which his biographer finds characteristic of Buchanan (McFarlane, 1981: 6). This generality of situation is valuable for the translator who is, inevitably, to some degree modernising as well as translating and, as we shall see, Garioch is able to subtly suggest that *Baptistes* offers parallels with situations that occurred later than Buchanan's lifetime.

Garioch's public role as a poet began when, as a student of Honours English at Edinburgh University, he stuck his poems on the English Library board. As he tells us, 'Vexed by the Englishness of other people's poems, I reacted by presenting "Fi'baw in the Street", glottal stops and all' (Garioch, 1979: 58). His earliest poetry therefore shows not only a reaction against the Englishness of other students' poetry but a willingness to use the most stigmatised form of Scots, the language of the streets. In his later work he continued to use Scots and never lost his ear for the language of ordinary people (as is evident in the translations of Belli which he worked on in the latter part of his life), but he also expanded his range of Scots, and wrote important poems in other registers. I have elsewhere (Tulloch, 1985: 53–69) described his work as exhibiting three main registers of Scots, which I have called *broad* (as in 'Fi'baw in the Street' ['Football in the Street']), *colloquial* (as mostly in the Belli sonnets and poems like 'Bingo Saith the Lord'), and *formal* (as in 'The Muir' ['The Moor']). This simplifies the situation somewhat but it makes clear that Garioch, as he himself told Duncan Glen (1977: 7), used 'Scots of different styles for different purposes'. As part of this use of 'different styles for different purposes', Garioch in *Jephthah* and *The Baptist* employed a formal register to translate the rather formal and declamatory style of Buchanan's originals.

While in his brief autobiographical account of his early life and in a response to Duncan Glen, Garioch made a few comments about his poetry, he seems, on the whole, to have been reticent in writing about his own work. To a large degree the poems and plays must speak for themselves. But Garioch was not working in a vacuum; he played a part in the wider literary movement of the Scottish Renaissance and, if Garioch himself tells us only a little about the movement's aims and aspirations, there are others who are more forthcoming. The driving force behind the movement was, of course, Hugh MacDiarmid. Although it would be wrong to see Garioch and other writers belonging to the Scottish Renaissance as simply slavishly implementing an agenda set by MacDiarmid, it is nevertheless easy to see that Garioch's work, and in particular his translations of Buchanan, did in fact fulfil some of the objectives of MacDiarmid's programme. In translating the work of a poet and dramatist of European renown, Garioch was embarking on the 'quest for new Continental affiliations, and a more or less conscious repudiation of the dominance of English influences' that MacDiarmid had described as an emerging feature of contemporary Scottish writing (including, and perhaps especially, his own) in the twenties.[4] We know from his own already-quoted words that Garioch's 'repudiation of the dominance of English influences' was entirely conscious. Equally conscious was his choice, in Buchanan, of a writer who had, in his affiliations with continental Europe, embodied quite other influences.[5] In his Preface to the translations, Garioch contrasts Buchanan with the new nineteenth-century breed of 'Scottish men of ingyne [genius]' who were 'lukan til [looking to] England, blate o [ashamed of] their fancied provincialism' and were 'nae langer citizens o Europe, as Buchanan and the lave [the rest] had been as a maitter o course' (Sutherland, 1959: 5). At the same time, by choosing a Scottish writer, Garioch was not simply replacing English cultural dominance with the dominance of another foreign country.

As is well known, the repudiation of English influences was only one part of MacDiarmid's programme. At least as important was the rejuvenation of Scots so that it could function as a fully developed language able to express all the concerns of modern Scotland. Writing in his own name as C.M. Grieve, he praised 'Mr. Hugh M'Diarmid' for having 'addressed himself to the question of the extendability (without psychological violence) of the Vernacular to embrace the whole range of modern culture'.[6] On the face of it, Garioch, in translating the work of a sixteenth-century poet, would not seem to be extending Scots to cover 'the whole range of modern culture'. This aim would seem to be rather better fulfilled in his long poem 'The Muir' where he writes about nuclear physics. But this is only superficially the case. Leaving aside the fact that some of Buchanan's concerns are relevant to modern life, Garioch was clearly working on extending Scots in a direction that enabled him to later write material such as 'The Muir'. By choosing formal literary tragedies for translation, he was forcing himself to move beyond the confines of subject matter and therefore of language that Scottish poets had set themselves in the long years of the dominance of the Burns tradition. For Scots to deal with the whole concerns of modern life it had first to break out of that confining mould. Formal, tragic and concerned with issues of contemporary relevance, Buchanan's plays were the very antithesis of the comic, sentimental and nostalgic verse that had dominated Scottish poetry for a hundred years after Burns.

Garioch was not the first Scottish writer to translate Buchanan's plays, as he was himself well aware. In 1750, Alexander Tait, a schoolmaster at Drummelzeir, published a translation of *Iephthes*, and this was followed by translations of both plays by Alexander Gibb in 1870 and by Archibald Brown, minister of Legerwood, in 1906. In the meantime A. Gordon Mitchell, the minister of Killearn, had published separate translations, of *Iepthes* in 1903 and *Baptistes* in 1904. What makes Garioch's work unique is his decision to use Scots: all the other translations are in English. In his Preface Garioch claims that the translations of Mitchell and Brown had been 'o muckle [great] help to me in this wark' (Sutherland, 1959: 7). However he did not fall into the trap of allowing intermediary English texts to interfere with his Scots, as has happened with many translators of the Bible into Scots (Tulloch, 1989). To avoid unintentional Anglicisation it is best to work from the original foreign-language text. This Garioch clearly did – even though in writing about his early life he was inclined to be modest about his competence in Latin (Garioch, 1979: 56) – as one can see from comparing his version with those of Mitchell and Brown. For instance, Garioch's translation of Buchanan's *'captatores alius captans'* (*Iephthes*, l. 1094) as 'Anither hunts the legacy-hunters' (Sutherland, 1959:

43) derives directly from the original, since the phrase has entirely disappeared from both the other versions. Garioch's independence is more fully illustrated by a longer example, as in the three renderings of the following extended simile:

> sed veluti sub luce maligna
> per secretos nemorum anfractus
> lubricus error mille viarum
> dubio occursu ludit euntes,
> inter varios semita flexus
> nulla placet neque displicet ulla;
> sic iter homines praeterpropter
> dubia incerti mente vagamur. (Iephthes, ll. 1082–9)[7]

Firstly, Brown:

> But, as the dim and scanty light,
> That half dispels the lingering night
> From underneath the leafy boughs
> Of the deep forest, dimly shows
> In interlaced perplexing maze
> The windings of a thousand ways
> That wind and part so endlessly
> The traveller knows not which to try,
> And wanders in the forest dim
> All paths become alike to him:
> So in life's journey still we stray,
> Uncertain where to choose our way. (Brown, 1906: 67–8)

Next Mitchell:

> But, as an elfin Light,
> that flits where secret ways through forest shadows wind,
> The traveller beguiles,
> And, by its cunning wiles,
> Conducts his erring feet
> To where, with doubtful course, a thousand pathways meet;
> And, while his footsteps wander
> Where devious tracks meander,
> A pleasing or displeasing road he cannot find:
> 'Tis so with every mortal wight;
> We wander here and there with doubtful mind,
> And cannot find a way to lead our feet aright. (Mitchell, 1903: 102)

Finally Garioch:

> Like a wannert man in the gloaming licht
> fanklit deep in a forest's labyrinth,
> aye taen-in by sliddery error,
> thousans o pathweys aa crisscrossing,
> tane nae better nor waur than the tither,
> sae we men unsiccarlie wanner,
> here and there, our minds in a swither. (Sutherland, 1959: 43)

[Like a bewildered man in the twilight light/entangled deep in a forest's labyrinth,/always duped by deceitful error,/thousands of pathways all crisscrossing,/the one no better or worse than the other,/so we men wander without certainty,/here and there, our minds in a state of confusion.]

There can be no doubt, with three such very different renderings, that Garioch is a fully independent translator. Apart from anything else, Garioch, perhaps because he is the only true poet amongst the three, is noticeably more succint.

None of the three translators sticks closely to the original at all times. In this passage, for instance, all three versions depart from the sentence structure of the original in which *error* is the subject of the first part of the sentence. Nevertheless, in most respects Mitchell and Garioch are somewhat closer to the original than Brown. It would have been very understandable if Garioch, confronting the difficulties inherent in using Scots for an unfamiliar purpose, had chosen to make life easier for himself by making a very free translation, especially as he had the example of Brown before him. But he chose otherwise and, rather than evade problems with a free, loose translation, he allowed reasonable adherence to the original to force him to search for appropriate Scots diction. Where that search led him is one of the most interesting aspects of his translation.

When Garioch came to create a Scots language for his translations, he was not operating all alone. The argument about the use of Synthetic Scots had been a public one for some time, and MacDiarmid and other poets had already demonstrated what could be done by poets willing to use the resources of Jamieson's *An Etymological Dictionary of the Scottish Language* (Jamieson, 1808), and other works on Scots, to expand the vocabulary of modern Scots and fit it for a wider range of subjects. Garioch's adherence to those who espoused the cause of Synthetic Scots is declared in his use in his Buchanan translations of some of their favourite words such as *cramosie* [crimson] and *howdumbdeid* [the depths, the darkest point]. *Cramosie* is found regularly in Scots from the later fifteenth century to the earlier eighteenth centuries, but is thereafter rare until revived by MacDiarmid

(1925: 1) in the very first line of his collection *Sangschaw*: 'Mars is braw [beautiful] in crammasy' (from 'The Bonnie Broukit Bairn'). After that, Sydney Goodsir Smith (1946: 33) used it in his poem 'Largo', published in 1946 in *The Deevil's Waltz*, before Garioch took it up in *Jephthah* (Sutherland, 1959: 13). *How-dumb-deid* is an even rarer term and derives from a phrase used by Thomas Gillespie in *Blackwood's Magazine* in 1820 : 'in the *how-dumb-dead* o' a caul' ha'rst [cold harvest] night'.[8] In 1825 Jamieson included *how-dumb-dead* in the *Supplement* to his dictionary and quoted Gillespie (Jamieson, 1825: 598). Jamieson is probably the source for the next recorded user, John Mackay Wilson ('Early Recollections of a Son of the Hills' in Wilson, n.d.: 290), and certainly the source for MacDiarmid (1925: 23) when he used the whole phrase quoted above as the first line of his poem 'The Eemis Stane'. After MacDiarmid it was taken up by William Soutar in 'Wintry Boughs' (Soutar, 1948: 60, l. 5). Similarly, *grugous* [grim], having been used by a few little-known writers at the end of the eighteenth and beginning of the nineteenth centuries, disappeared until it was revived in 1925 by MacDiarmid (very likely from Jamieson) in *A Drunk Man Looks at the Thistle* (MacDiarmid, 1987: 170 [first published 1926]). Subsequently it appeared in Garioch's *The Baptist* (Sutherland, 1959: 90). All three of these terms were thus identified with the use of Synthetic Scots before their use by Garioch.

Garioch, however, is very much his own man and clearly made his own direct use of the resources that MacDiarmid and others had plundered. For instance, it would seem that he took the phrase *play the jarg on* [play a trick on], from Jamieson who is the sole source for it cited in the *Scottish National Dictionary [SND]* (1925–75).[9] No doubt many of the words Garioch used are from Jamieson, but it is hard to demonstrate this except where a word is rare and unlikely to have been encountered elsewhere by Garioch. One such case is the verb *frivole*, which Jamieson (1825) glosses as 'annul, set aside'. Garioch has Herod say:

we are forced to mak fine promises,
in public aport gentil and amene,   [demeanour gentle and pleasant]
to defer the rage in our dissimillat hairt,   [dissembled heart]
and frivole our just anger for a fitter time.
                                    (Sutherland, 1959: 72).

While it is not impossible that Garioch had come across this word in Bellenden's translation of Livy (Craigie, 1901), which is Jamieson's only cited source, it is there used in quite a different way from the way Garioch uses it. Indeed, the *Dictionary of the Older Scottish Tongue [DOST]* (1925–2002) plausibly glosses the Bellenden usage, the only case of the verb that has been found, as 'To reject as frivolous'. It seems that Garioch's usage relies more on Jamieson's gloss than on the Bellenden passage; indeed, this and other cases strongly suggest that he used an abridged edition of Jamieson that did not include the quotations.[10]

Frivole is a Middle Scots word, and one of the advantages for Garioch of using a resource that includes Middle Scots is that it offers him a number of formal terms that he can revive. Over the last few centuries Scots has been particularly creative in colloquial language, and has become extremely rich in that register, but there has been a corresponding decline in distinctively Scots formal language. The text that Garioch was translating required some formal diction and there are a number of formal terms, many of them Latinate, which he revived from Middle Scots. In the passage just quoted there are, apart from *frivole*, *aport* [bearing], *amene* [pleasant], *dissimill* [dissemble]. Elsewhere we find such words as *apert* [open], *contumax* [contumacious], *engreve* [annoy], *felloun* [cruel], *preclair* [illustrious], and *verrayment* [truth]. There was also a place for less formal diction, some of which also came from Middle Scots, for instance *harsk* [harsh] and *swickfu* [deceitful]. Early Scots could also provide Garioch with some useful technical language, such as *schiltroun*. This word, which is not confined to Scots, though here given a Scots form, originally meant a close-packed body of men protected by their interlocked shields, and was useful for translating *phalanx*, as Garioch does when he renders Buchanan's '*fortium/densae phalanges militum*' (*Iephthes*, ll. 358–9) as 'serried schiltrouns o wicht [valiant] men' (Sutherland, 1959: 20). Using any particular source leads more or less inevitably to incorporating some of its errors. Jamieson is wrong in identifying French-derived *orphelin* [orphan] as a distinctively Scots term, even though he quotes John Knox. Knox was using a normal term of late Middle English and Early Modern English, but Garioch's use is not inappropriate. Had Scots continued to develop as a fully independent tongue, it may well have continued to use terms that were present in Middle Scots, whether they were also used in English or not. Garioch is acting as if this fully independent development had continued, just as, in translating Buchanan, he saw himself, as he says in his Preface, as resuming the interrupted Scottish tradition of translation from the classical authors into Scots and as producing 'the samyn strecht [same straight] line frae the point whaur it was broken-aff' (Sutherland, 1959: 6).

Revivals from later Scots tend to be more colloquial in tone, such as *yawp* [eager] and *skrip* [scoff], but, since some Scots formal diction survived into the eighteenth century, there are also such terms as *commove* [excite to passion]. Another likely borrowing from Jamieson is *gastrous* [monstrous], since it is otherwise attested only in relatively obscure sources. Here, too, as with the Middle Scots borrowings, we find a somewhat problematical word of French origin. The quotations in the *Oxford English Dictionary* (*OED*, 1989) suggest that *tourbillon* [whirlwind, vortex] may have been an accepted Standard English usage in the eighteenth and early nineteenth centuries. Alternatively its relative rareness and tendency to appear in italics may mean that it was never fully naturalised but, rather, continually readopted from French. Be that as it may, at least one edition of Jamieson's dictionary[11] evidently did not consider it to be Standard English and included it as an Ayrshire usage, while the *OED* quotes William Tennant as using it in a passage of Scots. English? Scots? foreign? – its status is uncertain. Whatever it might be, it fits neatly into the context of Garioch's translation:

Sae God birls about the affairs o men,   [spins]
as the tourbillon blaws the stour.   [blows the dust]
            (Sutherland, 1959: 43)

Synthetic Scots, as well as ranging in time, ranges in space. Garioch is no exception to this. His own dialect is that of Edinburgh but there is little to mark his language as distinctively of that area. He certainly shows no aversion to including words from other dialects. On the contrary, words that are labelled by the dictionaries at his disposal as belonging to another dialect area are freely introduced. I have already mentioned *play the jarg on* [play a trick on] as a revival of a word that had apparently not been used since its appearance in Jamieson. To those who would limit a Scots writer to the language of a particular time and place, *play the jarg on* is doubly inappropriate for Garioch to use, since it belongs neither to his time nor to his place: Jamieson (1808) gives it as only an Upper Clydesdale usage. So, too, we find him using *jauner* [idle talk], given in Jamieson as a Roxburghshire usage, and found by the *SND* (1925–76) only in Ayrshire and South-Western and Southern Scots.

Another way of expanding the vocabulary of modern Scots, also already practised by MacDiarmid, was to extend the meaning of existing words. It is always hard in such cases to know whether the extension is conscious or not, since such extensions can easily arise by mistake with any writer who makes use of a dictionary without quotations. For instance, when Garioch writes 'Soothfieness, shame and halieness avoke ye' [Truthfulness, shame and holiness avoid you] (Sutherland, 1959: 65) to translate the Latin '*te fugit verum pietas pudorque*' (*Baptistes*, l. 309), he seems to be using *avoke* in the sense of 'avoid' which is not otherwise recorded. It may well be that, having consulted an edition of Jamieson that does not include the quotations and having found the meaning 'to call away; to keep off', he took 'keep off' to mean 'avoid' whereas it actually means 'detain', as the quotation in the full version of the dictionary makes clear. Similarly, when John the Baptist is described as 'the skaithless prophet' (Sutherland, 1959: 64; for the Latin *'vatem innocentem'*, l. 298) the meaning of *skaithless* is apparently 'innocent' or 'harmless', whereas its normal meaning is 'unharmed'. Garioch is evidently relying on the meaning given in Jamieson, 'innocent; without culpability'. But editions of Jamieson that include the quotations make it clear that this is Jamieson's gloss on a particular passage in Chapter 9 of Sir Walter Scott's *The Black Dwarf* ('It was a' true ye tell'd me about Westburnflat; but he's sent back Grace safe and scaithless') (Jamieson, 1825) and that 'innocent' here means 'unharmed' in the sense of 'unsullied'.

Words can also be extended in meaning by figurative use. Garioch renders Buchanan's *'quibus in tenebris/degimus lapsu celeri fugacis/tempora vitae!'* (*Baptistes*, ll. 282–4) with the equally imposing

In what mirky corries
spend we our swithlie fuge and ever-dwynan
hantle o lifetime! (Sutherland, 1959: 64)

[In what gloomy hollows/spend we our swiftly flown and ever-dwindling/span of lifetime!]

Garioch's choice of *fuge* meaning 'transitory' is no doubt influenced by the Latin adjective *fugax,* but he could also cite the authority of Jamieson who quotes Gavin Douglas's translation of the *Aeneid* and gives the meaning as 'fugitive'. Garioch's use represents a figurative extension of Jamieson's meaning to cover the sense 'transitory'. However, the authenticity of this word is very doubtful. Jamieson quotes from Ruddiman's edition, based here on a reading in the Ruthven MS that is not shared by the other manuscripts.[12]

Finally, lexical resources can be expanded by the invention of new words. Pure creation, the creation of a new word that has no relation to existing words, is a rare activity in Scots as in other languages, but relatively straightforward derivatives are common enough. Garioch adopted at least one from MacDiarmid, *flegsom* [terrifying], but has some of his own such as *contramasty,* which apparently means 'perversity' and is formed from *contermashous* [perverse] and *mimness* [demureness] (Sutherland, 1959: 64, 65).

However, to concentrate on these unusual words is to give a false impression of Garioch's language, for he uses many more common words. Moreover, there is something of a tendency for the unusual words to occur in clumps: many of those cited above appear in a set piece of the chorus in

Scene II of *The Baptist*. The scene that immediately follows this begins with a speech from the queen which uses a much more ordinary kind of Scots:

> Are ye that dozent that ye dinna see
> royal authority is geynear in ruins?
> owre blind to see, at this time o the day,
> the foul plots preparing agen your heid?
> If this mob-leader lives anither year,
> your threits o prisoun, o raip and gallows,
> sall be in vain. He's already vauntie
> wi the sense o pouer, settin himsel up
> already wi his gang o ghillies
> abune the retainers o the royal court. (Sutherland, 1959: 66)
>
> [Are you that stupefied that you do not see/royal authority is very nearly in ruins?/too blind to see, at this time of the day,/the foul plots preparing against your head?/If this mob-leader lives another year,/your threats of prison, of rope and gallows,/will be in vain. He's already puffed-up/with the sense of power, setting himself up/already with his gang of followers/above the retainers of the royal court.]

This is more normal modern Scots but it is still distinctly literary, as indicated by the presence of *vauntie*, a word that the SND specifically marks as literary in register. The passage is clearly identified as Scots by its spelling, vocabulary and grammar, but the large amount of shared Scots–English diction is also characteristic of Garioch's language. Nor is this shared element confined to the common stock of words from which English and Scots separately developed, but includes more modern creations such as *mob-leader*. Here and elsewhere he also shows no reluctance to use formal Latinate diction such as *ascribe, calumny, clemency, conciliated, daedal, decency, equity, fascinate, immutable, impudent, innocent, insolence, prodigies, providence, redolent, regality, religion, sacrifice, sanction, seditious, singular, superstitions* and *trifurcate*. The problem for Scottish writers in using such terms is that, being formal, they are associated with English, the normal language of formal discourse. However, any writer who wishes to reclaim the full range of Scots diction needs to use them both as an essential part of a formal register and, in many of the cases listed above, as part of a register of religious language. Unlike such earlier translators as Waddell (1871), who in his translations into Scots of the Psalms and Isaiah went to great pains to avoid the word *sacrifice* and substituted for it his own creation *slachtir-tryst* (Psalms 51.17), Garioch happily uses such diction. As a result there are some sentences such as 'Ethical unity is an elementary quality' (Sutherland, 1959: 40) that consist almost totally of such diction but nevertheless do not seem out of place in their context. At the other end of the scale he is also ready to use English slang and colloquialisms, and includes such words as *grouse* [complain] and *dune-up* [decorated] (Sutherland, 1959: 30, 31). A somewhat similar justification for their use applies with these colloquialisms: Scots has been prolific in the formation of its own colloquial diction but it has also borrowed freely from English. To exclude such items would be to deny their use in Scottish speech. In this way, drawing on speech and particularly on written sources, Garioch is able to create a rich and varied Scots that can carry the weight of Buchanan's text. It is no small feat to have sustained this for a text of nearly one hundred pages.

Grammar and spelling are contrived to support the effect of the diction. The spelling conventions followed by Garioch are largely those suggested in *The Scots Style Sheet* adopted by the Makars' Club in 1947.[13] In particular Garioch abandons the eighteenth and nineteenth-century practice, found also in his own earlier collections of poems, of using apostrophes to indicate where Scots lacks a sound implied in the English spelling. Such apostrophes tend to suggest that Scots is just mispronounced English, and consequently need to be avoided by any writer keen to emphasise the independent status of Scots. Garioch's spelling of present participles and verbal nouns and adjectives is extremely inconsistent but, in so far as he does use the *-an* spelling, he once again signals the independence of Scots.[14] The grammar employs the traditional features expected in modern Scots texts (such as the verbal negative *-na*), but Garioch also makes a particularly strong use of the Latinate past participle ending in *-ate* or *-at*, as in Iphis's statement, 'I am dedicat til daith,/consecrat as a victim' (Sutherland, 1959: 49). This was a feature of Early Modern English, but survived rather longer in Scots. In the context of Garioch's general aims it has the great advantage of investing shared Scots–English formal diction with a specifically Scots quality. The formality of the language is reinforced by the occasional use of the very literary *wha* and, particularly, *wham* and *whase* as relative pronouns (colloquial Scots uses *at* or *that*), and by at least one case of the archaic use of *ane* as an indefinite article. On the other hand Garioch avoids the long-standing use of *-s* inflections after plural nouns and writes 'the warld's joys are sune wede awa [soon perish]' rather than 'is sune wede awa' (Sutherland, 1959: 89, 33). This is a stigmatised usage in modern Scots writing, no doubt because it could be seen as illiterate by English standards, but it has a long history in Scots and still strongly survives in Scottish speech.

Finding a serious formal language for his translation was not, of course, the only task confronting Garioch – though it was perhaps the most demanding. There were other features of the original plays that needed to be imitated. Buchanan uses several different metres in the two plays but Garioch makes no attempt to follow them closely, although he occasionally uses a shorter line when Buchanan does so as in Scene IV of *Iephthes*. Practical considerations preclude much more than this, but there is another feature of the plays that can be more easily imitated. Buchanan's language is full of echoes of classical authors. To take just a few examples from *Jephthah*, there are echoes of Virgil (ll. 292–5, 300, 359, 1082), Horace (ll. 413, 562), Ovid (ll. 802, 846, 870–71), Lucretius (l. 803), Ennius (l. 1088), and Seneca (ll. 1384–95).[15] In the Latin passage (ll. 1082–9) cited earlier there are, for instance, strong echoes of a famous passage in Virgil's *Aeneid*: '*quale per incertam lunam sub luce maligna/est iter in silvis*' (Book VI, ll. 270–71). Sometimes these echoes arise, one suspects, as much as anything from Buchanan's desire to imitate the best examples of classical Latinity, but in other cases the influence is more substantial. For example, in their edition of the plays, Sharratt and Walsh (1983: 266, note to ll. 1384–95) note that Seneca's *Troades* 'has exercised a strong influence' on the final act of *Jephthah*. Garioch could not provide a precise parallel to each of these echoes, but he could insert his own echoes into the text at other points so that his translations can be seen to belong to a Scots literary tradition just as Buchanan's original plays belong to a classical one. In *Jephthah*, no less than three times (Sutherland, 1959: 33, 42, 50), by using the phrase 'wede awa' Garioch recalls a very well-known line from Jane Elliot of Minto's 'The Flowers o' the Forest', as printed by Sir Walter Scott in his *Minstrelsy of the Scottish Border*: 'The flowers of the forest are a' wede awae'. Robert Burns's poem 'To a Louse' is evoked in 'Och, if some pouer wad gie til us the giftie/plainlie to see' (Sutherland, 1959: 65). Similarly, 'I prie ye ae thing, afore your anger/may garr ye gang onie mair agley' (Sutherland, 1959: 62), evokes Burns's oft-quoted lines in 'To a Mouse': 'the best-laid schemes o' mice an' men/gang aft agley'. At the same time, since Scots literature constantly interacts with English literature, it is appropriate for Garioch to incorporate an allusion to *Othello*, in a reference to 'the heid and front o the offending' (Sutherland, 1959: 68). Finally, he is able to draw on the English Bible for phrases such as 'the strecht gait o naukit virtue' [the straight path of naked virtue][16] and the description of the Jews as 'stiff-neckit' (Sutherland, 1959: 43, 11). Garioch's range of echoes is by no means as rich as Buchanan's but it is sufficient, as I have said, to serve the same purpose of setting his translations within a literary tradition.

Earlier I argued that Buchanan's plays were hard to tie to specific events, but were not without general allusions to contemporary life. Sometimes these allusions are still recognisable in the translation. When the pharisee Malchus exclaims, 'Sall I thole siccan flyting flyrit at my order?' [Shall I endure such reproach scorning my order?] (Sutherland, 1959: 78), we can still see the possibility of an implied comparison with the religious orders of Buchanan's time, a possibility that clearly lies within his original text. But Garioch's translation is an act of re-creation, implicitly claiming that the plays still have relevance; in those circumstances he can appropriately suggest his own comparisons with contemporary life. These comparisons carry us beyond Buchanan's time to the later development of the church in Scotland. By choosing to translate Buchanan's *'populus sanctus'* (the holy people) as 'your sancts o [saints of] the covenant', he applies to the Jews a phrase that has powerful associations with the persecution of the Covenanters in Scotland. Further, references to 'clarsachs' [small harps], 'ghillies' [followers], and the 'war-pipes' that 'skirl' [make a shrill sound], link the plays with the world of the Highlanders (Sutherland, 1959: 74, 21, 66, 91). In the same way, comparisons with the recent war in which Garioch had taken part, and about which he subsequently wrote (Garioch, 1975), are implied by references to 'infantry battalions' and 'squadrons o armoured cars' (Sutherland, 1959: 17) for Latin *'cohortes'* and *'turmae curules'* (ll. 243–4). By such means Buchanan's plays are brought into a modern and Scottish context, and allowed to speak to a new and more local audience just as they spoke originally to the international Latin culture of the European Renaissance.

When we consider a translation we usually consider what the new language brings to the text, but it is also often important to consider what the text brings to the new language. The use of Scots has revitalised these texts; it is true that the language of Buchanan's originals is very literary, but they were presumably always more often read than performed and Scots has given them new vitality as reading texts. It is always difficult to compare Scots and English translations of the same text, but to me it seems that Garioch's version of these two plays is superior in poetic power to the two English translations he consulted. Considered as poems, these translations must rank high amongst Garioch's achievements (as Garioch himself believed; see Findlay, 1998b). It is true that the voice we most commonly associate with Garioch, and perhaps the voice to which we are most strongly attracted, is the voice of the poet of Edinburgh, with its strong roots in the language of ordinary people. This is, moreover, the voice he was able to transfer to his highly successful translations of Belli. But he also had another voice, a serious and scholarly voice, which finds its expression in poems such as 'The Muir'. Following in the footsteps of MacDiarmid but never a mere imitator, Garioch was a key figure in the development of a new literary Scots capable of dealing with serious topics. This powerful poetic instrument is here put to the service of resurrecting Buchanan's plays. Though so different from the original language in which they were originally written, Scots provides an appropriate modern embodiment for Buchanan's work. The international Latin culture held its own for centuries but, as it began to decline, so the rise of nationalism promoted an interest in national and regional languages. It is fitting to the changed world of modern learning that Buchanan's transnational tragedies should rise again in the guise of dialect poetry written for a much more local audience.

But, if Scots brought something to the plays, the plays also brought something to Scots. In the last few centuries Scots has often been the language of sentimentality, but rarely the language of tragedy. The existence of these two tragedies in Scots changes our perceptions of what Scots can achieve and brings it closer to being a language that can deal with all the concerns of modern literature. In that sense Buchanan had as much to offer Garioch as Garioch had to offer Buchanan.[17]

Notes

1. Although Garioch's translations of Buchanan were published in one volume under his own name, I have referred to him in this essay under the name by which he was best known as a writer.
2. 'Garioch relished the technical challenge of translation and a full half of his total output [of poetry] comprises translations into Scots of poetry in Latin, Greek, French, German, Italian, Swedish and other languages.' (Findlay, 1998b: 58).
3. Elsewhere Buchanan seems to contradict this statement in part. (For a discussion, see Sharratt & Walsh, 1983: 2–4.)
4. C.M. Grieve [Hugh MacDiarmid], 'A Scotsman Looks at his World', in *Dunfermline Press*, 14 April 1923, p. 6; quoted from Glen (1964: 81).
5. For discussion of this, and of the 'programmes' of the MacDiarmid-led Scottish Renaissance helping to shape Garioch's motivation in translating Buchanan's Latin tragedies, see Findlay (1998b).
6. C.M. Grieve, 'Causerie', in *Scottish Chapbook*, 1: 3 (October 1922), pp. 62–3; quoted from Glen (1964: 77).
7. Quotations from Buchanan's originals are taken from Sharratt & Walsh (1983). Garioch evidently used Ruddiman's editions, but there are no serious textual variants in either of the two plays.
8. 'Sketches of Village Character. No. II', in *Blackwood's Edinburgh Magazine* 8 (44) (November 1820), p. 202. For the authorship see Strout (1959: 73).
9. Jamieson, rather than the *SND,* remained the major source of information about Scots at the time of Garioch's translation: by the time the the two plays appeared in 1959 the published part of the *SND* had reached only *ill-faured* and the *Dictionary of the Older Scottish Tongue* [*DOST*] (1925–2002) was not very far advanced either.
10. Interestingly, *dissimill,* used by Garioch in the previous line, also occurs in Bellenden's Livy, but it too could have been drawn from Jamieson.

11. The word is found in the one-volume abridged edition of Jamieson's dictionary (Paisley: Gardner, 1912) but not in the four-volume edition (Paisley: Gardner, 1879–82). These are the two editions most likely to have been readily available to Garioch; and the word's appearance only in the abridged version suggests this was the edition he was using.
12. The Ruthven MS stands alone here in reading 'Thay fage' (emended by Ruddiman to 'Ye fuge'), whereas the reading found in the other MSS and followed by the Scottish Text Society edition (Book 3, Canto 4, l. 75) is 'Theyfage', glossed by the Scottish Text Society editor as 'thieving'. See Coldwell (1957–64: I, 393, II, 122, 263).
13. For one of several printings of *The Scots Style Sheet*, see *Lines Review* 9 (August 1955), pp. 30–1.
14. *The Scots Style Sheet* had suggested using *-an* for present participles and *-in* for the verbal noun, but Garioch uses *-ing*, *-in*, *-and* and *-an* here in no consistent pattern.
15. I am indebted to Sharratt and Walsh (1983) for identification of these echoes. Their notes record many further echoes.
16. There seems a misremembering or misinterpretation by Garioch of the Bible's 'straight is the gate ... which leadeth unto life' (Matthew 7.14), where 'straight' means 'narrow'.
17. This chapter was completed before publication of Fulton (2002).

Chapter 10
Robert Garioch and Giuseppe Belli

CHRISTOPHER WHYTE

In 1941, amidst the grim realities of war and occupation, a doctor named Alexandre Roudinesco asked Paul Valéry to produce a line-for-line version of Virgil's *Eclogues*, to be published opposite the original text.[1] The French poet's reaction was hesitant. He appears to have undertaken the task with no great enthusiasm. The planned 1944 edition failed to materialise and the version did not see publication until 1953, when it was accompanied by an essay, 'Variations on the *Eclogues*', which constitutes Valéry's most sustained reflection on the art of translating poetry. In it he refuses to acknowledge any absolute boundary between translation and original composition:

> Writing anything at all, as soon as the act of writing requires a certain amount of thought and is not a mechanical and unbroken inscribing of spontaneous inner speech, is a work of translation exactly comparable to that of transmuting a text from one language into another. (Valéry, 1958: 299)[2]

Going even further, he affirms that:

> [t]he poet is a peculiar type of translator, who translates ordinary speech, modified by emotion, into 'language of the gods', and his inner labour consists less of seeking words for his ideas than of seeking ideas for his words and paramount rhythms. (Valéry, 1958: 301)

Valéry makes no secret of his lack of sympathy for pastoral as a literary mode, and protests at the senseless torment inflicted on generations of schoolchildren in the name of a classical education. Nevertheless, in the course of turning Virgil's verses into unrhymed French alexandrines, he claims that he experienced a kind of identification with the Latin poet, as if he could recreate or relive the moment in which the *Eclogues* were merely a tantalising possibility, suspended within reach of that long-dead consciousness:

Faced with my Virgil, I had the sensation (well known to me) of a poet at work. From time to time I argued absently with myself about this famous book, set in its millennial fame, with as much freedom as if it had been a poem of my own on the table before me. At moments, as I fiddled with my translation, I caught myself wanting to change something in the venerable text ... The work of translation, done with regard for a certain approximation of form, causes us in some way to try walking in the tracks left by the author; and not to fashion one text upon another, but from the latter to work back to the virtual moment of its formation, to the phase when the mind is in the same state as an orchestra whose instruments begin to waken, calling to each other and seeking harmony before beginning their concert. From that vividly imagined state one must make one's way down toward its resolution in a work in a different tongue. (Valéry, 1958: 302–4)

If 'original' composition means finding linguistic expression for a text that already exists on the subliminal plane, then the translator has, as it were, to unravel the fabric woven by his chosen poet to the point where he can rediscover this latent, 'virtual' text and set about manifesting it in a different linguistic medium.

Valéry is more renowned as a poet than as a translator. This makes his validation of the translator's task (provided that it is 'done with regard for a certain approximation of form') all the more striking. His reflections are a useful corrective in approaching the poetry of Robert Garioch, for it can be argued that Garioch's translations are his most significant achievement and that, among these, the 'Roman Sonnets frae Giuseppe Belli' deserve pride of place (Garioch, 1983: 215–80). The attitudes of readers of poetry (including critics) typically lag a generation or so behind the practice of poets themselves. As a result, the reception of even contemporary poets continues to be coloured by an aesthetic inherited from Romanticism that places a prime value on originality. The poem gushes out onto a virgin, completely blank page as the expression of the feelings and thoughts of a subject with a specific biography. Given that these feelings or thoughts are his (or her) individual property, unprecedented and unrepeatable, the resulting poem will also be completely new. One can argue that the artistic avant-garde that dominated the cultural scene in Western Europe and further afield between the wars and after exacerbated such an approach to the point where self-affirmation took the form of destroying and disowning what had gone before: supersession, not tradition. What a contrast to Anna Akhmatova's rueful, yet affectionate, admission in the 'First Dedication' to *Poem without a Hero* that,

> ... because I don't have enough paper,
> I am writing on your first draft.
> And here a strange word shows through
> and, like that snowflake on my hand long ago,
> melts trustingly, with no reproach. (Akhmatova, 1990: 403)

Even in 'original' composition, the page has already been written on, and the preceding text can never wholly be concealed. The analogy with Valéry's concept of translation could hardly be clearer.[3] Joseph Brodsky, considered by some a protégé of Akhmatova's, and certainly among her keenest admirers, has observed that 'poetry, in essence, is itself a certain other language – or a translation from such' (Brodsky, 1987: 234). His conviction that:

> verse metre is the equivalent of a certain psychological state, at times not of just one state but of several. The poet 'picks' his way toward the spirit of a work by means of the metre. (Brodsky, 1987: 208).

suggests that he would be sympathetic to attempts on the translator's part to reproduce, or at least to echo, the phonetic organisation of the original.

For Valéry to produce a version of Virgil's *Eclogues* had very different implications from Garioch's choice of the Roman dialect poet Giuseppe Belli (1791–1863). It is not just that in Valéry's case the language of the original was defunct and could therefore in no way 'answer back', or return the compliment. Translator and original always possess a precise collocation with linguistic, geographical and chronological coordinates. The act of translation establishes a connection between the two that can be visualised as lines plotted on several different graphs, and which are specific to every case.

Belli allowed only one of the 2,279 sonnets he composed in Roman dialect, or *romanesco*, to be published in his lifetime.[4] A note in his will of 1849 ordered his son to destroy 'all the vernacular verses in *romanesco* style so that they will never be known to the world, for they are scattered with shameful maxims, thoughts and words'. In that year Belli himself burned his papers, perhaps as a consequence of the turbulent political events connected with the proclamation of a Roman Republic. Copies appear to have survived in the hands of his friend and enlightened patron, Monsignor Vincenzo Tizzani. Belli's contradictory attitude may be attributed in part to an increasing political conservatism and in part to the fact that between 1838 and 1845 he worked as a civil servant in the papal administration, which now supplied him with a pension. Yet when Gregory XVI, whose 15-year reign provided the background to Belli's fresco of Roman life, died in 1846, the man who signed many of his sonnets *Peppe er tosto* (*tosto* is roughly equivalent to Scottish *gallus* [cocky and nonchalant]) is said to have remarked: 'I was fond of Pope Gregory because I had so much fun attacking him'. In 1852 he was given the task of vetting stage plays in order to ascertain their 'political morality'. His comments on *Macbeth* are indicative: '[A] benevolent monarch is betrayed in breach of the sacred laws of hospitality, his throat cut by a disloyal subject moved only by longing for power, an action which sets a dangerous example in any age, but especially in ours.' Belli presented Pius IX with a copy of his *romanesco* version of a hymn book in 1856, but declined to translate St Matthew's Gospel into dialect. This would have constituted in his opinion 'an irreverence towards the sacred text'. A widely read and travelled man, his *Zibaldone* or commonplace book ran to eleven sizeable volumes and he kept travel journals almost entirely in French. He was familiar with the writings of Scott, Rousseau and Madame de Staël. The discovery of Antonio Porta's dialect poetry on a visit to Milan in 1827 was a major influence for his own work in *romanesco*. The Russian novelist Gogol heard Belli recite sonnets in 1835, during his first journey to Italy, and spoke favourably of them to Sainte-Beuve in 1839. Giacomo Ferretti, the librettist of Rossini's hilarious *Cinderella*, was a close friend. In 1816 Belli married a woman 13 years his elder. The period until her death in 1837 was one of relative affluence and, in creative terms, the most fertile of Belli's life. Between 1830 and 1837 he wrote no fewer than 1,950 sonnets in *romanesco*: the figure for the years from 1838 to 1842 is merely 33.

A letter to another friend, Francesco Spada, dated 1831, contains the definitive version of the 'Introduction' to the sonnets. (Belli was to revise it at a later date, between 1839 and 1847). There he writes:

> Every neighbourhood in Rome, every one of its citizens from the middle class downwards, has provided me with episodes for my drama: the shopkeeper rubs shoulders with the servant, and the naked beggar appears next to the gullible little woman and the proud carter. Juxtaposing in this way the various classes of the people as a whole, and letting each one say what he knows, what he thinks and what he does, I have brought together the mass of customs and opinions of this populace, which is marked by the most singular contradictions. (Belli, 1984: 9)

Belli makes no secret of his ambition to furnish a kind of human comedy of Papal Rome in the years of its final decadence. He has no illusions as to the eloquence or expressiveness of the dialect he has chosen to write in:

Here I portray the ideas of a populace which is ignorant, yet for the most part pithy and acute, and portray them, I will say, without recourse to other than dialect, a broken and corrupt type of speech, a language which in sum is neither Italian nor Roman, but *romanesco*. Those who speak it know nothing or almost nothing: and what little they learn from tradition only serves to highlight their ignorance, such is the darkness of false beliefs which envelops them. Barren of ideas, its forms are limited and its vocabulary scant. A few terms of general application, frequently used, serve a wide range of purposes. (Belli, 1984: 8)

Robert Garioch did not so much choose Belli as have Belli chosen for him. Donald Carne-Ross wrote to him from the BBC in London to commission translations of three sonnets, providing English versions and suggesting that one at least should 'go I think into some kind of Scots'.[5] Almost without exception Garioch worked from line-for-line cribs. Carne-Ross supplied them for the sonnets published in *Selected Poems* (Garioch, 1966), Antonia Spadavecchia for those in *Doktor Faust in Rose Street* (Garioch, 1973), and Antonia Stott for the remainder, done between 1975 and Garioch's death in 1981, making a total of 120 in the *Complete Poetical Works* (Garioch, 1983).[6]

Valéry and Virgil both occupy central positions within the traditions to which they belong, and within the mainstream of Mediterranean and European verse. On the contrary, marginality is what characterises Belli and Garioch. Claims have been made for Porta and Belli as the major poets of the nineteenth century in Italy, yet Belli at least was recognised sooner abroad than in Italy. Moreover, in a linguistic culture that attributes a perhaps excessive importance to purism, it is hard to see how either, in employing dialect, can be integrated into the high tradition of Foscolo, Carducci and Pascoli. They are in a very real sense beyond the linguistic pale. Had Garioch been writing in the early years of Hugh MacDiarmid's Scottish Renaissance Movement, it is possible that he would have been drawn to translate poetry written in a recognised literary language as against poetry in dialect into Scots. Belonging as he does to the so-called second wave of that movement, he had to come to terms with the effective failure of MacDiarmid's struggle to promote Scots as a national language for poetry and the progressive marginalisation of work in Scots as against work in English. It is possible to read several major poems of Garioch's, most notably 'The Percipient Swan' (Garioch, 1983: 6–8), as responses to the predicament that writing in Scots presented him with. In the poem, the bird has clipped wings and is forced to swim round and round in the same confining pond. It threatens to escape eventually, but at a cost: the swan sings, by popular belief, at the moment of its death or destruction. The reductive idiom, the use of what poses as a speaking voice engaged in cutting pretensions down to size, is one of the most dangerous aspects of this predicament, and translation offered a means of escape. If what marks out dialect poetry as such is the intention of transcribing pre-existent speech, translation can never be that. It therefore liberates anyone using a stigmatised or reified linguistic medium, as one cannot, in a translation, be accused of writing what people would never say. A brief glance at Garioch's translation of Buchanan's Latin elegy 'The Humanists' Trauchles [Struggles] in Paris' (Garioch, 1983: 29–34), and the personal 'Repone [Reply]' he appended to it (1983: 35–7), proves the point. The translated elegy is, in linguistic terms, infinitely more experimental than the 'Repone'. It is also metrically more disciplined.

This is perhaps the stage at which to argue in some detail for the modernity of Garioch's project. In the discussion that follows, the Belli translations as a whole are considered to be a text with its own internal patterns of correspondence and ordering. While Garioch himself made little secret of his antipathy towards MacDiarmid, in both personal and cultural terms, a comparison between the older poet's *In Memoriam James Joyce* (MacDiarmid, 1955) and the Belli translations offers many useful insights. Each can be seen as operating a quintessentially post-modern deconstruction of received ideas about the literary text. Each is a compilation from pre-existing work, making no pretence to originality. At several points in the correspondence with Antonia Stott (Fulton, 1986: 148–71) Garioch can be seen engaged in the task of roving and selecting:

> I think we should not have too many of these anti-clerical ones, which are more removed from our life ... (15 December 1975; Fulton, 1986: 149)

> [W]e have enough anticlerical ones to be going on with, and should look at some others, especially the social ones, i.e. especially those that are mainly fun. (20 May 1976; Fulton, 1986: 154)

> [W]e can't exclude the obscene sonnets altogether, I agree. In an American university they would work out the right ratio by computer, but maybe we could have the obscene ones a little below the correct proportion. (12 March 1981; Fulton, 1986: 170)

Just as behind each single sonnet of Garioch's lies a *romanesco* source, so more and more of MacDiarmid's text turns out to have been 'lifted' from published books. Neither *In Memoriam James Joyce* nor the Belli translations can usefully be approached as an expression of or a key to the author's personality, or to the vicissitudes of his biography. In this sense both texts are truly authorless. Furthermore, both are 'open'. The major part of MacDiarmid's poem was composed (I choose the word deliberately) before the Second World War. When publication was mooted in the early 1950s, he saw no problem in replacing the missing sections with new material.[7] The text was in a process of uninterrupted becoming. One could even argue that publication was merely a stage in its history, rather than a definitive point of arrival. In an analogous fashion, one of the difficulties in comprehending Garioch's Belli translations is a simple question of ordering. We do not read them in the order of translation but according to the numerical sequence of the *romanesco* originals, which themselves are simply ordered according to the date that Belli appended to each one.[8] This means that each new version altered the text from within, as well as adding to it. The new material took its place, not at the end of the sequence, but internally, according to an order not established by Garioch or his helpers. If Garioch and Stott were able to choose which sonnets to translate, they could not choose the place they would take amongst the sonnets they had already translated into Scots. This 'open' quality is faithful to Belli's original, for he comments in his 'Introduction':

> Mine is a book to pick up and put down, as one does with pastimes, without needing progressively to reorder one's ideas. Each page is the beginning of the book, each page its end. (Belli, 1984: 9)

Had Garioch lived, say, for another five years, the full text of the Belli translations might be a very different one. The fact that he chose more traditional means of achieving results not dissimilar to those of MacDiarmid in *In Memoriam James Joyce*, should not lead us to underestimate the radical nature of his project. Neither should his apparent unawareness of it, evident in a characteristically self-deprecating observation such as the following, made to Antonia Stott:

> I should like to go on as long as you care to furnish me with cribs: it is frantic kind of fun, and keeps my hand in, now that my invention is showing signs of wear. (1 June 1976; Fulton, 1986: 155)

He is amazed by the facility with which the work proceeds:

> I can't guarantee to keep things up, but am delighted as well as surprised by the liveliness of the last week. It cheers me up especially as I have been so dull lately in the matter of any sort of writing. (16 December 1980; Fulton, 1986: 165)

Perhaps he saw the work on Belli as a substitute for failing inspiration. As readers we need not feel constrained to agree with him. Indeed, as readers, such a text sets us face to face with very complex problems. What is the correct way to read the Belli translations? From beginning to end? Dotting back and forth? Attempting to compare and contrast sonnets that are similar in tone or subject matter? In the order in which Garioch translated them? Who will read them more effectively: an audience that has no knowledge of the original, or one that can set Garioch's Scots against Belli's *romanesco*? I suspect the former public was the one Garioch had in mind, although, if I have been asked to write this essay, it is at least in part because I belong to the latter group. Rather than being dismayed at such questions, we should acknowledge them as symptomatic of the extraordinary semantic richness of the text that Garioch has produced.

To return to the question of metrics: if the curse of dialect writing is a perceived bondage to spoken practice, then the use of the sonnet form had an arbitrary, unjustifiable quality that brought with it its own kind of liberation. Whatever kind of language the populaces of Rome or Edinburgh may use, their utterances do not take the form of sonnets. Belli's claim in his 'Introduction' that he is effectively writing a kind of 'found poetry' has a strikingly modern ring to it:

> It is not my intention to present the poetry of the people, but to incorporate their speech in my own poetry. Metre and rhyme should emerge as if accidentally from an apparently casual juxtaposition of free sentences and current words never broken up, nor corrected, nor modelled, nor differently presented from what our ears can witness: so that verses thrown down with similar artifice, rather than provoking an impression, seem to revive a memory. (Belli, 1984: 6)

It is rarely other than misleading to portray the phonetic organisation of a poem as an attempt to represent something outside it – what is too often presented to schoolchildren as 'word painting' or onomatopoeia. Metrical codification cannot usefully be derived from the nature of the linguistic material to which it is applied, but constitutes an additional level, an application of further conventions or rules.[9] Garioch's preoccupation (one might almost say obsession), with metrical skill may well be an aspect of his reaction to the status of Scots at the time he was writing. Regular metrical patterns require agreement as to the interpretation of distinct features of a language.[10] Garioch was therefore always working at the cutting edge of the codified/non-codified nature of Scots, its ambivalent status as language and/or dialect. Seen from this angle, his poem 'Sisyphus' is a fascinating metrical pun. On the one hand, its metre can be passed off as merely an amusing evocation of the sound a boulder might make while rolling down a hill. On the other hand it is a stubbornly literal application of the Latin dactylic hexameter to a totally alien linguistic medium (even to the alternative of stressed or unstressed second syllables in the closing spondee, Garioch's equivalent for the alternative of a long or short vowel in the original Latin):

> Bumpity doun in the corrie gaed whuddran the pitiless whun stane,
> Sisyphus, pechan and sweitan, disjaskit, forfeuchan and broun'd-aff,
> sat on the heather a hanlawhile, houpan the Boss didna spy him,
> seein the terms of his contract includit nae mention of tea-breaks,
> syne at the muckle big scunnersom boulder he trauchlit aince mair.
> (Garioch, 1983: 28)
>
> [Bumpity down in the hillside hollow went rushing the pitiless whinstone,/ Sisyphus, panting and sweating, worn out, exhausted and browned-off,/sat on the heather a little while, hoping the Boss didn't spy him,/seeing the terms of his contract included no mention of tea-breaks,/then at the great big loathsome boulder he struggled once more.]

There is therefore a very real sense in which the Belli translations are an investigation of the Scots language, of its possibilities of regulation and codification. The presence of an original meant that Garioch was able to focus more closely than anywhere else in his work on this investigation. Again, little of this need have been conscious to him, although one glimpses the process in action when he observes to Antonia Stott:

> No. 358 has a good example of the BAD luck that sometimes attends Scots: *dead*, *head*, and *bed* all rhyme, but not *deid*, *heid* and *bed*. (But the luck often goes the other way.) (n.d.; Fulton, 1986: 149)

(The sonnet referred to here, 'The Reminder', is quoted in full later in this chapter).

I hope it is not too extreme to suggest a parallel with Johann Sebastian Bach's 48 'Preludes and Fugues' from *The Well-Tempered Clavier*, which investigate the expressive possibilities of a particular way of tuning the strings of a keyboard instrument. Bach is both inventing new music and discovering features of his chosen musical code. When given a Bach chorale to harmonise, music students traditionally begin at the end, deciding the cadences for each of the four phrases and then working back from these to the beginning. In a not-dissimilar fashion, Garioch would appear to have begun his sonnet translations by fixing on a rhyme scheme. Once he had an idea of the words terminating each line, he could then devise the remainder of the poem. In sonnet No. 125 he 'started off with a set of rhymes too difficult, if not impossible' (6 January 1976), and he complains in a later letter (25 November 1980) that:

> this rhyming is a desperate business, and there is a disheartening time when one is trying to lay out a set of rhymes for the two parts of a sonnet, and awful moments when one realises that two 'rhymes' are the very same word. (Fulton, 1986: 149, 162)

In a draft of sonnet No. 360, Garioch has written the rhyme pattern in the left margin of the English crib, then directly next to it a series of rhyming words. Interestingly, some of the planned rhymes come provided with enjambement, and there is even an alternative for the first line.[11]

His tour de force of enjambement is surely No. 1479, 'Ritual Questions':

> Whan thae twa meet, mind whit I say, Maria,
> Staund roun a corner, listen to their spiel.
> 'Eh-aeh, ma guid auld frien, Maister MacNeill.' –
> 'The same, yir hummil sairvant, Maister McKay.'
>
> Says he: 'Some sneeshin?' – 'Thanks,' he says, 'I'll try
> ae pinch. Hou're ye?' – 'Braw, and yirsel?' – 'Gey weill,
> thank ye.' – And syne he says: 'Hou dae ye feel,
> this weather?' – 'Garrs me cheenge ma sarks, och aye.'
>
> Says he: 'And hou's yir health?' – 'Soun as a bell,
> and yours?' – 'Thank Gode, I'm's weill as maist of men.' –
> 'Yir fowk?' – 'Graund; yours?' – 'The same, faur's I can tell.' –
>
> 'I'm glaid of that.' – 'And I, as ye may ken.' –
> 'Aweill, Maister MacNeill, luik eftir yirsel.' –
> 'Maister McKay ... till we meet again.' (Garioch, 1983: 263)

[When those two meet, remember what I say, Maria,/Stand round a corner, listen to their spiel./'Eh-aeh, my good old friend, Mister MacNeill.' –/'The same, your humble servant, Mister McKay.'//Says he: 'Some snuff?' – 'Thanks,' he says, 'I'll try/a pinch. How're you?' – 'Well, and yourself?' – 'Very well,/thank you.' – And then he says: 'How do you feel,/this weather?' – 'Makes me change my shirts, alas.'//Says he: 'And how's your health?' – 'Sound as a bell,/and yours?' – 'Thank God, I'm's well as most of men.' –/'Your folk?' – 'Grand; yours?' – 'The same, far's I can tell.' –//'I'm glad of that.' – 'And I, as you may know.' –/'Oh well, Mister MacNeill, look after yourself.' –/'Mister McKay ... till we meet again.']

Belli's original is entitled *'Le dimmane a testa per aria'* [roughly, 'Questions with the head in the air'] and is as follows:

Quanno lòro s'incontreno, Beatrice,
tu averessi da stà dietr'un cantone.
'Ôh caro sor Natale mio padrone!' –
'Umilissimo servo, sor Filice.' –

Dice: 'Ne prende?' – 'Grazzie tante,' dice. –
'Come sta?' – 'Bene, e lei?' – 'Grazzie, benone.' –
Dice: 'Come lo tratta sta staggione?' –
Dice: 'Accusí: mi fa mutà camice.' –

Dice: 'E la su' salute?' – 'Eh, nun c'è male.'
'E la sua?' dice. – 'Aringrazziam'Iddio.' –
'E a casa?' – 'Tutti. E a casa sua?' – 'L'uguale.' –

'Ne godo tanto.' – 'Se figuri io.' –
'Oh, dunque se conzervi, sor Natale.' –
'Ciarivediamo, sor Filice mio.' (Belli, 1965: III, 1560)

[When they meet each other, Beatrice,/You ought to stand behind a corner./ 'Oh dear Mr Natale my boss!'–/'Most humble servant, Mr Filice.'–//He says: 'Will you take some?'–'Many thanks,' he says.–/'How are you?'–'Well, and you?'–'Thank you, very well.'–/He says: 'How does this season treat you?'–/ He says: 'So-so: it makes me change my shirts.'–//He says: 'And your health?'– 'Ah, it's not bad.'/'And yours?' he says.–'Let us thank God.'–/'And at home?' –'Everyone. And in your home?' 'The same.'–//'It gives me such pleasure.'– 'Just imagine me.'–/ 'Oh, well, take care of yourself, Mr Natale.'–/'We'll see each other again, my Mr Filice.'] [Note: The dialect *'Sor'* is less formal and more affectionate than *'Mr'*, but throughout the conversation the two speakers address each other using the formal third person singular style – literally 'Will he take some?']

Belli's use of the form is much more traditional. There are no run-on lines. Indeed, the end of a line is marked not only by the end of a sentence, but in most cases also by a change of speaker. Where the pattern of Belli's conversation respects the divisions of the sonnet, Garioch runs his conversation against them. This highlights the unnaturalness, the unmotivated quality of the form, and also provokes a greater degree of excitement. For the point of the piece is that there is no point. The language communicates nothing. It is phatic language, not intended to transmit information, but to establish or, in this case, affirm, the nature of an interpersonal relationship. Garioch's choice of title, 'Ritual Questions', underlines this aspect. The two speakers are probably old men who repeat the same conversation every day. The deftness with which such a banal exchange is manoeuvred into the sonnet form emphasises the 'found' quality of the poem, as does the way the language is pointed to, almost placed upon a stage, by the opening couplet. The readers are, with Maria (or Beatrice), eavesdropping from behind the corner. Belli's original bears the date of 6 February 1835. Garioch projects it even further back, towards the eighteenth century, with his choice of language, while the name 'Maria' (presumably pronounced 'Mar - eye - a') serves to remind us that the poem is being translated, moved across from a Roman setting to a Scottish one, without being completely naturalised. Here as elsewhere, the conciseness of Scots forces him to come up with fillers not present in the original, such as 'mind whit I say' (l.1), 'listen to their spiel' (l.2), 'I'll try/ ae pinch' (ll.5–6). 'Soun as a bell' (l.9) offers a useful rhyme, while 'I'm's weill as maist of men' (l.10), like 'as ye may ken' (l.12), has absolutely no equivalent in Belli. The phrases serve a double purpose of padding (the term is not unkindly meant) and are of valuable assistance in carrying out Garioch's chosen rhyme scheme, in that they are not determined by the original. Because the sonnet is about banality, about set phrases that fill out a social slot as Garioch's fillers serve to complete his lines, the solution works excellently well here. This is not always the case with other sonnets.

If the first translations were indeed commissioned in 1958, then it is possible that Garioch was aware of Belli's work when he began his own sequence of 'Edinburgh Sonnets'.[12] 'Heard in the Cougate' (written in September 1962) pushes the premises of dialect writing almost to the limit by integrating into its metrical pattern phonic elements not normally considered a part of speech. But do they in fact convey any less information than the ritual questions in the sonnet we have just considered? There is the same provocative use of enjambement:

> 'Whu's aa thae fflag-poles ffur in Princes Street?
> Chwoich! Ptt! Hechyuch! Ab-boannie cairry-on.
> Seez-owre the wa'er. Whu' the deevil's thon
> inaidie, heh?' ... (Garioch, 1983: 83)

['What's all those fflag-poles ffor in Princes Street?/Chwoich! Ptt! Hechyuch! Ab-bonny carry-on./Pass over the water. What the devil's that/in aid of, heh?']

Is it fanciful to conclude that Garioch, here as in his Belli translations, is both acknowledging and challenging the limitations that the social realities of Scots usage threatened to impose upon his use of the language in poetry? A perception of Scots as intrinsically dialectal reduces the writer to the status of a scribe who represents on the page pre-existing linguistic practice. By pushing this rationale of representation to an extreme, and transcribing sounds not normally considered to be linguistic (that is, endowed with meaning) Garioch makes the limitations visible, ridicules and transcends them.

Garioch was not slavishly bound to the cribs furnished to him successively by his three collaborators. He tells Antonia Stott that:

> I can only just manage to read Italian with the help of a dictionary, and with the notes, which give the Italian equivalents of *romanesco* words. But if I have a literal translation I can see quite well where the meanings come from, so I'm not translating from the translation. (30 April 1975; Fulton, 1986: 148)

Still, he never quite managed to dispense with his intermediaries. Having sent Stott on 23 December 1979 a version of 'The Cholera Morbus', which he 'tried to translate all on my own, at the risk of making howlers', he apologises in the next letter:

> Yes, I had got things pretty far wrong with the two Christmassy sonnets, and it is good you were so patient about them. Still, they were well meant. But I shall let that be a lesson to me, very useful, and that is to keep the grammar-book in action (I have one) as well as the dictionary. (8 January 1980; Fulton, 1986: 161)

The two versions of the sonnet, before and after Antonia Stott's intervention, can be compared in *A Garioch Miscellany* (Fulton, 1986: 160–1). Antonia Stott's translation of No. 360 is as follows:

HE WHO WALKS BY NIGHT WALKS TO HIS DEATH

How accidents happen! This is the story:
In that hell-let-loose of a night
I was coming back in the small hours of the morning
From Split Head Street where Victoria lives.

I was just about to climb the steps of St Maria's
From Palazzo Doria, when I slip, have a hell of a fall,
And knock the back of my head.

I was lying on the ground, weeping like a broken vine,
When a high-class carriage
Passed by me slowly.

'Stop' shouted a servant to the driver;
But a sweet little voice coming from the carriage
Said to him: 'Go on, go on; who dies dies.'

To this she supplies two notes, both translated from Belli's own notes in Italian: 'Split Head Street' is 'Via Testa Spaccata, now no longer in existence. It is so called from a Roman statue now in the Museo delle Terme', and 'the back of my head' is 'called "memory" because it is popularly believed that memory resides in the nape of the neck'.[13] Here is what Garioch made of the sonnet in the printed version:

WHA GAES BY NICHT, GAES TIL HIS DAITH

Hou accidents will happen! Here's my story:
yon aafiest hellish nicht I iver saw,
coming hame frae Split Heid Street, in the smaa
hours of the morn, frae visiting Victoria,

jist as I mak my wey up frae the Doria
to sclimm St Mary Street, I skyte and faa,
Christ! whit a dunt! back of ma heid anaa,
it gied my harns a phantásmagória.

I'm doun, and weeping like a broken stick
of rhubarb, whan a cairriage, if you please,
a posh turn-out, gaes by, no very quick.

'Stop!' shouts a sairvant-laddie, whan he sees
the state I'm in; but a wee sweet-voiced chick
inside the coach says, 'Drive on; wha dee's dee's.' (Garioch, 1983: 234)

[WHO GOES BY NIGHT, GOES TO HIS DEATH: How accidents will happen! Here's my story:/that most hellish awful night I ever saw,/coming home from Split Head Street, in the small/hours of the morning, from visiting Victoria,//just as I make my way up from the Doria/to climb St Mary Street, I slip and fall,/Christ! what a thump! back of my head as well,/it gave my brains a phantasmagoria.//I'm down, and weeping like a broken stick/of rhubarb, when a carriage, if you please,/a posh turn-out, goes by, not very quickly.//'Stop!' shouts a servant-laddie, when he sees/the state I'm in; but a wee sweet-voiced chick/inside the coach says, 'Drive on; who dies dies.']

Attentive readers will have noticed that Stott compressed the second quatrain into three longish lines. Garioch's solution indicates that he went back to the original, which reads like this:

CHI VA LA NOTTE, VA A LA MORTE

Come sò le disgrazzie! Ecco l'istoria:
co quell' infern' uperto de nottata
me ne tornavo da Testa-spaccata
a sett'ora indov'abbita Vittoria.

Come lí propio dar Palazzo Doria
sò per salí Santa Maria 'nviolata,
scivolo, e te do un cristo de cascata,
e batto apparteddietro la momoria.

Stavo pe terra a piagne a vita mozza,
quanno ch'una carrozza da signore
me passò accanto a passo de barrozza.

'Ferma,' strillò ar cucchiero un zervitore;
ma un vocino ch'escí da la carrozza
je disse: 'Avanti, aló; chi more more.' (Belli, 1965: I, 390)

Stott had given Belli's fifth line in only three words: 'From Palazzo Doria'. Garioch, presumably for reasons of rhyme, restores it to its full length. But he has seen *'un cristo de cascata'* and replaced Stott's 'a hell of a fall' by the much more expressive 'Christ! whit a dunt!' Belli's joke at the end of line 6 is lost on both his translators. The church of Santa Maria stands in Via Lata, but his spelling is a visual pun with the meaning of 'undefiled', 'unviolated'. Garioch's eighth line is a splendid addition to both original and crib, skilfully incorporating the needed information from the note and introducing an exotic term that neatly completes his virtuosic series of rhymes: 'story – Victoria – Doria – phantasmagoria'. It is a triumphant solution to a problem he regularly faced, of finding his Scots version shrunken in size when compared with the original. In the first tercet, 'if you please' is an unashamed filler. The use of 'a posh turn-out' for 'high-class' effectively characterises the attitude and social position of his speaker, and the substitution of 'rhubarb' for 'vine' is another witty naturalisation (but do sticks of rhubarb weep?). Notice that, although Garioch Scotticises elements of his original, sufficient foreign elements are retained (here the Roman toponyms) to remind us we are not in Scotland. The resulting ambivalence was evidently precious to Garioch. Belli's *barrozza* is in Italian *baroccio*, a cart drawn by oxen. All Stott and Garioch retain of the comparison is the pace: the internal rhyme *mozza – carrozza – barrozza* in the first tercet is naturally lost. Garioch cuts the driver, adds 'whan he sees/the state I'm in' (again, the new material incorporates a rhyme and an enjambement) and turns the *vocino* (Stott's 'sweet' is not in Belli) into a person, a 'wee sweet-voiced chick' (in Belli it is the voice that is small). The French expression *aló* (from *allons*) is lost, but the switch of preposition in the closing line, 'inside' instead of 'from', is strikingly effective. It emphasises the invisibility of the girl, and therefore her power.

The poem is both funny and heartless, or about heartlessness, all the more surprising because it is demonstrated by a young woman who would stereotypically be seen as compassionate and tender. If it is fair to say that Belli's view of Rome is coloured by a bleak humour, the attractions of this stance for a poet such as Garioch are obvious. A sonnet like No. 358, 'The Reminder', is eloquent of the considerable, if not total, affinity between the two:

> D'ye mind of thon auldfarrant-leukan priest
> that learnt folk in their ain houses, him
> wi twa white linen bands about his kist,
> a muckle goun of some coorse kinna scrim?
>
> that stuid amang the heid-stanes, his lang, thin
> shanks like twa parritch-spirtles, niver missed
> a yirdin, him that gaed til the Sun Inn
> fir denner, and wad pey a hauf-croun, jist!
>
> Aweill, the ither day, they fand him deid
> and hingit, wi a raip about his throat
> tied til the crucifix-heuk abuin his bed.
>
> And this wee ploy of his meant sic a lot
> to him, to keep the maitter in his heid,
> he'd even tied his hankie in a knot. (Garioch, 1983: 233)

[D'you remember that old-fashioned-looking priest/who taught folk in their own houses, him/with two white linen bands about his chest,/a big gown of some coarse kind of scrim?//who stood among the head-stones, his long, thin/shanks like two porridge stirring-sticks, never missed a burial, /him who went to the Sun Inn/for dinner, and would pay a half-crown, only!//Well anyway, the other day, they found him dead/and hanged, with a rope about his throat/tied to the crucifix-hook above his bed.//And this wee plan of his meant such a lot/to him, to keep the matter in his head,/he'd even tied his handkerchief in a knot.]

The figure of the old world priest who scrapes a living from private lessons, is an enthusiastic attender of funerals, and finally takes his own life, putting a knot in his handkerchief to remind himself of his decision, is reminiscent of Garioch's outspoken sympathy for metaphysical despair, for a sense of homelessness and estrangement in the world – evident in, for example, his portrayal of Robert Fergusson's mental breakdown in 'The Muir' and 'To Robert Fergusson'. What attracts Belli, as it might well have attracted Garioch, is the oddness of such a mundane gesture in the context of an appalling resolution, as well as the rich irony of the man's hanging himself on the very hook where he hung the image of his God. All the rhymes in

Belli's original are on two syllables, and Garioch has negotiated with extreme deftness terms such as *cajellone* [dressed in a negligent or outdated fashion] or *stajole* [long, thin legs like the rods or *staggi* that hold up fishing-nets]. The latter is masterfully rendered as 'parritch-spirtles' [sticks for stirring porridge]. In the tercet, two details disappear in the Scots: the knot was tied the day before, and the rope was attached to the poor fellow's dog-collar. Yet to compensate, Garioch has found an appropriate Scots term: 'ploy', with its implication of mischievous fun, strikes a note of suppressed horror. With 'crucifix-heuk' he supplies in four Scots syllables the needed information about an alien world. Is it necessary to point out that, in Scots, the rhymes 'throat, lot, knot' are perfect?

The octave has an unusual rhyme scheme: *abab baba*. Garioch follows Belli faithfully here, as he does with another unusual pattern beloved of the *romanesco* poet: *abba baab*. The tercet follows the *cdc dcd* pattern favoured by Belli, one that Garioch complains of in his letters to Antonia Stott, given the difficulties of rhyming it presented to him.[14] Belli's innovations appear more regular when seen in terms of pairs of lines rather than single lines:

abab baba cdc dcd becomes AABB CCC (where A = *ab*, B = *ba*, and C = *cd*), and

abba baab cdc dcd becomes ABBA CCC (where A = *ab*, and B = *ba*).

The tone of voice in 'The Reminder' is not dissimilar to that in some of Garioch's Scots work, though it lacks his recurring overtones of aggression, the urge to cut pretension down to size. The Belli sonnets, however, present us with a range of characters and voices, male and female, ironic and tender. It is interesting to consider a case where, in my opinion, Garioch is less than successful in finding a Scots equivalent; No. 1677, 'The Puir Faimly' [The Poor Family]:

> Wheesht nou, my darling bairnies, bide ye quaet:
> yir faither's comin suin, jist bide a wee.
> Oh Virgin of the greitin, please help me,
> Virgin of waymenting, ye that can dae't.
>
> My hairts, I wuss that ye cuid ken hou great
> my luve is! Dinnae greit, or I sall dee.
> He'll bring us something hame wi him, you'll see,
> and we will get some breid, and ye will eat ...
>
> Whit's that ye're sayin, Joe? jist a wee while,
> my son, ye dinnae like the dark ava.
> Whit can I dae fir ye, if there's nay yle?

Puir Lalla, whit's the maitter? Oh my bairn,
ye're cauld? But dinnae staund agin the waa:
come and I'll warm ye on yir mammie's airm. (Garioch, 1983: 267)

[Shush now, my darling children, keep quiet:/your father's coming soon, just hold on a little./Oh Virgin of the crying, please help me,/Virgin of lamenting, you that can do't.//My sweethearts, I wish that you could know how great/ my love is! Don't cry, or I shall die./He'll bring us something home with him, you'll see,/and we will get some bread, and you will eat ... //What's that you're saying, Joe? Just a short while,/my son, you don't like the dark at all./ What can I do for you, if there's no oil?//Poor Lalla, what's the matter? Oh my child,/you're cold? But don't stand against the wall:/come and I'll warm you on your mummy's arm.]

There are many possible reasons for Garioch's comparative failure here. Even today, a spoken voice in Scots poetry may bear echoes of the eighteenth-century vernacular revival. Part of the ideological baggage of the mock elegies of Allan Ramsay and Robert Fergusson, however (most clamorously in 'Lucky Spence's Last Advice'; Kinghorn & Law, 1974: 13–17), is an emphasis on thrift, on the accumulation of material wealth. The mixture of tenderness, desperate piety and absolute destitution presented here may ring awkward because such a representation is alien to the Scots tradition. The technical weaknesses of the sonnet are either symptomatic of this awkwardness or contribute directly to it. I am thinking of the use of an unstressed syllable in rhyming position ('please help me' l. 3) and the flaccid corresponding rhymes in the second quatrain ('or I sall dee', 'you'll see'); the half rhyme on 'eat' at the end of the octave; the run-on between lines 5 and 6 ('hou great/my luve is') which gives an inappropriately rhetorical feel to the mother's declaration, with an implication of posturing and insincerity; and, again in rhyme position, the weakness of a filler like 'ava' (l. 10).

It is interesting to compare Belli's original here, '*La famija poverella*':

Quiete, crature mie, stateve quiete:
sí, fiji, zitti, ché mommó viè tata.
Oh Vergine der Pianto addolorata,
provedeteme voi che lo potete.

Nò, viscere mie care, nun piagnete:
nun me fate morí cusí accorata.
Lui quarche cosa l'averà abbuscata,
e pijeremo er pane, e magnerete.

Si capíssivo er bene che ve vojo!
Che dichi, Peppe? nun vòi stà a lo scuro?
Fijo, com'ho da fà si nun c'è ojo?
E tu, Lalla, che hai? Povera Lalla,
hai freddo? Ebbè, nun méttete lí ar muro:
viè in braccio a mamma tua che t'ariscalla. (Belli, 1965: III, 1763)

[Quiet, my creatures, keep quiet:/yes, children, silent, for Daddy's just arriving./ Oh dolorous Virgin of Tears,/provide for me, you who can do it.// No, my dear viscera, don't cry:/don't make me die heartstricken like this./He will have found something,/and we will take bread, and you will eat.//If you only knew how fond of you I am!... /What are you saying, Peppe? you don't want to be in the dark?/ Son, what am I to do if there's no oil?//And you, Lalla, what's the matter with you? Poor Lalla,/are you cold? Well, don't stay there by the wall:/come into your mother's arms and she will warm you.]

Belli's mother refers to her children as 'my creatures', 'my dear viscera', much more natural and stronger expressions than 'my darling bairnies' or 'my hairts'. The whole of her first two lines is aimed at quieting her children. She does not, like Garioch's mother, ask them to wait (something children are not good at doing). Garioch splits Belli's Virgin into two, again bringing a rhetorical flourish that sits ill with his subject matter. He transposes the first line in Belli's sestet to the second quatrain (losing the distinction in Italian between *amare* 'to love' and *voler bene* 'to be fond of'), and omits the manner of the mother's projected death: *accorata*, from *cuore* 'heart' ('heartstricken' could be one translation). The Scots reproduces the singular 'arm' of the original, when the meaning is clearly that the mother will embrace her shivering daughter with both arms. There may however be an unfairness in the comparison. The dialect supplies Belli with marvellously powerful polysyllables in rhyme position: *addolorata, magnerete, ariscalla*. The analytic nature of Scots, which excludes polysyllabic suffixes giving the person, mood and tense of a verse, and has instead strings of monosyllables, made it hard for Garioch to find any adequate equivalent.

The church, as both religious institution and civil government, is ever present in Belli's sonnets, sometimes in the foreground, sometimes in the background, conditioning the tone and the limits of what can be said. It may therefore be appropriate to close by examining two sonnets connected with it. In some ways it is the most alien element in the world that Garioch was transmuting into Scots. He did indeed have a long tradition of anti-Catholic polemic to draw on, stretching back to the time of the Reformation. But what characterises Belli's approach is that he uses the voice of the powerless, of the governed, who can respond with irony or sarcasm but cannot organise to bring about change, or criticise from the standpoint of a competing belief system. They have neither the linguistic resources nor the education required to do so. No. 811, 'The Relicschaw' [Relic Show], describes one of the aspects of Catholic practice most inimical to Protestant ideas. It also shows Garioch dealing with a list, a syntactical pattern that offered distinctive options to him as translator.[15]

> Amang thae relics thir's some ither trock:
> the Column, watter frae the Flood's on-ding,
> milk milkit frae Our Leddy, in a thing
> like a gless button, keepit fresh in stock.
>
> Syne thir's the Paschal Lamb, King Dauvit's sling,
> the kiss of Judas and St Peter's cock,
> and thir's the lint-white wig, set on its block,
> keepit aside the rod of Hevin's King.
>
> Thir's twa yairds of the eclipse at Calvary,
> and, juist to keep things gaein, suppose they swelt,
> a puckle life picked frae eternity.
>
> And thir's Gode's caunnle-end, that didnae melt
> whan he lit up the sun and said, 'Nou gie
> the bosses licht, and thaim that dae's they're tellt.' (Garioch, 1983: 242)

[Among those relics there's some other odds and ends:/the Column, water from the Flood's downpour,/milk milked from Our Lady, in a thing/like a glass button, kept fresh in stock.//Then there's the Paschal Lamb, King David's sling,/the kiss of Judas and St Peter's cock,/and there's the lint-white wig, set on its block,/kept beside the rod of Heaven's King.//There's two yards of the eclipse at Calvary,/and just to keep things going, in case they perished,/a little life picked from eternity.//And there's God's candle-end, that didn't melt/when he lit up the sun and said. 'Now give/the bosses light, and those that do as they're told.']

Belli's original is entitled '*La mostra de l'erliquie*':

> *Tra l'antre erliquie che t'ho dette addietro*
> *c'è l'agnello pasquale e la colonna:*
> *c'è er latte stato munto a la Madonna,*
> *ch'è sempre fresco in un botton de vetro.*
>
> *C'è l'acqua der diluvio: c'è la fionna*
> *der re Dàvide, e 'r gallo de san Pietro:*
> *poi c'è er bacio de Giuda, e c'è lo scetro*
> *der Padr'Eterno e la perucca bionna.*

Ce sò du parmi e mezzo de l'ecrisse
der Carvario, e c'è un po' de vita eterna
pe fà er lèvito in caso che finisse.
C'è er moccolo che aveva a la lenterna
Dio quanno accese er zole, e poi je disse:
'Va', illumina chi serve e chi governa.' (Belli, 1965: II, 862)

[Among the other relics I said to you before/there's the Easter lamb and the column:/there's the milk milked from the Madonna,/which is always fresh in a glass button.//There's the water of the flood: there's the sling/of King David, and the cock of Saint Peter:/then there's the kiss of Judas, and there's the sceptre/of the Eternal Father and the blonde wig.//There are two and a half palms of the eclipse/of Calvary, and there's a little eternal life/to serve as yeast if it should ever end.//There's the candle-end that was in the lantern/of God when he lit the sun, and then told it:/'Go, illuminate those who serve and those who govern.']

The rhyme pattern is the *abba baab* mentioned above. A list gives Garioch the opportunity to reorder elements: the flood water and the Easter lamb change places. Here as elsewhere, the elements he introduces tend to occupy rhyme slots ('some ither trock', 'the Flood's on-ding', 'in a thing', 'set on its block', 'that didnae melt'). More striking, however, is the fact that Garioch finds himself rendering the criticism more acute. In Belli's sonnet it is devastating but stated in such a way that, were one simply listening to the tone of the voice and not to what it says, it might escape one. The Madonna's milk is always fresh; one has to stop and ask oneself what Judas' kiss might look like; there is a beautiful touch of humour in describing the eternal life laid by as 'yeast', as if life itself were a kind of bread (the image is concrete enough to appeal to a popular audience); and God had a candle-end in his lantern when he lit the sun. The word *moccolo* can also mean 'snot', and the effect is hardly majestic.

The speaker never expresses scorn directly, whereas Garioch's Scots voice emphasises that the relics are 'trock' [worthless goods]; the container of the holy milk is 'a thing/like a gless button' and the milk itself is kept in 'stock' as if in a grocery store; even the addition 'didnae melt' serves to point out the lowering of sacred events that is practised all through the sonnet, by emphasising the diminutive nature of the wick that kindled the light of the universe. No doubt Garioch relished the chance to place St Peter's cock at the end of a line: the pun does not spring to mind in an Italian context, which has a plentiful range of other terms for the male member.

The contrast between original and translation can also be observed in the last line. Belli's could have an almost noble tone, the tell-tale detail being the ordering: the governors come last, in highlighted position, and therefore carry more weight. Garioch's speaker uses a rather heavy-handed irony which spells out the division of human society into two classes: 'those who govern' become 'the bosses', those who serve 'thaim that dae's they're tell't'. Interestingly, he also reverses the order of these two elements.

Comic lowering is explicit in one of the first sonnets Garioch translated, No. 273, 'Judgement Day':

> Fowre muckle angels wi their trumpets, stalkin
> til the fowre airts, sall aipen the inspection;
> they'll gie a blaw, and bawl, ilk to his section,
> in their huge voices: 'Come, aa yese, be wauken.'
>
> Syne sall crawl furth a ragment, a haill cleckin
> of skeletons yerkt out fir resurrection
> to tak again their ain human complexion,
> like choukies gaitheran roun a hen that's clockan.
>
> And thon hen sall be Gode the blissit Faither;
> he'll pairt the indwellars of mirk and licht,
> tane doun the cellar, to the ruiff the tither.
>
> Last sall come angels, swarms of them, in flicht,
> and, like us gaean to bed without a swither,
> they will blaw out the caunnles, and guid-nicht. (Garioch, 1983: 229)

[Four big angels with their trumpets, stalking/ to the four points, shall open the inspection;/they'll give a blow, and bawl, each to his section,/in their huge voices: 'Come, all you, awaken.'//Then shall crawl forth a long line, a whole litter/of skeletons pulled out for resurrection/to take again their own human complexion,/like chickens gathering round a broody hen.//And that hen will be God the blessed Father;/he'll part the inhabitants of dark and light,/the one down the cellar, to the roof the other.//Last will come angels, swarms of them, in flight,/and, like us going to bed without dithering,/they will blow out the candles, and good-night.]

It would be fascinating to compare Garioch's version with MacDiarmid's 1925 version of a Russian poem on the same subject but utterly different in effect, 'The Last Trump' (MacDiarmid, 1978: I, 29), from an original by Dmitry Merezhkovsky (1865–1941). Here is Belli's *romanesco* poem, *'Er giorno der giudizzio'*:

> *Quattro angioloni co le tromme in bocca*
> *se metteranno uno pe cantone*
> *a sonà: poi co tanto de vocione*
> *cominceranno a dí: 'Fora a chi tocca.'*

Allora vierà su una filastrocca
de schertri da la terra a pecorone,
pe ripijà figura de perzone,
come purcini attorno de la biocca.

E sta biocca sarà Dio benedetto,
che ne farà du' parte, bianca, e nera:
una pe annà in cantina, una sur tetto.

All'urtimo uscirà 'na sonajera
d'angioli, e, come si s'annassi a letto,
smorzeranno li lumi, e bona sera. (Belli, 1965: I, 299)

[Four big angels with trumpets in their mouths/will set themselves one at each corner/playing: then with a great big voice/will begin to say: 'Out those whose turn it is.'//Then there will come up a rigmarole/of skeletons from the ground on all fours,/to assume once more the shape of persons,/like chickens around the mother hen.//And this mother hen will be blessed God,/who will make two groups of them, white, and black:/one to go into the cellar, the other onto the roof.//Last of all will emerge a swarm/of angels, and, as if it were time for bed,/will put out the lights, and good evening.]

It is worth pausing to reflect on Belli's strategy here. In terms of preaching to an uneducated audience, it could hardly be faulted. The unconceivable events of the last day are recounted in terms of the ordinary and the familiar. But the effect, rather than making them real, is to make them ridiculous. Used in traditional fashion, the strategy could be condescending, a speaking down to those unable to grasp the content in another form. In Belli's hands, the satire moves in the opposite direction, undermining the ideology it purports to serve. Hell and Heaven are turned into the cellar and the roof of a house; God is a broody hen (what could be further from the image of the terrible judge?). And the lights of the created world are little more than a night-light to be snuffed out before going to sleep. Belli's chosen words have double meanings (in standard Italian, at least) that are faithful to his overall approach: *filastrocca* (1.5) is a children's nonsense rhyme, *sonagliera* (1.12) is a collar with bells of the kind that a jester might adopt,[16] and to address someone as *benedetto* (l. 9) can express a mixture of affection, exasperation and commiseration. As we have come to expect, Garioch adds a certain amount of material, preferably in line-end position: 'stalkin'', 'sall aipen the inspection', 'ilk to his section'. Oddly, in this case, the Scots tends to a majesty absent in the original. The alteration is evident in words like 'stalk', or 'inspection' and 'section' with their hint of military rigours. Belli's angels mention nothing so poetic as wakening. One almost has the impression that they are summoning children who have hidden away for fear of punishment. Understandably, Garioch dodges the problems of interpreting *filastrocca* and instead uses 'ragment' and 'cleckin' [a brood or litter; used derogatively when referring to human beings]. The latter, perhaps unfortunately, anticipates the hilarious hen and chicken image at the core of the sonnet. Nor does Garioch have his skeletons graphically crawl as they do for Belli. The same alteration of tone is evident in the sestet. Where Belli speaks of two 'parts', 'white' and 'black', Garioch impressively cites 'the indwellars of mirk and licht' [inhabitants of dark and light] ('indwellars' is a particularly archaic and uncolloquial term). The added, rhyming, terms include, alongside 'in flicht' and 'without a swither', the qualification of blessed God as a father, which again suggests majesty and authority.

There is no need to accuse Garioch of being unfaithful to his original or of misrepresenting it. But he is in effect producing a rather different poem: perhaps, after its fashion, one closer to MacDiarmid's Merezhkovsky translation than to Belli's sonnet. The virtuoso rhyming, at least in my view, contributes to the overall raising of tone: 'inspection – section – resurrection – complexion', 'stalkin – wauken – cleckin – clockan' and 'Faither – tither – swither'. The prevailing use of trisyllables and disyllables in rhyming position is considerably more marked in Scots than in *romanesco*. Is it inappropriate to see a reflection of Garioch's own religious scepticism, the metaphysical pessimism that surfaces in his untranslated poems, in that closing image of eternal darkness? After all, if the candles within are snuffed out, it is dark up on the roof as well.

The earlier version of this sonnet published in *Selected Poems* (Garioch, 1966: 22) has significant differences in two lines. In line 10 there is 'wha'll wale them out, the darkie frae the lichtie' [who'll pick them out, the dark one from the light one], much closer to the original, but with an awkwardness in the use of 'darkie' that troubled Garioch (Fulton, 1986: 151); and Carne-Ross's notion about the 'bell-collar' prompted 'angels in bell-ring'd flichtie [flight]' in line 12. The double rhyme meant that line 14 ended 'guid-nicht t'ye!' in this version. It is interesting that the later modifications allowed Garioch to alter this ending to a simple 'guid-nicht', much more in keeping with the generally more solemn tone he achieves.

Garioch's Belli translations are a double text in more ways than one. Behind the Scots version presented lurks at least one other text, be it the crib or (more cogently perhaps, since Garioch had access to them) the *romanesco* originals. At a deeper level, they present the double agenda characteristic of so much of this poet's work. His craftsmanlike attention to detail, the respect he shows for such apparently aleatory elements as the different rhyming patterns that Belli adopts in his octaves – these are in tune with an older, perhaps even an anachronistic concept of the poet as artisan, as someone who neither imposes his own personality nor feels constrained to 'Make it new!' but is willing to reproduce, or to appear to reproduce, the masterworks of an earlier generation.

Yet one could also argue that they offer, if not a substitute, then a transcendence, of the panorama of Edinburgh life that some might have expected, even demanded, from Garioch, and of which the Edinburgh sonnets are a mere truncated torso. They offer transcendence because, whatever angle they are seen from, the Belli sonnets are always something more. They are more than a portrait of Rome, because of the Scottish elements, and more than one of Edinburgh, because of the Roman. They are more than a translation because they are not enjoyed (and one suspects were not designed) as primarily a means of access to Belli's originals, but become something different while yet remaining linked and, in their way, faithful to those. They are more than an exercise in Scots because one is constantly aware of another presence, another language behind the lines. They are not about a language but about language or languages, and successfully enable Garioch to break free of the limitations of the stigmatised linguistic medium he had chosen, in a way that 'original' work of a 'purely Scottish' nature might never have allowed.

Notes

1. See Carena (1993). Roudinesco's 'Introduction' first appears in *Nouvelle revue française*, 1 August 1955, pp. 193–5.
2. The 1953 edition was reprinted in 1956: *Traduction en vers des Bucoliques de Virgile; précédé de Variations sur les Bucoliques,* [by] Paul Valéry (Paris: Gallimard). The quotations here are from *The Collected Works, Vol. 7: The Art of Poetry* translated by D. Foliott (see Valéry, 1958).
3. In 'The Task of the Translator', Walter Benjamin expresses views diametrically opposed to those of Valéry: 'As translation is a mode of its own, the task of the translator, too, may be regarded as distinct and clearly differentiated from the task of the poet.' He holds that 'a translation, instead of resembling the meaning of the original, must lovingly and in detail incorporate the original's mode of signification', and must also 'in large measure refrain from wanting to communicate something'. Garioch would hardly have understood his insistence that 'fidelity in reproducing the form impedes the rendering of the sense.' Limitations of space prevent me examining the contradiction between these two approaches. Benjamin's contention that '[t]he interlinear version of the Scriptures is the prototype or ideal of all translation' suggests that such an examination would not be without interest. (Benjamin, 1973: 76, 78, 82)
4. For the information in this paragraph see Belli (1984: lxv–xciv). The translations from the Italian are my own.

5. Letter dated 3 February (no indication of the year) in NLS [National Library of Scotland] MS 26595. Garioch comments elsewhere regarding this commission that 'away back in 1958 I think it must have been' (Fulton, 1986: 151).
6. See the 'Introduction by Antonia Stott' in *Complete Poetical Works* (Garioch, 1983: 217–20). The sonnets in *Selected Poems* (Garioch, 1966) are 273, 827, 1217 (here titled 'Respiscetto' [sic], later 'Deid'), 1517, 1942 and 2136; those in *Doktor Faust in Rose Street* (Garioch, 1973) are 43, 46, 54, 55, 861, 950, 1026, 1204, 1272, 1406, 1478 and 1723.
7. See the section entitled 'Composition and Publication' in Riach (1991: 60–7). Riach quotes a letter by MacDiarmid in 1956 confessing :

   I had great difficulty in recovering my mss – and did not recover it all. So I had to write fresh stuff to fill these gaps. Also in the interval some of my ideas had changed – and there had been developments in linguistic thought; so I had to do a considerable amount of amending, adding, etc. The same thing will happen with the unpublished sections of the whole poem when I lay my hands on the original drafts. (Riach, 1991: 64–65)

   The implication that the published poem is a provisional realisation of a continuing project could hardly be clearer.
8. For the troubled textual history of his sonnets see Belli (1965: I, lxxix–lxxx). This is the Italian edition that Garioch referred to, and Belli's texts are here quoted in the simplified orthography it uses.
9. Consider the view expressed by Tynianov in *The Problem of Verse Language*:

   [T]he outwardly easy and simple area of *motivated art* turns out to be quite complex and unfavourable material for study ... what is characteristic [of it] is the very motivation (the concealment of this [specific] 'plus' [of art]), which is a distinctive negative characteristic ... rather than a positive one. (Tynianov, 1981: 36)

   In other words, to perceive metre, or the phonetic organisation of poetry, as primarily representational is to conceal its actual function. In *The Structure of the Artistic Text*, Jurij Lotman (1977: 21) writes that '[l]iterature speaks in a special language which is superimposed as a secondary system on natural language'.
10. An indicative example is Garioch's interpretation, consistent throughout the sonnets, of words such as 'harns', 'learnt, and 'warlds' as disyllables for metrical purposes.
11. See National Library of Scotland MS 26595. The enjambements are 'smaa/hours', 'stick of/rhubarb', and the possible alternative 'bore ye (?)' for the final 'story' of the first line (respecting more closely the other words in this particular series: 'Victoria, Doria, phantasmagoria'). The sonnet is quoted in full later in the chapter.
12. Section III in *Complete Poetical Works* (Garioch, 1983: 81–91). There are 21 sonnets, written between March 1959 and March 1973 (Garioch, 1983: 281).
13. See National Library of Scotland MS 26595.
14. 'I am relieved when I find that a sestet rhymes *cdcede*' (18 March 1976). He writes of No. 163 on 21 September 1979: 'It has the *cdc, dcd*, but it can't be helped' (Fulton, 1986: 150, 157).
15. The most fascinating example of a translated list sonnet is 'Noah's Ark', No. 861 (Garioch, 1983: 244).

16. Garioch comments to Antonia Stott that 'Carne-Ross was never sure, I remember, ... about what he thought was some sort of bell-collar, in connection with the angels' (12 May 1976; Fulton, 1986: 151).

Chapter 11
The Puddocks *and* The Burdies *'by Aristophanes and Douglas Young'*

J. DERRICK MCCLURE

Of the many poet-translators who have given a cosmopolitan colouring to the Scots literary scene, none has ranged more widely in his choice of source languages than Douglas Young.[1] His volumes of poetry *Auntran Blads* (1943) and *A Braird o Thristles* (1947) feature translations into Scots from a wide variety of languages, including Greek, Latin, Scots and Irish Gaelic, Italian, French, German, Russian, Welsh, Lithuanian and Chinese. Young's most substantial exercises in translation, however, are not in the field of lyric but of dramatic poetry: *The Puddocks* (1958) and *The Burdies* (1959), from the two comedies of Aristophanes generally known in the English-speaking world as *The Frogs* and *The Birds*.

The Puddocks received its first performance in the Byre Theatre, St Andrews, in 1958: Young, then a lecturer in Greek at St Andrews University, wrote the translation for a student production. It was performed again the same year on the Edinburgh Festival Fringe, attracting wide and generally favourable attention; and the following year Young attempted to repeat his success with *The Burdies*, also produced as a Festival Fringe offering. Owing, apparently, to a poor production, this was not a success (Young & Murison, n.d.: 22). However, in 1966 it had the honour of being Edinburgh's new Royal Lyceum Theatre Company's first contribution to the Festival (a Festival which was on that occasion making Greek drama a special theme, with three other plays being produced in English and modern Greek translations). Reactions to this production were mixed. Nearly all critics were impressed by the costumes and setting, but many were quite patently puzzled by the mere fact of an attempt to recreate Aristophanes for a contemporary Scottish audience, with such mutations as Peisthetairos becoming Sir Wylie Bodie and Euelpides becoming Jock MacHowpfu. The language, too, presented difficulty to some reviewers. Harold Hobson, writing for the *BBC Arts Review*, admitted with disarming honesty:

The play has given – I was going to say all of us, but I alter it to most – [...] an inferiority complex. Having steeled ourselves to the unpalatable fact that we wouldn't understand it if it were played in Greek, it really is too humiliating to find that we don't understand it in Scots, either. And so we become angry. (Quoted in Young, 1966: 18)

Reviews in the Scottish press likewise included reservations regarding the language. For example, Peter Lewis in the *Scottish Daily Mail* wrote:

I cannot see what is funny about it in Douglas Young's adaptation in broad Scots either. Admittedly I don't speak even narrow Scots and some of it might as well have been in the original Greek for all I knew. (Quoted in Young, 1966: 13)

A more serious attack on the language, from a more formidable critic, was made in a BBC arts review programme when Young's fellow Scots-language poet and dramatist Alexander Scott expressed grave reservations on the translation. Young's vigorous response to this hostile criticism led not only to a protracted and very entertaining correspondence in *The Scotsman*, but to a devastating poetic onslaught on Young by Scott, 'Supermakar Story' (Robb, 1994: 101–4), whose concluding lines are:

But aye, albeid he spak through 's hat,   [although; spoke]
His buff was babbity bare.[2]   [bare as a child's]

Nonetheless, Young's daring experiment had enlightened many drama critics in England and further afield, as well as at home, to the potential of Scots as a dramatic medium.

The translation of literature is an act in which individual motives are liable to play an important role. Many, perhaps most, literary translators are attracted to specific projects by straightforward admiration for the source text. Having a personal love for some particular poem, play or whatever, they wish to enable others to share their own interest and enthusiasm. A translator may, particularly if his target language is relatively undeveloped, be acting as a language planner: his intention may be to extend the range of his native tongue and thus enhance its status as a literary medium. On a less altruistic level, though not necessarily a less respectable one, a translator may be responding to a challenge: that of exercising his own creative spirit, his skill in the foreign language, and his mastery of his own speech as a poetic vehicle, in the task of re-expressing in a new form and a new medium the poetic statement made by the original author. All these factors, we may readily assume, affected Douglas Young in his decision to translate the Aristophanic plays into Scots. As an internationally-renowned Greek scholar, an enthusiast for the Scots language, and a man of abounding intellectual enterprise and curiosity, Young could hardly, on the face of it, have failed to be attracted to the task. However, translation has another aspect – the public one. A translator, at least if he regards his work as more than a mere private hobby, must have some realistic expectation that it will be read (or, in the case of a play, performed) and appreciated by the target language's literate speakers.

From this point of view, Aristophanes is far from being an obvious candidate for admission to the literary culture of mid-twentieth-century Scotland. Study of the language and culture of ancient Greece had not, in the 1950s, declined to today's virtual non-existence. Yet it was scarcely to be expected that *many* people then would be familiar with Young's source texts, or have any knowledge whatever of the form and function of classical Greek comedy. Out of the multitudes who regularly used the phrase 'Cloud-Cuckoo-Land', or who had heard Gilbert and Sullivan's Major-General boast that he 'knew the croaking chorus from the *Frogs* of Aristophanes', only a small section could have had a clue regarding the origins of these references: or even, in the former case, known that a specific origin existed at all. And despite his enduringly high reputation and the popularity of some of his plays as texts for study, Aristophanes' influence on the subsequent development of the European comic tradition has not been great. *The Frogs* and *The Birds*, with their anarchic plots, headlong cataracts of characters and incidents interrupted by lengthy declamations, and their dialogue packed with local allusions, topical in-jokes and humorous devices ranging from sophisticated wordplay to infantile vulgarity, come from a world as alien to Douglas Young's Scotland as can be imagined.

And yet, the conclusion of Young's introduction to *The Burdies* is perfectly true: 'Its prime purpose was to be a funny play. And, by Bacchus, it still is a funny play' (Young, 1959: vi). A pair of renegade humans who organise the birds to build a city in the sky, thus preventing the gods from descending to earth for amorous encounters and starving them into submission by blocking off the sacrifices made by their worshippers – such a figment of inspired lunacy must surely appeal in any time and place. The techniques of political satire have not really changed much in two and a half millennia: make your target appear in a ridiculous garb, subject him to comic humiliations, attribute to him some absurd parody of what he said or, better still, take some of his actual words and put them in a grotesque context. The allure of slapstick is timeless. Any audience will be amused when a god has to prove his divinity by the unflinching endurance of skelps [smacks] on his backside, or when a fraudulent oracle-monger is kicked off the stage whether to words that mean 'Get to blazes out of here, will you?' (Sommerstein, 1987: 121, l. 990)[3] or, in Young's version, to 'Awa wi ye tae Freuchie, and fry mice' (*The Burdies*, l. 990). So too is the allure of bawdry and scatology: one of Aristophanes' stock-in-trade jokes is the bladding of one's breeks [shitting one's trousers] as a reaction to sudden fright:

>   EUELPIDES: Wi fricht I've turned til a Shittimite foul.
>   SERVANT: Blethers!
>   EUELPIDES: Aaricht. Juist luik what's on the grund here.
>   SERVANT: And him, – whatna burd's he? Will ye no tell me?
>   PEISTHETAIROS: Och me? I'm a dunglin frae Latrinia.
>   (*The Burdies*, ll. 65–8)[4]

[EU: With fright I've turned into a Shittimite fowl.//SER: Nonsense!//EU: All right. Just look what's on the ground here.//SER: And him, – what kind of bird's he? Won't you tell me?//PEI: You mean me? I'm a dun[g]lin from Latrinia.]

Young's treatment of names here shows real comic ingenuity, making a pun both rude and irreverent – i.e. doubly Aristophanic – on the Biblical Shittim and another on the name of the common shore-bird, *dunlin*.

Besides the features of Aristophanic drama that are funny simply because of what is unchanging in the make-up of the human psyche, it is hard not to imagine a special affinity between some of its characteristics and aspects of Scottish culture. A poetic tradition that includes 'The Gyre Carling', 'King Berdok', 'Kynd Kittock', 'Colkelbie's Sow' and the like, clearly belongs to a people with a well-developed taste for the grotesque and crazy – as Young, with his deep knowledge of Scottish literature, would have been well aware. Sir David Lindsay in *Ane Satyre of the Thrie Estaitis* (which had been revived by Tyrone Guthrie and Robert Kemp in 1948, a landmark event in Scottish theatrical history) mocks the establishment of his day, not only with the same energy and the same scathing wit as Aristophanes, but with the same reliance on invective, parody and scatological humour. Rabelais, who has often been compared to Aristophanes and was certainly influenced by him, inspired Sir Thomas Urquhart to produce one of the most remarkable translations in Scottish literature. And the vein of wild, grotesque and preposterous humour that characterises the Greek and French writers was developed still further by the Scot. Robert Burns, as has often been noted, includes a vein of exuberant anarchism in his multifaceted poetic personality. Young recalls this in echoes of his poetry when describing his birds as a 'hellish legion' and one of them as 'a chick o [of] Mars that has been in monie [many] wars'. In our own time the

Aristophanic mood surfaces regularly in poetry – most outstandingly, among the great post-MacDiarmid makars, in Sydney Goodsir Smith.

Nonetheless, in the late 1950s, when native-born (including vernacular) drama was, though far from negligible in quantity or quality, set firmly in the mould of traditional proscenium-arch theatre, the naturalising of Aristophanes was a bold experiment indeed. Linguistically, Young's response to the challenge was to employ a Scots which, though sometimes (for specific effects) venturing into exalted realms of aureation and polysyllabicity, is for the most part firmly grounded in vernacular speech and poetry of the Burns tradition. The opening of *The Puddocks* draws on an almost bathetically familiar vein of theatrical humour:

> XANTHIAS: Suld I come oot wi ane o the uisual jokes,
> maister, that gars the audience aye lauch?
>
> DIONYSOS: Onie ye like, by God, binna 'Ah'm owrewrocht.'
> Tak tent for that. It gars oor bluid fair byle.
>
> XANTHIAS: And nae ither baur?
>
> DIONYSOS: Ay, dinna say 'Ah'm forfochen.'
>   (Young, 1958; *The Puddocks*, ll. 1–5)[5]

[XA: Should I come out with one of the usual jokes,/master, which makes the audience always laugh?//DI: Any one you like, by God, bar 'I'm over-wrought.'/Look out for that. It makes our blood really boil.//XA: And any other joke?//DI: Yes, don't say 'I'm exhausted.']

The point of the joke is altered in that the words that the servant is forbidden to say in the original have a vulgar ring, whereas in the Scots version they are strongly marked Scotticisms that *could* be used facetiously; but the language itself is as plain as it could be.

Throughout both plays, what might be described as the basic register (against which passages in different styles stand out in relief) is this colloquial Scots, exploiting to the full the expressive vocabulary of the language but containing few of the archaisms and other lexical exotica often to be found in Young's poems. (Young's contemporary, Sydney Goodsir Smith, showed the same sense of dramatic realism by writing his play *The Wallace* (Smith, 1960) in a Scots that, compared to his poems, is much closer to a vernacular register.) This plain and unadorned language may be used simply for providing information:

> EUELPIDES: Nou, first, you was a man aince, juist like us;
> and you awed siller aince, juist like us;
> and ye likeit fine no peyin it, juist like us.
> Syne, whan ye tuik the natur o the burds,

> ye flew aa round the airth and sea attour,
> and ye hae aa the thochts o men and burds.
> (*The Burdies*, ll. 114–9)
>
> [EU: Now, first, you were a man once, just like us;/and you owed money once, just like us;/and you liked fine not paying it, just like us./Then, when you took the nature of the birds,/you flew all round the earth and sea besides,/and you have all the thoughts of men and birds.]

or for passages of humorous exchange which almost suggest the 'Scoatch coamic' tradition of music hall and pantomine:

> DIONYSOS: But shairlie the cuddie cairries the wecht you're cairryan?
> XANTHIAS: Losh no, Guidsakes, no what I've gotten tae cairry.
> DIONYSOS: But hou are you cairryan, whan you're cairryit yoursel?
> XANTHIAS: I dinna ken. But ma shouther here's owrewrocht.
> DIONYSOS: Aaricht, sin ye say the cuddie's nae uis tae ye,
> tak you your turn and cairry the cuddie nou. (*The Puddocks*, ll. 27–32)
>
> [**Di:** But surely the donkey carries the weight you're carrying?//**Xa:** Lord no, for God's sake, not what I've got to carry.//**Di:** But how can you be carrying, when you're being carried yourself?//**Xa:** I don't know. But my shoulder here's exhausted.//**Di:** All right, since you say the donkey's no use to you,/take you your turn and carry the donkey now.]

Also, by using colloquial language, and incorporating references to modern Scotland, Young can conjure up in rapid doggerel-patter a world which Aristophanes never knew:

> I the Wild Wast there's a region,   [In; West]
> caad the Gorbals, by the Clyde,   [called]
> whaur they breed a hero legion,–   [where]
> razor-slashin is their pride.
> Fans o Celtic and o Rangers
> like their bottles, fou or tuim,   [full or empty]
> bonnie fechters aa. But dangers   [good fighters all]
> dern in streets whaur lamps are dim.   [lurk; where]
> (*The Burdies*, ll. 1482–9)

However, Young readily elaborates on this plain language; and in both plays (but particularly in *The Burdies*, which is linguistically the more varied and imaginative of the two) many passages attest to his skill in handling the more distinctive registers of literary Scots. The remarkable variety of Scots bird names gave him, in a play about birds, opportunities of which he availed himself to the full:

Pyat, jay, and dou, and laivrock,
 shilfie, yalla-yite, and cushie,
gled and eagle, gowk and widgeon,
 reidshank, phalarope, and osprey,
purpie fink, and kestrel, diver,
 lintie, peregrine, wuidpyker ... (*The Burdies*, ll. 302–5)

[Magpie, jay, and dove, and lark,/chaffinch, yellow-hammer, and wood pigeon,/hawk and eagle, cuckoo and widgeon,/redshank, phalarope, and osprey,/purple finch, and kestrel, diver,/linnet, peregrine, woodpecker...]

(Not content with this, he adds a note saying '[Ye] micht add a wheen mair [few more]' and offering a further 48 bird names!) A well-known feature of Scots, its wealth of insult terms, affords him ample opportunity to reproduce the invective with which Aristophanes' characters pepper their dialogue: 'The sleekit deil' [sly devil], 'juist draff and druttle, bletherskytes' [just dregs and useless stuff, windbags], 'a doddy dowf doit [dull stupid thick] ignoramus', 'a fodyel gurk cam wauchlan up' [a fat short person came waddling up], 'Ye gomeril!' [you moron], 'Ye limmer!' [rascal], 'Ye creeshie sumph!' [greasy imbecile], 'Ye ill-deedie wratch!' [ill-behaved wretch], and 'Puir haiveral nyaff!' [poor foolish-talking nobody]. A deliberately over-written example is:

Ye scunnersome, ootrageous skellum, you,   [hideous; rascal]
mischievous villain, bluidie blagyart, you ...   [bloody blackguard]
 (*The Puddocks*, ll. 465–6)

By contrast, an increase in the density of Scots lexemes and a preponderance of archaic words can give a fine bombastic effect:

Siccar the dunneran makar 'll herbour a terrible anger,
suin as he sees his rival sherpan his tusk wi a clangour
shill and dirlan. Wud wi gram and teen,
Aeschylus will rowe his een.

Hech! sic a flytin we'll see, – bress helmets' gesserant flashin,
wallopan horsemane phrases, and skelves frae the chariots' bashin,
whan the chiseler fends the architect's
stallion-muntit word-effects. (*The Puddocks*, ll. 814–21)

[For certain the thundering poet'll harbour a terrible anger,/soon as he sees his rival sharpening his tusk with a clangour/shrill and reverberating. Mad with rage and resentment,/Aeschylus will roll his eyes.//Oh! such a violent altercation we'll see, – the glitter from brass helmets flashing,/galloping horse's-mane phrases, and splinters from the chariot's bashing,/when the chiseller protects the architect's/stallion-mounted word-effects.]

A speech from *The Burdies* begins in a measured and dignified tone, appropriate to a speech by a Herald, and immediately lapses into the vernacular with the insulting *clorty*, the undignified *crummocks* and the slangy *burdie-daft*:

> O, you that foondit the famed etherial city,
> ye kenna hou muckle honour ye win frae mortals,
> hou monie lovers are grienan for this country.
> For afore ye ever grundit this city here,
> the hale o mankind was daft on Spartan fashions.
> Lang-haired and hungert, clorty, juist like Socrates,
> they cairried crummocks. Nou they hae turned about;
> they're burdie-daft. (*The Burdies*, ll. 1277–84)
>
> [O, you that founded the famed ethereal city,/you do not know what great honour you receive from mortals,/how many lovers are yearning for this country./For before you ever established this city here,/the whole of mankind was besotted by Spartan fashions./Long-haired and famished, filthy, just like Socrates,/they carried sticks with crooked heads. Now they have turned about;/they're bird-crazy.]

The nightingale is summoned in an evocative passage, as serious in intent and effect as Young's translations from Dante or Homer:

> C'wa, nichtigal wife, gie owre your sleep.
> Lowse the melodies o halie sang,
> as frae yon ferly mou ye threep
> waefu Itys, my son and yours,
> dirlan aa owre as the sangspate poors
> frae your gleg broun hause, and the echoes gang
> clear throu the hinnysuckle bouers
> til the haas o Zeus on Olympus' steep ... (*The Burdies*, ll. 209–216)
>
> [Come away, nightingale wife, give over your sleep./Let loose the melodies of holy song,/as from that marvellous mouth you harangue/woeful Itys, my son and yours,/tremulous all over as the song-flood pours/from your keen brown neck, and the echoes go/clear through the honeysuckle bowers/to the halls of Zeus on Olympus' steep ...]

And immediately afterwards, the other birds are called in a much less melodious verse using vocabulary appropriate to the birds of nature instead of mythology:

> C'wa, burds o my fedder, flock thegidder,
> ye that pyke pleumen's weel-sawn ackers,
> ye coontless barley-guzzlan breeds,

and ye gleg clans that nibble seeds,
saft-chirplan i your swithwinged dackers ... (*The Burdies*, ll. 229–233)

[Come away, birds of my feather, flock together,/you that peck ploughmen's well-sown acres,/you countless barley-guzzling breeds,/and you nimble clans that nibble seeds,/softly twittering in your quick-winged wrangles ...]

In the celebrated *flyting* [quarrelling, using abusive language] of Aeschylus and Euripides, the climactic episode of *The Frogs*, Aristophanes produced virtuoso parodies of the various styles of both dramatists. This presented Young with an invitation – indeed, a positive obligation, if the joke was not to be lost entirely – to write passages that not only would be obviously unlike each other but would give unmistakable signs of not being seriously intended. He rises to the occasion with great panache, making Euripides mock his rival with a song in which polysyllabic words are clumsily strung together into clod-hopping dactylic lines, contorted in grammar and almost vacuous in sense:

'O Phthian Achilles, why ever, manslauchterous hearan,
Ho ro! trouble, stap ye na ben tae the rescue?
Hermes we venerate for oor forebear, the clan by the lochside.
Ho ro! trouble, stap ye na ben tae the rescue?'
...
'Maist famous Achaian, of Atreus the much-kingly, learn frae me, son.'
'Ho ro! trouble, stap ye na ben tae oor rescue?'
...
'Haud wheesht halie. The Beewarden priestesses Artemis' hoose apen
nearhaund.'
'Ho ro! trouble, stap ye na ben tae the rescue?'
(*The Puddocks*, ll. 1264–7, 1270–1, 1273–4)

[*manslauchterous hearan* = homicidal hearing; *stap ye na ben tae the rescue* = step you not inside to the rescue; *haud wheesht halie* = keep holy silence; *hoose apen nearhaund* = house open nearby]

He goes on to let Aeschylus respond with a psuedo-lament ludicrously juxtaposing classical names with banal vocabulary and atrocious rhymes:

Ye Cretan archers, bairns o Ben Ida, wi [children]
bows and arrows come and rescue me,
wi shanks at the dooble rin and circle this [legs; 'at the double']
hoose. And ye, Diktynna lass, bonnie Artemis,
gang aawhaur throu the haas wi your wee bitchies. [go everywhere; halls]
And ye, Zeus' dochter, wi torches' pitchiest [daughter]

flares i baith haunds, Hekate, gie us a licht tae Susie's,   [both hands]
sae I may search her hoosie wi a cruisie.   [oil-lamp]
(*The Puddocks*, ll. 1356–63)

In the *Scotsman* correspondence that followed the production of *The Burdies*, Young claimed (2 September 1966) that he was attempting to emulate Aristophanes' use of 'Greek of various periods and social strata'. Whether and to what extent Young's varieties of Scots correspond point for point to those in the Greek I am wholly unable to say; but that the attempt was made is unmistakable. The kaleidoscopic range of styles and registers in Young's Scots is obvious to any reader, and in some cases at least it makes for individual passages of high distinction.

Besides being linguistic *tours de force*, however, Aristophanes' plays are comedies; and Young's translations were written as the originals were, to make audiences (as well as readers) laugh. Simple horseplay, of which, as already noted, much of the humour consists, needs no translation; and the more sophisticated comedy of plot and situation (not *much* more sophisticated, it must be admitted, since plot-construction as understood and practised by dramatists of later times scarcely exists in Aristophanes) survives unchanged in the Scots versions. Aristophanes relies extensively, however, on wordplay, one of the most notorious challenges to any translator. Young tries manfully to reproduce, or at least to imitate, this feature, but with varying degrees of success. Some of his puns in performance, one suspects, would fly past unnoticed: 'Here's a houlet [owl]' – 'Hou'll it like an Embro [Edinburgh] diet ...?' (*The Burdies*, l. 301), or a reference to 'the camels coman' with a stage direction '*Bagpipe heard affstage* – "*The Campbells are comin*"' (*The Burdies*, l. 278). Not all of them rely on Scots words: 'Weary faa [bad luck to] the pouer [power] o the dolorous dollar!' (*The Puddocks*, l. 141); 'Are ye Leith Street policemen?' – 'Juist the opposite, we're West End types, non-lethal' (*The Burdies*, ll. 109–110); 'Ye'd wonder gin [if] there's a feat feet canna dae' (*The Burdies*, ll. 1147). In the last, the humour of the Greek line consists in the substitution of 'feet' for 'hands' in a well-known aphoristic phrase; and since no corresponding phrase exists in Scots, Young has tried – for good or ill – to make the line funny by other means. A cut above these in excruciating ingenuity is a line which follows a reference to Artemis: 'She'll be some artie miss frae the Schuil o Art' (*The Burdies*, l. 870). The Greek has an even more strained pun on a name for Artemis and the word for 'goldfinch'. At one point Young's fidelity to his original obliged him to add an apologetic note (in Scots): 'There is a puirlike pun i the Greek, hardly better than the Scots ane' (*The Burdies*, note to l. 815) – the Scots one being on 'Sparta' and 'sparty' (rope). A much more imaginative pun, in Scots this time, is 'Efter the storm ance mair I see a foumart' [Scots *foumart* = ferret, and *fou mart* = full marketplace] (*The Puddocks*, l. 304). Here, too, a note is called for: this pun has its origin in a slip of the tongue by which a Greek actor said the word for 'ferret' instead of the word for 'calm', to the great amusement of his audience; and Young's audience, not knowing the in-joke, would very probably miss an otherwise irrelevant pun. Sometimes, however, Young draws on a Scots homophony for a pun of classic stature, 'I'd blad the twa blads o my hairns' [I'd spoil the two parts of my brain] (*The Puddocks*, l. 134), or produces an embroidery so outrageous as to be memorable:

>   Triballi. Bally guid name tae.
>   As tribal allies they micht tribble ye.   [trouble you]
>   (*The Burdies*, ll. 1529–30)

One of his gems is the many-layered transcreation of a Greek pun in 'Auld Rockie'. This is a perfectly good translation of the original – a reference to Athens by a name that means 'rocky' – but is instantly funny because of its incongruous suggestion of Edinburgh's nickname, 'Auld Reekie' [Old Smoky]. Moreover, there are further resonances in that the character who says it is at that moment perched on a rock, and Auld Reekie has a rock, or rocks, of its own (Arthur's Seat and the Castle rock).

Another feature of Aristophanic comedy that is certain to vex a translator, but for a different reason, is fondness for the humorous possibilities of bodily functions. Here Young's problem was that of deciding what his audience would accept. Prudery has assuredly never been a special characteristic of Scottish writers; and it is not to be expected that Young would be reduced to Gilbert Murray's shift of making Dionysus say 'Don't ... say "I want to blow my nose"' and having Xanthias respond 'I shall sneeze' (Murray, 1912: 4), where a more accurate translation is 'Ye maunna [mustn't] ... cry out ye want the closet' (with 'ye want tae drite [defecate]' and 'ye need the bathruim' given in the notes as alternatives) and 'I'm like tae fert [fart]' (*The Puddocks*, l. 8 and l. 10). In an irresistible passage in the same play (ll. 542–8),[6] Young restores a 'chalmerpat' [chamberpot] that Murray found too indelicate to include, and his line 'kittlan [tickling excitedly] my dearest member' is even more explicit than Aristophanes. In fact, when lavatorial humour occurs in the originals, Young generally translates it faithfully. A reference to a singer who defiles the shrines of Hecate is changed by making the singer into a 'piper that messes his breeks [shits his trousers]' (*The Puddocks*, l. 366), and a similar defilement of a carved stone bearing a decree is rendered 'Mind hou ae nicht ye messed a kirkyaird dyke' [Remember how one night you fouled a churchyard wall] (*The Burdies*, l. 1054), but in both cases the defilement remains.

Sexual references and innuendoes, however, are often toned down from the Aristophanic robustness, or avoided altogether. Peisthetairos's (or Sir Wylie Bodie's) reaction to the beautiful nightingale, 'I'd like it fine tae cuddle her i ma airms' (*The Burdies*, l. 669), gives a very different impression from the original 'I'd have great pleasure in spreading her legs for her' (Sommerstein, 1987: 91–3, l. 669). A chorus in *The Puddocks* (ll. 409–13):

> Wow! there's a lassie I hae seen,
> a bonnie face tae charm your een, [eyes]
> and game for ploys. [amusements]
> Her gairit goun its duds atween [patched gown its tatters between]
> gies glisks o rarest joys. [gives glimpses of]
> (*The Puddocks*, ll. 409–13)

certainly conveys an inviting tone of cheerful sensuality; but what the Greek says in the last two lines is 'Through a tear in her little dress, her pretty breast bobbing out' (Stanford, 1958: 110). Peisthetairos/Sir Wylie insists that the birds 'never pyke [peck]/my sporran here' (*The Burdies*, ll. 441–2), substituting 'sporran' for the Greek word for 'bollocks'. In the exchange:

> PEISTHETAIROS: ... syne straucht aff aa the Phoenicians
> wad tak heuks and begin on the hairst o the wheat
> and the riggs o the birsslan barley.
>
> EUELPIDES: Ay, it's true, whan the gowk cries 'Gowk-oo' a wheen fowk
> faa tae wark on the riggs o the barley.
> (*The Burdies*, ll. 505–7)

[PE: ... then straight away all the Phoenicians/would take sickles and begin on the harvest of the wheat/and the strips of the bristling barley.//EU: Yes, it's true, when the cuckoo cries 'Cuckoo' a group of folk/fall to work on the strips of barley.']

a Scots reader (with memories of Burns in mind) *might* see a sexual suggestion in the response, and of course in performance an actor could make it very clear; but the Greek involves a whole series of bawdy puns that make the joke both more elaborate and much more explicit. The ready acceptance of homosexuality and paedophilia in classical Greece at one point presented Young with a test that he failed. In *The Burdies*, the Hoopoo (Tereus) asks Peisthetairos what kind of country he would like to live in, to which he replies:

A place whaur the daddie o a bonnie laddie
wad come tae me compleenan, wi a grievance like:
'Ye sleekit rogue, that's a braw wey tae treat　　　　[sly; fine way]
my laddie whan ye met him gangan hame　　　　　　[going]
frae the baths. Ye didna shak hands or say *"Hou d'ye dae?"*
or dunsh him i the ribs, altho you're a frien o the faimlie.'　[nudge him in]
(*The Burdies:* ll. 137–42)

This is simply pointless: why should Peisthetairos long to be rebuked for what appears to be merely a failure of common courtesy? In the original, however, the hypothetical father complains because he did not embrace and fondle the boy. Young was no doubt right in assuming that Edinburgh audiences in the 1950s would balk at such a suggestion, but it is surprising that he made no attempt to retain the humorous force of the passage – for example, by tacitly changing the bonnie laddie into a bonnie lassie!

This is a specific instance of a general problem that invariably confronts translators, to a degree directly related to the cultural distance between the world of the translator and that of the original writer. Any literary figure is, axiomatically, rooted in his own place and time; thus forcing a translator to decide how to present the culture-specific aspects of his model's work to his own contemporary audience. Aristophanes is, perhaps, a more-than-usually troublesome case, since his plays are packed with allusions to contemporary events and to individuals of whom, in some cases, all other records have vanished. Young's method is at first sight peculiar: some of the local and topical references in the original plays are left as they are; others are given Scots equivalents; resulting not only in some strange juxtapositions but in an overall sense of double vision. The denizens of Hades include an Aiakos and a Girzie [dimunitive of the previously common Scottish personal name *Grizel*]. The Loch Ness Monsteress (the suffix appears to be for no other reason than to make the line scan) joins with Gorgons (albeit from Crail) in a list of terrors. Jock MacHowpfu [MacHopeful] (Euelpides) asks the Hoopoo 'Hae ye nae Greek place, or Scots, tae tell us o?' (*The Burdies*, l. 148). Yet my purely intuitive impression on reading the translations is that the inconsistency would add a very effective dimension to the humour of the plays, by bringing ancient Greece and modern Scotland into laughably incongruous juxtaposition. Indeed, it is difficult to see what else, in principle, Young could have done. By retaining all the Greek allusions unchanged, he would of course have rendered many things in the plays unintelligible to his audiences. Conversely, a total Scotticisation would have resulted in a discordant cultural clash. Eric Linklater in his novel *The Impregnable Women* (Linklater,

1938) transferred the story of Aristophanes' *Lysistrata* in its entirety to modern Scotland; but *Lysistrata* contains no such elements as a sky-borne city (reachable on foot) or a literary contest between two dead dramatists with a return to life as the prize. Such notions could make sense as humorous fantasies in the intellectual, philosophical and religious setting of Athens in the late fifth century BC, but in Edinburgh in the mid-twentieth century AD they could make no sense whatever except as historical conceptions. By retaining in his translations something of the aura of ancient Greece, Young ensured that those ideas are still funny. They would not have been funny, merely senseless, if he had asked us to accept them as arising in a wholly Scottish setting.

Young has, nonetheless, taken the process of naturalising the plays in modern Scotland a very long way. His birds eat brambles, rowans, eemocks [ants], golochs [earwigs], clegs [horse flies], and midges; his puddocks lowp [frogs leap] through deer's hair and heather. The delicacies with which visitors to Hades are regaled include peasebrose, honie scones, rowies [small rolls], haggis, crowdie [soft cheese], Tay saumon [salmon], and Irish stew at five bob the plate; and Dionysus is sent home with 'a wee dram for the road' (*The Puddocks*, l. 1480). Buskit cockernonies [coiffed hairstyles], the bottle dungeon, Lammas Fair, the Brahan Seer, Finn MacCoul and Gow MacMorn flit unobtrusively across our field of vision. The city in the sky is styled Cloodiegowkburgh [Cloudy-cuckoo-burgh]: actually a better translation than the familiar 'Cloud-Cuckoo-Land', for the Greek name implies, and the place is clearly conceived as, not a country but a fortified city like Athens. The 'oil-cruse' [oil-flask] in the tag with which Aeschylus demolishes Euripides' prologues becomes a 'hipflask'. This is effective not only in providing a Scottish cultural equivalent of the article (because it is commonly used to keep whisky in a pocket), but in contributing to the metrical joke, since the tag '...tint his wee hipflask' requires to be scanned, not with its natural rhythm '*Tint* his wee *hip*-flask', but as '*Tint* his *wee* hip-*flask*':

EURIPIDES: 'Aigyptos, rins the maist disseminate tale,
wi fifty sons, propelled by mariner blade,
tuichan at Argos' ...

AESCHYLUS: tint his wee hipflask. (*The Puddocks*, ll. 1206–8)

[EU: 'Aigyptos, runs the most disseminated tale,/with fifty sons, propelled by mariner blade,/touching at Argos' ...//AE: lost his wee hipflask.]

This trick is played seven times in all, and as the repetitions accumulate, surely not only Aeschylus but his listeners on the stage, and even the audience, could hardly resist joining in the chant: 'tint his wee hip-FLASK!!!' Ironically enough, these almost timeless icons of Scottishness are interspersed with 1950s references that now give the translation itself a period flavour: rock 'n' rowe [roll], Licht Programme Variety, Teddy boys, MacMillan, President Nasser (the last to allow for a variation, 'President Basher'). Young in the notes to both plays, however, gives permission for producers to alter the allusions as they see fit (permission of which Tom Fleming, who directed the Lyceum *Burdies*, evidently took full advantage); and a contemporary production could readily find updated equivalents.

Geographical references familiar to Aristophanes' audience, of which there are many, are likewise often replaced with Scottish ones. Milesian rugs become Ayrshire blankets, and a Phrygian wool cloak becomes an Inverness cape. Acheron is 'as deep's Loch Ness', a purple-winged flamingo comes – or so we are told – 'frae Hebridean machars [seaside meadows]'. What appear in the originals to be crude personal references to individual citizens of little influence or importance are sometimes given not only a modern counterpart but a rather more dignified one: 'I abhor Lepreus because of Melanthius [a minor tragic dramatist with a disfiguring skin condition]' (Sommerstein, 1987: 33, l. 152) becomes 'Na, Langholm scunners me./It's the caufgrund o the makar Hugh MacDairymaid' [No, Langholm disgusts me./It's the birthplace of the poet Hugh MacDiarmid] (*The Burdies*, ll. 150–1). Among the most interesting of these naturalising touches are the equivalents found for the individuals – legendary heroes or contemporaries of more or less transient fame – to whom Aristophanes makes casual passing allusions. Theseus becomes Kenneth MacAlpin; the Athenian general Nicias becomes Robert Bruce; Prodicus, a philosopher with subversive views on religion, becomes Darwin; Phrynichus, a dramatist whom Aristophanes evidently respected highly, becomes the contemporary composer Cedric Thorpe Davie (the reference coming in rather incongruously in what is not a comic or satirical passage but a lyrical choral song: *The Burdies*, ll. 737–51). Diagoras, a poet eventually outlawed for his atheism, becomes 'Bolshie Hugh' [Hugh MacDiarmid]; and the versatile song-writer Simonides – of course – Rabbie Burns.

The platitude that the intellectual and literary achievement of ancient Greece is one of the foundations of Western culture receives, on the face of it, little support from Aristophanes. His plays emanate from a world in which all assumptions, including assumptions regarding the structure and purpose of drama, differ so radically from those of recent times in Europe that a major imaginative effort is required even to recognise the terms in which they can be understood. To render them capable of being not only understood in an academic sense but appreciated as the Athenian audience might have appreciated them (disregarding the religious context, which is self-evidently beyond recall) – that is, as colourful, rowdy, fast-paced, linguistically inventive, thought-provoking and above all funny stage spectacles – is a task from which a bold spirit might shrink. Douglas Young, fortunately, did not. His extensive scholarship, his ability to empathise with Aristophanes and his world, his mastery of the many registers of Scots, the verbal ingenuity that enabled him to compose in iambic pentameter, iambic heptameter, dactylic tetrameter, anapaestic heptameter, trochaic tetrameter or free verse, and above all his exuberant sense of humour, enabled him to produce a pair of brilliantly successful translations, which one would welcome the opportunity of seeing again on stage. It is no light matter to disagree with Alexander Scott, but Douglas Young's claim that his disapproving voice was decidedly at odds with other well-informed Scots critics[7] is true, and with good reason.

Notes

1. Edwin Morgan has translated from an even wider range of languages, but more often into English than into Scots.
2. The dates that Scott gives in his notes to the poem for the *Scotsman* letters are inaccurate, and should be emended as follows: Stanzas 1 and 2: for 3rd read 5th; Stanza 4: for 7th read 9th; Stanza 5: for 7th and 13th read 9th and 16th; Stanza 7: for 13th read 16th; Stanza 9: for 29th read 31st.
3. Knowing no Greek, I am obliged to rely on translations and commentaries for evidence regarding Young's treatment of his originals: for *The Frogs* I have used Murray (trans.), 1912; for *The Birds* I have used Sommerstein (trans.) (1987).
4. This and subsequent references to *The Burdies* are from Young (1959).
5. This and subsequent references to *The Puddocks* are from Young (1958).
6. The line numbers in Young's text appear to correspond to the Greek originals, but as the translation is not always line-for-line they do not necessarily correspond to the line-counting of the Scots text. The passage referred to is ten lines long.
7. In the *Scotsman* correspondence, especially the letters of 9 and 16 September 1966.

Chapter 12
Translation and Transplantation: Sir Alexander Gray's Danish Ballads

PETER GRAVES AND BJARNE THORUP THOMSEN

Sir Alexander Gray (1882–1968) was a Dundonian who went on via Dundee High School and the Universities of Edinburgh, Göttingen and the Sorbonne to become first a civil servant and then for 35 years Professor of Political Economy at the Universities of Aberdeen and Edinburgh in turn. He was also a poet and a translator from German and Danish into Scots. His two volumes of Danish ballads are *Four and Forty: A Selection of Danish Ballads Presented in Scots* (1954) and *Historical Ballads of Denmark* (1958). Both volumes are equipped with introductions. The introduction to *Historical Ballads* focuses on the nature of history in the ballad and has little of relevance to say in the present context. But in his introduction to *Four and Forty*, with a good deal of humour and an equal measure of self-deprecation, Gray justifies his translations into Scots:

> I have long been convinced that the Folk-poetry and the ballads of the Germanic and the Scandinavian peoples are untranslatable into standard English without the sacrifice of all the essential flavour which makes them what they are, and which alone lures the translator on to his perilous task. It may not be so with regard to the popular literature of the Romance languages: I am not, spiritually, sufficiently in tune with the French and Italian languages to express any opinion ... But when it comes to the ballads of the tougher north, I am sure that the medium into which they must be transferred, if they are not to be devalued in some mysterious way, must be a dialect. (Gray, 1954: xi–xiii)

Here we can, of course, see a late but clear reflex of those Victorian beliefs in the 'manly' vigour of the languages of the north, one that Gray underlines in a footnote in which he discusses various versions of 'Sir Halewyn'. 'Whereas the Dutch, the Danish and the German versions are stark and barbaric ... the French version seems made to be sung by little dancing schoolgirls, for whom Death is still but a word in a nursery rhyme' (Gray, 1954: p. xii). And it is a double reflex in that, implicitly, only a dialect of the north (i.e. Scots) can provide a suitable medium for this material: we are left to infer that a southern English version would go as 'trippingly' (Gray's word) as the French. Gray then considers earlier translators of the Danish ballads. He discusses Robert Buchanan's *Ballad Stories of the Affections* (1866), which he feels would have been better if Buchanan had followed his admitted intuition and gone for Scots rather than English, and Robert Jamieson's *Popular Ballads and Songs* (1806), which are, however, 'too excessively Scots, or too excessively Scots in the wrong direction. He is far more archaic, and therefore more difficult to read, than there is any need to be' (Gray, 1954: xiv).

Scots, then, is to be Gray's chosen medium. However, he takes an individualistic stance on how it may properly be described:

> But what, one may ask, is this 'Scots', this 'Doric', this 'Vernacular', this 'Lallans', this 'guid auld Scottis tongue', or whatever one may care to call it? And here, I need hardly add, I tremble on the brink of a controversy which recurrently strains the correspondence columns of *The Scotsman* and *The Glasgow Herald* to bursting-point.' (Gray, 1954: xvi)

Forswearing any desire to be a controversialist, Gray devotes his next ten pages to demonstrating that Scots never has been a language, never will be a language and, given the problems that writers from small language communities have in finding an audience, Scottish writers would only be disadvantaged were it ever to become one. Gray is quite emphatic, then, that his target language is a dialect. Fortunately, perhaps, that conviction is of no great relevance in the matter of the translation of Danish ballads into Scots. As to what kind of Scots Gray uses, J. Derrick McClure has shown that:

> Gray's poetic idiolect is the straightforward, unadorned Scots of a writer thoroughly at home in his dialect and grounded in the Scots poetic tradition, but intent on exploiting the natural genius of the tongue as actually used rather than extending it in artificial or experimental directions. (McClure, 1993)

Furthermore, on phonological grounds, McClure suggests that there is quite enough evidence to localise the origin of his dialect in Angus.[1]

In his introduction to *Four and Forty* Gray also discusses more specific matters. In the case of the almost-omnipresent refrain of Danish ballads, he will for the most part retain it. A little more complex is Gray's attitude to conventional formulae. He notes that the first couplet in each quatrain of four-line ballads frequently consists of only one semantic segment together with a conventional formula; this irritates him – particularly when it is repeated throughout the ballad. But if the formula is omitted the result is 'to telescope the first two lines into one, and the translator is left with a gap to be filled' (Gray, 1954: xxix). Gray also remarks on the frequency of 'conventional verses and stock phrases which belong to no one but are common property' (1954: xxx): we accept these as right in our own ballads, but will the reader tolerate them in translations? Implicitly, it seems that Sir Alexander hopes to avoid both padding and stock phrases while 'plead[ing] for tolerance' when they occur. In this area, central as it is to the ballad as genre, the introduction shows some lack of theoretical clarity, as indeed it does in the matter of Scots.

Gray's introduction, then, does not state, except in the most general way, why he chose Scots as the medium for his ballad translations. It is not difficult to justify the choice on his behalf, whether we view it from a linguistic, literary, or general cultural-historical perspective. The linguistic fit between Danish and English, both being Germanic languages in which the inflexional system has largely disappeared, is already close. The fit between Danish and Scots is a neater one still: according to Templeton (1975: 4), 'Scots goes back ultimately to Old Northumbrian' – that is, the northern dialect of Old English spoken between the Humber and the Forth, a dialect that was much influenced by Scandinavian settlement. Aitken goes so far as to refer to 'Scandinavianised Northern English' as 'Anglo-Danish', and writes:

> Early Scots shared much of its word-stock with contemporary Northern Middle English. This included virtually all its word-borrowings from Scandinavian, since these had originally reached Scotland as part of the Northern English speech of the Anglo-Danish immigrants. (Aitken, 1985: ix, xv)

As to literary fit, the existence of a considerable corpus of work of a generically and thematically similar (indeed, sometimes directly related) kind in both source and target languages gives the translator an enormous advantage in theory and in practice. In an elegant discussion of Douglas Young's translations into Scots from Gaelic, Italian and French, J. Derrick McClure has pointed out that:

> a fundamental fact is that during the process an implicit claim is being made for the target language: the status of being a fit vehicle for a literary text which will be – not equivalent, for such a concept is not even meaningful – but comparable, in factual, intellectual and emotional content, to the original poem ... and a translator working in a less comprehensively developed language, such as Scots, runs the risk

of making the defects of his medium painfully obvious. (McClure, 1987: 195)

Balladry having flourished vigorously on both sides of the North Sea, this is not a danger faced by the ballad translator, who in Scots may draw on a rich stock of suitable vocabulary and constructions at the same time as having access to the hoard of appropriate imagery and formulaic phrasing provided by the native ballad tradition.

In what follows we have chosen to study in detail four of Gray's texts in both their source and their target versions rather than to range piecemeal over all sixty ballads in the two volumes. The piecemeal approach would doubtless have provided us with a lengthy catalogue of felicities in Gray's work and a rather shorter one of infelicities. But it would have failed to elicit a full picture of the match between source and target in the case of any given text, and it would not have produced a conspectus of Gray's chosen strategies. We have chosen the texts with a view to representing different types of ballad, and we shall quote the source text, Gray's translation and, in square brackets, give a word-for-word translation of the source.

We should perhaps also nail our own colours to the mast by outlining our theoretical stance, since it is one that leads us to be inclined to question Gray's approach. The questioning and the criticism it leads to are, however, within the context of admiration for the high quality of Gray's work. For, were it not for an occasional alien name, readers would be unaware that they are enjoying translations: these ballads read well, both silently and aloud, and they give every appearance of being singable. And, in a literal sense, they are accurate renderings. They are therefore thoroughly convincing *as ballads*. It is when we ask the awkward questions 'What kind of ballad?' and 'Are they the same kind of ballad in Scots as they were in Danish?' that some problems arise. A clear example is offered by Gray's decision to relocate many of the ballads in Scotland. In 'Agnete and the Merman', for instance, the source text opens with Agnete walking on 'Højelands Bro' [Højeland Bridge] and refers later to *'de engelandske Klokkers Klang'* [the sound of the bells at Engeland]. Gray's version has Agnete walking 'alang the dunes' and later she hears 'the kirk-bells o' Forvie'. The new locus, then, is the Sands of Forvie on the Aberdeenshire coast, and, if the ballad has to be relocated, it would be difficult to find a more suitable home in view both of the strength of the genre in the North-East and of the particular traditions attached to the sand-inundated parish of Forvie, where the remains of the church may still be found among the dunes. In the introduction to *Four and Forty*, Gray writes of how his original aim had been '"transplantation" rather than translation', but he found that this had its limitations and:

> accordingly, I have increasingly tended to leave the heroes and heroines of these ballads the undisturbed enjoyment of their original and authentic names, as likewise I have refrained from geographical upheaval ... But I should add that on this point I am far from being a complete convert. (Gray, 1954: xiv–xv)

The issue of principle, however, concerns the purpose of literary translation: is that purpose primarily to enrich the literature of the target language or is it to make the literature of the source language accessible to those who do not speak that language? While recognising that both can be perfectly proper aims in different circumstances – and only rarely is it necessary for them to exclude one another – the present writers incline towards the latter view as a general principle unless there is good reason to deviate from it. Moreover, there seems no good reason for being motivated by the first-mentioned purpose in this case: Scots already has an outstanding ballad tradition that needs no reinforcement by 'transplantation'; Danish names are not so outlandish as to jar excessively on the Scots ear. Perhaps most importantly, there is arguably a certain condescension inherent in the thought that Scots readers are so *hameart* [devoted to home, or unsophisticated] that they would prefer the cultural and generic differences and distance (not very great anyway) to be ironed out.[3]

'*Harpens Kraft*'/'The Power of the Harp'

In respect of both its subject matter and its formal features, the ballad of '*Harpens Kraft*'/'The Power of the Harp' (Gray, 1954: 7–11) possesses characteristics that could be seen as almost archetypal of the subgenre of the Danish ballad known as *tryllevisen*, the supernatural ballad. This is a form of literature whose appeal arguably rests in its challenging combination of simplicity of expression and sophistication of meaning. '*Harpens Kraft*' discusses the complications of entering into a sustainable love relationship, giving in the process as much attention to the female as to the male. In the development of what could, with phraseology borrowed from the Danish scholar and poet Villy Sørensen,[4] be termed its theme of betrothal, or crossing over, the ballad constructs a stylised symbolical space that combines nature and 'supernature'. It depicts how a borderline in its landscape – a stream ironically named 'Blide' [the Gentle One] in which a troll lives – must be crossed via 'Blide-Bro' [Gentle Bridge] by the unnamed female protagonist on her 'way' to marrying a cultured and considerate male called Villemand. His name may be ironic, possibly pointing to 'wildness', which is not represented in the text by its male hero but by the troll and the stream, or to 'going wild', losing one's way – which does not happen to Villemand, but to his bride. Thus, the connotations of the proper names used in this ballad do not point straightforwardly, but rather by means of contrast or difference, to the qualities of the name-bearer, while at the same time throwing light on other areas of the text. By adding the information that two sisters of the bride 'sank down' (stanza 8) into the same stream on previous wedding journeys, the ballad on the one hand emphasises that the problem it discusses is a pattern of repetition inherent in the pre-wedding situation – a precarious point of transition from the 'first' family into the second – rather than an individual's particular predicament. On the other hand it offers an additional psychological explanation – the traumas of the past – as to why entering marriage is particularly complicated for the female protagonist.

In order to protect his 'beautiful bride' (st. 1) from the demonic forces of nature, Villemand spectacularly issues her with a guard of 212 horsemen to accompany her on the journey across the border. But such demonstration of male power proves to be to no avail: just as her sisters before her, the bride sinks into the rapid stream with none of the many riders able to help her. Only when Villemand has his golden harp brought and plays it both gently and vehemently by the riverside, is (super-)nature conquered: the troll is driven up from the bottom of the Blide, not only with Villemand's unharmed maiden in his mouth, but also with both her beautiful sisters. Thus, the hostages of the past are released, the pattern of repetition is broken, and Villemand can celebrate the wedding with his bride. In addition to its genre-typical features, *'Harpens Kraft'* is of special interest in that it addresses the theme of the 'exorcising' role of artistic (musical) creativity in such a foregrounded manner, and thereby arguably also draws attention to its own function or capabilities.

When translating a complex literary source text such as *'Harpens Kraft'*, which could be described (thus echoing its main theme) as a piece of 'crossover' fiction combining naturalism and symbolism, psychology and myth, light entertainment and life philosophy, the translator is asked to perform a difficult balancing act – to walk, as it were, a linguistic tightrope. It is very likely, perhaps inevitable, that he and his product will either lean in the 'normalising', 'naturalising' direction or push the symbolism too far. In either case he runs the risk of limiting the openness, relevance and ambiguity of the source text. There can be little doubt that Sir Alexander Gray's tendency, while skilfully rendering the Danish supernatural ballads into Scots, is to push in the normalising direction.

Choice of setting and naming is of obvious importance in translating *'Harpens Kraft'*. Although it could not be argued that the source text is set in an authenticised 'Danish' or 'Nordic' space, Gray decides to relocate the ballad to Scotland, substituting an authentic stream-name for the distinctly 'dis-authentic' Blide:

> But I greet because o' the dowie Dean,   [cry; sad, mournful, dismal]
> That I maun cross this day ere e'en.   [must]
> (Gray, 1954: 7–11, st. 7)

Interestingly, in his introduction to the translated ballad, Gray displays some hesitation as to whether 'the Dean is a somewhat insufficient stream to allow room for the kelpie's manoeuvres' but against this argues that the same stream is used as the location in a haunting and fatalistic rhyme of long ago, which he quotes:

> The dowie Dean
> Rins its lane;   [runs solitary]
> And ilka seven year,   [each]
> It taks ane.   [takes one]
> (Gray, 1954: 8)

Gray thus justifies his reuse of the location in a text with similar features. Although the textual effect of the choice arguably is different, Gray's translation, like its source text, pays particular attention to the connotations of the chosen setting. But in contrast, as far as the other central naming decision is concerned – finding a name for the male protagonist – it is more difficult to justify Gray's strategy. Although the two names sound alike, it is hardly a good 'fit' to replace, as Gray does, the arresting, ambiguous Villemand with the everyday William. Compared with the opening of the source text, in which attention is drawn to the male name through unusualness, foregrounding and stressed alliteration, in the target text the introduction of William (although vaguely alliterated with *wi'* [with]) goes considerably more unnoticed somewhere in the middle of the first line:

> *Villemand og hans væne Brud*
> *– Strengen er af Guld –*
> *de legte Guldtavl i hendes Bur.*
>
> [Villemand and his beautiful bride/– *the string is of gold* –/they played gold board in her bower.]

In her bower sat William wi' his May;
(*The strings are o' gowd.*) [of gold]
They played at the dice on their weddin' day. (st. 1)

It is also noteworthy that, whereas in Gray's text the opening line corresponds to a complete, harmonious sentence, the source text fragments its opening syntax by letting it run over into a new line. This delaying effect is made stronger by the interposing of the seemingly disconnected refrain line. Again, the result is the thematisation and isolation of the male and the female agent right at the beginning of the source text. It could also be pointed out that Gray adds a particularised time indication, 'on their weddin' day', to the opening stanza and 'tidies up' its rhyming scheme by substituting perfect rhyme ('May', 'day') for imperfect (*'Brud'*, *'Bur'*).

The differences between source and target text discussed thus far are not so much isolated occurrences as indications of Gray's translation strategy as a whole. This can be seen in more detail if we first briefly summarise some of the salient features of the literary language of the Danish ballad. This language is a spartan, economical voice that shuns elaboration and narratorial involvement. It is a language not particularly interested in variation of expressions, relying, rather, on repetition – of words, rhymes, lines, formulas – as one of its prime poetic devices. It is a condensed language that uses gaps to great effect, freely shifting scene or speaker without connecting passages. Similarly, it is a language that thrives on tensions: tension between the action- or plot-orientation of the core text and the more emotive tone of the refrain; tension between formulaic and non-formulaic language use; tension, even, between the tenses as the ballad voice utilises jumps from the past tense into the present to great effect. It is also a language that more than occasionally shows a liberal attitude to several aspects of standard grammatical practice. For example, it may position syntactic elements out of normal word order, particularly placing attributes *after* rather than *before* nouns, as in '*mine Søstre to*' [my sisters two; st. 8], '*Guldharpen min*' [the goldharp mine; st. 18], and '*Ganger graa*' [steed grey; st. 30]. It may also use a separate definite article in front of a noun (as in Scots or English and most other related languages) where standard Scandinavian would have an enclitic definite article (that is, as a noun ending). Not least significantly, it overuses the indefinite form of nouns, as in '*Da hun kom der midt paa* Bro' [when she came there on the middle of *bridge;* st. 13], and 'Jomfru *rakte op sin hvide Hand*' [*maiden* stretched up her white hand; st. 16]. These deviations often function, it would seem, as a means of manipulating rhyme and rhythm in the text; but at the same time they together contribute, at the micro level of language, to adding a distinct element of poetic 'strangeness' to a ballad voice which in other respects is fairly matter-of-fact.

It should be stressed that not all of these linguistic features could or should be translated into the target language. Translating is, after all, not always simply about establishing equivalence, as languages are not transparent systems but have different formal organisations and (therefore) different organisations of reality. How could Gray, to quote the most radical case, possibly be faithful to a pattern in the source text of not always adhering to an enclitic definite article that is non-existent in Scots? Also, it is quite likely that directly transferring bare nouns – or even sudden shifts between tenses – into the Scots version of the text might create *too* much strangeness in the target language. Nevertheless, it could be suggested as an ideal aim that the translator should attempt to create equivalence in the sense of reproducing the same general level of 'strangeness' found in the source text by using the formal means open to him in the target language.

In the main, Gray remains faithful to the artful language of Danish balladry outlined above. But when he deviates from it, his favoured direction is towards elaboration, harmonisation and specification, to some extent moving the target text away from the skeletal and the strange. Some examples might illlustrate this pattern. Firstly, Gray's use of adjectives is more generous – in their faceting, adorning, even judging – than found in the source text: '*hvide Hand*' [white hand; st. 16] becomes 'snaw-white hand'; '*Land*' [land; st. 16] becomes 'dry land'; '*Egetræ*' [oaktree; st. 22] becomes 'the gnarled aik [oak]'; '*Harpen*' [the harp; st.24] becomes 'the trummlin' [trembling] string'; and '*Trolden(s)*' [the troll(s); st. 24] becomes 'the evil thing'. Secondly, as a related point, the target text uses considerably more adjective-based adverbs than the source text. While this is arguably well suited for adding nuances to the description of events in a text, or for conveying the narrator's interpretation of occurrences, neither of these aims is significant in a fairly strict narrative economy such as the one suggested here. The target text, for example, contains 'sweetly' (second refrain line), 'stoutly' (st. 10), 'richt sharp and loud' (st. 18), 'sae saft, sae cunningly' (st. 20), 'angrily' (st. 21), and 'Blithely' (st. 29), for which only four corresponding words can be found in the source text, and some of these seem moreover of a less marked nature: '*liflig*' [sweetly; second refrain line], '*saa liste*' [so cleverly; st. 20], '*saa saare*' [so much; st. 21], '*gerne*' [gladly; st. 29]. Thirdly, in the three instances when the source text in its narrated passages switches into dramatic present, the target text ignores this in favour of a uniform use of the past tense. The first instance is the more telling of the three in that the shift of tense so obviously contributes to the production of textual meaning. It happens at the moment of transition and heightened suspense when the maiden sets off on her fateful journey towards Blide Bridge:

Han lod lægge under hendes Ganger de røde Guldsko,
og saa rider hun til Blide-Bro.

[He let put under her steed the red goldshoes,/and then rides she to Blide Bridge.]

Wi' gowden shoon her horse he shod;   [with golden shoes]
And to the Brig o' Dean they rode. (st. 12)

The target text here emphasises the continuity of the situation and the companionship ('they rode') of man and woman, whereas the source text highlights the isolation and exposed situation of the female ('she rides'). Fourthly, the target displays on one occasion an inclination to fill out a gap in the plot development of the source text by means of a one-line summary of the intervening action. Where in the Danish ballad there is a sudden, almost cinematic cut, between Villemand, in direct speech, ordering his servant boy to fetch the harp and then him holding it, in Gray's translation it is spelled out that the harp *has been brought to him* in the meantime:

...
'*Du hente mig ind Guldharpen min!*' (last line of st. 18)

Villemand tog Harpen i Hænde,
han gaar for Strømmen at stande. (st. 19)

['You fetch me in the goldharp mine!']
[Villemand took the harp in hand,/he goes by the stream to stand.]

'Gae, bring to me my harp o' gowd.'   [go; of gold]

And when the harp had been brocht to him,   [brought]
He stude close doon by the water's brim.

One could argue that a core aim, when translating a very dramatic genre such as the ballad, should be to respect such cuts between scenes. To continue the comparison to screen and stage, just as 'summary' is a narrative mode somewhat alien to filmic or dramatic story telling, so the explanatory, connecting passages like the one added by Gray in this example do not really ring true to ballad style. (We shall return to this in discussing 'Agnete and the Merman'.) As a fifth and final observation, it should be mentioned that 'The Power of the Harp', like most of Gray's other ballad translations, realises his stated ambition of minimising the use of formulaic expressions. For example, the repeated stock phrases of '*Vand under Ø*' [water below island], in stanzas 28 and 29 of the source text, are rendered with variation rather than repetition as 'waters here' and 'watery deep' respectively.

Taken in isolation, none of the examples of non-equivalence listed in this context are necessarily of any great significance; indeed some of them may smack of linguistic nit-picking. It could also be argued that, while Gray removes value from the ballad text, he also adds value – elegance, variation, completeness. Moreover, the discussion so far should not obscure the fact that, when it comes to plot development and conveying the drama and high entertainment value of the ballad genre, Gray's renderings are superb. Nevertheless, taken together, the examples quoted seem to suggest that Gray's own ideal of a ballad text – an ideal of which his translations could be seen to carry reflexes – is somewhat less skeletal and uneven than the source texts demand. The real irony is, however, that his stylistic 'improvements' of the texts do not just 'refine' but also remove meaning and sophistication.

'*Agnete og Havmanden*'/'Agnete and the Merman'

Gray's translation (Gray, 1954: 3–6) follows the original stanza by stanza – indeed, line by line for the most part – and he is accurate both in general and in detail without being craven. His solutions are never less than acceptable and, at best, they have a splendid vigour, as in stanza 4:

> *Han stoppcd hendes Øre, han stopped hendes Mund,*
> *saa førte han hende til Havsens Bund.*
>
> [He stopped up her ear, he stopped up her mouth,/then led he her to the sea's bottom.]
>
> Her lugs he has stappit; her mou' he has bound;   [ears; stopped; mouth]
> And guided her doon to the sea's saut ground.   [salt]

Gray's version of stanza 18 shows the same sort of quality, this time in a situation where the Danish source text uses a formulaic 'dear daughter' phrase. Unlike the foregoing example, a purist might argue in this case that Gray, by using 'tint your snude', is guilty of improving on the original (which, of course, he is) but the more pragmatic reader will applaud him because his change/addition is wholly within the meaning and spirit of the original:

> *Og, hør du, Agnete, kær Datter min,*
> *hvad gav han dig for Æren din?*

[And hear you, Agnete, dear daughter mine,/what gave he you for honour thine?]

Listen, Agnete; you've tint your snude; [lost your snood]
What gae he you for your maidenhude? [gave]

The excellence of these solutions is best appreciated by comparing them with the equally accurate but lifeless renderings offered by another translator:

Her ears he closed, her mouth he bound,
And bore her down through the sea to ground.

Harken, dear daughter, and fear no blame,
What did he give for thy maiden fame? (Smith-Dampier, 1939: 114)

Where Gray deviates, he does so mainly and understandably for purposes of metre and rhyme. In stanza 21, for instance, since the first line of his couplet covers the first line and a half of the Danish, the semantically redundant 'dowie' fills out the metre:

Og han gav mig en Harpe av Guld,
at jeg skulde spille paa, naar jeg var sorrigfuld.

[And he gave me a harp of gold,/that I should play on when I was sorrowful.]

And a gowden harp to harp upon, [golden]
When my hert was dowie and wae-begone. [heart; sad; woebegone]

In stanza 11 his addition of 'hod your face' both provides him with an easy rhyme and fills out the metre (though it is difficult to see any justification whether semantic, aesthetic or metrical for the 'in prayin'' in the first line of Gray's rendering):

Naar Præsten nævner den høje,
da maa du dig ikke nedbøje.

[When the priest names the High One,/then must you not bow down.]

When the priest names, in prayin', the name o' grace,
You maunna lout low, and hod your face. [mustn't bow down; hold]

The same double function is served by 'next the wa'' in stanza 27:

O tænk paa de store, og tænk paa de smaa,
og tænk paa den lille, som i Vuggen laa.

[O think of the big ones, and think of the small ones,/and think of the little one, who in the cradle lay.]

O, think on the big anes, and think on the sma',   [ones; small]
And the bairn in the cradle that sleeps next the wa'.   [child; wall]

A central feature of the way ballads tell their stories is their treatment of dialogue. Bengt R. Jonsson's description of the Swedish ballad is also valid for Danish ballads: 'The technique ... is better described as dramatic than as epic in the real sense of the word' (Jonsson, 1962: 15). M.J.C. Hodgart (1962: 28, note) makes the apt suggestion that ballad narrative may be compared to that of a strip cartoon. Thus dialogue in the ballad, as in the drama or strip cartoon, is not normally accompanied by such narratorial tags as 'he said', 'she whispered' and so on. The Danish source text *'Agnete og Havmanden'* contains no narratorial tags whatsoever. Gray, on the other hand, has introduced three of them. In stanza 3 the Danish has:

O ja saamænd, det vil jeg saa

[O yes indeed, that want I so much]

whereas Gray offers:

'Deed, ay!' quo' she, 'that will I dae'.

['Indeed, yes!' said she, 'that will I do.']

In stanza 7 the Danish has the characteristic abrupt shift to dialogue:

Agnete hun ganger for den Havmand at staa:
'Og maa jeg mig udi Kirken gaa?'

[Agnete she goes before the merman to stand: / 'And may I into the church go?']

whereas Gray gives:

She rase frae her liltin'. To the merman she spak:
'The kirk-bells are ringin'; fain wad I gae back.'   [would]

In stanza 8 the Danish merman responds directly to Agnete; that is, there is no marker that the speaker has changed between stanzas 7 and 8:

'O ja saamænd, det maa du saa,
naar du vill komme igen til Børnene smaa.'

['O yes indeed, that may you so, / if you will come again to the children small.']

But Gray's rendering is:

'You're welcome,' quo' he; 'but you'll no bide awa?   [not stay away]
You boot to come back, and tak care o' us a'.'   [are under compulsion to]

With the appearance of such tags, the ballad begins to slip along the scale in the direction of the 'literary' narrative poem and we, as readers or listeners, begin to lose the sense of being engaged by a dramatic enactment.

Alliteration, assonance and, to a lesser extent, internal rhyme are, of course, standard tools in the technical kit of the ballad poet whether Danish or Scots. *'Agnete og Havmanden'* makes frequent use of all three, as, for example, in stanza 9:

> Men naar du kommer paa Kirkegaard,
> da maa du ikke slaa ud dit favre gule Haar.
>
> [But when you come to churchyard,/then must you not let down your beautiful golden hair.]

If we take all three devices together we can find no fewer than 50 occurrences in the 28 stanzas of the Danish version. Gray's translation, however, adds another 15: not, perhaps, much in itself, but taken together with the other changes under discussion, it marks a further shift in the direction of literary retouching.

The metrical and rhyming scheme of *'Agnete og Havmanden'* is composed of a rhyming couplet followed by a refrain followed by a repetition of the second line of the couplet. Each line of the couplet has four beats (stressed syllables) and a total of 10–12 syllables. Thus stanza 26:

> 'Lad længes, lad længes, saa saare som de vil,
> slet aldrig kommer jeg mere dertil,
> – haa, haa, haa –
> slet aldrig kommer jeg mere dertil.'
>
> ['Let them long, let them long, as sorely as they want,/never ever come I again thither,/– haa, haa, haa –/never ever come I again thither.']

All the elements of this structural pattern, however, are treated with considerable licence in the Danish: six of the 28 stanzas have imperfect rhymes (stanza 1, for example, rhymes *'bro'* with *'op'*, and stanza 25 rhymes *'tren'* with *'omkring'*); a total of 14 lines have either three beats or five beats rather than the regular 4; line length measured in syllables ranges from 7 to 13 per line, and 15 of the couplets are composed of lines that differ by two or more syllables – frequently more than two. The metre of the Danish source text is best considered as strong-stress (or old native) metre; that is, a four beat line 'in which there is no fixed number of unaccented syllables to the foot' (Brooks & Warren, 1960: 568). As Brooks and Warren point out, it is sometimes possible to scan strong-stress metre in terms of iambs and anapaests but it involves 'a good deal of forcing'; this quickly becomes apparent when applied to *'Agnete og Havmanden'*. If we then examine Gray's text, we find that he has consistently regularised: all of his couplets have full rhyme, all of his lines have four beats, line length ranges from eight to twelve syllables, and only five couplets have lines that differ by two or more syllables. More significantly, the metre of the Scots rendering may be described quite conventionally as tetrameter couplets composed of either iambs or anapaests: over the ballad as a whole, the number of iambs (104) and anapaests (107) is effectively equal, though individual couplets tend to be either iambic or anapaestic. The effect of this regularity, especially when taken together with the jaunty effect induced by the frequency of anapaests, is to move the ballad along at an unvarying trot and, in spite of its subject matter, to give it a fairly light-hearted tone. The Danish text, on the other hand, is much more sedate, harsher in tone, and with more varied pace. One might suggest that, for all its good qualities, Gray's version is a fulfilment of his own statement that all ballads are destined to end up 'in the nursery, or ... round the camp-fire' (Gray, 1954: xii).

'Torbens Datter'/'Sir Walter's Daughter'

The Danish *'Torbens Datter og hendes Faderbane'* / 'Torben's Daughter and her Father's Slayer' (Gray, 1954: 40–42) is categorised as a *'riddarevise'* [ballad of chivalry], though we may feel it gives short shrift to chivalry. *'Torbens Datter'* reduces narrative to its bare bones: in 30 lines plus refrain it tells of the vengeance killing of Torben, the killer's visit to Torben's farm where he is welcomed by his victim's daughter, his revealing of his deed, and his carrying off of the girl. Depersonalisation is taken to its limits in this ballad: Torben is named, but not his killer and not his daughter; the events are not specifically localised; the cause of the feud is unmentioned; the formulaic phrases are commonplace – unmarked drawings on the standard storehouse such as *'favr og fin'* [fair and fine], *'saa væn en Maar'* [so fair a maid], *'Ganger graa'* [steed grey], or *'Kaaben blaa'* [cloak blue]. The power of *'Torbens Datter'* resides in its impersonality. Once the action begins, nothing detracts from the essence of the drama, as it is enacted with sombre and inevitable choreography. One segment alone breaches, and thus foregrounds, the impersonality of the rest and that is the lyrical (here, melancholy lyrical) tone of the introductory stanza so common among Danish ballads:

Vi vare saa mange Søskends smaa,
– under Lide –

saa aarlig faldt os Faderen fraa.
Der Dagen han dages, og Duggen den driver saa vide.

[We were so many children small,/– under the lea –/so early did we lose our father./Where the day it dawns, and the dew it drifts so wide.]

Gray's 'Sir Walter' (he has changed Torben's name) softens the starkness and introduces elements of the personal in a variety of ways. Firstly, he gives the ballad a location by telling us that the killer's party 'rade to the North, through the woods o' Buccleuch' (st. 2): the Danish anonymously locates the event 'by the northern forest'. Secondly, he has filled out the characters. The Danish Torben is simply addressed with the stereotyped *'Her gaar du, Hr. Torben, favr og fin'* [Here you walk, Sir Torben, fair and fine] whereas Sir Walter is rounded out to 'there you gae canty, like a douce man o' sense' [there you go cheerful, like a sedate man of sense]. Torben's daughter welcomes the killers and fills their goblets with a formulaic *'Lyst og Spil'* [merriment and sport], but of Sir Walter's daughter we hear: 'sae winsome she smiled, as she welcomed them a" (st. 9). Thirdly, there is a moderation of the impersonality by the voicing of a number of emotive phrases in Gray's version. Note the effect of the additions of 'dear lass' and 'bonnie' when the killer speaks to the daughter, for instance:

Havde jeg vidst, du havde været saa god,
aldrig skulde jeg set din Faders Hjerteblod.

[Had I known that you were so kind-natured,/never would I have seen your father's heart-blood.]

O, had I but kent you, sae bonnie and guid,   [known; good]
Dear lass, I had ne'er shed your father's bluid! (st. 10)

Note, too, the addition of 'wi' thae hands' and 'puir', and the doubling of 'sair', in the following couplet:

Og har I slaget min Fader til Død,
da har I gjort mig saa stor en Nød.

[And if you have killed my father,/then have you put me in such great distress.]

And hae you, wi' thae hands, garred my puir father dee?
O, sair, sair's the skaith you hae brocht upon me! (st. 11)

[And have you, with those hands, caused my poor father to die?/O, sore, sore's the hurt you have brought upon me!]

Similar breaches of impersonality result from the addition of descriptive adjectives to several formulaic phrases: '*Hjertblod*' [heart-blood] becomes 'reid [red] hert's-bluid' (st. 5); '*Ganger graa*' [steed grey] becomes 'fleet grey horse' (st. 13). Finally, one must point to what may be a misreading in the last stanza but, if it is a misreading, it is one that alerts us to the tenor of Gray's interpretation:

> *Saa red han over de sorte Heder,*
> [...]
> *aldrig saa hun sin Fader mere.*
>
> [So rode he over the black heaths,/never saw she her father again.]
>
> Awa ower the heathery road they fare;   [all over]
> [...]
> And her father she'll never see, never see mair.   (st.14)

That the killer and the daughter leave together is beyond doubt but the substitution of the plural pronoun 'they' for the singular 'he' of the Danish implies a degree of togetherness not expressed by the source text.

'*Dronning Dagmars Død*'/'The Death of Queen Dagmar'

If we have been correct in arguing that one of the thrusts of Gray's translations of the Danish ballads is a favouring of the authentic and the natural at the expense of the strange and the supernatural, it might be logically inferred that the subgenre of balladry known as the historical ballad would suit Gray's literary and translating temperament well. Although fiction that takes historical events as its subject matter is in a sense just as 'constructed' as any other form of fiction, and although even the historical ballad may contain the occasional magic component, the Danish historical ballads are nevertheless, as would be expected, clearly more authenticised and concerned with actuality than their supernatural and, to a lesser degree, their chivalrous counterparts. Their places are realistically localised, their plots parallel to some extent known historical events, and their characters mirror actual historical figures such as kings and queens. That there exists a rapport between this ballad form and Gray's general endeavours as a ballad translator seems validated by his fine rendering of '*Dronning Dagmars Død*'/'Queen Dagmar's Death' (Gray, 1958: 66–9) in *Historical Ballads of Denmark*.

Deservedly, '*Dronning Dagmars Død*' – based upon the demise of the Danish queen in 1212 – is one of the best known and most popular of the

Danish historical ballads. It is a moving exploration of pain, illness and death, but also of goodness, resurrection and eventual entry into Heaven. It is about female companionship and female expertise in the sense that it describes how the fatally ill queen summons to her sickbed in Ribe 'all' the country's wise ladies in an attempt to use their know-how to release her from a pain 'harder than iron' (st. 5). This linkage between 'all the ladies' and the attribute of wisdom is based upon a reading of the opening two stanzas of the source text:

> ...
> *alle de Fruer, i Danmark er,*
> *dem lader hun til sig hente.* (st. 1)
>
> *'I henter mig fire, I henter mig fem,*
> *I henter mig af de vise!*
> *I henter mig liden Kirsten,*
> *Hr. Karls Søster af Rise!'* (st. 2)

[... all the ladies in Denmark are,/them lets she [the queen] to her fetch.//'You fetch me four, you fetch me five,/You fetch me of the wise ones!/You fetch me little Kirsten,/Sir Karl's sister of Rise!']

An inference to be drawn here is that 'the wise ones' are women. However, in his translation Gray chooses to make them masculine:

> ...
> She has bidden the women o' Denmark come
> To bear her company. (st. 1)
>
> 'O bring me four, O bring me five
> Wise men o' lear and skill...' (st. 2) [learning]

Thus masculinity is prematurely inserted into the target text, which arguably weakens the significant gender distribution of behavioural characteristics found in a source text dominated by female action and, as it were, male reaction. Not that the remediable actions of the wise women help much, but then nothing can cure the queen. Since her condition, in Dagmar's euphemistic formulation, 'cannot become any better' (st. 7), her unnamed husband, the king, is eventually called in from elsewhere in the country – so only at this later point is masculinity admitted into the source text.

The ballads regularly feature a travel motif, but rarely is it used to greater effect than in *'Dronning Dagmars Død'*. The ballad is about Dagmar's travel out of this world and into the next and contains, even, an element of commuting between the two. But it is also more literally about the king's desperate traversing of Jutland in an attempt to arrive at Ribe before death and talk to his beloved wife one final time. Of course, the spartan ballad voice would not easily state straightforwardly that he loves her; instead, in order to convey a similar message, 'Dronning Dagmars Død' provides one among several effective realisations of the genre's common technique of creating what could be termed objective correlates to states of mind or heart:

> Der han red af Skanderborg,
> da fulgte ham hundred Svende;
> der han kom til Ribe,
> da var han mand alene. (st. 13)

> [When he [the king] rode out of Skanderborg,/then accompanied him hundred men;/when he came to Ribe,/then was he man alone.]

Or, in Gray's powerful version:

> As he rade oot o' Skanderborg,
> He rade wi' a hunder men;   [hundred]
> But long ere he got to Ribe wa's,   [walls]
> He was ridin' a' alane.   [all alone]

We see how the authentic, 'non-strange' place names used in this type of source text lead Gray to retain these in the target text. Thereby, ironically, he produces a somewhat more alien or exotic sounding setting than is the case with many of his relocated renderings of the stranger space of the supernatural ballads.

In a crucial coincidence Dagmar dies, however, at the very moment when the king rides up the streets of Ribe. Therefore he, the man alone, has to appeal to the gathered group of women to pray a prayer for him in order to enable him to speak with his wife. Dagmar then rises from her bier with blood-red eyes and does all the talking. She makes three requests to her husband, which in the source text are tied together through the device of the word 'Bøn' [request] being repeated in three consecutive stanzas (18, 19 and 20). By contrast, the target text, exhibiting the same striving for variation as witnessed in other of Gray's renderings, uses 'request', 'asking' and 'boon' respectively. All the queen's 'requests' could significantly be said to be concerned with regulating the lives of males. Firstly, all outlawed men should be let in peace and all prisoners released 'of iron' (st. 18) (a parallel to her own release from the pain that was earlier likened to iron). Secondly, the king should not marry Bengred after her, 'For she is a cankered bud' (st. 19), as the target text pointedly states. Finally, the king should let Knud, 'my youngest son' (st. 20), become king of Denmark. Having thus firmly said her say, it is then time for Dagmar to travel on:

I maun fare furth; it is decreed	[must travel forth]
That I bide nae langer here.	[remain]
The blessed angels wait for me,	
And the bells o' heaven ring clear. (st. 22)	

Writing of Sir Alexander Gray's translations of German poetry, J.D. McClure (1993) concludes: 'Many poetic translations, even excellent ones, fail to (or are not intended to) establish themselves within the poetic tradition associated with the target language. This is emphatically not true of Gray's work.'[5] This judgement also holds true for Gray's versions of the Danish ballads. What he has succeeded in doing in both *Four and Forty* and in *Historical Ballads of Denmark* is to create viable and authentic Scots ballads out of his source texts – that is, he has produced poems that can stand up 'within the poetic tradition associated with the target language'. But, in our comparisons of source and target versions, we have noted how cumulatively far he moved away from the source text in order to achieve this. In summary: he has personalised the impersonal; he has localised the general; he has relocated the local; he has fleshed out the skeletal; he has naturalised the supernatural; he has regularised the irregular. We have suggested earlier that we do not, in principle, favour the transplantation implied by these changes (however much we might applaud the results in practice). A more general thought, however, also arises from our comparisons: that the emotional registers of Danish and Scottish ballads might be rather more distinct than is commonly supposed.[6]

Notes

1. J. Derrick McClure, 'Alexander Gray's Translations from German Poetry'. We are grateful to the author for his permission to quote from this unpublished lecture delivered at the University of Freiburg in July 1993. See, too, his published paper on Gray's translations of German folk-songs (McClure, 1997).
2. Gray provides an appendix listing the Danish versions he has used, which are taken from the editions produced by either Axel Olrik or von der Recke. In the ballads discussed in this chapter we follow Gray in using Axel Olrik's *Danske Folkeviser i Udvalg* (Olrik, 1899).
3. For a stimulating discussion of this topic that takes the contrary view, see McClure (1995).
4. Villy Sørensen published his study of the Danish ballads, '*Folkeviser og forlovelser*' ['Ballads and Betrothals'], in his innovative volume of literary criticism *Digtere og Dæmoner* ['Writers and Demons'] (Sørensen, 1959). Sørensen's approach has since come under some criticism for reading a modern-

style psychological logic into the ballads. It is beyond doubt, however, that his study broke new ground for the appreciation of the complexities of the ballads as texts.
5. See note 1 above. For translations by Gray of balladry, poetry and folk song in German and other European languages, see Gray (1920, 1932, and 1949).
6. An earlier version of this essay, which was originally commissioned for this volume, was published in *Northern Studies* 34 (Graves & Thomson, 1999: 35–59). The notes were omitted in error and subsequently published as an addendum in *Northern Studies*, 35 (2000), pp. 155–6.

References

Aaltonen, S. (2000) *Time-Sharing on Stage: Drama Translation in Theatre and Society*. Clevedon: Multilingual Matters.
Aitken, A.J. (1985) A history of Scots. In *Concise Scots Dictionary* (pp. ix–xvi). Aberdeen: Aberdeen University Press.
Akhmatova, A. (1990) *The Complete Poems of Anna Akhmatova* (Vol. II) (J. Hemschemeyer, trans.; R. Reeder, ed.). Somerville, MA: Zephyr Press.
Alexander, R. (2000) Molière: Translated by Hector MacMillan. *Edinburgh Review* 105, 55–63.
Arnold, M. (1909) *The Poems of Matthew Arnold* (A.T. Quiller-Couch, intro.). London: Henry Frowde
Baker, H. and Miller, J. (trans) (1739/1956) *Molière's Comedies* (Vol. II). London: Dent.
Bakhtin, M.M. (1984) *Rabelais and his World*. (H. Iswolsky, trans.). Bloomington: Indiana University Press.
Barthes, R. (1972) Authors and writers. In R. Barthes *Critical Essays* (pp. 143–50). Evaston: Northwestern University. (The essay was first published in 1960.)
Bassnett, S. (2002) *Translation Studies* (3rd edn). London: Routledge.
Belli, G.G. (1965) *I sonetti* (M.T. Lanza, ed.; C. Muscetta, intro.). Milan: Feltrinelli.
Belli, G.G. (1984) *Sonetti* (P. Gibellini, ed.; G. Vigolo, commentary). Milan: Mondadori.
Benjamin, W. (1973) The task of the translator. In W. Benjamin *Illuminations* (H. Arendt, ed.; H. Zohn, trans.) (pp. 69–82). London: Fontana.
Besnier, P. (ed.) (1983) *Cyrano de Bergerac by Edmond Rostand*. Paris: Gallimard.
Boston, R. (ed.) (1975) *The Admirable Urquhart: Selected Writings*. London: Gordon Fraser.
Bowman, M. (1988) Joual/Scots: The language issue in Michel Tremblay's *Les Belles-Soeurs*. In I. Lockerbie (ed.) *Image and Identity: Theatre and Cinema in Scotland and Quebec* (pp. 42–55). Stirling: John Grierson Archive and Department of French, University of Stirling.
Bowman, M. (2000a) Traduire le théâtre de Michel Tremblay en écossais. *L'Annuaire théâtral* 27, 90–99.
Bowman, M. (2000b) Michel Tremblay in Scots translation: The critical response. *New Comparison* 29, 122–38.
Bowman, M. (2000c) Scottish horses and Montreal trains: The translation of vernacular to vernacular. In C-A. Upton (ed.) *Moving Target: Theatre Translation and Cultural Relocation* (pp. 25–33). Manchester: St Jerome.
Bowman, M. (2003) Michel Tremblay in Scots: Celebration and rehabilitation. In S. Grace and A-R. Glaap (eds) *Performing National Identities: International Perspectives on Contemporary Canadian Theatre* (pp. 38–50). Vancouver: Talonbooks.
Bowman, M. and Findlay, B. (1994) Québécois into Scots: Translating Michel Tremblay. *Scottish Language* 13, 61–81.

Brodsky, J. (1987) *Less than One: Selected Essays*. Harmondsworth: Penguin.
Brooks, C. and Warren, R.P. (1960) *Understanding Poetry* (3rd edn). New York: Holt, Rinehart and Winston.
Brown, A. (trans.) (1906) *The Sacred Dramas of George Buchanan*. Edinburgh: James Thin.
Buchanan, R. (1866) *Ballad Stories of the Affections*. London: Routledge.
Buck, P. (trans.) (1957) *All Men are Brothers [Shui hu chuan] by Shih Nai-an*. London: Methuen.
Burgess, A. (trans.) (1991) *Cyrano de Bergerac by Edmond Rostand*. London: Nick Hern Books.
Butcher, S.H. and Lang, A. (eds and trans) (1887) *The Odyssey of Homer done into English Prose*. London: Macmillan.
Carena, C. (ed.) (1993) *Bucoliche di Virgilio nella traduzione di Paul Valéry*. Torino: Einaudi.
Chen, X., Hou, Z. and Lu, Y. (eds) (1981) *Shuihu Zhuan Huiping Ben*. Beijing: Beijing University Press.
Coldwell, D.F.C. (ed.) (1957–64) *Virgil's Aeneid Translated into Scottish Verse by Gavin Douglas* (4 vols). Edinburgh: Scottish Text Society.
Coleridge, S.T. (1969/1978) *Coleridge: Poetical Works* (J. Coleridge, ed.). Oxford: Oxford University Press.
Coleridge, S.T. (1990) *The Collected Works of Samuel Taylor Coleridge 14: Table Talk* (Vol. 1) (C. Woodring, ed.). Princeton: Princeton University Press.
Concise Scots Dictionary (1985). Aberdeen: Aberdeen University Press.
Cooper, A. (trans.) (1973) *Li Po and Tu Fu: Poems*. Harmondsworth: Penguin.
Corbett, J. (1996) COMET and *The House Among the Stars*: Scottish Texts via the Internet. *The Glasgow Review* 4, 89–103.
Corbett, J. (1997) *Language and Scottish Literature*. Edinburgh: Edinburgh University Press.
Corbett, J. (1999) *Written in the Language of the Scottish Nation: A History of Literary Translation into Scots*. Clevedon: Multilingual Matters.
Craigie, W.A. (ed.) (1901) *Livy's History of Rome: The First Five Books, Translated into Scots by John Bellenden*. Edinburgh: Scottish Text Society/William Blackwood.
Craik, R.J. (1993) *Sir Thomas Urquhart of Cromarty (1611–1660), Adventurer, Polymath, and Translator of Rabelais*. Lampeter: Mellen Research University Press.
Crawford, R. (1990) 'To change/the unchangeable': The whole Morgan. In R. Crawford and H. Whyte (eds) *About Edwin Morgan* (pp. 10–24). Edinburgh: Edinburgh University Press.
Crawford, R. and Imlah, M. (eds) (2000) *The New Penguin Book of Scottish Verse*. London: Allen Lane/Penguin.
Crockett, S.R. (1895) *The Men of the Moss-Hags*. London: Bell.
Dars, J. (trans.) (c1978) *Au bord de l'eau: Shui-hu-zhuan by Shi Nai-an and Luo Guanzhong*. [Paris]: Gallimard.
Deleuze, G. (1988) *Le Pli: Liebniz et le baroque*. Paris: Les Editions de minuit.
Delisle, J-M. (2000) The Reel of the Hanged Man (M. Bowman and B. Findlay, trans). *Edinburgh Review* 105, 99–143.
Dent-Young, J. and A. (trans) (1994) *The Broken Seals: Part One of The Marshes of Mount Liang: A New Translation of the Shuihu Zhuan or Water Margin of Shi Naian and Luo Guanzhong*. Hong Kong: Chinese University Press.

Dent-Young, J. and A. (trans) (1997) *The Tiger Killers: Part Two of The Marshes of Mount Liang: A New Translation of the Shuihu Zhuan or Water Margin of Shi Naian and Luo Guanzhong.* Hong Kong: Chinese University Press.

Dent-Young, J. and A. (trans) (2001)*The Gathering Company: Part Three of The Marshes of Mount Liang: A New Translation of the Shuihu Zhuan or Water Margin of Shi Naian and Luo Guanzhong.* Hong Kong: Chinese University Press.

Dent-Young, J. and A. (trans) (2002a) *Iron Ox: Part Four of The Marshes of Mount Liang: A New Translation of the Shuihu Zhuan or Water Margin of Shi Naian and Luo Guanzhong.* Hong Kong: Chinese University Press.

Dent-Young, J. and A. (trans) (2002b) *The Scattered Flock: Part Five of The Marshes of Mount Liang: A New Translation of the Shuihu Zhuan or Water Margin of Shi Naian and Luo Guanzhong.* Hong Kong: Chinese University Press.

DOST (1925–2002) *Dictionary of the Older Scottish Tongue* (12 vols) (W.A. Craigie, *et al.*, ed.). London: Oxford University Press.

Douglas, H. and Stokes, T. (eds) (1994) *Water on the Border.* Yarrow: Weproductions.

Duncan, D. (1965) *Thomas Ruddiman: A Study in Scottish Scholarship of the Early Eighteenth Century.* Edinburgh: Oliver and Boyd.

Eliot, T.S. (1953) *Selected Prose* (J. Hayward, ed.). London: Penguin Books.

Evelyn-White, H.G. (ed. and trans.) (1936) *Hesiod: The Homeric Hymns and Homerica.* The Loeb Classical Library, 57. London: Heinemann.

Evgen'eva, A.P. (ed.) (1981) *Slovar' russkogo yazyka v chetyrekh tomakh.* Moscow: Izdatel'stvo 'Russkii yazyk'.

Farrell, J. (2000) Tallies and Italians: The Italian impact on Scottish drama. In V. Poggi and M. Rose (eds) *A Theatre That Matters: Twentieth-Century Scottish Drama and Theatre.* Milan: Unicopli.

Findlay, B. (1988) The Scots language context to translating *Les Belles-Soeurs*. In I. Lockerbie (ed.) *Image and Identity: Theatre and Cinema in Scotland and Quebec* (pp. 24–39). Stirling: John Grierson Archive and Department of French, University of Stirling.

Findlay, B. (1992) Translating Tremblay into Scots. *Theatre Research International* 17 (2), 138–45.

Findlay, B. (1993) Talking in tongues. *Theatre Scotland* 2 (6), 15–21.

Findlay, B. (1996a) Talking in tongues: Scottish translations 1970–1995. In R. Stevenson and G. Wallace (eds) *Scottish Theatre since the Seventies* (pp. 186–97). Edinburgh: Edinburgh University Press.

Findlay, B. (1996b) Translating into dialect. In D. Johnston (ed.) *Stages in Translation* (pp. 199–217). Bath: Absolute Press.

Findlay, B. (ed.) (1998a) *A History of Scottish Theatre.* Edinburgh: Polygon.

Findlay, B. (1998b) Robert Garioch's *Jephthah and The Baptist*: Why he considered it 'my favourite work'. *Scottish Literary Journal* 25 (2), 45–66.

Findlay, B. (1998c) Silesian into Scots: Gerhart Hauptmann's *The Weavers. Modern Drama* 41 (1), 90–104.

Findlay, B. (2000a) Translations into Scots. In P. France (ed.) *The Oxford Guide to Literature in English Translation* (pp. 36–8). Oxford: Oxford University Press.

Findlay, [B.]W. (2000b) Motivation and method in Scots translations, versions, and adaptations of plays from the historic repertoire of continental European drama. Unpublished doctoral thesis (2 vols). Queen Margaret University College, Edinburgh.

Findlay, B. (2000c) Translating standard into dialect: Missing the target? In C-A. Upton (ed.) *Moving Target: Theatre Translation and Cultural Relocation* (pp. 35–46). Manchester: St Jerome.
Findlay, B. (ed.) (2001a) *Scots Plays of the Seventies*. Dalkeith: Scottish Cultural Press.
Findlay, B. (2001b) Motivation and mode in Victor Carin's stage translations into Scots. In M. Rose and E. Rossini (eds) *Italian Scottish Identities and Connections* (pp. 121–42). Edinburgh: Italian Cultural Institute.
Findlay, B. (2004, forthcoming) The founding of a modern tradition: Robert Kemp's Scots translations of Molière at the Gateway. In I. Brown (ed.) *Journey's Beginning: The Gateway Theatre Building and Company, 1884–1965*. Bristol: Intellect.
Fleming, T. (1965) A theatre is people. In *The Twelve Seasons of the Edinburgh Gateway Company 1953–1965* (pp. 24–30). Edinburgh: St Giles Press.
Fo, D. (1974) *Mistero Buffo*. Verona: Bertani.
Fo, D. (1988) *Mistero Buffo* (E. Emery, trans.; S. Hood, intro. and ed.). London: Methuen. [An appendix, pp.120–2, gives a section of the play translated into Scots by Stuart Hood.]
Fo, D. (1990) *Dialogo provocatorio sul comico*. Rome: Laterza.
Foucheraux, J. (1995) Traduire/trahir *Le Vrai monde?* de Michel Tremblay: *The Real World?/The Real Wurld? Québec Studies* 20, 86–96.
Frame, D. (trans.) (1967) *Tartuffe and Other Plays by Molière*. New York: The New American Library.
France, P. and Glen, D. (eds) (1989) *European Poetry in Scotland: An Anthology of Translations*. Edinburgh: Edinburgh University Press.
Fry, C. (trans.) (1975) *Cyrano de Bergerac: A Heroic Comedy in Five Acts by Edmond Rostand*. Oxford: Oxford University Press.
Fulton, R. (ed.) (1986) *A Garioch Miscellany*. Edinburgh: Macdonald.
Fulton, R. (2002) 'Tak him awa again': Notes on Robert Garioch's Scots versions of George Buchanan's Latin plays. *Translation and Literature* 11 (2), 195–205.
Garioch, R. (1966) *Selected Poems*. Edinburgh: Macdonald.
Garioch, R. (1973) *Doktor Faust in Rose Street*. Loanhead: Macdonald.
Garioch, R. (1975) *Two Men and a Blanket: A Prisoner of War's Story*. Edinburgh: Southside.
Garioch, R. (1979) Early days in Edinburgh. In M. Lindsay (ed.) *As I Remember* (pp. 45–58). London: Hale.
Garioch, R. (1983) *Complete Poetical Works* (R. Fulton, ed.). Edinburgh: Macdonald.
Gibb, A. (trans.) (1870) *The Jephthah and Baptist by George Buchanan*. Edinburgh: Miller.
Glen, D. (1964) *Hugh MacDiarmid (Christopher Murray Grieve) and the Scottish Renaissance*. Edinburgh: Chambers.
Glen, D. (1977) Editorial: Poetry or 'Scot lit'? *Akros* 11 (33), 7.
Graham, A.C. (trans.) (1981) *Chuang-tzu: The Seven Inner Chapters and Other Writings*. London: Allen and Unwin.
Graham, W.S. (1986) Notes on a poetry of release. *Edinburgh Review* 72, 42–5.
Graves, P. and Thomsen, B.T. (1999) Translation and transplantation: Sir Alexander Gray's Danish ballads. *Northern Studies* 34, 35–59. [Notes omitted, but published in *Northern Studies* 35 (2000), 155–6.]
Gray, A. (trans.) (1920) *Songs and Ballads, Chiefly from Heine*. London: Grant Richards.
Gray, A. (trans.) (1932) *Arrows: A Book of German Ballads and Folk-Songs Attempted in Scots*. Edinburgh: Grant & Murray.

Gray, A. (trans.) (1949) *Sir Halewyn: Examples in European Balladry and Folk Song*. Edinburgh: Oliver and Boyd.
Gray, A. (trans.) (1954) *Four and Forty: A Selection of Danish Ballads Presented in Scots*. Edinburgh: Edinburgh University Press.
Gray, A. (trans.) (1958) *Historical Ballads of Denmark*. Edinburgh: Edinburgh University Press.
Hampton, C. (trans.) (1984) *Molière's Tartuffe or The Impostor*. London: Faber and Faber.
Hartnoll, P. (ed.) (1983) *The Oxford Companion to the Theatre*. Oxford: Oxford University Press.
Harvie, J. (1995) The real nation? Michel Tremblay, Scotland and cultural translatability. *Theatre Research in Canada* 16 (1–2), 5–25.
Hastie, D. (2000) The Québécois phenomenon. *Chapman* 95, 23–9.
Hawkes, D. and Minford, J. (trans) (1973–1986) *The Story of the Stone by Cao Xueqin* (5 vols). Harmondsworth: Penguin Books.
Hawkes, D. (trans.) (1989) *Songs of the South*. Harmondsworth: Penguin Books.
Henryson, R. (1968) *Testament of Cresseid* (D. Fox, ed.). London: Nelson.
Hinton, D. (trans.) (1989) *The Selected Poems of Tu Fu*. London: Anvil.
Hodgart, M.J.C. (1962) *The Ballads*. London: Hutchinson.
Hogg, J. (1972) *The Three Perils of Man* (D. Gifford, ed.). Edinburgh: Scottish Academic Press
Holquist, M. (ed.) (1981) *The Dialogic Imagination: Four Essays by M.M. Bakhtin*. Austin: University of Texas Press.
Holton, B. (trans.) (1981) *Men o the Mossflow* [Chapter 1, part 1]. *Cencrastus* 7, 2–5.
Holton, B. (trans.) (1982) *Men o the Mossflow* [Chapter 1, part 2]. *Cencrastus* 8, 32–5.
Holton, B. (trans.) (1984) *Men o the Mossflow* [Chapter 2]. *Cencrastus* 16, 28–30.
Holton, B. (trans.) (1986) *Men o the Mossflow* [Chapter 3]. *Edinburgh Review* 74, 18–30.
Holton, B. (trans.) (1987) *Men o the Mossflow* [Chapter 4]. *Edinburgh Review* 76, 73–89.
Holton, B. (trans.) (1993) *Men o the Mossflow* [Chapter 5]. *Edinburgh Review* 89, 97–111.
Holton, B. (trans.) (1995a) *Men o the Mossflow* [Chapter 4]. In M. MacDonald (ed.) *Nothing is Altogether Trivial: An Anthology of Writing from Edinburgh Review*. Edinburgh: Edinburgh University Press. [Reprint from *Edinburgh Review*, 76. See Holton, 1987.]
Holton, B. (trans.) (1995b) 'Shuitin Geese' by Qiao Jifu. *Gairfish* 9, 69–70.
Hood, S. (1963) *Pebbles From My Skull*. London: Hutchinson.
Huang, R. (c1981) *1587, A Year of No Significance: The Ming Dynasty in Decline*. New Haven: Yale University Press.
Hutchison, D. (1987) Scottish Drama 1900–1950. In C. Craig (ed.) *The History of Scottish Literature* (Vol. 4): *Twentieth Century* (pp. 163–77). Aberdeen: Aberdeen University Press.
Jack, R.D.S. (1972) *The Italian Influence on Scottish Literature*. Edinburgh: Edinburgh University Press.
Jack, R.D.S. (1986) *Scottish Literature's Debt to Italy*. Edinburgh: Italian Institute and Edinburgh University Press.
Jackson, J.H. (trans.) (1963) *The Water Margin [Shui hu chuan] by Shih Nai-an*. Hong Kong: Commercial Press.
Jamieson, J. (1808) *An Etymological Dictionary of the Scottish Language* (2 vols). Edinburgh: Creech.

Jamieson, J. (1825) *Supplement to the Etymological Dictionary of the Scottish Language* (2 vols). Edinburgh: Tait.
Jamieson, J. (1879–82) *An Etymological Dictionary of the Scottish Language to Which is Prefixed a Dissertation on the Origin of the Scottish Language* (4 vols). Paisley: Gardner.
Jamieson, J. (1912) *A Dictionary of the Scottish Language, Abridged by J. Johnson and Revised and Enlarged by Dr Longmuir*. Paisley: Gardner.
Jamieson, R. (1806) *Popular Ballads and Songs* (2 vols). Edinburgh: Constable.
Jones, C. (ed.) (1997) *The Edinburgh History of the Scots Language*. Edinburgh: Edinburgh University Press.
Jonsson, B.R. (ed.) (1962) *Svenska medeltidsballader*. Stockholm: Natur och kultur.
Kelman, J. (1994) *How Late It Was, How Late*. London: Secker and Warburg.
Kemp, R. (trans.) (1983) *Let Wives Tak Tent*. Glasgow: Brown, Son & Ferguson.
Kemp, R. (trans.) (1987) *The Laird o' Grippy*. Glasgow: Brown, Son & Ferguson.
Kinghorn, A.M. and Law, A. (eds) (1974) *Poems by Allan Ramsay and Robert Fergusson*. Edinburgh: Scottish Academic Press.
Kinloch, D. (1998) 'Lazarus at the Feast of Love': Morgan's *Cyrano de Bergerac*. *Scotlands* 5 (2), 34–54.
Kinloch, D. (2000) Le chant de la flûte en os. Traductions en écossais des pièces de Michel Tremblay. In D. Kinloch and R. Price (eds) *La Nouvelle Alliance: Influences francophones sur la littérature écossaise moderne* (pp. 211–40). Grenoble: Ellug, Université Stendhal.
Kinloch, D. (2002) Questions of status: *Macbeth* in Québécois and Scots. *The Translator* 8 (1), 73–100.
Leonard, T. (1976) Honest. In A. Hamilton, J. Kelman and T. Leonard, *Three Glasgow Writers* (pp. 46–9). Glasgow: Molendinar.
Leonard, T. (1984) *Intimate Voices: Selected Works 1965–1983*. Newcastle upon Tyne: Galloping Dog.
Liddell, H.G. and Scott, R. (1895) *A Greek–English Lexicon* (rev. 8th edn). Oxford: Clarendon.
Linklater, E. (1938) *The Impregnable Women*. London: Cape.
Lochhead, L. (trans.) (1985) *Tartuffe: A Translation into Scots from the Original by Molière*. Glasgow: Third Eye Centre/Polygyon.
Lochhead, L. (trans.) (2002) *Miseryguts & Tartuffe: Two Plays by Molière*. London: Nick Hern Books.
Lockerbie, I. (2000a) La réception de Michel Tremblay et de Robert Lepage en Écosse. *L'Annuaire théâtral* 27, 221–28.
Lockerbie, I. (2000b) The place of vernacular languages in the cultural identities of Quebec and Scotland. Unpublished conference paper given at 'Scotland–Quebec: An Evolving Comparison', Centre of Canadian Studies, University of Edinburgh, 5–6 May.
Lorimer, R.L.C. (trans.) (1992) *Shakespeare's Macbeth Translated into Scots*. Edinburgh: Canongate.
Lorimer, W.L. (trans.) (1983) *The New Testament in Scots*. Edinburgh: Southside.
Lotman, J. (1977) *The Structure of the Artistic Text* (R. Vroon, trans.). Ann Arbor: University of Michigan Press.
MacDiarmid, H. (1925) *Sangschaw*. Edinburgh: Blackwood.
MacDiarmid, H. (ed.) (1940/1948) *The Golden Treasury of Scottish Poetry*. London: MacMillan.
MacDiarmid, H. (1955) *In Memoriam James Joyce*. Glasgow: MacLellan.

MacDiarmid, H. (1978) *Complete Poems 1920–1976* (Vols I and II) (M. Grieve and W.R. Aitken, eds). London: Martin Brian and O'Keefe.
MacDiarmid, H. (1926/1987) *A Drunk Man Looks at the Thistle* (K. Buthlay, ed.). Edinburgh: Scottish Academic Press.
MacDiarmid, H. (1997) *The Raucle Tongue: Hitherto Uncollected Prose* (Vol. 2) (A. Calder, G. Murray and A. Riach, eds). Manchester: Carcanet.
Macdonald, J. (ed.) (1937) Ewen MacLachlan's Gaelic verse: Comprising a translation of Homer's *Iliad* Books I–VIII and original compositions. *Aberdeen University Studies 114*. Inverness: Carruthers.
Mac Gilleathain, I. [John Maclean] (trans.) (1976) *Odusseia Homair*. Glasgow: Gairm.
Mayakovsky, V. (1958) *Vladimir Mayakovskii: Polnoe sobranie sochinenii v trinadtsati tomakh* (13 vols). Moscow: Gosudarstvennoe izdatel'stvo khudozhestvennoi literatury.
McClure, J.D. (1987) Three translations by Douglas Young. In C. Macafee and I. Macleod (eds) *The Nuttis Schell: Essays on the Scots Language* (pp. 195–210). Aberdeen: Aberdeen University Press.
McClure, J.D. (1993) Alexander Gray's translations from German poetry. Unpublished lecture delivered at the University of Freiburg.
McClure, J.D. (1995) Canto uno chato de Prouvénço: Thoughts on translating Mistral's *Mireille*. In I. Masson and C. Pagnouelle (eds) *Cross Words: Issues and Debates in Literary and Non-literary Translating* (pp. 145–57). Liège: University of Liège English Department.
McClure, J.D. (1997) Alexander Gray's translations of German folk-songs. In I. Navrátil and R.B. Pynsent (eds) *Appropriations and Impositions: National, Regional and Sexual Identity in Literature* (pp. 83–93). Proceedings of the Fifth International Conference on the Literature of Region and Nation. Bratislava: Národne literárne centrum.
McFarlane, I.D. (1981) *Buchanan*. London: Duckworth.
Meredith, G. (1912/1928) *The Poetical Works of George Meredith, With Some Notes by G.M. Trevelyan*. London: Constable.
Mitchell, A.G. (trans.) (1903) *Jephthah: A Drama (Translated from the Latin of George Buchanan)*. Paisley: Gardner.
Mitchell, A.G. (trans.) (1904) *John the Baptist: A Drama (Translated from the Latin of George Buchanan)*. Paisley: Gardner.
Mitchison, R. (1971) *A History of Scotland*. London: Methuen.
Molière, J.B.P. de (1950) *The Misanthrope* (M. Malleson, trans.). London: Samuel French.
Molière, J.B.P. de (1954) *The School for Wives* (M. Malleson, trans.). London: Samuel French.
Molière, J.B.P. de (1973) *The Misanthrope* (T. Harrison, trans.). London: Rex Collings.
Molière, J.B.P. de (1990) *Le Tartuffe ou l'imposteur* (G. Ferreyrolles, ed.). Paris: Larousse.
Morgan, E. (trans.) (1972) *Wi the Haill Voice: 25 Poems by Vladimir Mayakovsky Translated into Scots by Edwin Morgan*. South Hinksey, Oxford: Carcanet.
Morgan, E. (1988) Interview with Robert Crawford. *Verse* 5 (1), 27–42. [Repr. in R. Crawford, H. Hart, D. Kinloch and R. Price (eds) (1995) *Talking Verse: Interviews with Poets* (pp. 146–61). St Andrews and Williamsburg: Verse.]
Morgan, E. (1990a) *Collected Poems*. Manchester: Carcanet.

Morgan, E. (1990b) The translation of poetry. In H. Whyte (ed.) *Nothing Not Giving Messages: Reflections on Work and Life': Edwin Morgan* (pp. 232–5). Edinburgh: Polygon. [First published in 1976 in *Scottish* Review 2 (5), 18–23.]
Morgan, E. (trans.) (1992a) *Edmond Rostand's Cyrano de Bergerac*. Manchester: Carcanet.
Morgan, E. (1992b) The third tiger: The translator as creative communicator. In P. Hobsbaum, P. Lyons and J. McGhee (eds) *Channels of Communication: Papers from the Conference of Higher Education Teachers of English* (pp. 43–59). Glasgow: Department of English Literature, University of Glasgow.
Morgan, E. (trans.) (2000) *Jean Racine's Phaedra: Translated from the French into Scots by Edwin Morgan*. Manchester: Carcanet.
Moss, J. (1996) Québécois theatre: Michel Tremblay and Marie Laberge. *Theatre Research International* 21 (3), 196–207.
Murison, D. (1979) The historical background. In A.J. Aitken and T. McArthur (eds) *Languages of Scotland* (pp. 2–13). Edinburgh: Chambers.
Murray, A.T. (ed. and trans.) (1919) *Homer: The Odyssey* (2 vols). The Loeb Classical Library, 104–105. London: Heinemann.
Murray, G. (trans.) (1912) *The Frogs, by Aristophanes*. London: Allen.
Nabokov, V.D. (trans.) (1964) *Eugene Onegin, a Novel in Verse by Aleksandr Pushkin* (4 vols). London: Routledge and Kegan Paul.
Neill, W. (trans.) (1992) *Tales Frae the Odyssey o Homer Owreset intil Scots*. Edinburgh: Saltire Society.
Neill, W. (trans.) (1995) *A Hantle o Romanesco Sonnets bi Giuseppe Gioachino Belli set ower intil Scots bi William Neill*. Castle Douglas: Burnside Press.
Neill, W. (trans.) (1998) *Seventeen Sonnets by G.G. Belli Translated from the Romanesco by William Neill*. Kirkcaldy: Akros.
Ogston, D. (1988) William Lorimer's *New Testament in Scots*: An appreciation. In D.F. Wright (ed.) *The Bible in Scottish Life and Literature* (pp. 53–61). Edinburgh: Saint Andrew Press.
Olrik, A. (1899) *Danske Folkeviser i Udvalg*. Copenhagen: Gyldendal.
OED (1989) *The Oxford English Dictionary* (2nd edn, 20 vols) (J.A. Simpson and E.S.C. Weiner, eds). Oxford: Clarendon Press.
Pautz, D. (2000) The men behind McTremblay. *The Globe and Mail* [Toronto], 1 June, R1–R2.
Peacock, N. (1993) *Molière in Scotland 1945–1990*. Glasgow: University of Glasgow French and German Publications.
Peacock, N. (1994) Cent ans de recherches sur Molière. *Le Nouveau Moliériste* 1, 45–61.
Poole, A. and Maule, J. (eds) (1995) *The Oxford Book of Classical Verse in Translation*. Oxford: Oxford University Press.
Pope, A. (1965) An essay on criticism. In D. Grant (ed.) *Pope: Selected Poems* (pp. 36–59). Oxford: Oxford University Press.
Pound, E. (1975) *The Cantos of Ezra Pound*. London: Faber.
Prévot, J. (ed.) (1977) *Oeuvres Complètes, by Cyrano de Bergerac*. Paris: Belin.
Purves, D. (trans.) (1992) *The Tragedie o Macbeth: A Rendering into Scots of Shakespeare's Play*. Edinburgh: Rob Roy Press.
Pushkin, A.S. (1984) *Evgenni Onegin*. Blackwell Russian Texts. Oxford: Blackwell.
Riach, A. (1991) *Hugh MacDiarmid's Epic Poetry*. Edinburgh: Edinburgh University Press.

Richards, I.A. (1932) *Mencius on the Mind: Experiments in Multiple Definition*. London: K. Paul, Trench, Trubner & Co.
Robb, D.S. (ed.) (1994) *The Collected Poems of Alexander Scott*. Edinburgh: Mercat Press.
Rolston, D.L. (ed.) (1990) *How to Read the Chinese Novel*. Princeton: Princeton University Press.
Salter, D. (1993) Who's speaking here? Tremblay's Scots voice. *Canadian Theatre Review* 74, 40–5.
Savage, R. (1987) Molière in English and Scots. Programme note in the Royal Lyceum Theatre Company Edinburgh programme for the revived production of Liz Lochhead's translation of Molière's *Tartuffe*. Private copy.
SND (1925–75) *Scottish National Dictionary* (10 vols) (W. Grant and D.D. Murison, eds). Edinburgh: Scottish National Dictionary Association.
Shapiro, S. (trans.) (1981) *Outlaws of the Marsh, by Shi nai'an and Luo Guanzhong*. Beijing: Foreign Languages Press.
Sharratt, P. and Walsh, P.G. (eds) (1983) *George Buchanan Tragedies*. Edinburgh: Scottish Academic Press.
Sima, Q. (1974) *The Warlords* (W. Dolby and J. Scott, trans). Edinburgh: Canongate.
Smart, H. (1993) In *Lines Review* 125, 52–54.
Smith, J.M. (1934) *The French Background of Middle Scots Literature*. Edinburgh: Oliver and Boyd.
Smith, S.G. (1946) *The Deevil's Waltz*. Glasgow: MacLellan.
Smith, S.G. (1960) *The Wallace*. Edinburgh: Oliver and Boyd.
Smith-Dampier, E.M. (trans.) (1939) *A Book of Danish Ballads, by Axel Olrik*. Princeton: Princeton University Press.
Sommerstein, A.H. (trans.) (1987) *The Birds, by Aristophanes*. Warminster: Aris and Phillips.
Sørensen, V. (1959) *Digtere og Daemoner* [Writers and Demons]. Copenhagen: Gyldendal.
Soutar, W. (1948) *Collected Poems* (H. MacDiarmid, ed.). London: Dakers.
STA (various) Scottish Theatre Archive, Department of Special Collections, Glasgow University Library.
Stanford, W.B. (ed.) (1958) *The Frogs, by Aristophanes*. London: Macmillan.
Stevenson, R. (1993). Re-enter houghmagandie: Language as performance in Liz Lochhead's *Tartuffe*. In R. Crawford and A. Varty (eds) *Liz Lochhead's Voices* (pp. 109–23). Edinburgh: Edinburgh University Press.
Stevenson, R. and Wallace, G. (eds) (1996) *Scottish Theatre Since the Seventies*. Edinburgh: Edinburgh University Press.
Strout, A.L. (1959) *A Bibliography of Articles in Blackwood's Magazine 1817–1825*. Lubbock, TX: Texas Technological College Library.
Sutherland, R.G. [Robert Garioch] (trans.) (1959) *George Buchanan's Jephthah and The Baptist translatit frae Latin in Scots*. Edinburgh: Oliver and Boyd.
Templeton, J.M. (1975) Scots: An outline history. In A.J. Aitken (ed.) Lowland Scots (pp. 4–13). *Association for Scottish Literary Studies Occasional Papers No. 2*. Edinburgh: Association for Scottish Literary Studies.
Tremblay, M. (1988) *The Guid Sisters* (M. Bowman and B. Findlay, trans). Toronto: Exile Editions.
Tremblay, M. (1989) Interview with Michel Tremblay. *Cencrastus* 32, 30–3.
Tremblay, M. (1991) *The Guid Sisters and Other Plays* (title play: M. Bowman and B. Findlay, trans). London: Nick Hern Books.

Tremblay, M. (1996) *Messe solennelle pour une pleine lune d'été*. Ottawa: Leméac.
Tremblay, M. (2000) *Solemn Mass for a Full Moon in Summer* (M. Bowman and B. Findlay, trans). London: Nick Hern Books.
Tulloch, G. (1985) Robert Garioch's different styles of Scots. *Scottish Literary Journal* 12 (1), 53–69.
Tulloch, G. (ed.) (1987) *The Psalms in Scots: Reprint of P. Hately Waddell's The Psalms: Frae Hebrew intil Scottis first published in 1871*. Aberdeen: Aberdeen University Press.
Tulloch, G. (1989) *A History of the Scots Bible*. Aberdeen: Aberdeen University Press.
Tynianov, Y. (1981) *The Problem of Verse Language* (M. Sosa and B. Harvey, ed. and trans). Ann Arbor: Ardis.
Valéry, P. (1956) *Traduction en vers des Bucoliques de Virgil: Précéde de Variations sur les Bucoliques*. Paris: Gallimard.
Valéry, P. (1958) *The Collected Works of Paul Valéry* (vol. 7): *The Art of Poetry* (D. Folliott, trans.). London: Routledge.
Waddell, P.H. (1871) *The Psalms frae Hebrew intil Scottis*. Edinburgh: Menzies. [Reprinted by Tulloch, 1987.]
Wang, J. (n.d.) *Jin Sheng-T'an*. New York: Twayne.
Wang, S. (1968) *The Romance of the Western Chamber* (Hsiung Shih-I, trans.). New York: Columbia University Press.
Wilbur, R. (trans.) (1982) Tartuffe. In A. Drury and R. Wilbur (trans) *Five Plays: Jean Baptiste Poquelin de Molière*. London: Methuen. [First published by Faber and Faber in 1964.]
Wilson, J.M. (ed.) (n.d.) *Historical, Traditionary and Imaginative Tales of the Borders, and of Scotland* (Vol. IV). Manchester: Ainsworth.
Woodsworth, J. (1996) Language, translation and the promotion of national identity: Two test cases. *Target: International Journal of Translation Studies* 8 (2), 211–38.
Woollen, G. (ed.) (1994) *Cyrano de Bergerac, by Edmond Rostand*. Bristol: Bristol Classical Press.
Yang, Lian (1994) *Non-Person Singular* (B. Holton, trans.). London: WellSweep.
Yang, Lian (1995) *Where the Sea Stands Still* (B. Holton, trans.). London: WellSweep.
Yang, Lian (1999) *Where the Sea Stands Still: New Poems by Yang Lian* (B. Holton, trans.). Newcastle: Bloodaxe.
Young, C. and Murison, D. (eds) (n.d.) *A Clear Voice: Douglas Young, Poet and Polymath*. Loanhead: Macdonald.
Young, D. (1943) *Auntran Blads*. Glasgow: MacLellan.
Young, D. (1945) Letter to Hugh MacDiarmid, 1940. In M. Lindsay (ed.) *Poetry Scotland: Second Collection* (pp. 25–9). Glasgow: MacLellan.
Young, D. (1947) *A Braird o Thristles*. Glasgow: MacLellan.
Young, D. (1949) *The Use of Scots for Prose*. Greenock: Greenock Philosophical Society.
Young, D. (trans.) (1958) *The Puddocks: A Verse Play in Scots from the Greek of Aristophanes* (2nd edn). Tayport: The author.
Young, D. (trans.) (1959) *The Burdies: A Comedy in Scots Verse from the Greek of Aristophanes* (1st edn). Tayport: The author.
Young, D. (1966) *Scots Burds and Edinburgh Reviewers: A Case Study in Theatre Critics and Their Contradictions*. Edinburgh: Macdonald.

Contributors

Martin Bowman teaches at Champlain Regional College, St Lambert, Quebec. With Bill Findlay he has translated into Scots Jeanne-Mance Delisle's *The Reel of the Hanged Man* (Stellar Quines), and eight plays by Michel Tremblay: *The Guid Sisters*, *The Real Wurld?* and *Hosanna* (Tron Theatre); *The House Among the Stars* and *Solemn Mass for a Full Moon in Summer* (Traverse Theatre); *Forever Yours, Marie-Lou* (LadderMan); *Albertine in Five Times* (Clyde Unity Theatre); *If Only...* (Royal Lyceum Theatre). With Wajdi Mouawad he translated into French for theatres in Montreal and Brussels, respectively, the stage adaptation of Irvine Welsh's *Trainspotting* and Enda Walsh's play *Disco Pigs*.

Bill Findlay is Research Fellow in the School of Drama and Creative Industries, Queen Margaret University College, Edinburgh. He is editor of *A History of Scottish Theatre* (1998) and *Scots Plays of the Seventies* (2001). He has published widely on the use of Scots in stage translation, and has had staged over a dozen translations of plays into Scots, including, in collaboration with Martin Bowman (see above), nine from Québécois.

Peter Graves is Senior Lecturer in Swedish in the Scandinavian Studies section of the School of European Languages and Culture at the University of Edinburgh. His research and publications are mainly focused on nineteenth- and twentieth-century Scandinavian literature, and on literary relations between Scandinavia and Britain. He has also published a number of translations of Scandinavian literature.

Brian Holton taught Chinese language and literature at Newcastle and Durham Universities, and is currently Assistant Professor in the Department of Chinese and Bilingual Studies at Hong Kong Polytechnic University. He has published translations of classical and modern Chinese literature into both Scots and English, most recently the collections *Notes of a Blissful Ghost: Selected Poems by Yang Lian* and *Where the Sea Stands Still: New Poems by Yang Lian* (a UK Poetry Book Society Recommended Translation).

Stuart Hood was Controller of Programmes at BBC Television, and Professor of Film and Television at the Royal College of Art. He has written widely on the media and media sociology, and has published several novels, one of which, *A Storm from Paradise* (1985), won the Scottish Book of the Year Award. He has translated widely from Italian, French, Russian and German (particularly the poetry of Erich Fried and works by Ernst Jünger). His translations from Italian include the work of Pasolini, Dino Celati, Aldo Busi and Dario Fo.

David Kinloch is Senior Lecturer in French Studies at the University of Strathclyde. He is author of *The Thought and Art of Joseph Joubert* (1992) and co-editor of *La Nouvelle Alliance: Influences francophones sur la littérature écossaise moderne* (2000). His volumes of poetry include *Paris-Forfar* (1994) and *Un Tour d'Ecosse* (2001). He is co-founder of the poetry magazine *Verse*.

J. Derrick McClure is Senior Lecturer in the Department of English at the University of Aberdeen. He is the Chairman of the Forum for Research in the Languages of Scotland and Ulster, and editor of the journal *Scottish Language*. In addition to editing books, he is author of *Why Scots Matters* (1988), *Scots and Its Literature* (1995), *Poetry and Nationhood: Scots as a Poetic Language from 1878 to the Present* (2000) and *Doric: The Dialect of North-East Scotland* (2002). He contributed the chapter 'English in Scotland' to the *Cambridge History of the English Language* (Vol. 5). He has published a collection of Scots translations from contemporary Gaelic poetry, *Scotland o Gael an Lawlander* (1996), and has as a work-in-progress translating Mistral's *Mireille* into North-East Scots.

Stephen Mulrine was formerly Head of Historical and Critical Studies at Glasgow School of Art. He began translating from Russian in the late 1980s, mainly drama, and his published and produced work now ranges from translations of Pushkin, Gogol, Ostrovsky, Turgenev and Chekhov, to the contemporary plays of Gelman and Petrushevskaya. His dramatisation of Venedikt Yerofeev's cult novel *Moscow Stations* has been staged in Edinburgh, London and New York. Other adaptations include Bulgakov's *Heart of a Dog* and Leskov's *Lady Macbeth of Mtsensk*.

William Neill studied Celtic languages and English at Edinburgh University, then taught for some years in Galloway where he now lives. One of Scotland's senior poets, his trilingual work includes several collections of verse in Gaelic, Scots and English. He won the National Gaelic Mod's bardic crown in 1969. His *Tales frae the Odyssey o Homer owreset intil*

Scots was published by the Saltire Society in 1992. His readings of those translations (and verse by him) are available on Scotsoun. His *Selected Poems* were published in 1996.

Noël Peacock is Marshall Professor of French at the University of Glasgow. He has published extensively on Molière: a monograph entitled *Molière in Scotland* (1993), critical editions of *La Jalousie du Barbouillé et George Dandin* (1984) and *Dépit amoureux* (1990), critical guides on *L'École des femmes* (1988) and *Les Femmes savantes* (1990), and around forty articles and reviews. He is co-director and co-founder of a new international journal, *Le Nouveau Moliériste*, the first for over a hundred years to be devoted to Molière. In 1993 he was made a *Chevalier dans l'Ordre des Palmes académiques* for services to French culture, and in 2002 he was created a *Chevalier dans l'Ordre des Arts et des Lettres*.

Randall Stevenson is Reader in the Department of English Literature at the University of Edinburgh. He is author of *The British Novel Since the Thirties* (1986), *Modernist Fiction* (1992, 1998), *A Reader's Guide to the Twentieth-Century Novel in Britain* (1993), and *The Oxford English Literary History, volume 12: 1960–2000* (forthcoming 2004). He co-edited *The Scottish Novel since the Seventies* (1993), *Scottish Theatre since the Seventies* (1996), and *Twentieth-Century Scottish Drama: An Anthology* (2001). He regularly reviews Scottish theatre for *The Times Literary Supplement*.

Bjarne Thorup Thomsen is Senior Lecturer in Danish in the Scandinavian Studies section of the School of European Languages and Cultures at the University of Edinburgh. He is co-editor of *Northern Studies*, the journal of the Scottish Society for Northern Studies. His research and publications are mainly focused on nineteenth- and early twentieth-century Scandinavian literature (Selma Lagerlöf and Hans Christian Andersen in particular), but also include translation studies and film studies.

Graham Tulloch is Professor of English at the Flinders University of South Australia. He has written extensively on the Scots language and is the author of *The Language of Walter Scott* (1980), *A History of the Scots Bible* (1989), and the editor of P. Hately Waddell's *The Psalms in Scots* (1987). More recently he has edited *Ivanhoe* (1998) for the *Edinburgh Edition of the Waverley Novels* and contributed to the *Edinburgh History of the Scots Language* (1997).

Christopher Whyte taught at the University of Rome from 1977 to 1985 and is currently Reader in the Department of Scottish Literature at the University of Glasgow. He is editor of *Gendering the Nation: Studies in Modern Scottish Literature* (1995), and a bilingual anthology of contemporary Gaelic poetry *An Aghaidh na Sìorraidheachd/In the Face of Eternity: Eight Gaelic Poets* (1991). His critical edition of Sorley Maclean's *Dàin do Eimhir* was published in 2002. His first volume of poems, *Uirsgeul/Myth: Poems in Gaelic with English Translations* (1991), won a Saltire Award. His debut novel *Euphemia MacFarrigle and the Laughing Virgin* was published in 1995, followed by *The Warlock of Strathearn* (1997), *The Gay Decameron* (1998) and *The Cloud Machinery* (2000) – all published by Gollancz.

Index

accent
- Bearsden 119, 122 n.5
- Buchan 29
- Glasgow 134
- Scottish 73
Aeschylus 5, 221, 223, 228
Ainslie, H.
- 'The Hint o Hairst' 62
Akhmatova, A. 164, 189-90
Anglo-Danish 233
Anglo-Irish translations 104
Ariosto, L.
- *Orlando Furioso* 2
Aristophanes
- *Lysistrata* 228
- *The Puddocks* & *The Burdies* 5, 9, 39, 215-30
Arnold, M. 138
Auld Alliance 100, 112

Bach, J.S. 196
Bain, S. 39
Bakhtin, M. 119-20
ballads
- Border ballads 40
- Danish ballads 231-51
- 'The Douglas Tragedy' 40
- 'Fair Helen of Kirkconnel' 40
- Germanic ballads 231
- historical ballad 247
- *riddarevise* (ballad of chivalry) 245
- Scandinavian ballads 231
- Scots and ballad language 11, 231-4, 250
- Scottish ballads 11, 233, 234, 235, 250
- 'Sir Patrick Spens' 40
- Swedish ballads 243
- 'Tam Linn' 40
- 'True Thomas' 40
- *tryllevisen* (supernatural ballad) 235
- 'The Wife of Usher's Well' 40
Barbour, J.
- *The Brus* 32-3
Barthes, R. 124, 126
Bassnett, S. 107
BBC 192, 216

Beaumarchais, P. 5
Beethoven, L. van 38
Bellenden, J.
- *see* Livy
Belli, G. 4, 9, 39, 52 n.1, 172, 174, 185, 188-214 *passim*
Benjamin, W. 35-6, 138, 212 n.3
Beowulf 40
Berlioz, H. 75
Besnier, P. 126, 134
Bible 184, 187 n.16, 218
Bible into Scots 175, 182
Blackwood's Magazine 178
Blin Hary [Blind Harry]
- *The Wallace* 32
Boece, H.
- *The History and Chronicles of Scotland* 2
Bowman, M. 10
Braxfield, Lord 51
Brecht, B. 5
Brodsky, J. 190
Brooks, C. & Warren, R.P. 244
Brown, A. 175-7
Brown, G.D.
- *The House with the Green Shutters* 161
Bruce, G. 40, 49
Buchanan, G. 5, 6, 8, 9, 193
- *Alcestis* 172-3
- *Franciscanus* 173
- Latin tragedies into Scots 171-87
- *Medea* 172-3
Buchanan, R.
- *Ballad Stories of the Affections* 232
Buck, P. 36 n.5
Burel, J.
- *Pamphilus speakand of Lufe* 2, 6
Burgess, A.
- *Cyrano de Bergerac* 126, 131, 137, 140
Burns, R. 2, 18, 32, 43, 48, 51, 62, 99, 121, 166, 175, 218, 219, 226, 229
- 'Holy Willie's Prayer' 107
- 'On Captain Grose's Peregrinations through Scotland' 37 n.13
- 'To a Louse' 184

266

Index

– 'To a Mouse' 184
Byre Theatre 215
Byron, Lord 121

Carducci, G.192
Carin, V. 12 n.5
Carne-Ross, D. 192, 211, 214 n.16
Castalian Band 2
Catalan 12 n.6
Chekhov, A. 5, 71
Chen, K.
– *Farewell My Concubine* 37 n.11
Coffey, D. 110
Coleridge, S.T. 39, 42
'Colkelbie's Sow' 218
commedia dell'arte 109-10, 113, 118
Communicado Theatre Company 134
Confucius
– *Analects* 21
Connolly, B. 56
Constructivist 153
Corbett, J. 6, 74
– *Written in the Language of the Scottish Nation* 1
Cormann, E. 5
Corneille, P. 93, 113
Cousse, R. 5
Covenanters 185
Crawford, R. 124, 125
Crockett, S.R. 32
– *Men of the Mosshags* 36 n.4

Danis, D. 5
Dante 39, 222
Dars, J. 36 n.5
D'Aubigné, A. 127
De Staël, Madame 191
Deleuze, G. 130, 132-3
Delisle, J.-M. 5
Dent-Young, J. & A. 36 n.5
Desbiens, J.-P. 68
Dinglichkeit 159
Douglas, G. 2, 3, 38
– *Aeneid* 39, 172, 181
Du, F. 22
Du Bartas, G. de S.
– *Uranie* 2
Dunbar, W. 2, 51, 166

Early Modern English 179, 183
Edinburgh Festival Fringe 215
Edinburgh International Festival 87, 98, 101, 215
Eliot, T.S.

– 'Reflections on *Vers Libre*' 42
Elliot, J., of Minto
– 'The Flowers o' the Forest' 184
Embassy Theatre 99
Ennius 184
Esenin, S. 153
Estienne, H. 171
Euripides 5, 173, 223, 228

Farrell, J. 65 n.2
Farrow, K.
– *Iliad* 52 n.2
Faure, F. 123
Feng, M. 21
Fergusson, R. 2, 18, 32, 62, 205
Ferretti, G. 191
Findlay, B. 10, 87, 106, 121, 125
Fingal 39
Finland 104, 122 n.6
Fionn ann an Taigh a' Bhlàir Bhuidhe 39
Fleming, T. 98, 101, 229
Fo, D. 5
– *Mistero Buffo* 11, 53-65
Formby, G. 121
Foscolo, U. 192
Franco-Prussian War 123
Fry, C. 143
Fulton, R. 102, 104, 110
– *A Wee Touch o' Class* 104, 110
Futurists 153, 160

Gaelic 1, 3, 28, 31, 39, 40, 41, 47, 48, 50, 51, 52, 215, 233
Galt, J. 2, 32
Garioch, R. 3, 4, 8, 9, 32, 62
– 'Anatomy of Winter' 39, 46
– 'Bingo Saith the Lord' 174
– Buchanan's tragedies 8, 9, 171-87
– 'The Cholera Morbus' 200
– 'Edinburgh Sonnets' 199
– 'Fi'baw in the Street' 173, 174
– 'Garioch's Repone til George Buchanan' 172, 193
– 'Heard in the Cougate' 199-200
– 'The Humanists' Trauchles in Paris' 172, 193
– 'Judgement Day' 209-11
– 'The Muir' 174, 175, 185, 203
– 'Noah's Ark' 213 n.15
– 'The Percipient Swan' 192-3
– 'The Puir Faimly' 204-6
– 'The Relicschaw' 207-9
– 'The Reminder' 196, 203-4
– 'Ritual Questions' 197-9

- 'Roman Sonnets frae Giuseppe Belli'
  188-214
- 'Sisyphus' 41, 195-6
- 'To Robert Fergusson' 203
- 'Whae Gaes by Nicht, Gaes til his Daith'
  197, 200-3, 213 n.11
Gascon identity 136
Gateway Theatre Company 98
Gibb, A. 175
Gillespie, T. 178
Glen, D. 174
Gogol, N. 5, 191
Goldoni, C. 5, 12 n.5, 109
Gorky, M. 5
Graham, W.S. 34
Graves, P. 11
Gray, Sir A. 4, 11, 62
- 'Agnete and the Merman' 234-5, 240, 241-5
- 'The Death of Queen Dagmar' 247-50
- 'The Power of the Harp' 235-41
- 'Sir Halewyn' 231-2
- 'Sir Walter's Daughter' 245-7
Gregory, Lady 104
Gregory XVI, Pope 190-1
Grieve, C.M.
- *see* 'MacDiarmid, H.'
'The Gyre Carling' 218

Hampton, C.
- *Tartuffe* 111-15, 117, 122
Harrison, T.
- *The Misanthrope* 105
Hartnol, P. 106
Hauptmann, G. 5, 12 n.5
Hawkes, D. 27
Hazlitt, W. 105 n.3
Heine, H.
- *Dichterliebe* 62
Henryson, R. 2, 36, 51
- 'The Testament of Cresseid' 37 n.14, 62
Herbert, W.N. 32
Hesiod
- *Work and Days* 39, 46
Hodgart, M.J.C. 243
Hogg, J. 2, 32
- *The Three Perils of Man* 17
Holberg, L. 5
Holloway, S. 121
Holton, B. 10, 11
- *Men o the Mossflow* 5, 8, 15-37
Homer 222
- *The Iliad* 39, 45, 52 n.2
- *The Odyssey* 4, 9, 11, 38-52

Hood, S. 11
Horace 184
Hutchison, D. 110, 116

Ibsen, H. 5, 71
Ionesco, E. 71
Isaiah into Scots 182

Jackson, J.H. 36 n.5
Jacob, V.
- 'Tam i' the Kirk' 62
James VI, King of Scots 2, 3, 173
Jamieson, J.
- *An Etymological Dictionary of the Scottish Language* 63, 177, 178, 179, 180, 181, 186 n.9, 187 n.11
Jamieson, R.
- *Popular Ballads and Songs* 232
Jin, R. 21
Jin, S. 37 n.6
- *Shuihu Zhuan* 21-4
Johnson, Dr S. 45
Johnson, K. 61
Jonsson, B.R. 243
joual 68-9, 70, 71, 73, 78, 82
Jouvet, L. 87-8, 89, 91

Kelman, J.
- *How Late It Was, How Late* 61
Kemp, A. 88, 104 n.1
Kemp, R. 3, 5, 6, 8, 11, 110, 218
- *The Laird o' Grippy* 87-105 *passim*
- *Let Wives Tak Tent* 6, 87-105 *passim*
'King Berdok' 218
Kinloch, D. 10, 11
Kleist, H. von 5, 12 n.5
Knox, J. 179
Kohout, P. 5
'Kynd Kittoch' 218

Landsmaal 7, 12 n.6
Lang Johnnie Moir 44
Langham, M. 137
Laurendeau, A. 68
Laurie, J. 103
Leibniz, G.W. 132
Leonard, T. 134
- 'Honest' 79
- 'The Voyeur' 165, 170 n.6
Lindsay, Sir D. 2
- *Ane Satyre of the Thrie Estaitis* 218
Ling, M. 21
Linklater, E.
- *The Impregnable Women* 227-8

Livy
- *History of Rome* 2, 178-9, 186 n.10
Lochhead, L. 5, 125
- *Tartuffe* 6, 9, 10, 11, 104, 106-22
Lockerbie, I. 69
Lorca, F.G. 71
Lorimer, W.L.
- *The New Testament in Scots* 5, 12 n.4, 62
Lotman, J. 213 n.9
Lubkiewicz, T. 5
Lucretius 184
Luo, G. 21

McClure, J.D. 9, 232, 233, 250, 250 n.1, 250 n.3
MacDiarmid, H. 2-4, 5, 6, 9, 12 n.6, 17, 32, 51, 62, 63, 104, 166, 174-5, 177, 180, 181, 185, 186 n.4-6, 192, 193, 219, 229
- 'The Bonnie Broukit Bairn' 178
- *A Drunk Man Looks at the Thistle* 178
- 'The Eemis Stane' 178
- *In Memoriam James Joyce* 193-4, 213 n.7
- 'The Last Trump' 209, 211
Mac Gilleathain, I.
- *see* MacLean, J.
MacIntyre, D.B. 40
MacLachlan, E. 41, 50
- *Iliad* 39
Maclean, J. 41
- *Odusseia Homair* 1, 39, 50, 52
Maclean, S. 52
McLellan, R. 32
MacMillan, H. 87, 125
- *Le Bourgeois gentilhomme* 104
- *The Hypochondriak* 104, 122
'MacMolière' 10, 67, 87
Macrae, D. 88, 110
'McTremblay' 67
Machiavelli, N.
- *Il Principe* 2
Makars 16, 32, 172
Makars' Club 183
- *see also* Scots Style Sheet
Malleson, M. 89
Mary, Queen of Scots 173
Mayakovsky, V. 4, 5, 9, 10, 124
- *see also* Morgan, E.
Meredith, G. 41
Merezhkovsky, D. 209, 211
Middle English 179
Mistral 12 n.6
Mitchell, A.G. 175-7
Molière, J.B.P. de 5, 6, 8, 10, 11, 12 n.5
- reasons for Scottish appeal 107-12

- *see also* Kemp, R. *and* Lochhead, L. *montréalais*
- see *joual*
Morgan, E. 4, 5, 9, 10, 87, 230 n.1
- 'Anent the Deeference o Tastes' 159-60
- 'The Atlantic' 153-4, 156-7
- 'Awa wi it!' 167
- 'Ay, but can ye?' 150-1
- 'The Ballad o the Rid Cadie' 155-6, 163-4
- 'Brooklyn Brig' 157-8
- 'Che' 125
- 'Cinquevalli' 125
- 'Comrade Teenager' 164-5
- *Cyrano de Bergerac* 6, 9-10, 11, 121, 123-44
- 'The Death of Marilyn Monroe' 125
- 'Eupatoria' 154-5
- 'Fiddle-ma-fidgin' 162-3
- 'Goavy-dick!' 164, 166-7
- 'I'm aff' 158-9
- 'Loch Ness Monster's Song' 136
- 'Mandment No. 2 to the Army o the Arts' 146
- 'May Day' 149-50, 164
- 'Mayakonferensky's Anectidote' 165, 168-9
- *Phaedra* 12 n.8
- 'A Richt Respeck for Cuddies' 160-2
- 'To the Bourgeoisie' 150
- 'Versailles' 151-2, 164
- 'Vladimir's Ferlie' 148-9
- 'Wi the Haill Voice' 147-8, 153, 164
Mulrine, S. 10
Murray, C.
- *Hamewith* 62
Murray, G. 225, 230 n.3
Murray, J.A.H.
- *The Dialect of the Southern Counties of Scotland* 32
music hall & variety 110-12, 220

Nabokov, V. 145-6, 167, 170
Nash, O. 121
Neill, W. 4, 9, 11
Northern Middle English 233

Old Northumbrian English 233
Olivier, L. 101
Olrik, A. 250 n.2
Ovid 184

pantomime 110-12, 113, 220
Para Handy 32
Pascoli, G. 192
Pasolini, P.P. 60

Peacock, N. 8, 11
– *Molière in Scotland 1945-1990* 109, 110
Petrarch
– *Trionfi* 2
Petrushevskaya, L. 5
Pitcairn's *Trials* 32
Plautus 109
Pléiade 2
Pope, A.
– 'An Essay on Criticism' 112
Porta, A. 191, 192
Pound, E. 40, 42
Proust, M. 134
Provençal 12 n.6
Psalms into Scots 182
Pushkin, A.
– *Eugene Onegin* 145-6, 170

Qiao, J. 31
Qu, Y.
– *Encountering Sorrows* 22

Rabelais 93, 120, 169, 218
Racine, J. 5, 12 n.8, 96
Rame, F. 65
Ramsay, A. 2, 18, 62, 95, 205
Reformation 206
register
– colloquial register in Scots 8, 18, 179, 219-20
– creating a high register in Scots 26, 27, 174, 179, 182
– key to success/failure in Scots translation 10, 17
– loss of high register in Scots 5, 8, 18, 179
– opportunities for register shifts offered by Scots 7, 9, 11, 66-83 *passim*, 94, 96, 119-20, 135, 219-24
– religious register 27, 80, 182
– signalled by phonetic spelling 78
– standard language 75-6 (*see also* Standard English)
– translating register in source text 17, 60-83,
Renaissance
– European 2, 172, 185
– French 172
– Scottish (16th & 20th centuries) *see* Scottish Renaissance
Révolution tranquile 68
Richards, I.A. 35
Roman dialect
– *see romanesco*
Romance of the Western Chamber 22

romanesco 188-214 *passim*
Romanticism 189
Ronsard, P. de 2, 135
Rossini, G. 191
ROSTA 150, 170 n.5
Rostand, E. 5
– *see also Cyrano de Bergerac* at Morgan, E.
Roudinesco, A. 188
Rousseau, J.J. 191
Royal Lyceum Theatre 106, 114, 215, 229
Royal Shakespeare Company 111, 112
Ruddiman, T. 172, 181, 186 n.7
Russian Futurists 153
Ruthven MS 181, 187 n.12

St Matthew's Gospel 191
Sainte-Beuve, C.A. 191
Saurat, D. 2
Savage, R. 106, 112, 118, 121
Schiller, F. 42
'Scoatch coamic' tradition 220
Scots language: characteristics
– analytic 206
– combative 11, 38, 49, 134, 136, 221
– conciseness 114, 199
– concreteness 10, 11, 141, 147, 157, 159-60, 162, 168
– directness/immediacy 11, 19, 39, 49, 159, 168
– earthiness 11, 19, 54-5, 116, 135
– elegant 25
– emotional range 11, 134
– emotional temperature rises 10, 11, 82, 119, 162
– energy 68, 115, 117, 136, 166
– familiarity 15, 18-19, 116, 121, 161-2, 246-7
– figurative 83 n.4
– flippant 11, 134
– folk voice 10, 11, 39-40, 167
– gutsy/pungent 11, 116-18, 120
– idiomatic 83 n.4
– lyrical power 11, 68, 73, 134, 143
– malleable 25
– nostalgic 11, 134
– precise 38, 45-7, 160, 163
– sense of community *see* familiarity *above*
– spiky rhythms 11, 19
– strong/vivid imagery 11, 19, 38, 151-2, 166-7
– use of diminutives 164
Scots language: styles & varieties
– Aberdeenshire 43
– accents *see* accent (*main entry*)
– Angus 61-4, 232

Index

- Ayrshire 43, 48, 88, 180
- ballad Scots *see* ballads *(main entry)*
- Border 16
- broad 174
- colloquial/vernacular 6, 9, 48, 88, 113, 117-18, 174, 179, 183, 193, 219, 232
- country 6, 70, 73-4
- demotic/urban 4, 6, 68, 71, 73-4, 79, 81, 121, 173
- Early Scots 179, 233
- eclectic *see* synthetic
- Edinburgh 180, 185
- experimental 4-5, 6, 9, 193
- formal (*see also* Translating into Scots, elevated/formal register) 174
- Glasgow 79, 83 n.1, 134
- 'invented' 121, 122, 181
- Lallans 63, 88, 232
- legal 17, 96, 169
- literary *see* synthetic
- localised 6, 62
- Lothian standard 16
- Mid Scots 62
- Middle Scots 172, 179, 180
- North East 43, 88
- reconstructed 18th-century 104, 199, 205
- register shifts *see* register *(main entry)*
- religious 51, 182
- Roxburghshire 180
- Shetland 29
- South-Western 180
- Southern 180
- Stirling 62
- synthetic (*see also* Translating into Scots, base medium employed in synthesis) 2, 4-5, 6, 9, 43, 62, 88, 104, 168, 177-83, 185-6, 219-20
- 'theatrical' 6, 9, 117, 121
- 'traditional' 6
- Upper Clydesdale 180
- West Fife 83 n.1
- West-of-Scotland 118
Scots Language Society 44
Scots Style Sheet 16, 36 n.1, 183, 187 n.13, 187 n.14
Scott, A. 230
- 'Supermakar Story' 216, 230 n.2
Scott, J. 36 n.4
Scott, Sir W. 2, 17, 18, 32, 191
- *The Black Dwarf* 181
- *Minstrelsy of the Scottish Border* 184
Scotticisms 6, 219
Scottish Renaissance
- 16th-century 4

- 20th-century 2-4, 5, 172, 174, 186 n.5, 192
Scottish Standard English 6, 40, 69, 70, 81
Scottish Theatre Company 101, 102, 104, 110
Seneca 184
Shakespeare, W. 18, 42, 71, 90, 106, 118
- *Macbeth* 5, 191
- *Othello* 184
Shapiro, S. 36 n.5
Sherek Players 91
Shi, N. 21
Shuihu Zhuan
- *see* Men o the Mossflow at Holton, B.
Sima, Q.
- *Historical Records* 22
Smart, H. 52
Smith, S.G. 219
- 'Largo' 178
- *The Wallace* 219
Socrates 45, 222
Sommerstein, A.H. 218, 226, 229, 230 n.3
Song, J. 20, 36 n.3
Sophocles 5
Sørensen, V. 235, 250 n.4
Soutar, W. 62
- 'Wintry Boughs' 178
Spada, F. 191
Spadavecchia, A. 192
Stair, Viscount
- *Institutes* 32
Standard English 5, 81, 82, 117, 119, 180
- comparison with Scots 10, 11, 39, 40, 51, 54, 23, 121, 134, 136, 165, 168
- Scots speaker's options 38, 40
- Scottish Standard English 6, 40, 69, 70, 81
- Scottish translator's options (*see also* comparison with Scots) 6, 9, 10, 70, 82, 113
- *see also* register *(main entry)*
Stanford, W.B. 226
Stevenson, R. 10, 11, 68
Stevenson, R.L. 2, 25
- *Weir of Hermiston* 61
Stott, A. 192, 193-4, 196, 200-2, 204, 214 n.16
Sutherland, R.G.
- *see* Garioch, R.
Swan, A. 32

Tait, A. 175
Templeton, J.M. 233
Tennant, W. 180
Terence 109
Thatcherism 109
Thomsen, B.T. 11
Tizzani, V. 190
Translating into Scots

– actorly considerations 88, 105 n.4, 110, 118
– adaptation/relocation to Scotland 89-104 *passim*, 215-30 *passim*, 234-50 *passim*
– advance status of Scots 2, 3-4, 6, 24-5, 233
– archaisms 62, 63-4, 221, 232
– avoiding English options 66, 175
– base medium employed in synthesis 9, 16, 43, 48, 61-2, 88, 113, 219
– contribution to national culture/literature 7, 116, 184, 235, 250
– culturo-patriotic-political act 2, 3, 7, 12 n.6, 142-3, 174
– diversity/flexibility of medium 6, 7, 9, 10, 11, 17, 28-9, 38, 70-82 *passim*, 94, 96, 118-21, 127, 134-6, 174, 219-230 *passim*
– elevated/formal register 8, 12 n. 8, 17, 25, 96, 174-5, 179, 182, 185-6
– enlarged choice of vocabulary, pronunciation, rhymes 7, 113-16, 136, 204
– extend creative capacities of Scots 3, 5, 6, 8, 9, 11, 24-5, 35, 68, 75, 125, 142-3, 175, 177-83, 196, 199-200, 212
– fit with Scottish context 50-1, 54-5, 67-83 *passim*, 106-12, 123, 184-5, 199, 202, 212, 218
– fit with source culture/language 7, 10, 11, 38, 45, 49, 60-1, 65, 68, 67-83 *passim*, 231-4, 250
– more appropriate/effective than English 7, 10, 11, 16, 18-19, 38, 39, 43, 49, 54, 61, 65, 70, 82, 108-13, 121, 134, 136, 165, 185, 231
– names, forms of address, titles 26-8, 31-2, 89-90, 218, 229, 237
– neologisms 134, 152, 153, 154, 163
– obscurities 31
– opportunity to be inventive 8, 9, 18, 34, 193, 212
– otherness/strangeness 8, 19, 24, 199, 202, 212, 239, 249
– performative dimension 11, 115, 118, 119-20
– proverbs & saws 29-30
– puns 30-1, 134, 208, 218, 224-7
– return to 'Good Europeanism' 3-4, 174
– Scots a defective medium 8, 18, 24-5, 96, 175, 179, 186, 193, 233-4
– Scots translation unsatisfactory: critics' comments 98-100, 103-4, 215-6
– Scots translation unsatisfactory: instances 10, 41-2, 81-3, 96-7, 111, 136, 146, 148-50, 156, 166, 204-6, 224, 226-7, 234-50 *passim*
– sound 7, 12 n.7, 20, 29-30, 33, 38, 40, 44, 47, 51, 81-2, 83 n.3, 113, 128, 134, 153, 158, 162, 183,199, 204

– spelling 16, 44, 51, 62-3, 78-82, 83 n.1, 182, 183
– verse form problems 41-2, 88, 96, 112-15, 184, 196-9, 211, 223, 230, 232-3, 242-5
– Why Scots? 15, 24-5, 38, 54-5, 67-8, 123-5, 136, 231-2
– wordplay 66, 135, 140, 147, 153, 155-6, 168, 224
Tremblay, M. 5, 10, 67
– *The Guid Sisters* 67, 68, 69, 70-1, 75, 83 n.1
– *The House Among the Stars* 73-4
– *If Only...* 71-3
– *The Real Wurld?* 67
– *Solemn Mass for a Full Moon in Summer* 67, 68, 75-83
Tulloch, G. 8, 9
Tynianov, Y. 213 n.9

Union of Crowns 5, 18
Union of Parliaments 5, 18
Urquhart, Sir T. 169, 218

Valéry, P. 188-90, 192, 212 n.3
vernacular revival (18th-century) 18, 205
Vettese, R. 62
Vinaver, M. 5
Virgil 192
– *Aeneid* 2, 172, 184
– *Eclogues* 188-90

Waddell, P.H. 182
Waley, A. 17
The Water Margin
– see *Men o the Mossflow* at Holton, B.
Welsh, I. 32
Whitman, W. 152
Whyte, C. 9
Wilbur, R.
– *Tartuffe* 112, 114
Williams, T. 71
Wilson, J.M.
– *Tales of the Borders* 32, 178
Woollen, G. 126, 127, 131, 132, 133, 137, 139, 141

Yang, L. 18
– 'Whaur the Deep Sea Devauls' 19
Young, D. 3-4, 9, 12 n.3, 233
– *Auntran Blads* 215
– *A Braird o Thristles* 215
– 'Letter to Hugh MacDiarmid, 1940' 3
– *The Puddocks & The Burdies* 9, 39, 215-30

Zhuangzi 22